青が散る

宮本 輝一

Italo Calvino Il vi

Gabriel García Márquez

А.С. ПУШКИН

CAMINHO

José Saramago

Caligrafia

英汉对照

唐诗三百首新译

围城 钱锺书

THE
top10★
OF EVERYTHING
2001

THE top10

OF EVERYTHING

2001

RUSSELL ASH

DK

A Dorling Kindersley Book

Contents

Dorling **DK** Kindersley

LONDON, NEW YORK, SYDNEY, DELHI,
PARIS, MUNICH, and JOHANNESBURG

Project Editor David Tombesi-Walton
Senior Designer Tracy Hambleton-Miles

DTP Designer Jason Little
Production Silvia La Greca, Elizabeth Cherry
Picture Research Anna Grapes

Managing Editor Stephanie Jackson
Managing Art Editor Nigel Duffield

Produced for Dorling Kindersley by
Cooling Brown, 9–11 High Street,
Hampton, Middlesex TW12 2SA

Editor Alison Bolus
Designers Tish Mills, Elaine Hewson
Creative Director Arthur Brown

Author's Research Manager Aylla Macphail

First American Edition, 2000
00 01 02 03 04 05 10 9 8 7 6 5 4 3 2 1

Published in the United States by Dorling Kindersley Publishing, Inc.,
95 Madison Avenue, New York, New York 10016

DK Publishing offers special discounts for bulk purchases for sales promotions
or premiums. Specific, large-quantity needs can be met with special editions,
including personalized covers, excerpts of existing guides, and corporate imprints.
For more information, contact Special Markets Department, Dorling Kindersley
Publishing Inc., 95 Madison Avenue, New York, NY 10016 Fax: 800-600-9098.

Library of Congress Cataloging-in-Publication Data
Ash, Russell.
    The Top 10 of everything 2001 / Russell Ash. -- 1st American ed.
    p. cm.
    ISBN 0-7894-5960-4 (hardcover). -- ISBN 0-7894-6132-3 (pbk.)
    1. Curiosities and wonders. 2. World records--Miscellanea.
I. Title. II. Title: Top ten of everything 2001.
AG243.A69 2000
031.02--dc21   2000-23292
                                                    CIP

Reproduction by Colourpath, London
Printed and bound by Printer Barcelona, Spain

See our complete catalog at
www.dk.com

Culture & Learning

THE YEAR 2000

Music

Stage & Screen

The Commercial World

On the Move

Sports

Introduction

Looking Back

This is the 12th annual edition of *The Top 10 of Everything* and the first to be published in the new century and the new millennium. We start with a look back at the 20th century in A Century of Change before moving on to chart many of the developments of the 1990s.

Information Overload?

The Internet is a mixed blessing: on the one hand, it gives increased access to information, especially official figures; on the other, we are increasingly overwhelmed by the sheer volume of data. Perhaps today more than ever the value of *The Top 10 of Everything* is that it distills down all this available information to a manageable level, which is why, despite the Internet, books like this still have a place.

Listomania

During the past dozen years, the number of published lists has increased inexorably, and the 20th century ended with a tidal wave of lists of the best movies, books, and recordings of all time. Scarcely a day goes by when I am not inspired with an idea for a new list, such as the top advertising campaigns, leading fat consumers, latest assassinated monarchs, deadliest serial killers, fastest roller coasters, largest mollusks, and champion cowboys, as featured here.

Not Just the Best

The book focuses on superlatives in numerous categories and also contains a variety of "firsts" or "latests," which recognize the pioneers and the most recent achievers in various fields of endeavor. Lists of movies are based on worldwide box-office income, and those on recorded music, videos, and books are based on sales, unless otherwise stated.

History in the Making

The Top 10 of Everything now spans three decades and has become a historical resource. Schools use back numbers when undertaking projects on social changes, while others buy *Top 10* to commemorate births and other family events, as a "time capsule" of the year.

A Never-ending Task

While I endeavor to ensure that all the information is as up to date as possible, certain statistics are slow to be collated and published. At the same time, lists relating to bestsellers and sporting achievements can change almost daily. Even lists that one would not expect to alter do: a revised height for Everest was published while I was at work on this book.

The Research Network

Compiling *The Top 10 of Everything* has been a pleasure and a revelation to me: in the course of my work on it and the associated television series, and through publicity tours in the UK and US, I have discovered numerous interesting facts, increased my library, and, in particular, met many people who have become consultants on the book. My thanks to all of them and to everyone who has contacted me with helpful information.

Keep in touch

If you have any list ideas or comments, please write to me c/o the publishers or email me direct at ash@pavilion.co.uk.

Other Dorling Kindersley books by Russell Ash:
The Factastic Book of Comparisons
The Factastic Book of 1,001 Lists
Factastic Millennium Facts
Great Wonders of the World

Special Features

• More than 1,000 lists make this the most wide-ranging
Top 10 of Everything ever.

• A Century of Change surveys some of the fascinating
Top 10s of the 20th century.

• Double the number of pages have been devoted to
some of the most popular subjects.

• Illustrated SnapShots add extra information to many lists.

• "Did You Know?" entries offer unusual sidelights
on the subjects explored.

• "Why Do We Say?" features explain the origins of
popular words and phrases.

• Quiz questions with multiple-choice answers appear
throughout the book.

• Dramatic vertical format spreads add to the visual appeal.

A Century of Change

TOP 10 ★ MOST HIGHLY POPULATED COUNTRIES, 1900–2000

	1900	1950	2000
1	China	China	China
2	India	India	India
3	Russia	USSR	US
4	US	US	Indonesia
5	Germany	Japan	Brazil
6	Austria	Indonesia	Russia
7	Japan	Germany	Pakistan
8	UK	UK	Bangladesh
9	Turkey	Brazil	Japan
10	France	Italy	Nigeria

TEEMING MILLIONS

China began the 20th century with some 400 million inhabitants and ended it with 1.2 billion, about one-fifth of the world's population.

TOP 10 ★ MOST HIGHLY POPULATED CITIES, 1900

	CITY/LOCATION	POPULATION*
1	**London**, UK	6,581,000
2	**New York**, US	3,437,000
3	**Paris**, France	2,714,000
4	**Berlin**, Germany	1,889,000
5	**Chicago**, US	1,699,000
6	**Vienna**, Austria	1,675,000
7	**Wuhan**, China	1,500,000
8	**Tokyo**, Japan	1,440,000
9	**Philadelphia**, US	1,294,000
10	**St. Petersburg**, Russia	1,265,000

* Including adjacent suburban areas

Censuses and population estimates conducted around 1900 indicated that these cities, plus just three others (Constantinople in Turkey, Moscow in Russia, and Xian in China), were the only ones with populations in excess of 1 million. As we enter the 21st century, there are over 400 world cities with million-plus populations.

★ A CENTURY OF SPEED: THE PROGRESSION OF THE LAND SPEED RECORD

			SPEED	
DECADE*	DRIVER	COUNTRY	MPH	KM/H
1900	Camille Jenatzy	Belgium	65.792	105.882
1910	Barney Oldfield	US	131.275	211.267
1920	Tommy Milton	US	155.343	250.000
1930	Henry Segrave	UK	231.567	372.671
1940	John Cobb	UK	369.741	595.041
1950	John Cobb	UK	393,827	633.803
1960	Mickey Thompson	US	406,600	654.359#
1970	Gary Gabelich	US	630,389	1,014.513
1980	Gary Gabelich	US	630,389	1,014.513
1990	Richard Noble	UK	634.052	1,020.408
2000	Andy Green	UK	763.035	1,227.985

* As of the first year of each decade

 # Based on flying mile; all others over flying km

A CENTURY OF US POPULATION
(Year/population)

1900 75,994,575 **1910** 91,972,266 **1920** 105,710,620
1930 122,775,046 **1940** 131,669,275 **1950** 150,697,361
1960 179,323,175 **1970** 203,302,031 **1980** 226,542,199
1990 248,709,873 **2000*** 274,634,000

* Estimated

The greatest rate of increase in the US population within a decade occurred not in this century but in the first decade of the 19th century, when it expanded by 36.4 percent. The lowest growth rate during the past 200 years was registered in the 1930s, at just 7.2 percent.

A CENTURY OF UK POPULATION
(Year/population)

1901 38,237,000 **1911** 42,082,000 **1921*** 44,027,000
1931* 46,038,000 **1941** 48,216,000 **1951** 50,225,000
1961 52,709,000 **1971** 55,928,000 **1981** 56,352,000
1991 57,808,000, **2001#** 59,994,000

* Figures for Northern Ireland estimated

 # Estimated

Did You Know? United Nations estimates for world population in 2050 predict a 50 percent increase on today's 6 billion, bringing the total to about 9 billion.

TOP 10 ⭐
MOST EXPENSIVE MOVIES OF THE 20TH CENTURY

	DECADE	MOVIE/YEAR	COST $
1	1900–09	*For the Term of His Natural Life** (1908)	34,000
2	1910–19	*A Daughter of the Gods* (1916)	1,000,000
3	1920–29	*Ben-Hur* (1925)	3,900,000
4	1930–39	*Gone With the Wind* (1939)	4,250,000
5	1940–49	*Joan of Arc* (1948)	8,700,000
6	1950–59	*Ben-Hur* (1959)	15,000,000
7	1960–69	*Cleopatra* (1963)	44,000,000
8	1970–79	*Superman* (1978)	55,000,000
9	1980–89	*Who Framed Roger Rabbit* (1988)	70,000,000
10	1990–99	*Titanic* (1997)	200,000,000

* Australian; all others US

FRANKLY, MY DEAR...
Gone With the Wind, *starring Clark Gable and Vivien Leigh, was the most expensive movie ever made, allowing for inflation. It was also the most successful.*

TOP 10 ⭐
SUCCESSIVE HOLDERS OF THE TITLE "WORLD'S TALLEST HABITABLE BUILDING" IN THE 20TH CENTURY

	BUILDING/LOCATION	YEAR	STORIES	FT	M
1	**City Hall**, Philadelphia	1901	7	511	155
2	**Singer Building***, New York	1908	34	656	200
3	**Metropolitan Life**, New York	1909	50	700	212
4	**Woolworth Building**, New York	1913	59	792	241
5	**40 Wall Street**, New York with spire	1929	71	854 / 927	260 / 282
6	**Chrysler Building**, New York with spire	1930	77	925 / 1,046	282 / 319
7	**Empire State Building**, New York with spire	1931	102	1,250 / 1,472	381 / 449
8	**World Trade Center**, New York with spire	1973	110	1,362 / 1,710	415 / 521
9	**Sears Tower**, Chicago with spires	1974	110	1,454 / 1,707	443 / 520
10	**Petronas Towers**, Kuala Lumpur, Malaysia	1996	96	1,482	452

* Demolished 1970

UNBEATEN CITY HALL
Once the world's tallest building, Philadelphia City Hall remains the largest and most expensive municipal building in the US.

The Universe & The Earth

Star Gazing

TOP 10 STARS NEAREST TO THE EARTH*

	STAR	LIGHT YEARS	MILES (MILLIONS)	KM (MILLIONS)
1	Proxima Centauri	4.22	24,792,500	39,923,310
2	Alpha Centauri	4.35	25,556,250	41,153,175
3	Barnard's Star	5.98	35,132,500	56,573,790
4	Wolf 359	7.75	45,531,250	73,318,875
5	Lalande 21185	8.22	48,292,500	77,765,310
6	Luyten 726-8	8.43	49,526,250	79,752,015
7	Sirius	8.65	50,818,750	81,833,325
8	Ross 154	9.45	55,518,750	89,401,725
9	Ross 248	10.40	61,100,000	98,389,200
10	Epsilon Eridani	10.80	63,450,000	102,173,400

Excluding the Sun

A spaceship traveling at 25,000 mph (40,237 km/h) – which is faster than any human has yet reached in space – would take more than 113,200 years to reach the Earth's closest star, Proxima Centauri. While the nearest stars in this list lie just over four light years away from the Earth, others within the Milky Way lie at a distance of 2,500 light years.

CLOSE TO THE EARTH

The name of Proxima Centauri, a red dwarf star in the constellation of Centaurus, literally means "nearest of Centaurus," and it is indeed the Earth's closest star beyond the Sun.

TOP 10 ★
BODIES FARTHEST FROM THE SUN*

	BODY	AVERAGE DISTANCE FROM THE SUN MILES	KM
1	Pluto	3,675,000,000	5,914,000,000
2	Neptune	2,794,000,000	4,497,000,000
3	Uranus	1,784,000,000	2,871,000,000
4	Chiron	1,740,000,000	2,800,000,000
5	Saturn	887,000,000	1,427,000,000
6	Jupiter	483,600,000	778,300,000
7	Mars	141,600,000	227,900,000
8	Earth	92,900,000	149,600,000
9	Venus	67,200,000	108,200,000
10	Mercury	36,000,000	57,900,000

In the Solar System, excluding satellites and asteroids

Chiron, a "mystery object" which may be either a comet or an asteroid, was discovered on November 1, 1977, by American astronomer Charles Kowal. It measures 124–186 miles (200–300 km) in diameter.

AMERICAN DISCOVERY

The Solar System's smallest planet, Pluto, found in 1930, is the only planet to have been discovered by an American – Clyde Tombaugh.

TOP 10 ★
BRIGHTEST STARS*

	STAR/CONSTELLATION	APPARENT MAGNITUDE#
1	**Sirius**, Canis Major	-1.46
2	**Canopus**, Carina	-0.73
3	**Alpha Centauri**, Centaurus	-0.27
4	**Arcturus**, Boötes	-0.04
5	**Vega**, Lyra	+0.03
6	**Capella**, Auriga	+0.08
7	**Rigel**, Orion	+0.12
8	**Procyon**, Canis Minor	+0.38
9	**Achernar**, Eridanus	+0.46
10	**Beta Centauri**, Centaurus	+0.61

* Excluding the Sun

\# Based on apparent visual magnitude as viewed from the Earth – the lower the number, the brighter the star

At its brightest, the star Betelgeuse is brighter than some of these, but its variability disqualifies it from the Top 10. More distant stars naturally appear fainter. To compensate for this effect, absolute magnitude estimates the brightness of a star at an imaginary fixed distance of 10 parsecs, or 32.6 light years, enabling comparison between the "true" brightness of different stars.

RINGS OF ICE

Saturn's ring system was not discovered until 1656. Composed of ice, the rings are up to 167,770 miles (270,000 km) in diameter.

TOP 10 ★
LARGEST BODIES IN THE SOLAR SYSTEM

	BODY	MAXIMUM DIAMETER MILES	KM
1	**Sun**	865,036	1,392,140
2	**Jupiter**	88,846	142,984
3	**Saturn**	74,898	120,536
4	**Uranus**	31,763	51,118
5	**Neptune**	30,778	49,532
6	**Earth**	7,926	12,756
7	**Venus**	7,520	12,103
8	**Mars**	4,222	6,794
9	**Ganymede**	3,274	5,269
10	**Titan**	3,200	5,150

Most of the planets are visible with the naked eye and have been observed since ancient times. The exceptions are Uranus, discovered on March 13, 1781 by British astronomer Sir William Herschel; Neptune, found by German astronomer Johann Galle on September 23, 1846; and, outside the Top 10, Pluto, located using photographic techniques by American astronomer Clyde Tombaugh. Its discovery was announced on March 13, 1930; its diameter is uncertain but is thought to be about 1,430 miles (2,302 km).

TOP 10 ★
LONGEST DAYS IN THE SOLAR SYSTEM

	BODY	LENGTH OF DAY* DAYS	HOURS	MINS
1	**Venus**	244	0	0
2	**Mercury**	58	14	0
3	**Sun**	25#	0	0
4	**Pluto**	6	9	0
5	**Mars**		24	37
6	**Earth**		23	56
7	**Uranus**		17	14
8	**Neptune**		16	7
9	**Saturn**		10	39
10	**Jupiter**		9	55

* Period of rotation, based on 23-hour, 56-minute sidereal day

\# Variable

TOP 10 ★
GALAXIES NEAREST TO THE EARTH

	GALAXY	DISTANCE LIGHT YEARS
1	**Large Cloud of Magellan**	169,000
2	**Small Cloud of Magellan**	190,000
3	**Ursa Minor dwarf**	250,000
4	**Draco dwarf**	260,000
5	**Sculptor dwarf**	280,000
6	**Fornax dwarf**	420,000
7 =	**Leo I dwarf**	750,000
=	**Leo II dwarf**	750,000
9	**Barnard's Galaxy**	1,700,000
10	**Andromeda Spiral**	2,200,000

These and other galaxies are members of the so-called "Local Group," although with vast distances such as these, "local" is a relative term.

TOP 10 ★
MOST MASSIVE BODIES IN THE SOLAR SYSTEM*

	BODY	MASS#
1	**Sun**	332,800.000
2	**Jupiter**	317.828
3	**Saturn**	95.161
4	**Neptune**	17.148
5	**Uranus**	14.536
6	**Earth**	1.000
7	**Venus**	0.815
8	**Mars**	0.10745
9	**Mercury**	0.05527
10	**Pluto**	0.0022

* Excluding satellites

\# Compared with the Earth = 1; the mass of the Earth is approximately 80 million trillion tons

When was Halley's Comet last seen?   **A** 1976
see p.14 for the answer   **B** 1986
   C 1996

13

Asteroids, Meteorites & Comets

MOST RECENT OBSERVATIONS
OF HALLEY'S COMET

1 1986
The Japanese *Suisei* probe passed within 93,827 miles (151,000 km) of its 9-mile (15-km) nucleus on March 8, 1986, revealing a whirling nucleus within a hydrogen cloud emitting 20–50 tons of water per second. The Soviet probes *Vega 1* and *Vega 2* passed within 5,524 miles (8,890 km) and 4,990 miles (8,030 km) respectively. The European Space Agency's *Giotto* passed as close as 370 miles (596 km) on March 14 of the same year. All were heavily battered by dust particles, and it was concluded that Halley's comet is composed of dust bonded by water and carbon dioxide ice.

2 1910
Predictions of disaster were widely published, with many people convinced that the world would come to an end. Mark Twain, who had been born at the time of the 1835 appearance and who believed that his fate was linked to that of the comet, died when it reappeared in this year.

3 1835
Widely observed but noticeably dimmer than in 1759.

4 1759
The comet's first return, as predicted by Halley, thus proving his calculations correct.

5 1682
Observed in Africa and China and extensively in Europe, where it was observed on September 5–19 by Edmund Halley, who predicted its return.

6 1607
Seen extensively in China, Japan, Korea, and Europe, described by German astronomer Johannes Kepler and its position accurately measured by amateur Welsh astronomer Thomas Harriot.

7 1531
Observed in China, Japan, Korea, and in Europe on August 13–23 by Peter Appian, German geographer and astronomer, who noted that comets' tails point away from the Sun.

8 1456
Observed in China, Japan, Korea, and by the Turkish army, which was threatening to invade Europe. When the Turks were defeated by Papal forces, it was seen as a portent of the latter's victory.

9 1378
Observed in China, Japan, Korea, and Europe.

10 1301
Seen in Iceland, parts of Europe, China, Japan, and Korea.

Before Edmund Halley (1656–1742) studied and foretold the return of the famous comet that now bears his name, no one had succeeded in proving that comets travel in predictable orbits. The dramatic return in 1759 of the comet Halley had observed in 1682 established the science of cometary observation. There have been about 30 recorded appearances of Halley's comet. The most famous occurred in 1066, when William of Normandy (later known as William the Conqueror) regarded it as a sign of his imminent victory over King Harold at the Battle of Hastings; it is clearly shown in the Bayeux Tapestry.

TOP 10 MOST FREQUENTLY
SEEN COMETS
(Comet/years between appearances)

1. **Encke**, 3.302
2. **Grigg-Skjellerup**, 4.908
3. **Honda-Mrkós-Pajdusáková**, 5.210
4. **Tempel 2**, 5.259
5. **Neujmin 2**, 5.437
6. **Brorsen**, 5.463
7. **Tuttle-Giacobini-Kresák**, 5.489
8. **Tempel-L. Swift**, 5.681
9. **Tempel 1**, 5.982
10. **Pons-Winnecke**, 6.125

COMETS COMING
CLOSEST TO THE EARTH

	COMET	DATE*	DISTANCE AU#
1	Lexell	July 1, 1770	2.3
2	Tempel-Tuttle	Oct 26, 1366	3.4
3	Halley	Apr 10, 837	5.0
4	Biela	Dec 9, 1805	5.5
5	Grischow	Feb 8, 1743	5.8
6	Pons-Winnecke	June 26, 1927	5.9
7	La Hire	Apr 20, 1702	6.6
8	Schwassmann-Wachmann	May 31, 1930	9.3
9	Cassini	Jan 8, 1760	10.2
10	Schweizer	Apr 29, 1853	12.6

* Of closest approach to the Earth

Astronomical Units: 1 AU = mean distance from the Earth to the Sun (92,955,900 miles/149,598,200 km)

ROCK OF AGES

Visitors are encouraged to touch the 11-ft (3.4-m) Ahnighito, the largest meteorite on public display, and to appreciate that it is as old as the Solar System – some 4.5 billion years.

THE 10 ★
FIRST ASTEROIDS TO BE DISCOVERED

ASTEROID/DISCOVERER	DISCOVERED
1 **Ceres**, Giuseppe Piazzi	Jan 1, 1801
2 **Pallas**, Heinrich Olbers	Mar 28, 1802
3 **Juno**, Karl Ludwig Harding	Sep 1, 1804
4 **Vesta**, Heinrich Olbers	Mar 29, 1807
5 **Astraea**, Karl Ludwig Hencke	Dec 8, 1845
6 **Hebe**, Karl Ludwig Hencke	July 1, 1847
7 **Iris**, John Russell Hind	Aug 13, 1847
8 **Flora**, John Russell Hind	Oct 18, 1847
9 **Metis**, Andrew Graham	Apr 25, 1848
10 **Hygeia**, Annibale de Gasparis	Apr 12, 1849

Asteroids, sometimes known as "minor planets," are fragments of rock orbiting between Mars and Jupiter. There are perhaps 45,000 of them, but fewer than 10 percent have been named.

ASTEROIDS

Since the discovery of Ceres, the first and largest asteroid, over 6,000 have been found, 26 of them larger than 120 miles (200 km) in diameter. Gaspra, pictured here, measures only 12 x 7 miles (20 x 12 km), but was closely studied by the *Galileo* spacecraft in 1991. The total mass of all the asteroids is less than that of the Moon. It is believed that, on average, one asteroid larger than ¼ mile (0.4 km) strikes the Earth every 50,000 years. As recently as 1994, a small asteroid with the temporary designation 1994XM, measuring a modest 33 ft (18 m) in diameter, came within 69,594 miles (112,600 km) of the Earth – making it the closest recorded near-miss.

SNAP SHOTS

TOP 10 ★
LARGEST METEORITES EVER FOUND

SITE/LOCATION	ESTIMATED WEIGHT TONS
1 **Hoba West**, Grootfontein, Namibia	over 60.0
2 **Ahnighito ("The Tent")**, Cape York, West Greenland	57.3
3 **Campo del Cielo**, Argentina	41.4
4 **Canyon Diablo***, Arizona	30.0
5 **Sikhote-Alin**, Russia	27.0
6 **Chupaderos**, Mexico	24.2
7 **Bacuberito**, Mexico	22.0
8 **Armanty**, Western Mongolia	20.0
9 **Mundrabilla**#, Western Australia	17.0
10 **Mbosi**, Tanzania	16.0

* *Formed Meteor Crater; fragmented – total in public collections is around 11.5 tons*

In two parts – 11.5 and 6.1 tons

The Hoba meteorite was found on a farm in 1920. A 9 x 8 ft (2.73 x 2.43 m) slab, it consists of 82 percent iron and 16 percent nickel. In 1989, 36 Malaysian soldiers with the UN Peacekeeping Force attempted to hack pieces off it as souvenirs, causing an outcry. "The Tent," known by its original Inuit name of Ahnighito, was discovered in 1894 by the American Arctic explorer Admiral Robert Peary. Now in the Hayden Planetarium at the New York Museum of Natural History, it is the largest meteorite in the world on exhibition.

TOP 10 ★
LARGEST METEORITES EVER FOUND IN THE US

SITE/LOCATION	ESTIMATED WEIGHT TONS
1 **Canyon Diablo***, Arizona	30.00
2 **Willamette**, Oregon	15.00
3 **Old Woman**, California	2.75
4 **Brenham**, Kansas	2.40
5 **Navajo**, Arizona	2.18
6 **Quinn Canyon**, Nevada	1.45
7 **Goose Lake**, California	1.17
8 **Norton County**, Kansas	1.00
9 **Tucson**, Arizona	0.97
10 **Sardis**#, Georgia	0.80

* *Formed Meteor Crater; fragmented – total in public collections is around 11.5 tons*

Now badly corroded

It has been suggested that the weight of a meteorite discovered at Cosby's Creek, Tennessee, was 0.958 tons, but only 95 kg of it has been accounted for. There are approximately 1,200 meteorites known in the US; by comparison, there have been only 17 definite meteorites found in the UK. The number of meteorites falling has been calculated to amount to some 500 a year across the whole globe, although many fall in the ocean and unpopulated areas, where their descent goes unnoticed. There is no record of anyone being killed by a meteorite.

Did You Know? A car damaged by a 22-lb (10-kg) meteorite in Peekskill, New York, in 1992 was sold to the Montana Meteorite Lab for $69,000 – complete with the meteorite.

Space Firsts

THE 10 ★ FIRST BODIES TO HAVE BEEN VISITED BY SPACECRAFT

	BODY	SPACECRAFT	COUNTRY	YEAR
1	Moon	Pioneer 4	US	1959
2	Venus	Mariner 2	US	1962
3	Mars	Mariner 4	US	1965
4	Sun	Pioneer 7	US	1966
5	Jupiter	Pioneer 10	US	1973
6	Mercury	Mariner 10	US	1974
7	Saturn	Pioneer 11	US	1979
8	Comet Giacobini-Zinner	International Sun–Earth Explorer 3 (International Cometary Explorer)	US	1985
9	Uranus	Voyager 2	US	1986
10	Halley's Comet	Giotto	Europe	1986

THE 10 ★ FIRST ANIMALS IN SPACE

	NAME/ANIMAL	COUNTRY	DATE
1	Laika, dog	USSR	Nov 3, 1957
2=	Laska and Benjy, mice	US	Dec 13, 1958
4=	Able and Baker, female rhesus monkey and female squirrel monkey	US	May 28, 1959
6=	Otvazhnaya, female Samoyed husky, and an unnamed rabbit	USSR	July 2, 1959
8	Sam, male rhesus monkey	US	Dec 4, 1959
9	Miss Sam, female rhesus monkey	US	Jan 21, 1960
10=	Belka and Strelka, female Samoyed huskies	USSR	Aug 19, 1960

TOP 10 ★ FIRST WOMEN IN SPACE

	NAME/SPACECRAFT	DATE
1	Valentina V. Tereshkova, *Vostok 6*	June 16–19, 1963
2	Svetlana Savitskaya, *Soyuz T7*	Aug 19, 1982
3	Sally K. Ride, *Challenger STS-7*	June 18–24, 1983
4	Judith A. Resnik, *Discovery STS-41-D*	Aug 30–Sep 5, 1984
5	Kathryn D. Sullivan, *Discovery STS-41-G*	Oct 5–13, 1984
6	Anna L. Fisher, *Discovery STS-51-A*	Nov 8–16, 1984
7	Margaret R. Seddon, *Discovery STS-51-D*	Apr 12–19, 1985
8	Shannon W. Lucid, *Discovery STS-41-G*	June 17–24, 1985
9	Bonnie J. Dunbar, *Discovery STS-61-A*	Oct 30–Nov 6, 1985
10	Mary L. Cleave, *Discovery STS-61-B*	Nov 26–Dec 3, 1985

On May 18, 1991, Helen Sharman, a 27-year-old chemist, became Britain's first astronaut and the 15th woman in space when she went on a seven-day mission on Soyuz TM12 to the Mir space station.

TOP 10 ★ FIRST MOONWALKERS

	ASTRONAUT/SPACECRAFT	TOTAL EVA* HR:MIN	MISSION DATES
1	Neil A. Armstrong, *Apollo 11*	2:32	July 16–24, 1969
2	Edwin E. ("Buzz") Aldrin, *Apollo 11*	2:15	July 16–24, 1969
3	Charles Conrad, Jr., *Apollo 12*	7:45	Nov 14–24, 1969
4	Alan L. Bean, *Apollo 12*	7:45	Nov 14–24, 1969
5	Alan B. Shepard, *Apollo 14*	9:23	Jan 31–Feb 9, 1971
6	Edgar D. Mitchell, *Apollo 14*	9:23	Jan 31–Feb 9, 1971
7	David R. Scott, *Apollo 15*	19:08	July 26–Aug 7, 1971
8	James B. Irwin, *Apollo 15*	18:35	July 26 –Aug 7, 1971
9	John W. Young, *Apollo 16*	20:14	Apr 16–27, 1972
10	Charles M. Duke, *Apollo 16*	20:14	Apr 16–27, 1972

* Extra Vehicular Activity (i.e. time spent out of the lunar module on the Moon's surface)

MOON ROCKET

Apollo 11 blasts off from Cape Canaveral on July 16, 1969. Aboard are Americans Neil Armstrong and "Buzz" Aldrin, destined to be the first men to walk on the Moon.

★ THE 10

FIRST COUNTRIES TO HAVE ASTRONAUTS OR COSMONAUTS IN ORBIT

	COUNTRY/ASTRONAUT OR COSMONAUT	DATE*
1	**USSR**, Yuri A. Gagarin	Apr 12, 1961
2	**US**, John H. Glenn	Feb 20, 1962
3	**Czechoslovakia**, Vladimir Remek	Mar 2, 1978
4	**Poland**, Miroslaw Hermaszewski	June 27, 1978
5	**East Germany**, Sigmund Jahn	Aug 26, 1978
6	**Bulgaria**, Georgi I. Ivanov	Apr 10, 1979
7	**Hungary**, Bertalan Farkas	May 26, 1980
8	**Vietnam**, Pham Tuan	July 23, 1980
9	**Cuba**, Arnaldo T. Mendez	Sep 18, 1980
10	**Mongolia**, Jugderdemidiyn Gurragcha	Mar 22, 1981

* Of first space entry of a national of that country

★ THE 10

FIRST SPACEWALKERS

	ASTRONAUT	SPACECRAFT	EVA* HR:MIN	EVA DATE
1	**Alexei Leonov**	*Voskhod 2*	0:23	Mar 18, 1965
2	**Edward H. White**	*Gemini 4*	0:36	June 3, 1965
3	**Eugene A. Cernan**	*Gemini 9*	2:07	June 3, 1966
4	**Michael Collins**	*Gemini 10*	0:50	July 19, 1966
5	**Richard F. Gordon**	*Gemini 11*	0:33	Sep 13, 1966
6	**Edwin E. ("Buzz") Aldrin**	*Gemini 12*	2:29	Nov 12, 1966
7=	**Alexei Yeleseyev**	*Soyuz 5*	0:37	Jan 16, 1969
=	**Yevgeny Khrunov**	*Soyuz 5*	0:37	Jan 16, 1969
9=	**Russell L. Schweickart**	*Apollo 9*	0:46	Mar 6, 1969
=	**David R. Scott**	*Apollo 9*	0:46	Mar 6, 1969

* *Extravehicular Activity*

Leonov's first spacewalk almost ended in disaster when his spacesuit "ballooned" and he was unable to return through the air-lock into the capsule until he had reduced the pressure in his suit to a dangerously low level. Edward H. White was killed in the *Apollo* spacecraft fire of January 27, 1967.

★ TOP 10

FIRST PEOPLE TO ORBIT THE EARTH

	NAME/SPACECRAFT	COUNTRY OF ORIGIN	DATE
1	**Yuri A. Gagarin**, *Vostok I*	USSR	Apr 12, 1961
2	**Gherman S. Titov**, *Vostok II*	USSR	Aug 6–7, 1961
3	**John H. Glenn**, *Friendship 7*	US	Feb 20, 1962
4	**M. Scott Carpenter**, *Aurora 7*	US	May 24, 1962
5	**Andrian G. Nikolayev**, *Vostok III*	USSR	Aug 11–15, 1962
6	**Pavel R. Popovich**, *Vostok IV*	USSR	Aug 12–15, 1962
7	**Walter M. Schirra**, *Sigma 7*	US	Oct 3, 1962
8	**L. Gordon Cooper**, *Faith 7*	US	May 15–16, 1963
9	**Valeri F. Bykovsky**, *Vostok V*	USSR	June 14–19, 1963
10	**Valentina V. Tereshkova**, *Vostok VI*	USSR	June 16–19, 1963

Yuri Gagarin, at the age of 27, orbited the Earth once, taking 1 hour 48 minutes. Titov, the youngest-ever astronaut at 25 years 329 days, performed 17 orbits during 25 hours. The first American to orbit the Earth, John Glenn, is the oldest on this list at 40; he has since gone on to become the oldest astronaut of all time.

FIRST IN SPACE

In 1961, Soviet cosmonaut Yuri Gagarin became the first human to enter space and orbit the Earth. His flight aboard Vostok 1 lasted just 108 minutes. After receiving his country's highest honors, Gagarin was killed in a MiG-15 plane crash in 1968.

Space Explorers

SPACELINK

In 1995, the US's 100th crewed flight, Atlantis STS-71, linked up with Russian space station Mir for the first time, exchanging astronauts and cosmonauts between the two spacecraft.

TOP 10 ★
MOST EXPERIENCED SPACEMEN*

	SPACEMAN	MISSIONS	TOTAL DURATION OF MISSIONS DAYS	HOURS	MINS	SECS
1	Sergei V. Avdeyev	3	747	14	22	47
2	Valeri V. Polyakov	2	678	16	33	18
3	Anatoli Y. Solovyov	5	651	0	11	25
4	Viktor M. Afanasyev	3	545	2	34	41
5	Musa K. Manarov	2	541	0	29	38
6	Alexander S. Viktorenko	4	489	1	35	17
7	Sergei K. Krikalyov	4#	483	9	37	26
8	Yuri V. Romanenko	3	430	18	21	30
9	Alexander A. Volkov	3	391	11	52	14
10	Vladimir G. Titov	5#	387	0	51	03

* To January 1, 2000

\# Including flights aboard US space shuttles

All the missions listed were undertaken by the USSR (and, latterly, Russia). In recent years, a number of US astronauts have added to their space logs by spending time on board the Russian *Mir* space station, but none has matched the records set by Russian cosmonauts. While Valeri Polyakov holds the record for the longest continuous space flight, Sergei Avdeyev exceeded Polyakov's cumulative record on June 20, 1999, by spending his 679th day in space.

TOP 10 ★
MOST EXPERIENCED SPACEWOMEN*

	SPACEWOMAN#	MISSIONS	TOTAL DURATION OF MISSIONS DAYS	HOURS	MINS	SECS
1	Shannon W. Lucid	5	223	2	52	26
2	Yelena V. Kondakova	2	178	10	41	31
3	Tamara E. Jernigan	5	63	1	25	40
4	Bonnie J. Dunbar	5	50	8	24	44
5	Marsha S. Ivins	4	43	0	27	43
6	Kathryn C. Thornton	4	40	15	15	18
7	Janice E. Voss	4	37	21	10	18
8	Wendy B. Lawrence	3	37	5	23	20
9	Susan J. Helms	3	33	20	16	31
10	Nancy J. Currie	3	30	17	23	46

* To January 1, 2000

\# All US except 2 (Russian)

Shannon Lucid became both America's most experienced astronaut and the world's most experienced female astronaut in 1996. She took off in US space shuttle *Atlantis STS-76* on March 22, and transferred to the Russian *Mir* Space Station, returning on board *Atlantis STS-79* on September 26 after traveling 75.2 million miles (121 million km) in 188 days, 4 hours, 0 minutes, 14 seconds – also a record duration for a single mission by a US astronaut.

Did You Know? The greatest number of people in space at the same time was 13, when, on March 14, 1995, a space shuttle, a Russian spacecraft, and the *Mir* space station orbited simultaneously.

TOP 10 ⭐
OLDEST US ASTRONAUTS*

ASTRONAUT	LAST FLIGHT	AGE#
1 John H. Glenn	Nov 6, 1998	77
2 F. Story Musgrave	Dec 7, 1996	61
3 Vance D. Brand	Dec 11, 1990	59
4 Karl G. Henize	Aug 6, 1985	58
5 Roger K. Crouch	July 17, 1997	56
6 William E. Thornton	May 6, 1985	56
7 Don L. Lind	May 6, 1985	54
8 Henry W. Hartsfield	Nov 6, 1988	54
9 John E. Blaha	Dec 7, 1996	54
10 William G. Gregory	Mar 18, 1995	54

* *Including payload specialists, etc., to January 1, 2000*

Those of apparently identical age have been ranked according to their precise age in days at the time of their last flight.

At 53, Shannon Lucid (born January 14, 1943, last flight March 31, 1996) holds the record as the oldest woman in space.

TOP 10 ⭐
YOUNGEST US ASTRONAUTS*

ASTRONAUT	FIRST FLIGHT	AGE#
1 Kenneth D. Bowersox	June 25, 1984	28
2 Sally K. Ride	June 18, 1983	32
3 Tamara E. Jernigan	June 5, 1991	32
4 Eugene A. Cernan	June 3, 1966	32
5 Koichi Wakata	Jan 11, 1996	32
6 Steven A. Hawley	Aug 30, 1984	32
7 Mary E. Weber	July 13, 1995	32
8 Kathryn D. Sullivan	Oct 5, 1984	33
9 Ronald E. McNair+	Feb 3, 1984	33
10 George D. Nelson	Apr 6, 1984	33

* *To January 1, 2000*

Those of apparently identical age have been ranked according to their precise age in days at the time of their first flight.

+ *Killed in Challenger disaster, January 28, 1986*

TOP 10 ⭐
LONGEST SPACE MISSIONS*

NAME/MISSION DATES	DAYS
1 Valeri V. Polyakov Jan 8, 1994–Mar 22, 1995	437.7
2 Sergei V. Avdeyev Aug 13, 1998–Aug 28, 1999	379.6
3 = Musa K. Manarov Dec 21, 1987–Dec 21, 1988	365.9
= Vladimir G. Titov Dec 21, 1987–Dec 21, 1988	365.9
5 Yuri V. Romanenko Feb 5–Dec 5, 1987	326.5
6 Sergei K. Krikalyov May 18, 1991–Mar 25, 1992	311.8
7 Valeri V. Polyakov Aug 31, 1988–Apr 27, 1989	240.9
8 = Oleg Y. Atkov Feb 8–Oct 2, 1984	237.0
= Leonid D. Kizim Feb 8–Oct 2, 1984	237.0
= Anatoli Y. Solovyov Feb 8–Oct 2, 1984	237.0

* *To January 1, 2000*

Space medicine specialist Valeri V. Polyakov (born April 27, 1942) spent his 52nd birthday in space during his record-breaking mission aboard the *Mir* space station.

"ASTRONAUT"

In a pioneering science-fiction novel, *Across the Zodiac*, published in 1880, British writer Percy Greg (1836–89) presented the first fictional account of interplanetary travel by space ship, calling his vessel *Astronaut* (from the Greek for "star sailor"). By the late 1920s, the word had become used to mean a space *traveler*, rather than his ship, and, once the space age began, it was this sense that became established in the West, with cosmonaut as the Russian equivalent.

WHY DO WE SAY?

SPACE-AGE WOMAN

With three further missions since her first flight aboard Space Shuttle Endeavor STS-57 in 1993, NASA astronaut Janice Voss has earned a place among the world's most experienced spacewomen.

Waterworld

DEEPEST OCEANS AND SEAS

OCEAN OR SEA	GREATEST DEPTH FT	M	AVERAGE DEPTH FT	M
1 Pacific Ocean	35,837	10,924	13,215	4,028
2 Indian Ocean	24,460	7,455	13,002	3,963
3 Atlantic Ocean	30,246	9,219	12,880	3,926
4 Caribbean Sea	22,788	6,946	8,685	2,647
5 South China Sea	16,456	5,016	5,419	1,652
6 Bering Sea	15,659	4,773	5,075	1,547
7 Gulf of Mexico	12,425	3,787	4,874	1,486
8 Mediterranean Sea	15,197	4,632	4,688	1,429
9 Japan Sea	12,276	3,742	4,429	1,350
10 Arctic Ocean	18,456	5,625	3,953	1,205

The deepest point in the deepest ocean is the Marianas Trench in the Pacific at a depth of 35,837 ft (10,924 m). The Pacific is so vast that it contains more water than all the world's other seas and oceans put together.

LONGEST RIVERS

RIVER	LOCATION	LENGTH MIILES	KM
1 Nile	Tanzania/Uganda/Sudan/Egypt	4,145	6,670
2 Amazon	Peru/Brazil	4,007	6,448
3 Yangtze–Kiang	China	3,915	6,300
4 Mississippi–Missouri–Red Rock	US	3,710	5,971
5 Yenisey–Angara–Selenga	Mongolia/Russia	3,442	5,540
6 Huang Ho (Yellow River)	China	3,395	5,464
7 Ob'-Irtysh	Mongolia/Kazakhstan/Russia	3,362	5,410
8 Congo	Angola/Dem. Rep. of Congo	2,920	4,700
9 Lena–Kirenga	Russia	2,734	4,400
10 Mekong	Tibet/China/Myanmar (Burma)/Laos/Cambodia/Vietnam	2,703	4,350

LONGEST GLACIERS

GLACIER	LOCATION	LENGTH MILES	KM
1 Lambert-Fisher	Antarctica	320	515
2 Novaya Zemlya	Russia	260	418
3 Arctic Institute	Antarctica	225	362
4 Nimrod-Lennox-King	Antarctica	180	290
5 Denman	Antarctica	150	241
6 =Beardmore	Antarctica	140	225
=Recovery	Antarctica	140	225
8 Petermanns	Greenland	124	200
9 Unnamed	Antarctica	120	193
10 Slessor	Antarctica	115	185

LARGEST FRESHWATER LAKES IN THE US*

LAKE	LOCATION	APPROX. AREA SQ MILES	SQ KM
1 Michigan	Illinois/Indiana/Michigan/Wisconsin	22,400	58,016
2 Iliamna	Alaska	1,000	2,590
3 Okeechobee	Florida	700	1,813
4 Becharof	Alaska	458	1,186
5 Red	Minnesota	451	1,168
6 Teshepuk	Alaska	315	816
7 Naknek	Alaska	242	627
8 Winnebago	Wisconsin	215	557
9 Mille Lacs	Minnesota	207	536
10 Flathead	Montana	197	510

Excluding those partly in Canada

TOP 10 DEEPEST DEEP-SEA TRENCHES

(Trench/ocean/deepest point in ft/m)

1 Marianas, Pacific, 35,837/10,924 **2** Tonga*, Pacific, 35,430/10,800 **3** Philippine, Pacific, 34,436/10,497 **4** Kermadec*, Pacific, 32,960/10,047 **5** Bonin, Pacific, 32,786/9,994 **6** New Britain, Pacific, 32,609/9,940 **7** Kuril, Pacific, 31,985/9,750 **8** Izu, Pacific, 31,805/9,695 **9** Puerto Rico, Atlantic, 28,229/8,605 **10** Yap, Pacific, 27,973/8,527

Some authorities consider these parts of one feature

JUNGLE FEEDER

It was not until 1953 that the source of the Amazon was identifed as a stream called Huarco, flowing from the Misuie glacier in the Peruvian Andes mountains. It joins the Amazon's main tributary at Ucayali, Peru.

COUNTRIES WITH THE GREATEST AREAS OF INLAND WATER

	COUNTRY	PERCENTAGE OF TOTAL AREA	WATER AREA SQ MILES	SQ KM
1	Canada	7.60	291,573	755,170
2	India	9.56	121,391	314,400
3	China	2.82	104,460	270,550
4	US	2.20	79,541	206,010
5	Ethiopia	9.89	46,680	120,900
6	Colombia	8.80	38,691	100,210
7	Indonesia	4.88	35,908	93,000
8	Russia	0.47	30,657	79,400
9	Australia	0.90	26,610	68,920
10	Tanzania	6.25	22,799	59,050

Large areas of some countries are occupied by major rivers and lakes. Lake Victoria, for example, raises the water area of Uganda to 15.39 percent of its total. In Europe, three Scandinavian countries have considerable percentages of water: Sweden 8.68 percent, Finland 9.36 percent, and Norway 5.05 percent.

HIGHEST WATERFALLS

	WATERFALL	LOCATION	TOTAL DROP FT	M
1	Angel	Venezuela	3,212	979*
2	Tugela	South Africa	3,107	947
3	Utigård	Norway	2,625	800
4	Mongefossen	Norway	2,540	774
5	Yosemite	California	2,425	739
6	Østre Mardøla Foss	Norway	2,152	656
7	Tyssestrengane	Norway	2,120	646
8	Cuquenán	Venezuela	2,000	610
9	Sutherland	New Zealand	1,904	580
10	Kjellfossen	Norway	1,841	561

* Longest single drop 2,648 ft (807 m)

FALL AND ANGEL

Angel Falls in Venezuela were discovered in 1933 by American adventurer James Angel, after whom they are named. Their overall height is equivalent to two-and-a-half Empire State Buildings.

DEEPEST FRESHWATER LAKES

	LAKE	LOCATION	GREATEST DEPTH FT	M
1	Baikal	Russia	5,371	1,637
2	Tanganyika	Burundi/ Tanzania/Dem. Rep. of Congo/ Zambia	4,825	1,471
3	Malawi	Malawi/ Mozambique/Tanzania	2,316	706
4	Great Slave	Canada	2,015	614
5	Matana	Celebes, Indonesia	1,936	590
6	Crater	Oregon, US	1,932	589
7	Toba	Sumatra, Indonesia	1,736	529
8	Hornindals	Norway	1,686	514
9	Sarez	Tajikistan	1,657	505
10	Tahoe	California/ Nevada, US	1,645	501

LARGEST LAKES

	LAKE	LOCATION	APPROX. AREA SQ MILES	SQ KM
1	Caspian Sea	Azerbaijan/ Iran/Kazakhstan/ Russia/Turkmenistan	143,205	371,000
2	Superior	Canada/US	31,820	82,413
3	Victoria	Kenya/ Tanzania/Uganda	26,570	68,800
4	Huron	Canada/US	23,010	59,596
5	Michigan	US	22,400	58,016
6	Aral Sea	Kazakhstan/ Uzbekistan	15,444	40,000
7	Tanganyika	Burundi/ Tanzania/Dem. Rep. of Congo/Zambia	13,860	32,900
8	Great Bear	Canada	12,030	31,150
9	Baikal	Russia	11,775	30,500
10	Great Slave	Canada	11,030	28,570

LARGEST LAKES IN NORTH AMERICA

	LAKE	LOCATION	APPROX. AREA SQ MILES	SQ KM
1	Superior	Canada/US	31,820	82,413
2	Huron	Canada/US	23,010	59,596
3	Michigan	US	22,400	58,016
4	Great Bear	Canada	12,030	31,150
5	Great Slave	Canada	11,030	28,570
6	Erie	Canada/US	9,930	25,719
7	Winnipeg	Canada	9,094	24,553
8	Ontario	Canada/US	7,520	19,477
9	Athabasca	Canada	3,058	7,920
10	Reindeer	Canada	2,444	6,330

The Great Lakes together form the largest area of freshwater on the Earth. They comprise Superior, Huron, Michigan, Erie, and Ontario, which together have an area of 94,616 sq miles (245,055 sq km).

Where in the Solar System does a day last 244 Earth days?
see p.13 for the answer

A Pluto
B Neptune
C Venus

TOP 10 LARGEST VOLCANIC ISLANDS

ISLAND/LOCATION	STATUS	APPROX. AREA SQ MILES	SQ KM
1 **Sumatra**, Indonesia	Active volcanic	171,068.7	443,065.8
2 **Honshu**, Japan	Volcanic	87.182.0	225,800.3
3 **Java**, Indonesia	Volcanic	53.588.5	138,793.6
4 **North Island**, New Zealand	Volcanic	43.082.4	111,582.8
5 **Luzon**, Philippines	Active volcanic	42.457.7	109,964.9
6 **Iceland**, Indonesia	Active volcanic	39,315.2	101,826.0
7 **Mindanao**, Philippines	Active volcanic	37,656.5	97,530.0
8 **Hokkaido**, Japan	Active volcanic	30,394.7	78,719.4
9 **New Britain**, Papua New Guinea	Volcanic	13,569.4	35,144.6
10 **Halmahera**, Indonesia	Active volcanic	6,965.1	18,039.6

Source: *United Nations*

TOP 10 ⭐ LARGEST ISLANDS

ISLAND/LOCATION	APPROX. AREA* SQ MILES	SQ KM
1 **Greenland**	840,070	2,175,600
2 **New Guinea**, Papua New Guinea/Indonesia	309,000	800,000
3 **Borneo**, Indonesia/Malaysia/Brunei	287,300	744,100
4 **Madagascar**	226,657	587,041
5 **Baffin Island**, Canada	195,875	507,450
6 **Sumatra**, Indonesia	164,000	424,760
7 **Honshu**, Japan	89,176	230,966
8 **Great Britain**	88,787	229,957
9 **Victoria Island**, Canada	83,896	217,206
10 **Ellesmere Island**, Canada	75,767	196,160

* *Mainlands, including areas of inland water, but excluding offshore islands*

Australia is regarded as a continental land mass rather than an island: otherwise it would rank first at 2,941,517 sq miles (7,618,493 sq km), or 35 times the size of Great Britain. The largest US island is Hawaii, which measures 4,037 sq miles (10,456 sq km), and the largest off mainland US is Kodiak, Alaska, at 3,672 sq miles (9,510 sq km).

TOP 10 ⭐ LARGEST ISLANDS IN EUROPE

ISLAND/LOCATION	AREA SQ MILES	SQ KM
1 **Great Britain**, North Atlantic	88,787	229,957
2 **Iceland**, North Atlantic	39,769	103,000
3 **Ireland**, North Atlantic	32,342	83,766
4 **West Spitsbergen**, Arctic Ocean	15,200	39,368
5 **Sicily**, Mediterranean Sea	9,807	25,400
6 **Sardinia**, Mediterranean Sea	9,189	23,800
7 **North East Land**, Barents Sea	5,792	15,000
8 **Cyprus**, Mediterranean Sea	3,572	9,251
9 **Corsica**, Mediterranean Sea	3,367	8,720
10 **Crete**, Mediterranean Sea	3,189	8,260

Great Britain became an island only after the end of the last ice age, some 8,000 years ago, when the land bridge that had previously existed was inundated and the North Sea became connected with the English Channel. Until then the Dogger Bank, now a notable fishing ground, was land, and the Thames River was a tributary of the Rhine.

TOP 10 ⭐ LARGEST ISLANDS IN THE US

ISLAND/LOCATION	AREA SQ MILES	SQ KM
1 **Hawaii**, Hawaii	4,037	10,456
2 **Kodiak**, Alaska	3,672	9,510
3 **Prince of Wales**, Alaska	2,587	6,700
4 **Chicagof**, Alaska	2,085	5,400
5 **Saint Lawrence**, Alaska	1,710	4,430
6 **Admiralty**, Alaska	1,649	4,270
7 **Baranof**, Alaska	1,636	4,237
8 **Nunivak**, Alaska	1,625	4,210
9 **Unimak**, Alaska	1,606	4,160
10 **Long Island**, New York	1,401	3,269

Did You Know? The volcanic island of Surtsey emerged from the sea to the south of Iceland in 1963. It was named after the Norse god Surtur.

UNDER THE VOLCANO

Volcanic Sumatra's tallest peak, Gunung Kerinici, is a 12,484-ft (3,805-m) active volcano that was first climbed in 1877. Southeast Asia has more active volcanoes than any other part of the world.

TOP 10 HIGHEST ISLANDS

(Island/location/highest elevation in ft/m)

1 **New Guinea**, Papua New Guinea/Indonesia, 16,503/5,030
2 **Akutan**, Alaska, 14,026/4,275 **3** **Borneo**, Indonesia/Malaysia/Brunei, 13,698/4,175 **4** **Hawaii**, 13,678/4,169 **5** **Formosa**, China, 13,114/3,997 **6** **Sumatra**, Indonesia, 12,480/3,804 **7** **Ross**, Antarctica, 12,448/3,794 **8** **Honshu**, Japan, 12,388/3,776 **9** **South Island**, New Zealand, 12,349/3,764 **10** **Lombok**, Lesser Sunda Islands, Indonesia, 12,224/3,726

Source: *United Nations*

TOP 10 ★
LARGEST LAKE ISLANDS

	ISLAND	LAKE/LOCATION	AREA SQ MILES	SQ KM
1	Manitoulin	Huron, Ontario, Canada	1,068	2,766
2	Vozrozhdeniya	Aral Sea, Uzbekistan/Kazakhstan	888	2,300
3	René-Lavasseur	Manicouagan Reservoir, Quebec, Canada	780	2,020
4	Olkhon	Baykal, Russia	282	730
5	Samosir	Toba, Sumatra, Indonesia	243	630
6	Isle Royale	Superior, Michigan	209	541
7	Ukerewe	Victoria, Tanzania	205	530
8	St. Joseph	Huron, Ontario, Canada	141	365
9	Drummond	Huron, Michigan	134	347
10	Idjwi	Kivu, Dem. Rep. of Congo	110	285

Not all islands are surrounded by sea: many sizeable islands are situated in lakes. The second largest in this list, Vozrozhdeniya, is growing as the Aral Sea contracts, and is set to link up with the surrounding land as a peninsula.

TOP 10 LARGEST ISLANDS IN THE UK

(Island/location/area in sq miles/sq km)

1 **Lewis and Harris**, Outer Hebrides, 859/2,225
2 **Skye**, Inner Hebrides, 643/1,666 **3** **Mainland**, Shetland, 373/967 **4** **Mull**, Inner Hebrides, 347/899 **5** **Anglesey**, Wales, 276/714 **6** **Islay**, Inner Hebrides, 247/639 **7** **Isle of Man**, England, 221/572 **8** **Mainland**, Orkney, 207/536 **9** **Arran**, Inner Hebrides, 168/435 **10** **Isle of Wight**, England, 147/381

MALTESE SQUEEZE

Close-packed high-rise housing in the capital, Valetta, exemplifies Malta's status as the world's most densely populated island country. Over 383,000 people are packed into just 122 sq miles (316 sq km).

TOP 10 ★
MOST DENSELY POPULATED ISLAND COUNTRIES

	ISLAND	AREA SQ MILES	SQ KM	POPULATION*	POPULATION PER SQ MILE	SQ KM
1	Malta	122	316	383,285	3,142	1,213
2	Bermuda	21	53	62,912	2,996	1,187
3	Maldives	115	298	310,425	2,699	1,042
4	Bahrain	268	694	641,539	2,394	924
5	Mauritius	720	1,865	1,196,172	1,661	642
6	Taiwan	13,800	35,742	22,319,222	1,617	624
7	Barbados	166	430	259,248	1,562	603
8	Tuvalu	10	25	10,730	1,073	429
9	Marshall Islands	70	181	68,088	973	376
10	Japan	143,939	372,801	126,434,470	878	339

* *Estimated for the year 2000*   Source: *United Nations*

The Face of the Earth

TOP 10 ★
DEEPEST DEPRESSIONS

	DEPRESSION/LOCATION	MAXIMUM DEPTH BELOW SEA LEVEL FT	M
1	**Dead Sea**, Israel/Jordan	1,312	400
2	**Turfan Depression**, China	505	154
3	**Qattâra Depression**, Egypt	436	133
4	**Poluostrov Mangyshlak**, Kazakhstan	433	132
5	**Danakil Depression**, Ethiopia	383	117
6	**Death Valley**, US	282	86
7	**Salton Sink**, US	235	72
8	**Zapadny Chink Ustyurta**, Kazakhstan	230	70
9	**Prikaspiyskaya Nizmennost'**, Kazakhstan/Russia	220	67
10	**Ozera Sarykamysh**, Turkmenistan/Uzbekistan	148	45

LYING LOW

The shore of the Dead Sea is the lowest exposed ground below sea level, but the bed of the sea actually reaches 2,388 ft (728 m) below sea level. Much of Antarctica is also below sea level.

TOP 10 ★
HIGHEST ACTIVE VOLCANOES

	VOLCANO	LOCATION	LATEST ACTIVITY	HEIGHT FT	M
1	**Guallatiri**	Chile	1987	19,882	6,060
2	**Lááscar**	Chile	1991	19,652	5,990
3	**Cotopaxi**	Ecuador	1975	19,347	5,897
4	**Tupungatito**	Chile	1986	18,504	5,640
5	**Popocatépetl**	Mexico	1995	17,887	5,452
6	**Ruiz**	Colombia	1992	17,716	5,400
7	**Sangay**	Ecuador	1988	17,159	5,230
8	**Guagua Pichincha**	Ecuador	1988	15,696	4,784
9	**Purace**	Colombia	1977	15,601	4,755
10	**Kliuchevskoi**	Russia	1995	15,584	4,750

This list includes all volcanoes that have been active at some time during the 20th century. The tallest currently active volcano in Europe is Mt. Etna.

TOP 10 ★
LARGEST DESERTS

	DESERT	LOCATION	APPROX. AREA SQ MILES	SQ KM
1	**Sahara**	North Africa	3,500,000	9,000,000
2	**Australian**	Australia	1,470,000	3,800,000
3	**Arabian**	Southwest Asia	502,000	1,300,000
4	**Gobi**	Central Asia	400,000	1,036,000
5	**Kalahari**	Southern Africa	201,000	520,000
6	**Turkestan**	Central Asia	174,000	450,000
7	**Takla Makan**	China	125,000	327,000
8=	**Namib**	Southwest Africa	120,000	310,000
=	**Sonoran**	US/Mexico	120,000	310,000
10=	**Somali**	Somalia	100,000	260,000
=	**Thar**	Northwest India/Pakistan	100,000	260,000

Did You Know? Analysis of the latest data concerning Everest indicates that the mountain is growing higher and moving north-east at a rate of 2.4 in (6 cm) per year.

TOP 10 ⭐
LONGEST CAVES

CAVE/LOCATION	TOTAL KNOWN LENGTH	
	MILES	KM
1 **Mammoth cave system,** Kentucky	352	567
2 **Optimisticeskaja,** Ukraine	125	201
3 **Jewel Cave,** South Dakota	108	174
4 **Hölloch,** Switzerland	103	166
5 **Lechuguilla Cave,** New Mexico	100	161
6 **Siebenhengsteholen-system,** Switzerland	87	140
7 **=Fisher Ridge cave system,** Kentucky	78	126
=Wind Cave, South Dakota	78	126
9 **Ozernay,** Ukraine	69	111
10 **Gua Air Jernih,** Malaysia	68	109

Source: *Tony Waltham, BCRA, 1999*

TOP 10 ⭐
DEEPEST CAVES

CAVE SYSTEM/ LOCATION	TOTAL KNOWN DEPTH	
	FT	M
1 **Lampreschtsofen,** Austria	5,354	1,632
2 **Gouffre Mirolda,** France	5,282	1,610
3 **Réseau Jean Bernard,** France	5,256	1,602
4 **Shakta Pantjukhina,** Georgia	4,948	1,508
5 **Sistema Huautla,** Mexico	4,839	1,475
6 **Sistema del Trave,** Spain	4,737	1,444
7 **Boj Bulok,** Uzbekistan	4,642	1,415
8 **Puerto di Illamina,** Spain	4,619	1,408
9 **Lukina Jama,** Croatia	4,567	1,392
10 **Sistema Cheve,** Mexico	4,547	1,386

Source: *Tony Waltham, BCRA, 1999*

TOP 10 ⭐
HIGHEST MOUNTAINS

MOUNTAIN/LOCATION	HEIGHT*	
	FT	M
1 **Everest,** Nepal/Tibet	29,022	8,846
2 **K2,** Kashmir/China	28,250	8,611
3 **Kangchenjunga,** Nepal/Sikkim	28,208	8,598
4 **Lhotse,** Nepal/Tibet	27,890	8,501
5 **Makalu I,** Nepal/Tibet	27,790	8,470
6 **Dhaulagiri I,** Nepal	26,810	8,172
7 **Manaslu I,** Nepal	26,760	8,156
8 **Cho Oyu,** Nepal	26,750	8,153
9 **Nanga Parbat,** Kashmir	26,660	8,126
10 **Annapurna I,** Nepal	26,504	8,078

* *Height of principal peak; lower peaks of the same mountain are excluded*

In November 1999 it was announced that an analysis of data beamed from sensors on Everest's summit to GPS satellites had claimed a new height of 29,035 ft (8,850 m). This height has been accepted by the National Geographic Society but awaits confirmation as the official figure.

TOP 10 ⭐
COUNTRIES WITH THE HIGHEST ELEVATIONS*

COUNTRY/PEAK	HEIGHT	
	FT	M
1 **Nepal#,** Everest	29,022	8,846
2 **Pakistan,** K2	28,250	8,611
3 **India,** Kangchenjunga	28,208	8,598
4 **Bhutan,** Khula Kangri	24,784	7,554
5 **Tajikistan,** Mt. Garmo (formerly Kommunizma)	24,590	7,495
6 **Afghanistan,** Noshaq	24,581	7,490
7 **Kyrgystan,** Pik Pobedy	24,406	7,439
8 **Kazakhstan,** Khan Tengri	22,949	6,995
9 **Argentina,** Cerro Aconcagua	22,834	6,960
10 **Chile,** Ojos del Salado	22,588	6,885

* *Based on the tallest peak in each country*

Everest straddles Nepal and Tibet, which, now known as Xizang, is a province of China

TOP 10 LARGEST METEORITE CRATERS
(Crater/location/diameter in miles/km)

1 = **Sudbury,** Ontario, Canada, 87/140; = **Vredefort,** South Africa, 87/140 **3** **Manicouagan,** Quebec, Canada, 62/100; = **Popigai,** Russia, 62/100 **5** **Puchezh-Katunki,** Russia, 50/80 **6** **Kara,** Russia, 37/60 **7** **Siljan,** Sweden, 32/52 **8** **Charlevoix,** Quebec, Canada, 29/46 **9** **Araguainha Dome,** Brazil, 25/40 **10** **Carswell,** Saskatchewan, Canada, 23/37

METEORITE CRATERS

Unlike on the Solar System's other planets and moons, many astroblemes (collision sites) on the Earth have been weathered over time. Geologists are thus unsure whether or not certain craterlike structures are of meteoric origin or are the remnants of extinct volcanoes. The Vredefort Ring, for example, was thought to be volcanic but has since been claimed as a definite meteor crater. Barringer Crater in Arizona (0.79 miles/1.265 km) is, however, the largest that all scientists agree is an astrobleme. The original diameter of many craters, such as Manicouagan (seen from a space shuttle), has been reduced by erosion.

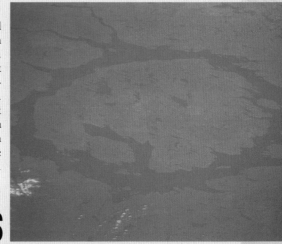

SNAP SHOTS

Background image: **NAMIB DESERT**

World Weather

COLDEST PLACES IN THE US

WEATHER STATION/STATE	MEAN TEMPERATURE °F	°C
1 **International Falls**, Minnesota	36.8	2.67
2 **Duluth**, Minnesota	38.5	3.61
3 **Caribou**, Maine	38.8	3.78
4 **Marquette**, Michigan	39.1	3.94
5 **Sault St. Marie**, Michigan	39.7	4.28
6 **Fargo**, North Dakota	41.0	5.00
7 **Alamosa**, Colorado	41.1	5.05
8 = **Saint Cloud**, Minnesota	41.5	5.28
= **Williston**, Maryland	41.5	5.28
10 **Bismark**, North Dakota	41.6	5.33

Source: National Climatic Data Center

HOTTEST CITIES IN THE US

CITY/STATE	AVERAGE ANNUAL TEMPERATURE °F	°C
1 **Key West**, Florida	77.8	25.4
2 **Miami**, Florida	75.9	24.2
3 **West Palm Beach**, Florida	74.7	23.7
4 = **Fort Myers**, Florida	74.4	23.3
= **Yuma**, Arizona	74.4	23.3
6 **Brownsville**, Texas	73.8	23.1
7 = **Tampa**, Florida	72.4	22.4
= **Vero Beach**, Florida	72.4	22.4
9 **Corpus Christi**, Texas	71.6	22.3
10 **Daytona Beach**, Florida	70.4	21.3

Source: National Climatic Data Center

WETTEST CITIES IN THE US

CITY/STATE	MEAN ANNUAL PRECIPITATION IN	MM
1 **Quillayute**, Washington	105.18	2,672
2 **Astoria**, Oregon	66.40	1,687
3 **Tallahassee**, Florida	65.71	1,669
4 **Mobile**, Alabama	63.96	1,625
5 **Pensacola**, Florida	62.25	1,581
6 **New Orleans**, Louisiana	61.88	1,572
7 **Baton Rouge**, Louisiana	60.89	1,547
8 **West Palm Beach**, Florida	60.75	1,543
9 **Meridian**, Mississippi	56.71	1,440
10 **Tupelo**, Mississippi	55.87	1,419

Source: National Climatic Data Center

COLDEST INHABITED PLACES

WEATHER STATION/LOCATION	AVERAGE TEMPERATURE °F	°C
1 **Norilsk**, Russia	12.4	−10.9
2 **Yakutsk**, Russia	13.8	−10.1
3 **Yellowknife**, Canada	22.3	−5.4
4 **Ulan-Bator**, Mongolia	23.9	−4.5
5 **Fairbanks**, Alaska	25.9	−3.4
6 **Surgut**, Russia	26.4	−3.1
7 **Chita**, Russia	27.1	−2.7
8 **Nizhnevartovsk**, Russia	27.3	−2.6
9 **Hailar**, Mongolia	27.7	−2.4
10 **Bratsk**, Russia	28.0	−2.2

COLD COMFORT

Yakutsk, Siberia, a port with a population of 200,000, experiences some of the world's coldest winters, but receives surprisingly little precipitation – just 8.39 in (213 mm) a year.

TOP 10 DRIEST CITIES IN THE US

(City/state/mean annual precipitation in in/mm)

1 Yuma, Arizona, 3.17/80.5 **2 Las Vegas**, Nevada, 4.13/104.9 **3 Bishop**, California, 5.37/136.4 **4 Bakersfield**, California, 5.72/145.3 **5 Reno**, Nevada, 7.53/191.3 **6 Alamosa**, Colorado, 7.57/192.3 **7 Phoenix**, Arizona, 7.66/194.6 **8 Yakima**, Washington, 7.97/202.4 **9 Winslow**, Arizona, 8.04/204.2 **10 Winnemucca**, Nevada, 8.23/209.0

Source: National Climatic Data Center

TOP 10 ⭐
HOTTEST INHABITED PLACES

WEATHER STATION/LOCATION	AVERAGE TEMPERATURE °F	°C
1 Djibouti, Djibouti	86.0	30.0
2 =Timbuktu, Mali	84.7	29.3
=Tirunelevi, India	84.7	29.3
=Tuticorin, India	84.7	29.3
5 =Nellore, India	84.6	29.2
=Santa Marta, Colombia	84.6	29.2
7 =Aden, South Yemen	84.0	28.9
=Madurai, India	84.0	28.9
=Niamey, Niger	84.0	28.9
10 =Hudaydah, North Yemen	83.8	28.8
=Ouagadougou, Burkina Faso	83.8	28.8
=Thanjavur, India	83.8	28.8
=Tiruchirapalli, India	83.8	28.8

HOT SPOT
A small town at the end of a Saharan caravan route, Timbuktu in Mali is one of the world's hottest places, coming second only to Djibouti.

TOP 10 ⭐
WETTEST INHABITED PLACES

WEATHER STATION/LOCATION	AVERAGE ANNUAL RAINFALL IN	MM
1 Buenaventura, Colombia	265.47	6,743
2 Monrovia, Liberia	202.01	5,131
3 Pago Pago, American Samoa	196.46	4,990
4 Moulmein, Myanmar	191.02	4,852
5 Lae, Papua New Guinea	182.87	4,645
6 Baguio, Luzon Island, Philippines	180.04	4,573
7 Sylhet, Bangladesh	175.47	4,457
8 Conakry, Guinea	170.91	4,341
9 =Padang, Sumatra Island, Indonesia	166.34	4,225
=Bogor, Java, Indonesia	166.34	4,225

The total annual rainfall of the Top 10 wettest locations is equivalent to over 26 6-ft (1.83-m) adults standing on top of each other. The greatest rainfall in a 12-month period was 1,041.75 in (26,461 mm) at Cherrapunji, India.

TOP 10 ⭐
DRIEST INHABITED PLACES

WEATHER STATION/LOCATION	AVERAGE ANNUAL RAINFALL IN	MM
1 Aswan, Egypt	0.02	0.5
2 Luxor, Egypt	0.03	0.7
3 Arica, Chile	0.04	1.1
4 Ica, Peru	0.09	2.3
5 Antofagasta, Chile	0.19	4.9
6 Minya, Egypt	0.20	5.1
7 Asyut, Egypt	0.21	5.2
8 Callao, Peru	0.47	12.0
9 Trujilo, Peru	0.54	14.0
10 Fayyum, Egypt	0.75	19.0

The total annual rainfall of the Top 10 driest inhabited places, as recorded over long periods, is just 2½ in (64.8 mm) – the average length of an adult little finger. The Atacama Desert often receives virtually no rain for years on end.

⭐ **Did You Know?** The highest temperatures recorded in the US and Europe are 118°F (47.8°C) (Phoenix, Arizona) and 117°F (47.2°C) (Seville, Spain).

Out of This World

HEAVIEST ELEMENTS

	ELEMENT	DISCOVERER/COUNTRY	YEAR DISCOVERED	DENSITY*
1	Osmium	S. Tennant, UK	1804	22.59
2	Iridium	S. Tennant	1804	22.56
3	Platinum	J. C. Scaliger[#], Italy/France	1557	21.45
4	Rhenium	W. Noddack *et al.*, Germany	1925	21.01
5	Neptunium	Edwin M. McMillan/ Philip H. Abelson, US	1940	20.47
6	Plutonium	G. T. Seaborg *et al.*, US	1940	20.26
7	Gold	–	Prehistoric	19.29
8	Tungsten	J. J. and F. Elhuijar, Spain	1783	19.26
9	Uranium	M. J. Klaproth, Germany	1789	19.05
10	Tantalum	A. G. Ekeberg, Sweden	1802	16.67

* *Grams per cu cm at 20°C*
[#] *Earliest reference to this element*

LIGHTEST ELEMENTS*

	ELEMENT	DISCOVERER/COUNTRY	YEAR DISCOVERED	DENSITY[#]
1	Lithium	J. A. Arfvedson, Sweden	1817	0.533
2	Potassium	Sir Humphry Davy, UK	1807	0.859
3	Sodium	Sir Humphry Davy	1807	0.969
4	Calcium	Sir Humphry Davy	1808	1.526
5	Rubidium	R. W. Bunsen/G. Kirchoff, Germany	1861	1.534
6	Magnesium	Sir Humphry Davy	1808[+]	1.737
7	Phosphorus	Hennig Brandt, Germany	1669	1.825
8	Beryllium	F. Wöhler, Germany/ A. A. B. Bussy, France	1828[*]	1.846
9	Cesium	R. W. Bunsen/G. Kirchoff	1860	1.896
10	Sulfur	–	Prehistoric	2.070

* *Solids only* [#] *Grams per cu cm at 20°C* [+] *Recognized by Joseph Black, 1755, but not isolated* [*] *Recognized by Nicholas Vauquelin, 1797, but not isolated*

TOP 10 MOST EXTRACTED METALLIC ELEMENTS

(Element/estimated annual extraction in tons)

1 Iron, 789,247,000 **2** Aluminum, 16,535,000 **3** Copper, 7,209,000
4 Manganese, 6,856,000 **5** Zinc, 5,534,000 **6** Lead, 3,086,000 **7** Nickel, 562,000
8 Magnesium, 358,000 **9** Sodium, 220,000 **10** Tin, 182,000

Certain metallic minerals are extracted in relatively small quantities, while compounds containing these elements are major industries: contrasting with 220,500 tons of metallic sodium, 185 million tons of salt are extracted annually; metallic calcium is represented by about 2,210 tons, contrasting with some 123 million tons of lime (calcium carbonate); and 220 tons of the metal potassium contrast with 56 million tons of potassium salts.

METALLIC ELEMENTS WITH THE GREATEST RESERVES

	ELEMENT	ESTIMATED GLOBAL RESERVES (TONS)
1	Iron	121,254,200,000
2	Magnesium	22,046,200,000
3	Potassium	11,023,100,000
4	Aluminum	6,613,800,000
5	Manganese	3,698,300,000
6	Zirconium	over 1,102,300,000
7	Chromium	1,102,300,000
8	Barium	496,000,000
9	Titanium	485,000,000
10	Copper	341,700,000

This list includes accessible reserves of commercially mined metallic elements, but excludes two, calcium and sodium, that exist in such vast quantities that their reserves are considered "unlimited" and unquantifiable.

COPPER TO SPARE

Copper is among the world's most extracted elements. Bingham Copper Mine, Utah, is the largest manmade excavation in the world.

TOP 10 ★
MOST COMMON ELEMENTS IN THE EARTH'S CRUST

	ELEMENT	PARTS PER MILLION*
1	Oxygen	474,000
2	Silicon	277,100
3	Aluminum	82,000
4	=Iron	41,000
	=Calcium	41,000
6	=Magnesium	23,000
	=Sodium	23,000
8	Potassium	21,000
9	Titanium	5,600
10	Hydrogen	1,520

* mg per kg

TOP 10 ★
MOST COMMON ELEMENTS IN THE UNIVERSE

	ELEMENT	PARTS PER MILLION
1	Hydrogen	739,000
2	Helium	240,000
3	Oxygen	10,700
4	Carbon	4,600
5	Neon	1,340
6	Iron	1,090
7	Nitrogen	970
8	Silicon	650
9	Magnesium	580
10	Sulfur	440

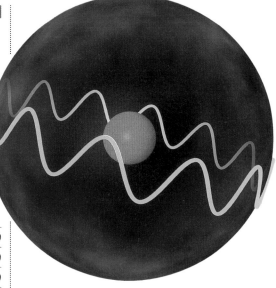

IT'S ELEMENTARY

The gas hydrogen is the simplest and most abundant element. This computer-generated image shows a hydrogen atom with a nucleus and orbiting electron.

TOP 10 PRINCIPAL COMPONENTS OF AIR
(Component/volume percent)

1 Nitrogen, 78.110 **2** Oxygen, 20.953 **3** Argon, 0.934 **4** Carbon dioxide, 0.01–0.10 **5** Neon, 0.001818 **6** Helium, 0.000524 **7** Methane, 0.0002 **8** Krypton, 0.000114 **9** = Hydrogen, 0.00005; = Nitrous oxide, 0.00005

THE 10 DEGREES OF HARDNESS*
(Substance)

1 Talc **2** Gypsum **3** Calcite **4** Fluorite **5** Apatite **6** Orthoclase **7** Quartz **8** Topaz **9** Corundum **10** Diamond

* According to the Mohs Scale, in which No. 1 is the softest mineral and No. 10 is the hardest

TOP 10 ★
MOST EXTRACTED NONMETALLIC ELEMENTS

	ELEMENT	ESTIMATED ANNUAL EXTRACTION (TONS)
1	Hydrogen	386,000,000,000
2	Carbon*	18,000,000,000
3	Chlorine	185,000,000
4	Phosphorus	168,000,000
5	Oxygen	110,000,000
6	Sulfur	59,000,000
7	Nitrogen	48,000,000
8	Silicon#	4,282,000
9	Boron	1,102,000
10	Argon	777,000

* Carbon, natural gas, oil, and coal

 # Various forms

CRYSTAL BOMB

Known since ancient times, sulfur is extracted in large quantities for use in many industrial and chemical processes, including making explosives.

THE GOLD RUSH

In August 1896, 35-year-old George Washington Carmack struck gold while panning the Rabbit (later Bonanza) Creek, south of the Yukon at Klondike near the Canadian/Alaskan border. When news of his discovery reached the outside world, it sparked the world's biggest gold rush since the California stampede of 1849. More than 100,000 prospectors traveled to the inhospitable region to seek their fortunes, and in the first year alone some $22 million worth of Klondike gold was shipped out. Most of the gold-seekers failed, however, with many dying from the freezing winter conditions or else returning home empty-handed. In 1976 much of the area was designated as the Klondike Gold Rush Historical Park.

SNAP SHOTS

Which is the world's highest island? *see p.23 for the answer* **A** Sumatra **B** Hawaii **C** New Guinea

Natural Disasters

WORST EARTHQUAKES OF THE 20TH CENTURY

	LOCATION	DATE	ESTIMATED NO. KILLED
1	**Tang-shan**, China	July 28, 1976	242,419
2	**Nan-Shan**, China	May 22, 1927	200,000
3	**Kansu**, China	Dec 16, 1920	180,000
4	**Messina**, Italy	Dec 28, 1908	160,000
5	**Tokyo/Yokohama**, Japan	Sep 1, 1923	142,807
6	**Kansu**, China	Dec 25, 1932	70,000
7	**Yungay**, Peru	May 31, 1970	66,800
8	**Quetta**, India*	May 30, 1935	50–60,000
9	**Armenia**	Dec 7, 1988	over 55,000
10	**Iran**	June 21, 1990	over 40,000

* Now Pakistan

Reaching 7.2 on the Richter scale, the earthquake that struck Kobe, Japan, on January 17, 1995 was exceptionally precisely monitored by the rescue authorities. It left a total of 3,842 dead and 14,679 injured.

WORST AVALANCHES AND LANDSLIDES OF THE 20TH CENTURY*

	LOCATION	INCIDENT	DATE	ESTIMATED NO. KILLED
1	**Yungay**, Peru	Landslide	May 31, 1970	17,500
2	**Italian Alps**	Avalanche	Dec 13, 1916	10,000
3	**Huarás**, Peru	Avalanche	Dec 13, 1941	5,000
4	**Nevada Huascaran**, Peru	Avalanche	Jan 10, 1962	3,500
5	**Medellin**, Colombia	Landslide	Sep 27, 1987	683
6	**Chungar**, Peru	Avalanche	Mar 19, 1971	600
7	**Rio de Janeiro**, Brazil	Landslide	Jan 11, 1966	550
8	=**Northern Assam**, India	Landslide	Feb 15, 1949	500
	=**Grand Rivière du Nord**, Haiti	Landslide	Nov 13/14, 1963	500
10	**Blons**, Austria	Avalanche	Jan 11, 1954	411

* Excluding those where most deaths resulted from flooding, earthquakes, etc., associated with landslides

The worst incident of all, the destruction of Yungay, Peru, in May 1970, was only part of a much larger cataclysm that left a total of up to 70,000 dead. Following an earthquake and flooding, the town was wiped out by an avalanche that left just 2,500 survivors out of a population of 20,000. Among the most tragic landslide disasters of this century occurred at Aberfan, Wales, on October 20, 1966. Weakened by the presence of a spring, a huge volume of slurry from a 800-ft (244-m) high heap of coal-mine waste suddenly flowed down and engulfed the local school, killing 144 people.

TURKISH EARTHQUAKE

The earthquake that occurred in Turkey on August 17, 1999 was the second worst of the decade, resulting in a death toll unofficially estimated at between 30,000 and 40,000. It lasted only 45 seconds but measured 7.4 on the Richter scale. Its epicenter was 7 miles (11 km) southeast of Izmit, an industrial area 50 miles (90 km) east of Istanbul, where many multistory concrete apartment buildings collapsed into rubble. Most had been poorly constructed with inferior materials and little regard for the area's known vulnerability to earthquakes. In this and the surrounding area, some 20,000 structures were destroyed or damaged, while the country's industrial infrastructure was severely damaged. The Tüpras oil refinery in Korfez was set ablaze, Turkey's electricity supply cut, and water and road networks disrupted.

SNAP SHOTS ★

THE 10 ★
COSTLIEST HURRICANES TO STRIKE THE US

	HURRICANE	YEAR	DAMAGE ($)*
1	Andrew	1992	30,475,000,000
2	Hugo	1989	8,491,561,181
3	Agnes	1972	7,500,000,000
4	Betsy	1965	7,425,340,909
5	Camille	1969	6,096,287,313
6	Diane	1955	4,830,580,808
7	Frederic	1979	4,328,968,903
8	New England	1938	4,140,000,000
9	Fran	1996	3,200,000,000
10	Opal	1995	3,069,395,018

* Adjusted to 1996 dollars

Source: *The National Hurricane Center*

THE 10 WORST EPIDEMICS OF ALL TIME

	EPIDEMIC	LOCATION	DATE	ESTIMATED NO. KILLED
1	Black Death	Europe/Asia	1347–51	75,000,000
2	Influenza	Worldwide	1918–20	21,640,000
3	Plague	India	1896–1948	12,000,000
4	AIDS	Worldwide	1981–	11,700,000
5	Typhus	Eastern Europe	1914–15	3,000,000
6 =	"Plague of Justinian"	Europe/Asia	541–90	millions*
=	Cholera	Worldwide	1846–60	millions*
=	Cholera	Europe	1826–37	millions*
=	Cholera	Worldwide	1893–94	millions*
10	Smallpox	Mexico	1530–45	>1,000,000

* No precise figures available

THE 10 ★
WORST VOLCANIC ERUPTIONS OF ALL TIME

LOCATION/DATE/INCIDENT	EST. NO. KILLED

1 Tambora, Indonesia, Apr 5–12, 1815 — 92,000
The eruption on the island of Sumbawa killed about 10,000 islanders immediately, with a further 82,000 dying subsequently from disease and famine resulting from crops being destroyed. An estimated 1,700,000 tons of ash was hurled into the atmosphere, blocking out the sunlight.

2 Miyi-Yama, Java, 1793 — 53,000
The volcano dominating the island of Kiousiou erupted, engulfing all the local villages in mudslides and killing most of the rural population.

3 Mont Pelée, Martinique, May 8, 1902 — 40,000
After lying dormant for centuries, Mont Pelée began to erupt in April 1902.

4 Krakatoa, Sumatra/Java, Aug 26–27, 1883 — 36,380
Krakatoa exploded with what may have been the biggest bang ever heard by humans, audible up to 3,000 miles (4,800 km) away.

5 Nevado del Ruiz, Colombia, Nov 13, 1985 — 22,940
The hot steam, rocks, and ash ejected from Nevado del Ruiz melted its icecap, resulting in a mudslide that completely engulfed the town of Armero.

6 Mount Etna, Sicily, Mar 11, 1669 — over 20,000
Europe's largest volcano has erupted frequently, but the worst instance occurred in 1669, when the lava flow engulfed the town of Catania.

7 Laki, Iceland, Jan–June 1783 — 20,000
An eruption on the Laki volcanic ridge culminated on June 11, with the largest ever recorded lava flow. It engulfed many villages in a river of lava up to 50 miles (80 km) long and 100 ft (30 m) deep, releasing poisonous gases that killed those who escaped.

8 Vesuvius, Italy, Aug 24, 79 — 16–20,000
The Roman city of Herculaneum was engulfed by a mud flow, while Pompeii was buried under a vast and preserving layer of pumice and volcanic ash.

9 Vesuvius, Italy, Dec 16–17, 1631 — up to 18,000
The next major cataclysm was almost as disastrous, when lava and mudflows gushed down onto the surrounding towns, including Naples.

10 Mount Etna, Sicily, 1169 — over 15,000
Large numbers died in Catania cathedral, where they believed they would be safe, and more were killed when a tidal wave caused by the eruption hit the port of Messina.

THE 10 ★
WORST FLOODS AND STORMS OF THE 20TH CENTURY

	LOCATION	DATE	ESTIMATED NO. KILLED
1	Huang He River, China	Aug 1931	3,700,000
2	Bangladesh	13 Nov 1970	300–500,000
3	Henan, China	Sep 1939	over 200,000
4	Bangladesh	30 Apr 1991	131,000
5	Chang Jiang River, China	Sep 1911	100,000
6	Bengal, India	15–16 Nov 1942	40,000
7	Bangladesh	1–2 June 1965	30,000
8	Bangladesh	28–29 May 1963	22,000
9	Bangladesh	11–12 May 1965	17,000
10	Morvi, India	11 Aug 1979	5–15,000

No. 4 was omitted previously because the total number of fatalities combines the effects of storm, flood and tidal wave, and it is impossible to isolate the figures for just those deaths attributable to the storm and flood aspects of the disaster. On balance, I think it deserves to be recorded.

Background image: **INFLUENZA VIRUSES**

Where is the world's highest waterfall?
see p.21 for the answer
A Venezuela
B India
C China

Life on Earth

Extinct & Endangered

THE 10 ⭐ COUNTRIES WITH THE MOST ASIAN ELEPHANTS

COUNTRY	NUMBER*
1 India	24,000
2 Myanmar	6,000
3 Indonesia	4,500
4 Laos	4,000
5 Sri Lanka	3,000
6 = Thailand	2,000
= Cambodia	2,000
9 = Borneo	1,000
= Malaysia	1,000
10 Vietnam	400

* Based on maximum estimates

The total numbers of Asian elephants is put at anything from a minimum of 37,860 to a maximum 48,740. Estimates of populations of Asian elephants are notoriously unreliable as this species is exclusively a forest animal and its numbers cannot be sampled using aerial survey techniques.

Source: *International Union for the Conservation of Nature*

COME INTO MY PARLOR ...

Listed as "vulnerable" by the International Union for the Conservation of Nature, the distinctive Dolomedes Great raft or Fishing spider can sit on water as it awaits its prey.

THE 10 ⭐ MOST ENDANGERED BIG CATS*

1	Amur leopard
2	Anatolian leopard
3	Asiatic cheetah
4	Eastern puma
5	Florida cougar
6	North African leopard
7	Siberian tiger
8	South Arabian leopard
9	South China tiger
10	Sumatran tiger

* In alphabetical order

Source: *International Union for the Conservation of Nature*

All 10 of these big cats are classed by the International Union for Conservation of Nature as being "critically endangered," that is, facing an extremely high risk of extinction in the wild in the immediate future.

THE 10 ⭐ MOST ENDANGERED SPIDERS

SPIDER	COUNTRY
1 Kauai cave wolf spider	US
2 Doloff cave spider	US
3 Empire cave pseudoscorpion	US
4 Glacier Bay wolf spider	US
5 Great raft spider	Europe
6 Kocevje subterranean spider (*Troglohyphantes gracilis*)	Slovenia
7 Kocevje subterranean spider (*Troglohyphantes similis*)	Slovenia
8 Kocevje subterranean spider (*Troglohyphantes spinipes*)	Slovenia
9 Lake Placid funnel wolf spider	US
10 Melones cave harvestman	US

Source: *International Union for the Conservation of Nature*

The first spider on this list is considered by the IUCN as "endangered" (facing a very high risk of extinction in the wild in the near future), and the others as "vulnerable" (facing a high risk of extinction in the wild in the medium-term future). Some exist exclusively in one habitat, making them especially susceptible to environmental threats.

THE 10 ⭐ MOST RECENTLY EXTINCT ANIMAL SPECIES

1	Partula Tree Snails from Hawaii
2	Palos Verde Blue Butterfly
3	Canary Islands Blackfly
4	Lord Howe Islands Phasmid Fly
5	Dusky Seaside Sparrow
6	Colombian Grebe and Atitlan Grebe
7	Glaucous Macaw
8	Hawaiian Honey Creeper
9	Pohmpei (Caroline Island bird)
10	Bali Tiger

The saddest thing about this list is that by the time you read it, it will be out of date because yet another species will have become extinct, usually as a direct result of human intervention.

Did You Know? Once thought extinct but later rediscovered, the Kakapo parrot cannot fly, but instead climbs trees and glides down to the ground.

When Portuguese sailors first encountered a large, flightless bird on the island of Mauritius, they were struck by its ludicrous clumsy appearance and the ease with which they were able to catch it; so they christened it the "doudo," the Portuguese word for "stupid." Even its Latin name emphasizes its silliness – *Didus ineptus*. As doudos, or dodos, tasted delicious, they were hunted down; and by 1681, when the last was seen by English naturalist Benjamin Harry, they were completely extinct – hence the expression, "as dead as a dodo."

WHY DO WE SAY?

THE 10 ★
COUNTRIES WITH THE MOST THREATENED SPECIES

	COUNTRY	MAMMALS	BIRDS	REPTILES	AMPHIBIANS	FISH	INVERTEBRATES	TOTAL
1	US	35	50	28	24	123	594	854
2	Australia	58	45	37	25	37	281	483
3	Indonesia	128	104	19	0	60	29	340
4	Mexico	64	36	18	3	86	40	247
5	Brazil	71	103	15	5	12	34	240
6	China	75	90	15	1	28	4	213
7	South Africa	33	16	19	9	27	101	205
8	Philippines	49	86	7	2	26	18	188
9	India	75	73	16	3	4	22	193
10=	Japan	29	33	8	10	7	45	132
=	Tanzania	33	30	4	0	19	46	132

THE 10 ★
MOST ENDANGERED MAMMALS

	MAMMAL	ESTIMATED NO.
1=	Tasmanian wolf	?
=	Halcon fruit bat	?
=	Ghana fat mouse	?
4	Javan rhinoceros	50
5	Iriomote cat	60
6	Black lion tamarin	130
7	Pygmy hog	150
8	Kouprey	100–200
9	Tamaraw	200
10	Indus dolphin	400

The first three mammals on the list have not been seen for many years and may well be extinct.

TOP 10 COUNTRIES WITH THE MOST AFRICAN ELEPHANTS

(Country/elephants)

1 Tanzania, 73,459* **2** Dem. Rep. of Congo, 65,974# **3** Botswana, 62,998*
4 Gabon, 61,794+ **5** Zimbabwe, 56,297* **6** Congo, 32,563# **7** Zambia, 19,701*
8 Kenya, 13,834* **9** South Africa, 9,990* **10** Cameroon, 8,824#

* Definite # Possible + Probable
Source: *International Union for the Conservation of Nature*

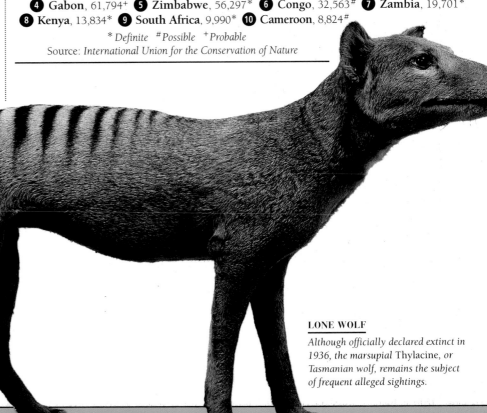

LONE WOLF
Although officially declared extinct in 1936, the marsupial Thylacine, or Tasmanian wolf, remains the subject of frequent alleged sightings.

Land Animals 1

HEAVIEST TERRESTRIAL MAMMALS

MAMMAL	LENGTH* FT	LENGTH* M	WEIGHT LB	WEIGHT KG
1 African elephant	24	7.3	14,432	7,000
2 White rhinoceros	14	4.2	7,937	3,600
3 Hippopotamus	13	4.0	5,512	2,500
4 Giraffe	19	5.8	3,527	1,600
5 American bison	13	3.9	2,205	1,000
6 Arabian camel (dromedary)	12	3.5	1,521	690
7 Polar bear	8	2.6	1,323	600
8 Moose	10	3.0	1,213	550
9 Siberian tiger	11	3.3	661	300
10 Gorilla	7	2.0	485	220

* From head to toe or head to tail

The list excludes domesticated cattle and horses. It also avoids comparing close kin, such as the African and Indian elephants.

SLEEPIEST ANIMALS*

ANIMAL	AVERAGE HOURS OF SLEEP PER DAY
1 Koala	22
2 Sloth	20
3 =Armadillo	19
=Opossum	19
5 Lemur	16
6 =Hamster	14
=Squirrel	14
8 =Cat	13
=Pig	13
10 Spiny anteater	12

* Excluding periods of hibernation

SLEEPYHEAD

The eastern Australian koala (which is actually a marsupial, not a bear), sleeps almost constantly to conserve the little energy it has.

HEAVIEST PRIMATES

PRIMATE	LENGTH* IN	LENGTH* CM	WEIGHT LB	WEIGHT KG
1 Gorilla	79	200	485	220
2 Man	70	177	170	77
3 Orangutan	54	137	165	75
4 Chimpanzee	36	92	110	50
5 =Baboon	39	100	99	45
=Mandrill	37	95	99	45
7 Gelada baboon	30	75	55	25
8 Proboscis monkey	30	76	53	24
9 Hanuman langur	42	107	44	20
10 Siamung gibbon	35	90	29	13

* Excluding tail

The longer, leaner, and lighter forms of the langurs, gibbons, and monkeys – evolved for serious monkeying around in trees – contrast sharply with their heavier great ape cousins.

GENTLE GIANT

The largest of all primates, the gorilla has a menacing appearance that has been exploited in such films as King Kong. In fact, gorillas are usually docile.

TOP 10 ★
HEAVIEST CARNIVORES

CARNIVORE	LENGTH		WEIGHT	
	FT	M	LB	KG
1 Southern elephant seal	21	6.5	7,716	3,500
2 Walrus	12	3.8	2,646	1,200
3 Steller sea lion	9	3.0	2,425	1,100
4 Grizzly bear	9	3.0	1,720	780
5 Polar bear	8	2.6	1,323	600
6 Tiger	9	2.8	661	300
7 Lion	6	1.9	551	250
8 American black bear	6	1.8	500	227
9 Giant panda	5	1.5	353	160
10 Spectacled bear	6	1.8	309	140

Of the 273 mammal species in the order *Carnivora*, or meat-eaters, many (including its largest representatives on land, the bears) are in fact omnivorous, and around 40 specialize in eating fish or insects. All, however, share a common ancestry indicated by the butcher's-knife form of their canine teeth. As the Top 10 would otherwise consist exclusively of seals and related marine carnivores, only three have been included in order to enable the terrestrial heavyweight division to make an appearance. The polar bear is probably the largest land carnivore if shoulder height (when the animal is on all fours) is taken into account: it tops an awesome 5.3 ft (1.6 m), compared with the 4 ft (1.2 m) of its nearest rival, the grizzly.

TOP BEAR

Although among the heaviest carnivores, many records of giant grizzlies have been exaggerated by hunters and showmen for prestige.

"GORILLA"

"Gorilla" was adopted in 1847 as part of the original scientific name for the large ape, *Troglodytes gorilla*. The word was coined by Dr. Thomas Staughton Savage, an American missionary in Africa, who had heard of the Gorillai, a mythical African tribe of hairy women, imaginatively described in a 5th- or 6th-century BC Greek account of the voyages of Hanno the Carthaginian.

WHY DO WE SAY?

Did You Know? Giant pandas spend up to 15 hours a day eating, consuming as much as 99 lb (45 kg) of bamboo shoots a day.

Land Animals 2

"WHITE ELEPHANT"

The rare albino or white elephant was considered sacred to the people of Siam (now Thailand). Legend has it that the king would sometimes present such an elephant to an unpopular courtier. Decorum would have meant that the courtier could not refuse the gift, but the immense cost of looking after the beast would have ruined him financially. A "white elephant" thus became a synonym for a burdensome gift that one could not dispose of.

WHY DO WE SAY?

TOP 10 MOST INTELLIGENT MAMMALS

① Human **②** Chimpanzee **③** Gorilla
④ Orangutan **⑤** Baboon **⑥** Gibbon
⑦ Monkey **⑧** Smaller-toothed
whale **⑨** Dolphin **⑩** Elephant

This list is based on research conducted by Edward O. Wilson, Professor of Zoology at Harvard University, who defined intelligence as speed and extent of learning performance over a wide range of tasks, also taking account of the ratio of the animal's brain size to its body bulk.

TOP 10 ★ MOST PROLIFIC WILD MAMMALS

	ANIMAL	AVERAGE LITTER
1	Malagasy tenrec	25.0
2	Virginian opossum	22.0
3	Golden hamster	11.0
4	Ermine	10.0
5	Prairie vole	9.0
6	Coypu	8.5
7=	European hedgehog	7.0
=	African hunting dog	7.0
9=	Meadow vole	6.5
=	Wild boar	6.5

The prairie vole probably holds the world record for most offspring produced in a season. It has up to 17 litters in rapid succession, bringing up to 150 young into the world.

DEADLY CHARM

Traditionally used by Indian snake charmers, the menacingly hooded Indian cobra's venom is sufficiently powerful to kill an elephant.

TOP 10 ★ MOST VENOMOUS CREATURES

	CREATURE*	TOXIN	FATAL AMOUNT MG#
1	Indian cobra	Peak V	0.009
2	Mamba	Toxin 1	0.02
3	Brown snake	Texilotoxin	0.05
4=	Inland taipan	Paradotoxin	0.10
=	Mamba	Dendrotoxin	0.10
6	Taipan	Taipoxin	0.11
7=	Indian cobra	Peak X	0.12
=	Poison arrow frog	Batrachotoxin	0.12
9	Indian cobra	Peak 1X	0.17
10	Krait	Bungarotoxin	0.50

* *Excluding bacteria*
\# *Quantity required to kill one average-sized human adult*

The venom of these creatures is almost unbelievably powerful: 1 milligram of Mamba Toxin 1 would be sufficient to kill 50 people. Such creatures as scorpions (0.5 mg) and black widow spiders (1.0 mg) fall just outside the Top 10.

PENSIVE PRIMATE

Numbered among the most intelligent mammals, and noted for its use of tools, the forest-dwelling orangutan's name derives from the Malay words for "man of the woods."

TOP 10 ★
LONGEST LAND ANIMALS

	ANIMAL*	LENGTH# FT	M
1	Royal python	35	10.7
2	Tapeworm	33	10.0
3	African elephant	24	7.3
4	Estuarine crocodile	19	5.9
5	Giraffe	19	5.8
6	White rhinoceros	14	4.2
7	Hippopotamus	13	4.0
8	American bison	13	3.9
9	Arabian camel (dromedary)	12	3.5
10	Siberian tiger	11	3.3

* Longest representative of each species

\# Head to toe or head to tail

GROWING FAST

The giraffe is the tallest of all living animals. In 1937 a calf giraffe that measured 5 ft 2 in (1.58 m) at birth was found to be growing at an astonishing 0.5 in (1.3 cm) per hour.

TOP 10 ★
FASTEST MAMMALS

	MAMMAL	MAXIMUM RECORDED SPEED MPH	KM/H
1	Cheetah	65	105
2	Pronghorn antelope	55	89
3 =	Mongolian gazelle	50	80
=	Springbok	50	80
5 =	Grant's gazelle	47	76
=	Thomson's gazelle	47	76
7	Brown hare	45	72
8	Horse	43	69
9 =	Greyhound	42	68
=	Red deer	42	68

QUICK OFF THE MARK

The speedy cheetah can accelerate to 60 mph (96 km/h) in just three seconds.

TOP 10 ★
DEADLIEST SNAKES

	SNAKE	MAXIMUM DEATHS PER BITE	MORTALITY RATE RANGE (PERCENT)
1	Black mamba	200	75–100
2	Forest cobra	50	70–95
3	Russell's viper	150	40–92
4	Taipan	26	10–90
5	Common krait	60	70–80
6	Jararacussa	100	60–80
7	Terciopelo	40	Not known
8	Egyptian cobra	35	50
9	Indian cobra	40	30–35
10	Jararaca	30	25–35

What is special about Kitti's hognosed bat?
see p.42 for the answer

A It is the rarest
B It is the lightest
C It is the fastest

Marine Animals

TOP 10 HEAVIEST MARINE MAMMALS

	MAMMAL	LENGTH FT	LENGTH M	WEIGHT TONS
1	Blue whale	110.0	33.5	143.3
2	Fin whale	82.0	25.0	49.6
3	Right whale	57.4	17.5	44.1
4	Sperm whale	59.0	18.0	39.7
5	Gray whale	46.0	14.0	36.0
6	Humpback whale	49.2	15.0	29.2
7	Baird's whale	18.0	5.5	12.1
8	Southern elephant seal	21.3	6.5	4.0
9	Northern elephant seal	19.0	5.8	3.7
10	Pilot whale	21.0	6.4	3.2

Probably the largest animal that ever lived, the blue whale dwarfs the other whales listed here, all but one of which far outweigh the biggest land animal, the elephant.

TOP 10 ★ HEAVIEST SHARKS

	SHARK	WEIGHT LB	WEIGHT KG
1	Whale shark	46,297	21,000
2	Basking shark	32,000	14,515
3	Great white shark	7,300	3,314
4	Greenland shark	2,250	1,020
5	Tiger shark	2,070	939
6	Great hammerhead shark	1,860	844
7	Six-gill shark	1,300	590
8	Gray nurse shark	1,225	556
9	Mako shark	1,200	544
10	Thresher shark	1,100	500

As well as specimens that have been caught, estimates have been made of beached examples, but such is the notoriety of sharks that many accounts of their size are exaggerated, and this list should be taken as an approximate ranking based on the best available evidence.

MARINE MONSTER

There are several species of right whale, with exceptional specimens reputedly exceeding 70 tons.

TOP 10 FISHING COUNTRIES

(Country/annual catch in tons)

1. China, 36,549,637
2. Peru, 10,493,199
3. Chile, 8,365,223
4. Japan, 7,448,229
5. US, 6,187,216
6. India, 5,796,982
7. Indonesia, 4,850,937
8. Russia, 4,819,957
9. Thailand, 4,019,985
10. Norway, 3,093,291

TOP 10 ★ HEAVIEST TURTLES

	TURTLE	WEIGHT LB	WEIGHT KG
1	Pacific leatherback turtle	1,908	865
2	Atlantic leatherback turtle	1,000	454
3	Green sea turtle	900	408
4	Loggerhead turtle	850	386
5	Alligator snapping turtle	403	183
6	Black sea turtle	278	126
7	Flatback turtle	185	84
8	Hawksbill turtle	150	68
9=	Kemps ridley turtle	110	50
=	Olive ridley turtle	110	50

Background image: SCHOOL OF MACKEREL

TOP 10 ★
HEAVIEST SPECIES
OF FRESHWATER FISH CAUGHT

	SPECIES	ANGLER/LOCATION/DATE	LB	OZ	KG
1	White sturgeon	Joey Pallotta III, Benicia, California, July 9, 1983	468	0	212.28
2	Alligator gar	Bill Valverde, Rio Grande, Texas, Dec 2, 1951	279	0	126.55
3	Beluga sturgeon	Merete Lehne, Guryev, Kazakhstan, May 3, 1993	224	1	101.97
4	Nile perch	Adrian Brayshaw, Lake Nasser, Egypt, Dec 18, 1997	213	0	96.62
5	Flathead catfish	Ken Paulie, Withlacoochee River, Florida, May 14, 1998	123	9	56.05
6	Blue catfish	William P. McKinley, Wheeler Reservoir, Tennessee, July 5, 1996	111	0	50.35
7	Chinook salmon	Les Anderson, Kenai River, Alaska, May 17, 1985	97	4	44.11
8	Giant tigerfish	Raymond Houtmans, Zaire River, Zaire, July 9, 1988	97	0	44.00
9	Smallmouth buffalo	Randy Collins, Athens Lake, Arkansas, June 6, 1993	82	3	37.28
10	Atlantic salmon	Henrik Henrikson, Tana River, Norway (date unknown) 1928	79	2	35.89

Source: *International Game Fish Association*

TOP 10 ★
HEAVIEST SPECIES
OF SALTWATER FISH CAUGHT

	SPECIES	ANGLER/LOCATION/DATE	LB	OZ	KG
1	Great white shark	Alfred Dean, Ceduna, South Australia, Apr 21, 1959	2,664	0	1,208.39
2	Tiger shark	Walter Maxwell, Cherry Grove, California, June 14, 1964	1,780	0	807.4
3	Greenland shark	Terje Nordtvedt, Trondheims-fjord, Norway, Oct 18, 1987	1,708	9	775.00
4	Black marlin	A. C. Glassell, Jr., Cabo Blanco, Peru, Aug 4, 1953	1,560	0	707.62
5	Bluefin tuna	Ken Fraser, Aulds Cove, Nova Scotia, Canada, Oct 26, 1979	1,496	0	678.59
6	Atlantic blue marlin	Paulo Amorim, Vitoria, Brazil, Feb 29, 1992	1,402	2	635.99
7	Pacific blue marlin	Jay W. de Beaubien, Kaaiwi Point, Kona, May 31, 1982	1,376	0	624.15
8	Swordfish	L. Marron, Iquique, Chile, May 7, 1953	1,182	0	536.16
9	Mako shark	Patrick Guillanton, Black River, Mauritius, Nov 16, 1988	1,115	0	505.76
10	Hammerhead shark	Allen Ogle, Sarasota, Florida, May 20, 1982	991	0	449.52

Source: *International Game Fish Association*

TOP 10 ★
SPECIES OF FISH
MOST CAUGHT

	SPECIES	TONS CAUGHT PER ANNUM
1	Anchoveta	13,110,282
2	Alaska pollock	4,737,078
3	Chilean jack mackerel	4,688,601
4	Silver carp	2,571,703
5	Atlantic herring	2,078,487
6	Grass carp	2,007,409
7	South American pilchard	1,976,354
8	Common carp	1,793,172
9	Chubb mackerel	1,661,261
10	Skipjack tuna	1,611,825

Some 3 million tons of shrimps and prawns, and a similar amount of squid, cuttlefish, and octopuses, are caught annually.

SPEEDY SWIMMER

The highly streamlined sailfish is acknowledged as the fastest over short distances, with anglers reporting them capable of unreeling 300 ft (91 m) of line in three seconds.

TOP 10 FASTEST FISH
(Fish/recorded speed in mph/km/h)

1 Sailfish, 68/110 **2** Marlin, 50/80 **3** Bluefin tuna, 46/74 **4** Yellowfin tuna, 44/70
5 Blue shark, 43/69 **6** Wahoo, 41/66 **7** = Bonefish, 40/64; = Swordfish, 40/64
9 Tarpon, 35/56 **10** Tiger shark, 33/53

Flying fish have a top speed in the water of only 23 mph (37 km/h), but airborne they can reach 35 mph (56 km/h). Many sharks qualify for the list; only two are listed here to prevent the list becoming overly shark-infested.

From which play does the phrase "in the doghouse" come?

see p.45 for the answer

A *Peter Pan*
B *A Midsummer Night's Dream*
C *The Importance of Being Earnest*

Flying Animals

TOP 10 ISLANDS WITH THE MOST ENDEMIC BIRD SPECIES*

(Island/species)

1 New Guinea, 195 **2** Jamaica, 26
3 Cuba, 23 **4** New Caledonia, 20
5 Rennell Solomon Islands, 15
6 São Tomé, 14 **7** = Aldabra,
Seychelles, 13; = Grand Cayman,
Cayman Islands, 13 **9** Puerto Rico, 12
10 New Britain, Papua New Guinea, 11

* Birds that are found uniquely on these islands.
Source: *United Nations*

TOP 10 MOST COMMON NORTH AMERICAN GARDEN BIRDS

(Bird/percentage of feeders visited)

1 Dark-eyed junco, 83 **2** House
finch, 70 **3** = American goldfinch, 69;
= Downy woodpecker, 69 **5** Blue jay, 67
6 Mourning dove, 65 **7** Black-capped
chickadee, 60 **8** House sparrow, 59
9 Northern cardinal, 56
10 European starling, 52

Source: *Project FeederWatch/
Cornell Lab of Ornithology*
These are the birds that watchers are most likely
to see at their feeders in North America.

TINSELTOWN BIRD

*One of the most common garden
birds, finches were spread
from the western American
states in the 1940s
by dealers who
sold them as
"Hollywood
Finches."*

TOP 10 ★ LIGHTEST BATS

BAT/HABITAT	LENGTH IN	CM	WEIGHT OZ	G
1 Kitti's hognosed bat (*Craseonycteris thonglongyai*), Thailand	1.10	2.9	0.07	2.0
2 Proboscis bat (*Rhynchonycteris naso*), Central and South America	1.50	3.8	0.09	2.5
3 =Banana bat (*Pipistrellus nanus*), Africa	1.50	3.8	0.11	3.0
=Smoky bat (*Furiptera horrens*), Central and South America	1.50	3.8	0.11	3.0
5 =Little yellow bat (*Rhogeessa mira*), Central America	1.57	4.0	0.12	3.5
=Lesser bamboo bat (*Tylonycteris pachypus*), Southeast Asia	1.57	4.0	0.12	3.5
7 Disc-winged bat (*Thyroptera tricolor*), Central and South America	1.42	3.6	0.14	4.0
8 =Lesser horseshoe bat (*Rhynolophus hipposideros*), Europe and Western Asia	1.46	3.7	0.18	5.0
=California myotis (*Myotis californienses*), North America	1.69	4.3	0.18	5.0
10 Northern blossom bat (*Macroglossus minimus*), Southeast Asia to Australia	2.52	6.4	0.53	15.0

This list focuses on the smallest example of 10 different bat families. The weights shown are typical, rather than extreme – and since a bat can eat more than half its own weight, the weights of individual examples may vary considerably. The smallest of all weighs less than a table-tennis ball, and even the heaviest listed here weighs less than an empty aluminum drink can. Length is of head and body only, since tail lengths vary from zero (as in Kitti's hognosed bat and the Northern blossom bat) to long (as in the Proboscis bat and Lesser horseshoe bat).

TOP 10 ★ FASTEST BIRDS

BIRD	RECORDED SPEED MPH	KM/H
1 Spine-tailed swift	106	171
2 Frigate bird	95	153
3 Spur-winged goose	88	142
4 Red-breasted merganser	80	129
5 White-rumped swift	77	124
6 Canvasback duck	72	116
7 Eider duck	70	113
8 Teal	68	109
9 =Mallard	65	105
= Pintail	65	105

This list picks out star performers among the medium- to large-sized birds that can hit their top speed without help from wind or gravity. Fastest among swimming birds is the gentoo penguin at 22.3 mph (35 km/h), while the speediest of flightless birds is the ostrich at 45 mph (72 km/h).

TOP 10 ★ RAREST BIRDS

BIRD/COUNTRY	ESTIMATED NO.*
1 = Spix's macaw, Brazil	1
=Cebu flower pecker, Philippines	1
3 Hawaiian crow, Hawaii	5
4 Black stilt, New Zealand	12
5 Echo parakeet, Mauritius	13
6 Imperial Amazon parrot, Dominica	15
7 Magpie robin, Seychelles	20
8 Kakapo, New Zealand	24
9 Pink pigeon, Mauritius	70
10 Mauritius kestrel, Mauritius	100

* Of breeding pairs reported since 1986

Several rare bird species are known from old records or from only one specimen, but must be assumed to be extinct in the absence of recent sightings or records of breeding pairs. Rare birds come under most pressure on islands like Mauritius, where the dodo met its fate.

What is an Australian trumpet?
see p.49 for the answer

A A swan
B A marine snail
C A venomous spider

OCEAN FLYER

Featuring in Coleridge's poem The Rime of the Ancient Mariner, *the albatross has a massive wingspan and can soar over the oceans for days at a time.*

TOP 10 BIRDS WITH THE LARGEST WINGSPANS

(Bird/wingspan in ft/m)

❶ **Marabou stork**, 13/4.0 ❷ **Albatross**, 12/3.7 ❸ **Trumpeter swan**, 11/3.4
❹ = **Mute swan**, 10/3.1; = **Whooper swan**, 10/3.1; = **Grey pelican**, 10/3.1;
= **California condor**, 10/3.1; = **Black vulture**, 10/3.1
❾ = **Great bustard**, 9/2.7; = **Kori bustard**, 9/2.7

TOP 10 ★
HEAVIEST FLIGHTED BIRDS

BIRD	WINGSPAN FT	WINGSPAN M	WEIGHT LB	WEIGHT OZ	WEIGHT KG
1 Great bustard	9	2.7	46	1	20.9
2 Trumpeter swan	11	3.4	37	1	16.8
3 Mute swan	10	3.1	35	15	16.3
4 =Albatross	12	3.7	34	13	15.8
=Whooper swan	10	3.1	34	13	15.8
6 Manchurian crane	7	2.1	32	14	14.9
7 Kori bustard	9	2.7	30	0	13.6
8 Grey pelican	10	3.1	28	11	13.0
9 Black vulture	10	3.1	27	8	12.5
10 Griffon vulture	7	2.1	26	7	12.0

Wing size does not necessarily correspond to weight in flighted birds. The 13-ft (4-m) wingspan of the marabou stork beats all the birds listed here, yet its body weight is normally no heavier than any of these. When laden with a meal of carrion, however, the marabou can double its weight and may fail to take off.

"A LITTLE BIRD TOLD ME"

This phrase is often used to announce that one has information but may not be willing to reveal the source of it. Birds as messengers are legendary, but this expression, like so many others, has its origin in the Bible. In the Book of Ecclesiastes (9:20), the writer warns those who complain against kings and the rich and powerful that "a bird of the air shall carry the voice, and that which hath wings shall tell the matter."

WHY DO WE SAY?

TOP 10 ★
MOST COMMON BIRDS IN THE US

BIRD
1 Red-winged blackbird
2 European starling
3 American robin
4 Mourning dove
5 Common grackle
6 American crow
7 Western meadowlark
8 House sparrow
9 Northern cardinal
10 Cliff sparrow

Source: *US Fish and Wildlife Service*

SWANNING AROUND

A heavyweight among flighted birds, exceptional specimens of the mute swan may top 49 lb 10 oz (22.5 kg) and have wingspans of up to 12 ft (3.7 m).

Cats, Dogs & Pets

MOVIES STARRING DOGS

MOVIE	YEAR
1 *101 Dalmatians*	1996
2 *One Hundred and One Dalmatians**	1961
3 *Lady and the Tramp**	1955
4 *Oliver & Company**	1988
5 *Turner & Hooch*	1989
6 *The Fox and the Hound**	1981
7 *Beethoven*	1992
8 *Homeward Bound II: Lost in San Francisco*	1996
9 *Beethoven's 2nd*	1993
10 *K-9*	1991

* Animated

Man's best friend has been stealing scenes since the earliest years of moviemaking, with the 1905 low-budget *Rescued by Rover* standing as one of the most successful productions of the pioneer period. The numerous silent era movies starring Rin Tin Tin, an ex-German army dog who emigrated to the US, and his successor, Lassie, whose long series of feature and TV movies date from the 1940s onward, are among the most enduring in cinematic history.

TOP 10 DOGS' NAMES IN THE US

1 Max **2** Buddy **3** Molly **4** Maggie
5 Bailey **6** Jake **7** Lucy **8** Sam
9 Bear **10** Shadow

Based on a database of 117,000 I.D. tag records.
Source: American Pet Classics

TOP DOGS

Labrador retrievers are the most popular pedigree dogs in both the US and the UK, where they were first bred as gundogs in the 19th century.

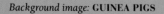

Background image: **GUINEA PIGS**

44

DOG BREEDS IN THE US

BREED	NO. REGISTERED*
1 Labrador retriever	154,897
2 Golden retriever	62,652
3 German shepherd	57,256
4 Dachsund	50,772
5 Beagle	49,080
6 Poodle	45,852
7 Chihuahua	42,013
8 Rottweiler	41,776
9 Yorkshire terrier	40,684
10 Boxer	34,998

* By American Kennel Club, Inc., 1999

Source: *The American Kennel Club*

The Labrador retriever tops the list for the eighth consecutive year. This breed is also No. 1 in the UK. New to this year's Top 10 is the boxer, while the rottweiler drops from fourth place in 1998 down to No. 8 in 1999.

CAT BREEDS IN THE US

BREED	NO. REGISTERED*
1 Persian	30,656
2 Maine coon	4,642
3 Siamese	2,389
4 Exotic	2,188
5 Abyssinian	1,962
6 Oriental	1,210
7 Birman	1,017
8 Scottish fold	1,007
9 American shorthair	986
10 Burmese	923

* Year ending December 31, 1999

Source: *Cat Fanciers' Association*

Some people consider that the Maine coon is so called because it resulted from crossbreeding a cat and a racoon.

MOST INTELLIGENT DOG BREEDS

1	Border collie
2	Poodle
3	German shepherd (Alsatian)
4	Golden retriever
5	Doberman pinscher
6	Shetland sheepdog
7	Labrador retriever
8	Papillon
9	Rottweiler
10	Australian cattle dog

Source: *Stanley Coren, The Intelligence of Dogs*

TOP 10 CATS' NAMES IN THE US

1 Tiger **2** Max **3** Tigger **4** Sam **5** Kitty
6 Sammy **7** Smokey **8** Shadow
9 Misty **10** Fluffy

Based on a database of
117,000 I.D. tag records.
Source: American Pet Classics

WHAT'S NEW, PUSSYCAT?

*Although their role as household mouse
exterminators is less significant today, cats maintain
their place among the world's favorite
animals.*

TOP 10 ★ PETS IN THE US

PET	ESTIMATED NO.*
1 Cat	66,150,000
2 Dog	58,200,000
3 Small animal pet#	12,740,000
4 Parakeet	11,000,000
5 Freshwater fish	10,800,000
6 Reptile	7,540,000
7 Finch	7,350,000
8 Cockatiel	6,320,000
9 Canary	2,580,000
10 Parrot	1,550,000

Source: *Pet Industry Joint Advisory Council*

* *Number of households owning, rather than
individual specimens*

*Includes small rodents: rabbits, ferrets,
hamsters, guinea pigs, and gerbils*

"IN THE DOGHOUSE"

In J. M. Barrie's famous children's play *Peter
Pan* (1904), irascible Mr. Darling mistreats
the dog-nursemaid, Nana, as a result of which
the Darling children – Wendy, John, and
Michael – leave home. As a penance, Mr.
Darling lives in the doghouse until the
children return. Mr. Darling was based on
Arthur Llewelyn Davies, the real-life father of
the boys on whom
Barrie based the story,
and Nana was Barrie's
own dog, Luath.

WHY DO WE SAY?

TOP 10 RABBITS' NAMES IN THE US

1 Thumper **2** Flopsy **3** Charlie **4** Fudge
5 Rosie **6** Smokey **7** Snowy
8 Daisy **9** George **10** Molly

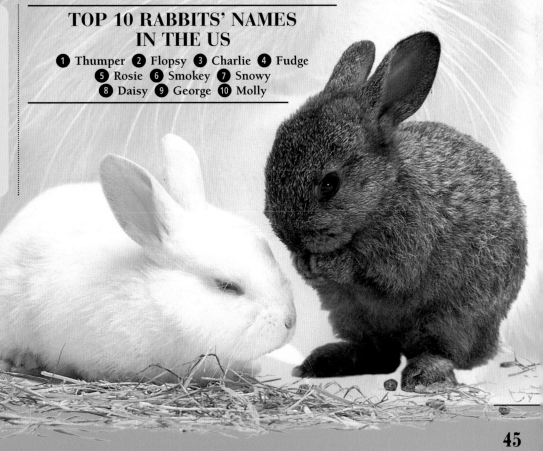

FURRY FAVORITES

*Although Flopsy is second choice,
Beatrix Potter's more famous creations of
Peter and Benjamin are surprisingly absent
from the Top 10 rabbits' names.*

TOP 10 ★
FASTEST FLYING INSECTS

SPECIES	MPH	KM/H
1 **Hawkmoth** (*Sphingidaei*)	33.3	53.6
2 =**West Indian butterfly** (*Nymphalidae prepona*)	30.0	48.0
=**Deer bot fly** (*Cephenemyia pratti*)	30.0	48.0
4 **Deer bot fly** (*Chrysops*)	25.0	40.0
5 **West Indian butterfly** (*Hesperiidae sp.*)	18.6	30.0
6 **Dragonfly** (*Anax parthenope*)	17.8	28.6
7 **Hornet** (*Vespa crabro*)	13.3	21.4
8 **Bumblebee** (*Bombus lapidarius*)	11.1	17.9
9 **Horsefly** (*Tabanus bovinus*)	8.9	14.3
10 **Honeybee** (*Apis millefera*)	7.2	11.6

Few accurate assessments of these speeds have been attempted, and this list reflects only the results of those scientific studies recognized by entomologists.

BEETLE BEATS ALL

This red-spotted longhorn beetle is one of about 400,000 beetles identified so far. This makes the beetle the most common known species of insect.

TOP 10 ★
LARGEST MOTHS

	WINGSPAN	
MOTH	IN	MM
1 **Atlas moth** (*Attacus atlas*)	11.8	300
2 **Owlet moth** (*Thysania agrippina*)*	11.4	290
3 *Haematopis grataria*	10.2	260
4 **Hercules emperor moth** (*Coscinocera hercules*)	8.3	210
5 **Malagasy silk moth** (*Argema mitraei*)	7.1	180
6 *Eacles imperialis*	6.9	175
7 =**Common emperor moth** (*Bunaea alcinoe*)	6.3	160
=**Giant peacock moth** (*Saturnia pyri*)	6.3	160
9 **Gray moth** (*Brahmaea wallichii*)	6.1	155
10 =**Black witch** (*Ascalapha odorata*)	5.9	150
=**Regal moth** (*Citheronia regalis*)	5.9	150
=**Polyphemus moth** (*Antheraea polyphemus*)	5.9	150

* *Exceptional specimen measured at 12¼ in (308 mm)*

TOP 10 ★
MOST COMMON INSECTS*

SPECIES	APPROXIMATE NO. OF KNOWN SPECIES
1 **Beetles** (*Coleoptera*)	400,000
2 **Butterflies and moths** (*Lepidoptera*)	165,000
3 **Ants, bees, and wasps** (*Hymenoptera*)	140,000
4 **True flies** (*Diptera*)	120,000
5 **Bugs** (*Hemiptera*)	90,000
6 **Crickets, grasshoppers, and locusts** (*Orthoptera*)	20,000
7 **Caddisflies** (*Trichoptera*)	10,000
8 **Lice** (*Phthiraptera/Psocoptera*)	7,000
9 **Dragonflies and damselflies** (*Odonata*)	5,500
10 **Lacewings** (*Neuroptera*)	4,700

* *By number of known species*

This list includes only species that have been discovered and named: it is surmised that many thousands of species still await discovery.

Did You Know? The heaviest of all insects is the Goliath beetle, which can weigh up to 3½ oz (100 g), or more than twice the weight of a golf ball.

LEGGING IT TO THE TOP

The Haplophilus subterraneus *centipede measures up to 2¾ in (70 mm) and has 89 pairs of legs. It is interesting to note that all centipedes always have an odd number of body segments (although the number of legs is, of course, always even!).*

TOP 10 ★

CREATURES WITH THE MOST LEGS

	CREATURE	AVERAGE NO. OF LEGS
1	Millipede *Illacme plenipes*	750
2	Centipede *Himantarum gabrielis*	354
3	Centipede *Haplophilus subterraneus*	178
4	Millipedes*	30
5	Symphylans	24
6	Caterpillars*	16
7	Woodlice	14
8	Crabs, shrimps	10
9	Spiders	8
10	Insects	6

* Most species

Because "centipede" means 100 feet and "millipede" 1,000 feet, many people believe that centipedes have 100 legs and millipedes 1,000. However, despite their names and depending on their species, centipedes have anything from 28 to 354 legs and millipedes up to 400, with the record standing at more than 700. The other principal difference between them is that each body segment of a centipede has two legs, while that of a millipede has four.

BIG WING

Male African giant swallowtails, Papilio antimachus, are Africa's largest butterflies, with wingspans of up to an impressive 9⅛ in (230 mm).

TOP 10 ★

LARGEST BUTTERFLIES

	BUTTERFLY	WINGSPAN IN	MM
1	Queen Alexandra's birdwing	11.0	280
2	African giant swallowtail	9.1	230
3	Goliath birdwing	8.3	210
4 =	*Trogonoptera trojana*	7.9	200
=	Buru opalescent birdwing	7.9	200
=	*Troides hypolitus*	7.9	200
7 =	*Ornithoptera lydius*	7.5	190
=	Chimaera birdwing	7.5	190
=	*Troides magellanus*	7.5	190
=	*Troides miranda*	7.5	190

Creepy Crawlies 2

TOP 10 LARGEST SNAILS

(Species/length in in/mm)

1 **Australian trumpet** (*Syrinx aruanus*), 30¼/770 **2** **Horse conch**
(*Pleuroploc filamentosa*), 22¾/580 **3** **= Baler shell** (*Voluta amphora*), 18¾/480;
= **Triton's trumpet** (*Charonia tritonis*), 18¾/480 **5** **Beck's volute** (*Voluta becki*), 18½/470
6 **Umbilicate volute** (*Voluta umbilicalis*), 16½/420 **7** **Madagascar helmet**
(*Cassis madagascariensis*), 16/409 **8** **Spider conch** (*Lambis truncata*), 15¾/400
9 **Knobbly trumpet** (*Charonia nodifera*), 15¼/390 **10** **Goliath conch**
(*Strombus goliath*), 15/380

TOP 10 ★
DEADLIEST SPIDERS

SPIDER/LOCATION

1 **Banana spider** (*Phonenutria nigriventer*),
Central and South America

2 **Sydney funnel web** (*Atrax robustus*), Australia

3 **Wolf spider** (*Lycosa raptoria/erythrognatha*),
Central and South America

4 **Black widow** (*Latrodectus species*), worldwide

5 **Violin spider/Recluse spider**, worldwide

6 **Sac spider**, Southern Europe

7 **Tarantula** (*Eurypelma rubropilosum*), Neotropics

8 **Tarantula** (*Acanthoscurria atrox*), Neotropics

9 **Tarantula** (*Lasiodora klugi*), Neotropics

10 **Tarantula** (*Pamphobeteus species*), Neotropics

This list ranks spiders according to their "lethal potential" – their
venom yield divided by their venom potency. The Banana spider, for
example, yields 6 mg of venom, with 1 mg the estimated lethal dose in
man. However, few spiders are capable of killing humans – there were
just 14 recorded deaths caused by black widows in the US in the
whole of the 19th century.

READY TO STRIKE
*Found only in New South Wales, male
Sydney funnel web spiders are, unusually,
more dangerous than the females.*

TOP 10 ★
MOST POPULAR US STATE INSECTS

INSECT/STATES	NO.
1 **Honeybee**, Arkansas, Georgia, Kansas, Louisiana, Maine, Mississippi, Missouri, Nebraska, New Hampshire, New Jersey, North Carolina, South Dakota, Utah, Vermont, Wisconsin	15
2 **Swallowtail butterfly**, Florida (giant/zebra longwing), Georgia (tiger), Mississippi (spicebush), Ohio (tiger), Oklahoma (black), Oregon (Oregon), Virginia (tiger), Wyoming (western)	8
3 **Ladybird beetle/ladybug**, Delaware (convergent), Iowa, Massachusetts, New York (nine-spotted), New Hampshire (two-spotted), Ohio, Tennessee (ladybug)	7
4 **Monarch butterfly**, Alabama, Idaho, Illinois, Texas, Vermont	5
5 **Firefly**, Pennsylvania, Tennessee	2
6 **=Baltimore checkerspot butterfly**, Maryland	1
=California dogface butterfly, California	1
=Carolina mantis, South Carolina	1
=Colorado hairstreak butterfly, Colorado	1
=European praying mantis, Connecticut	1
=Four-spotted skimmer dragonfly, Alaska	1
=Green darner dragonfly, Texas	1
= Karner blue butterfly, New Hampshire	1
= Tarantula hawk wasp, New Mexico	1
= Viceroy butterfly, Kentucky	1

SNAIL'S PACE

Although exceeded by marine species, the Giant African snail is the largest terrestrial mollusk. Exceptional specimens may reach almost 15.5 in (400 mm) in length and weigh 2 lb (900 g).

THE 10 COUNTRIES WITH THE MOST THREATENED INVERTEBRATES

(Country/threatened invertebrate species)

1 US, 594 **2** Australia, 281 **3** South Africa, 101 **4** Portugal, 67 **5** France, 61 **6** Spain, 57 **7** Tanzania, 46 **8** = Japan, 45; = Dem. Rep. of Congo, 45 **10** = Austria, 41; = Italy, 41

Source: International Union for the Conservation of Nature

TOP 10 ★
LARGEST MOLLUSKS*

SPECIES	CLASS	LENGTH IN	LENGTH MM
1 Giant squid (*Architeuthis sp.*)	Cephalopod	660	16,764#
2 Giant clam (*Tridacna gigas*)	Marine bivalve	51	1,300
3 Australian trumpet	Marine snail	30	770
4 *Hexabranchus sanguineus*	Sea slug	20	520
5 *Carinaria cristata*	Heteropod	19	500
6 Steller's coat of mail shell (*Cryptochiton stelleri*)	Chiton	18	470
7 Freshwater mussel (*Cristaria plicata*)	Freshwater bivalve	11	300
8 Giant African snail (*Achatina achatina*)	Land snail	7	200
9 Tusk shell (*Dentalium vernedi*)	Scaphopod	5	138
10 Apple snail (*Pila werneri*)	Freshwater snail	4	125

* *Largest species within each class*

\# *Estimated; actual length unknown*

Which breed of dog is regarded as the most intelligent?
see p.44 for the answer
A Border collie
B Saint Bernard
C Afghan hound

Trees & Forests

TOP 10 TALLEST TREES IN THE US*

	TREE	LOCATION	HEIGHT FT	M
1	**Coast Douglas fir**	Coos County, Oregon	329	100.3
2	**Coast redwood**	Prairie Creek Redwoods State Park, California	313	95.4
3	**General Sherman, giant sequoia**	Sequoia National Park, California	275	83.8
4	**Noble fir**	Mount St. Helens National Monument, Washington	272	82.9
5	**Grand fir**	Redwood National Park, California	257	78.3
6	**Western hemlock**	Olympic National Park, Washington	241	73.5
7	**Sugar pine**	Dorrington, California	232	70.7
8	**Ponderosa pine**	Plumas National Forest, California	223	68.0
9	**Port-Orford cedar**	Siskiyou National Forest, Oregon	219	66.8
10	**Pacific silver fir**	Forks, Washington	217	66.1

By species (i.e., the tallest known example of each of the 10 tallest species)
Source: American Forests

ON TAP

In the 20th century, annual world demand for natural rubber, especially from the automotive industry, increased from under 50,000 to over 6 million tons.

TOP 10 ★ RUBBER-PRODUCING COUNTRIES

	COUNTRY	1998 PRODUCTION TONS
1	**Thailand**	2,382,976
2	**Indonesia**	1,723,885
3	**Malaysia**	1,192,804
4	**India**	597,284
5	**China**	495,900
6	**Philippines**	220,400
7	**Vietnam**	199,131
8	**Côte d'Ivoire**	127,466
9	**Sri Lanka**	116,572
10	**Nigeria**	99,180
	World total	7,471,658

Source: Food and Agriculture Organization of the United Nations

TOP 10 ★ TIMBER-PRODUCING COUNTRIES

	COUNTRY	1998 PRODUCTION CU FT	CU M
1	**US**	17,478,536,826	494,937,000
2	**China**	11,054,092,059	313,017,000
3	**India**	10,822,357,195	306,455,000
4	**Brazil**	7,780,280,892	220,313,000
5	**Indonesia**	7,168,471,891	202,988,500
6	**Canada**	6,751,387,981	191,178,000
7	**Nigeria**	4,145,483,167	117,387,000
8	**Russia**	2,965,302,211	83,968,000
9	**Sweden**	2,126,790,686	60,224,000
10	**Ethiopia**	1,847,310,388	52,310,000
	World total	119,562,158,989	3,385,623,000

Source: Food and Agriculture Organization of the United Nations

TREE TOPS
The US leads the world in timber production, supplying the requirements of industries such as construction and paper manufacture.

TOP 10 ★
MOST COMMON TREES IN THE US

	TREE
1	Silver maple
2	Black cherry
3	Boxelder
4	Eastern cottonwood
5	Black willow
6	Northern red oak
7	Flowering dogwood
8	Black oak
9	Ponderosa pine
10	Coast douglas fir

Source: *American Forests*

TOP 10 ★
COUNTRIES WITH THE LARGEST AREAS OF FOREST

	COUNTRY	SQ MILES	AREA SQ KM
1	Russia	2,957,203	7,659,120
2	Canada	1,907,345	4,940,000
3	Brazil	1,884,179	4,880,000
4	US	1,142,824	2,959,900
5	Dem. Rep. of Congo	671,046	1,738,000
6	Australia	559,848	1,450,000
7	China	503,848	1,304,960
8	Indonesia	431,562	1,117,740
9	Peru	327,415	848,000
10	India	264,480	685,000
	World total	15,976,944	41,380,090

The world's forests occupy some 28 percent of the total land area of the planet. Almost 45 percent of the area of Russia is forested, representing a total area that is almost the size of Australia.

NATURAL BEAUTY
The largest National Forest in the US, the Tongass in Alaska, is a magnificent wilderness that encompasses mountains, rivers, glaciers, and islands. This vast forest is over three times the size of the next forest in the Top 10.

TOP 10 ★
LARGEST NATIONAL FORESTS IN THE US

	FOREST	LOCATION	SQ MILES	AREA SQ KM
1	Tongass National Forest	Sitka, Alaska	25,937	67,177
2	Chugach National Forest	Anchorage, Alaska	8,281	21,448
3	Toiyabe National Forest	Sparks, Nevada	5,000	12,950
4	Tonto National Forest	Phoenix, Arizona	4,531	11,735
5=	Boise National Forest	Boise, Idaho	4,218	10,925
=	Gila National Forest	Silver City, New Mexico	4,218	10,925
7=	Humboldt National Forest	Elko, Nevada	3,906	10,116
=	Challis National Forest	Challis, Idaho	3,906	10,116
9=	Shoshone National Forest	Cody, Wyoming	3,750	9,712
=	Flathead National Forest	Kalispell, Montana	3,750	9,712

Source: *Land Areas of the National Forest System*

Did You Know? A vast area of the Tunguska Forest of Siberia was flattened in an instant on June 30, 1908, when a meteorite – or perhaps part of Encke's comet – exploded in the sky above it.

The Human World

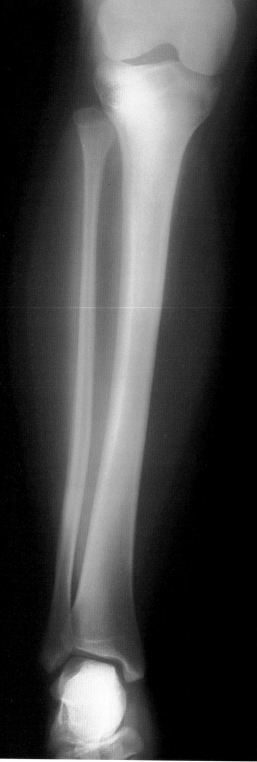

THE WINNING LEG

The second longest bone, the tibia is named after the Latin word for a flute, which it resembles in shape and length. The three longest bones are all in the leg.

TOP 10 ★
COUNTRIES THAT SPEND THE MOST ON HEALTH CARE

	COUNTRY	HEALTH SPENDING PER CAPITA ($)
1	US	4,093
2	Switzerland	3,603
3	Germany	2,677
4	Norway	2,622
5	Japan	2,442
6	Denmark	2,388
7	France	2,349
8	Sweden	2,222
9	Austria	2,012
10	Netherlands	1,978

Source: *World Bank,* World Development Indicators 1999

THE 10 ★
MOST COMMON REASONS FOR VISITS TO A PHYSICIAN

	REASON FOR VISIT	VISITS, 1997
1	General medical examination	59,796,000
2	Progress visit, not otherwise specified	28,583,000
3	Cough	25,735,000
4	Routine prenatal examination	22,979,000
5	Postoperative visit	18,861,000
6	Symptoms referable to throat	17,151,000
7	Well baby examination	15,526,000
8	Vision dysfunctions	13,443,000
9	Earache or ear infection	13,359,000
10	Back symptoms	12,863,000

Source: *National Ambulatory Medical Care Survey/ Center for Disease Control/National Center for Health Statistics*

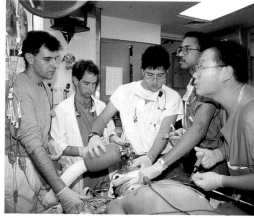

ER, US

The world's hospital emergency rooms have to be equipped to treat victims of everything from minor injuries to major traumas.

TOP 10 ★
LONGEST BONES IN THE HUMAN BODY

	BONE	AVERAGE LENGTH IN	CM
1	**Femur** (thighbone)	19.88	50.50
2	**Tibia** (shinbone)	16.94	43.03
3	**Fibula** (outer lower leg)	15.94	40.50
4	**Humerus** (upper arm)	14.35	36.46
5	**Ulna** (inner lower arm)	11.10	28.20
6	**Radius** (outer lower arm)	10.40	26.42
7	**7th rib**	9.45	24.00
8	**8th rib**	9.06	23.00
9	**Innominate bone** (hipbone)	7.28	18.50
10	**Sternum** (breastbone)	6.69	17.00

THE 10 MOST COMMON HOSPITAL ER CASES
(Reason for visit/visits, 1997)

① **Stomach and abdominal pain,** 5,527,000 **②** **Chest pain and related symptoms,** 5,315,000 **③** **Fever,** 4,212,000 **④** **Headache,** 2,518,000 **⑤** **Injury – upper extremity,** 2,383,000 **⑥** **Shortness of breath,** 2,242,000 **⑦** **Cough,** 2,220,000 **⑧** **Back symptoms,** 2,073,000 **⑨** **Pain, nonspecific site,** 2,040,000 **⑩** **Symptoms referable to throat,** 1,953,000

Source: *Center for Disease Control/ National Center for Health Statistics*

THE 10 ★
MOST COMMON TYPES OF ILLNESS

TYPE	NEW CASES ANNUALLY
1 Diarrhea (including dysentery)	4,002,000,000
2 Malaria	up to 500,000,000
3 Acute lower respiratory infections	395,000,000
4 Occupational injuries	350,000,000
5 Occupational diseases	217,000,000
6 Trichomoniasis	170,000,000
7 Mood (affective) disorders	122,865,000
8 Chlamydial infections	89,000,000
9 Alcohol dependence syndrome	75,000,000
10 Gonococcal (bacterial) infections	62,000,000

Source: *World Health Organization*

TOP 10 ★
MOST COMMON PHOBIAS

OBJECT OF PHOBIA	MEDICAL TERM
1 Spiders	Arachnephobia or arachnophobia
2 People and social situations	Anthropophobia or sociophobia
3 Flying	Aerophobia or aviatophobia
4 Open spaces	Agoraphobia, cenophobia or kenophobia
5 Confined spaces	Claustrophobia, cleisiophobia, cleithrophobia, or clithrophobia
6 =Vomiting	Emetophobia or emitophobia
=Heights	Acrophobia, altophobia, hypsophobia, or hypsiphobia
8 Cancer	Carcinomaphobia, carcinophobia, carcinomatophobia, cancerphobia, or cancerophobia
9 Thunderstorms	Brontophobia or keraunophobia
10 =Death	Necrophobia or thanatophobia
=Heart disease	Cardiophobia

TOP 10 ★
MOST COMMON ELEMENTS IN THE HUMAN BODY

ELEMENT	AVERAGE WEIGHT* OZ	AVERAGE WEIGHT* G
1 Oxygen	1,608	45,500
2 Carbon	445	12,600
3 Hydrogen	247	7,000
4 Nitrogen	74	2,100
5 Calcium	37	1,050
6 Phosphorus	25	700
7 Sulfur	6	175
8 Potassium	5	140
9 =Chlorine	4	105
=Sodium	4	105

* Average in 154 lb (70 kg) person

The Top 10 elements account for more than 99 percent of the total, with the balance comprising minute quantities of metallic elements including iron, zinc, tin, and aluminum. Each has one or more specific functions: oxygen is essential for energy production, carbon and hydrogen are major cell components, while nitrogen is vital for DNA and most body functions.

WEIGHTY MATTER

The modern technique of Magnetic Resonance Imaging (MRI) enables us to view the human brain, the human body's third-largest organ.

TOP 10 ★
LARGEST HUMAN ORGANS

ORGAN		AVERAGE WEIGHT OZ	G
1 Skin		384.0	10,886
2 Liver		1,560	55.0
3 Brain	male	49.7	1,408
	female	44.6	1,263
4 Lungs	right	20.5	580
	left	18.0	510
	total	38.5	1,090
5 Heart	male	11.1	315
	female	9.3	265
6 Kidneys	right	4.9	140
	left	5.3	150
	total	10.2	290
7 Spleen		6.0	170
8 Pancreas		3.5	98
9 Thyroid		1.2	35
10 Prostate (male only)		0.7	20

This list is based on average immediate postmortem weights, as recorded by St. Bartholemew's Hospital, London, and other sources during a 10-year period. Various instances of organs far in excess of the average have been recorded, including male brains of over 70.6 oz (2,000 g). The Victorians believed that the heavier the brain, the greater the intelligence, and were impressed by the recorded weights of 58 oz (1,658 g) for author William Makepeace Thackeray.

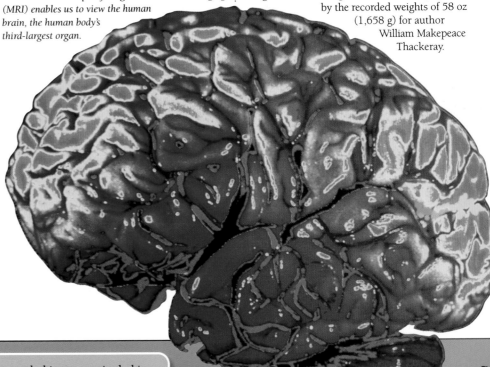

Did You Know? Among the least-common phobias are geniophobia (fear of eggshells,) barophobia (gravity), apeirophobia (infinity), and linonophobia (string).

55

Diet & Fitness

US CITIES WITH THE FEWEST OBESE PERSONS

	CITY/STATE	PERCENTAGE OBESE
1	**Denver**, Colorado	22.10
2	**Minneapolis**, Minnesota	22.63
3	**San Diego**, California	22.91
4	**Washington, D.C.**	23.84
5	**Phoenix**, Arizona	24.36
6	**St. Louis**, Missouri	24.78
7	**Tampa**, Florida	24.91
8	**San Francisco**, California	25.16
9	**Los Angeles**, California	25.22
10	**Atlanta**, Georgia	25.49

Source: *National Center for Health Statistics*

These cities were ranked at the bottom of the NCHS's survey of obesity in the US's 33 largest metropolitan areas. As well as such considerations as regional food styles, the survey pointed to the tendency of residents in Denver to engage in outdoor activities, including hiking and skiing, giving them a figure that compares favorably with the national average (which encompasses smaller metropolitan and rural areas). The same survey also found that 54 percent of all US adults were overweight (with a Body Mass Index of over 25).

TOP 10 ACTIVITIES FOR WEIGHT MANAGEMENT

1 Walking 2 Cycling 3 Swimming
4 Active hobbies (gardening, DIY, etc.)
5 Low-impact aerobics
6 Jogging 7 Weight training
8 Vigorous sports 9 Housework
10 Switching off the television

Source: Slimming World

PROTEIN CONSUMERS

	COUNTRY	PROTEIN CONSUMPTION PER CAPITA PER DAY OZ	GM
1	**Greece**	4.05	114.9
2	**Portugal**	4.00	113.5
3	**Iceland**	3.99	113.3
4	**France**	3.98	113.1
5	**US**	3.96	112.3
6	**Ireland**	3.90	110.6
7	**Malta**	3.88	110.0
8	**Cyprus**	3.85	109.3
9	**Italy**	3.83	108.6
10	**New Zealand**	3.81	108.1
	World average	2.60	73.9

Source: *Food and Agricultural Organization of the UN*

LEAST PROTEIN CONSUMERS

	COUNTRY	PROTEIN CONSUMPTION PER CAPITA PER DAY OZ	GM
1	**Dem. Rep. of Congo**	0.99	28.1
2	**Mozambique**	1.23	34.9
3	**Liberia**	1.28	36.5
4	**Angola**	1.42	40.5
5	**Haiti**	1.44	41.0
6	**Comoros**	1.51	42.9
7	**Republic of Congo**	1.52	43.1
8	**Sierra Leone**	1.53	43.6
9	**Djibouti**	1.54	43.7
10	**Central African Republic**	1.54	43.8

Source: *Food and Agricultural Organization of the UN*

US CITIES WITH THE MOST OBESE PERSONS

	CITY/STATE	PERCENTAGE OBESE
1	**New Orleans**, Louisiana	37.55
2	**Norfolk**, Virginia	33.94
3	**San Antonio**, Texas	32.96
4	**Kansas City**, Kansas	31.66
5	**Cleveland**, Ohio	31.50
6	**Detroit**, Michigan	31.01
7	**Columbus**, Georgia	30.75
8	**Cincinnati**, Ohio	30.71
9	**Pittsburgh**, Philadelphia	29.99
10	**Houston**, Texas	29.19

Source: *National Center for Health Statistics*

A 1997 NCHS interview considered the weights of people in the US's 33 largest metropolitan areas. "Obeseity" was defined as 20 percent over the weight recommended by standard health charts, or a Body Mass Index greater than 30. Health officials consider that as many as 280,000 US deaths a year result from obesity-related disabilities.

LEAST FAT CONSUMERS

	COUNTRY	FAT CONSUMPTION PER CAPITA PER DAY OZ	GM
1	**Burundi**	0.38	11.0
2	**Eritrea**	0.68	19.5
3	**Bangladesh**	0.77	22.0
4	**Rwanda**	0.79	22.4
5	**Ethiopia**	0.80	22.7
6	**Afghanistan**	0.84	24.0
7	**Laos**	0.90	25.7
8	**Dem. Rep. of Congo**	0.95	27.7
9	**Uganda**	0.98	28.0
10	**Zambia**	1.04	29.7

Source: *Food and Agricultural Organization of the UN*

SINK OR SWIM

Swimming promotes all-around fitness with reduced danger of muscle strain, and is thus considered one of the most valuable activities for dieters.

Background image: **LETTUCE**

TOP 10 ★
MOST FATTENING FOODS*

FOOD	ENERGY DENSITY KCALS PER 100G
1 Cooking oils/fats#	891–899
2 Butter/margarine+	739
3 Hollandaise sauce	707
4 Mayonnaise	691
5 Creamed coconut	669
6 French dressing	651
7 Nuts★	630
8 Peanut butter	623
9 Tahini paste	607
10 Pork rinds	606

* Based on most concentrated source of Calories

\# Including coconut, cod liver, olive, lard, and dripping

\+ Margarine 737 kcals

★ Average

Source: Slimming World

TOP 10 ★
LEAST FATTENING FOODS*

FOOD	ENERGY DENSITY KCALS PER 100G
1 =Celery	7
=Rhubarb	7
=Chicory, boiled	7
4 =Globe artichoke, boiled	8
=Oyster mushrooms	8
6 Marrow, boiled	9
7 =Cucumber	10
=Canned beansprouts, drained	10
9 =Mushrooms, boiled	11
=Fennel, boiled	11
=Rutabaga, boiled	11
=Canned bamboo shoots	11

* Based on least concentrated source of Calories

Source: Slimming World

TOP 10 ★
FAT CONSUMERS

COUNTRY	FAT CONSUMPTION PER CAPITA PER DAY OZ	GM
1 France	5.78	164.0
2 Austria	5.69	161.4
3 Belgium and Luxembourg	5.63	159.6
4 Greece	5.41	153.4
5 Italy	5.18	146.8
6 Cyprus	5.17	146.7
7 Spain	5.10	144.7
8 Germany	5.09	144.4
9 Switzerland	5.06	143.6
10 US	5.03	142.8
World average	2.53	71.7

Source: *Food and Agricultural Organization of the UN*

PORTUGUESE PLATTER

This traditional beef, egg, and fried potato dish is a component of Portugal's high per capita Calorie consumption.

TOP 10 ★
CALORIE CONSUMERS

COUNTRY	AVERAGE DAILY PER CAPITA CONSUMPTION
1 US	3,699.1
2 Portugal	3,667.0
3 Greece	3,648.6
4 Belgium and Luxembourg	3,619.2
5 Ireland	3,565.1
6 Austria	3,535.8
7 Turkey	3,524.7
8 France	3,518.4
9 Italy	3,506.9
10 Cyprus	3,429.2

Source: *Food and Agricultural Organization of the UN*

The Calorie requirement of the average man is 2,700 and that of the average woman is 2,500. Inactive people need less, while those engaged in heavy labor might require to increase, perhaps even to double, these figures. Calories that are not consumed as energy turn to fat.

Births, Marriages & Deaths

COUNTRIES WITH THE HIGHEST FEMALE LIFE EXPECTANCY

	COUNTRY	LIFE EXPECTANCY AT BIRTH (YEARS), 1998
1	Japan	83.59
2	Switzerland	81.90
3	France	81.86
4	Sweden	81.53
5	Norway	81.07
6	Australia	81.05
7	Canada	80.89
8	Italy	80.74
9	Belgium	80.61
10	Iceland	80.59
	US	78.9

Source: UN Demographic Yearbook

YOUNG AT HEART

In the past century, female life expectancy in Japan has increased by almost 40 years, from 44.3 years in 1900 to its present 83.59.

COUNTRIES WITH THE LOWEST BIRTH RATE

	COUNTRY	1998 LIVE BIRTHS PER 1,000
1	Bulgaria	7.4
2	Latvia	7.9
3	Estonia	8.6
4	Ukraine	8.7
5	=Belarus	8.8
	=Czech Republic	8.8
7	Spain	9.0
8	Russia	9.2
9	Hong Kong	9.3
10	=Italy	9.4
	=Slovenia	9.4
	US	14.8

Source: UN Demographic Yearbook

COUNTRIES WITH THE HIGHEST MALE LIFE EXPECTANCY

	COUNTRY	LIFE EXPECTANCY AT BIRTH (YEARS), 1998
1	Luxembourg	77.87
2	Japan	77.01
3	Sweden	76.51
4	Iceland	76.20
5	Switzerland	75.70
6	Greece	75.62
7	Norway	75.37
8	Israel	75.30
9	Australia	75.22
10	Malta	74.94
	US	72.5

Source: UN Demographic Yearbook

Half a century ago, the vast majority of the global population died before the age of 50. Today, the great majority survive well beyond that age. Between 1980 and 1995, global average life expectancy increased by an average of 4.6 years and is now 64 years for men, 67 for women.

THE 10 COUNTRIES WITH THE HIGHEST DEATH RATE

(Country/1998 death rate per 100,000)

1. **Rwanda**, 44.6 2. **Sierra Leone**, 29.6
3. **Liberia**, 27.9 4. **Malawi**, 22.4
5. = **Guinea Bissau**, 21.8; = **Uganda**, 21.8
7. **Afghanistan**, 21.7 8. **Guinea**, 20.3
9. **Burundi**, 19.6 10. **The Gambia**, 19.2
US, 8.8

Source: UN Demographic Yearbook

THE 10 COUNTRIES WITH THE MOST DEATHS FROM HEART DISEASE

(Country/1998 death rate per 1,000)

1. **Ukraine**, 534.1 2. **Estonia**, 438.8
3. **Lithuania**, 418.3 4. **Belarus**, 382.7
5. **Moldova**, 381.0 6. **Russia**, 356.4
7. **Georgia**, 328.1 8. **Hungary**, 304.4
9. **Bulgaria**, 267.9 10. **Finland**, 267.7

Source: UN Demographic Yearbook

COUNTRIES WITH THE HIGHEST BIRTH RATE

	COUNTRY	1998 LIVE BIRTHS PER 1,000
1	Niger	52.5
2	=Angola	50.8
	=Mali	50.8
	=Uganda	50.8
5	=Guinea	50.6
	=Malawi	50.6
7	Afghanistan	49.7
8	Sierra Leone	49.0
9	Ethiopia	48.9
10	Yemen	48.7
	US	14.8

Source: UN Demographic Yearbook

The countries with the highest birth rates are among the poorest countries in the world. In these countries, people often want to have large families so that the children can help to earn income for the family when they are older. The 10 countries with the highest birth rate therefore correspond very closely with those countries with the highest fertility rate.

THE 10 ⭐
MOST COMMON CAUSES OF DEATH

	CAUSE	APPROXIMATE NO. OF DEATHS PER ANNUM
1	Ischaemic heart disease	7,375,000
2	Cancers*	7,229,000
3	Cerebrovascular disease	5,106,000
4	Acute lower respiratory infection	3,452,000
5	HIV/AIDS	2,285,000
6	Chronic obstructive pulmonary disease	2,249,000
7	Diarrhea (including dysentery)	2,219,000
8	Childhood diseases#	1,651,000
9	Tuberculosis	1,498,000
10	Road traffic accidents	1,171,000

* Lung cancer deaths alone number 1,244,000

\# Including pertussis, polio, diptheria, measles, and tetanus

Source: WHO World Health Report 1999

TOP 10 ⭐
PROFESSIONS OF COMPUTER-DATING MEMBERS IN THE US

WOMEN'S PROFESSIONS	PERCENTAGE OF THOSE REGISTERED		PERCENTAGE OF THOSE REGISTERED	MEN'S PROFESSIONS
Teachers/lecturers	7.8	1	6.1	Engineers
Nurses	5.2	2	5.3	Computer professionals
Women at home	4.8	3	4.8	Teachers/lecturers
Secretaries	4.5	4	4.5	Company directors
Civil servants	3.9	5	4.3	Accountants
Social workers	3.8	6	4.2	Doctors
Lawyers	3.5	7	4.0	Managers
Accountants	3.1	8	3.7	Civil servants
Doctors	2.8	9	2.5	Architects
Students	1.3	10	1.4	Farmers

Source: *Dateline International*

TOP 10 COUNTRIES WITH THE HIGHEST MARRIAGE RATE

(Country/1998 marriages per 1,000)

1 Antigua and Barbuda, 21.0 **2** Maldives, 19.7 **3** Bermuda, 15.7 **4** Barbados, 13.5 **5** Liechtenstein, 12.9 **6** Seychelles, 11.4 **7** Bangladesh, 9.7 **8** Mauritius, 9.5 **9** = Bahamas, 9.3; = Sri Lanka, 9.3

US, 8.8   Source: UN Demographic Yearbook

The highest marriage rates in the world are actually recorded in places that are not independent countries. Gibraltar, for example, has a marriage rate of 26.7 per 1,000.

TOP 10 ⭐
COUNTRIES WITH THE HIGHEST DIVORCE RATE

	COUNTRY	1998 DIVORCE RATE PER 1,000
1	Maldives	10.75
2	= Belarus	4.63
	= China	4.63
4	Russia	4.51
5	US	4.33
6	Surinam	4.26
7	Estonia	3.85
8	Cuba	3.72
9	Ukraine	3.71
10	Puerto Rico	3.49

Source: UN Demographic Yearbook

WEDDED BLISS?
Cuba once featured prominently among countries with a high marriage rate, but today ranks among the world's foremost countries for divorce.

Did You Know? In Rwanda, the death rate at 44.6 per 1,000 people is actually greater than the birth rate, which is 43.9 per 1,000 people.

What's in a Name?

FIRST NAMES IN ENGLAND & WALES

GIRLS		BOYS
Chloe	1	Jack
Emily	2	Thomas
Megan	3	James
Olivia	4	Joshua
Sophie	5	Daniel
Charlotte	6	Matthew
Lauren	7	Samuel
Jessica	8	Joseph
Rebecca	9	Callum
Hannah	10	William

FIRST NAMES IN SCOTLAND

BOYS		GIRLS
Jack	1	Chloe
Lewis	2	Rebecca
Ryan	3	Lauren
Cameron	4	Emma
Ross	5	Amy
James	6	Megan
Andrew	7	Caitlin
Liam	8	Rachel
Scott	9	Erin
Connor	10	Sophie

As in England and Wales, Jack and Chloe remained the top names in Scotland in 1999. Among boys' names, Liam experienced the greatest increase in popularity, rising seven places on the previous year to enter the Top 10, while Lauren underwent the greatest rise among girls, moving up five places. Outside the Top 10, the unisex name Morgan rose by a remarkable 32 places among boys and seven places among girls, reaching nos. 73 and 18 respectively. It should be noted that there are considerable variations between regions.

FIRST NAMES IN IRELAND

GIRLS		BOYS
Chloe	1	Conor
Ciara	2	Sean
Sarah	3	Jack
Aoife	4	James
Emma	5	Adam
Niamh	6	Aaron
Rachel	7	Dylan
Megan	8	David
Rebecca	9	Michael
Lauren	10	Daniel

FIRST NAMES IN NORTHERN IRELAND

GIRLS		BOYS
Chloe	1	Matthew
Emma	2	Ryan
Rebecca	3	James
Amy	4	Jack
Lauren	5	Conor
Hannah	6	Adam
Shannon	7	Jordan
Sarah	8	Michael
Rachel	9	David
Megan	10	Christopher

A comparative survey of names recorded in both 1975 and 1998 showed that none of the Top 10 1998 girls' names appeared in the earlier list, while three boys' names (James, Michael, and David) were in both.

TOP 10 SURNAMES IN SCOTLAND*

1 Smith 2 Brown 3 Wilson
4 Thomson 5 Robertson
6 Campbell 7 Stewart 8 Anderson
9 Macdonald 10 Scott

* Based on a survey of names appearing on birth and death registers, and both names on marriage registers

TOP 10 SURNAMES IN THE UK

(Surname/number)

1 Smith, 538,369 2 Jones, 402,489
3 Williams, 279,150 4 Brown, 260,652
5 Taylor, 251,058 6 Davies/
Davis, 209,584 7 Wilson, 191,006
8 Evans, 170,391 9 Thomas, 152,945
10 Johnson, 146,535

This survey of British surnames is based on an analysis of almost 50 million names appearing on the British electoral rolls.

FIRST NAMES IN WALES

GIRLS		BOYS
Chloe	1	Thomas
Megan	2	Jack
Emily	3	Joshua
Sophie	4	Daniel
Lauren	5	Callum
Jessica	6	James
Georgina	7	Liam
Ffion	8	Samuel
Hannah	9	Ryan
Rebecca	10	Matthew

FIRST NAMES IN AUSTRALIA*

GIRLS		BOYS
Emily	1	Joshua
Jessica	2	Matthew
Sarah	3	Daniel
Emma	4	James
Hannah	5	Jake
Samantha	6	Benjamin
Georgia	7	Lachlan
Rebecca	8	Nicholas
Amy	9	Jack
Sophie	10	Thomas

* Based on births registered in New South Wales

"WENDY"

Like Pamela, Lorna, Thelma, and Mavis, Wendy is one of a group of girls' names invented by authors. Margaret, the infant daughter of writer W. E. Henley, called family friend J. M. Barrie her "friendy," pronouncing it as "wendy," a nickname she then acquired. Margaret died aged 5 in 1894, but her name lived on as Wendy Darling in Barrie's 1904 play *Peter Pan*. The popularity of the play and 1911 book ensured that Wendy became a common first name in both the UK and US.

WHY DO WE SAY?

TOP 10 ★
FIRST NAMES IN CANADA*

GIRLS		BOYS
Emily	1	Matthew
Sarah	2	Joshua
Emma	3	Nicholas
Jessica	4	Ryan
Taylor	5	Alexander
Hannah	6	Tyler
Megan	7	Michael
Samantha	8	Brandon
Ashley	9	Jacob
Nicole	10	Kyle

* Based on births in British Columbia

TOP 10 ★
FIRST NAMES IN NORWAY

GIRLS		BOYS
Ingrid	1	Andreas
Ida	2	Markus
Marte	3	Kristian
Karoline	4	Martin
Silje	5	Kristoffer
Julie	6	Thomas
Camila	7	Jonas
Kristine	8	Fredrik
Maria	9	Daniel
Vilde	10	Marius

TOP 10 SURNAMES IN THE MANHATTAN TELEPHONE DIRECTORY

1 Smith **2** Brown **3** Williams **4** Cohen **5** Lee **6** Johnson **7** Rodriguez **8** Green **9** Davis **10** Jones

TOP 10 ★
MOST COMMON SURNAMES IN THE US

	NAME	% OF ALL US NAMES
1	Smith	1.006
2	Johnson	0.810
3	Williams	0.699
4	=Brown	0.621
	=Jones	0.621
6	Davis	0.480
7	Miller	0.424
8	Wilson	0.339
9	Moore	0.312
10	=Anderson	0.311
	=Taylor	0.311
	=Thomas	0.311

The Top 10 (or, in view of those in equal 10th place, 12) US surnames together make up over 6 percent of the entire US population – in other words, one American in every 16 bears one of these names. Extending the list, some 28 different names make-up 10 per cent of the entire population, 115 names 20 percent, 315 names 30 percent, 755 names 40 percent, 1,712 names 50 percent, and 3,820 names 60 percent.

TOP 10 TERMS OF ENDEARMENT USED IN THE US

1 Honey **2** Baby **3** Sweetheart **4** Dear **5** Lover **6** Darling **7** Sugar **8** = Angel; = Pumpkin **10** = Beautiful; = Precious

A survey of romance conducted by a US champagne company concluded that 26 percent of American adults favored "honey" as their most frequently used term of endearment. Curiously, identical numbers were undecided whether to call their loved one an angel or a pumpkin....

TOP 10 ★
BOYS' NAMES IN THE US, 1989–99

1989		1999
Michael	1	Jacob
Christopher	2	Michael
Joshua	3	Matthew
Matthew	4	Nicholas
David	5	Christopher
Daniel	6	Joshua
Andrew	7	Austin
Joseph	8	Tyler
Justin	9	Brandon
John	10	Joseph

TOP 10 ★
GIRLS' NAMES IN THE US, 1989–99

1989		1999
Jessica	1	Emily
Ashley	2	Sarah
Amanda	= 3	Brianna
Brittany	=	
	4	Samantha
Sarah	5	Hailey
Jennifer	6	Ashley
Stephanie	7	Kaitlyn
Samantha	8	Madison
Elizabeth	9	Hannah
Lauren	10	Alexis

TOP 10 SURNAMES IN CHINA

1 Zhang **2** Whang **3** Li **4** Zhao **5** Chen **6** Yang **7** Wu **8** Liu **9** Huang **10** Zhou

Which country was the first to ratify the UN Charter?
see p.64 for the answer
A US
B Nicaragua
C China

World Royalty

LONGEST-REIGNING BRITISH MONARCHS

	MONARCH	REIGN	AGE AT ACCESSION	AGE AT DEATH	REIGN YEARS
1	Queen Victoria	1837–1901	18	81	63
2	King George III	1760–1820	22	81	59
3	King Henry III	1216–72	9	64	56
4	King Edward III	1327–77	14	64	50
5	Queen Elizabeth II	1952–	25	—	48
6	Queen Elizabeth I	1558–1603	25	69	44
7	King Henry VI	1422–61*	8 months	49	38
8	King Henry VIII	1509–47	17	55	37
9	King Charles II	1649–85	19	54	36
10	King Henry I	1100–35	31–32#	66–67#	35

* Henry VI was deposed; he died in 1471.

Henry I's birthdate is unknown, so his age at accession and death are uncertain.

This list excludes the reigns of monarchs before 1066, so excludes such rulers as Ethelred II, who reigned for 37 years.

FIRST IN LINE TO THE BRITISH THRONE

	SUCCESSOR	BORN
1	HRH The Prince of Wales (Prince Charles Philip Arthur George)	Nov 14, 1948
2	HRH Prince William of Wales (Prince William Arthur Philip Louis)	June 21, 1982
3	HRH Prince Henry of Wales (Prince Henry Charles Albert David)	Sep 15, 1984
4	HRH The Duke of York (Prince Andrew Albert Christian Edward)	Feb 19, 1960
5	HRH Princess Beatrice of York (Princess Beatrice Elizabeth Mary)	Aug 8, 1988
6	HRH Princess Eugenie of York (Princess Eugenie Victoria Helena)	Mar 23, 1990
7	HRH Prince Edward (Prince Edward Antony Richard Louis)	Mar 10, 1964
8	HRH The Princess Royal (Princess Anne Elizabeth Alice Louise)	Aug 15, 1950
9	Master Peter Mark Andrew Phillips	Nov 15, 1977
10	Miss Zara Anne Elizabeth Phillips	May 15, 1981

LONGEST-REIGNING QUEENS*

	QUEEN	COUNTRY	REIGN	REIGN YEARS
1	Victoria	Great Britain	1837–1901	63
2	Wilhelmina	Netherlands	1890–1948	58
3	Wu Chao	China	655–705	50
4	Elizabeth II	UK	1952–	48
5	Salote Tubou	Tonga	1918–65	47
6	Elizabeth I	England	1558–1603	44
7	Maria Theresa	Hungary	1740–80	40
8	Maria I	Portugal	1777–1816	39
9	Joanna I	Italy	1343–81	38
10=	Suiko Tenno	Japan	593–628	35
=	Isabella II	Spain	1833–68	35

* Queens and empresses who rule (or ruled) in their own right, not as consorts of kings or emperors

LONG TO REIGN OVER US

If Queen Elizabeth II is on the throne on September 11, 2015, she will have beaten Queen Victoria's record by one day and will become the world's longest-reigning queen.

THE 10 ⭐
LATEST WORLD MONARCHS TO COME TO POWER

MONARCH/COUNTRY	ACCESSION
1 King Sayyidi Muhammad VI ibn al-Hasan, Morocco	July 23, 1999
2 Sultan Tuanku Salehuddin Abdul Aziz Shah ibni al-Marhum Hisamuddin Alam Shah, Malaysia	Apr 26, 1999
3 Emir Sheikh Hamad ibn 'Isa al-Khalifah, Bahrain	Mar 6, 1999
4 King Abdallah (II) ibn al-Hussein al-Hashimi, Jordan	Feb 7, 1999
5 King Letsie III, Lesotho	Feb 7, 1996
6 Emir Sheikh Ahmad ibn Khalifa al-Thani, Qatar	June 27, 1995
7 King Albert II, Belgium	Aug 9, 1993
8 King Preah Baht Samdach Preah Norodom Sihanuk Varmn, Cambodia	Sep 24, 1993*
9 King Harald V, Norway	Jan 17, 1991
10 Prince Hans Adam II, Liechtenstein	Nov 13, 1989

* Elected king

TOP 10 ⭐
LONGEST-REIGNING LIVING MONARCHS*

MONARCH/COUNTRY	DATE OF BIRTH	ACCESSION
1 King Bhumibol Adulyadej, Thailand	Dec 5, 1927	June 9, 1946
2 Prince Rainier III, Monaco	May 31, 1923	May 9, 1949
3 Queen Elizabeth II, UK	Apr 21, 1926	Feb 6, 1952
4 King Malietoa Tanumafili II, Western Samoa	Jan 4, 1913	Jan 1, 1962#
5 Grand Duke Jean, Luxembourg	Jan 5, 1921	Nov 12, 1964
6 King Taufa'ahau Tupou IV, Tonga	July 4, 1918	Dec 16, 1965
7 King Haji Hassanal Bolkiah, Brunei	July 15, 1946	Oct 5, 1967
8 Sultan Sayyid Qaboos ibn Said al-Said, Oman	Nov 18, 1942	July 23, 1970
9 Queen Margrethe II, Denmark	Apr 16, 1940	Jan 14, 1972
10 King Birendra Bir Bikram Shah Dev, Nepal	Dec 28, 1945	Jan 31, 1972

* Including hereditary rulers of principalities, dukedoms, etc.

\# Sole ruler since April 15, 1963

There are 29 countries that have emperors, kings, queens, princes, dukes, sultans, or other hereditary rulers as their heads of state. The current Sultan of Oman took control of the country by ousting his own father in a palace coup.

THE 10 ⭐
LATEST WORLD MONARCHS TO BE ASSASSINATED

MONARCH/COUNTRY	DATE OF DEATH
1 King Faisal ibn Abdul Aziz, Saudi Arabia *Murdered by his nephew during an audience with the Kuwaiti oil minister.*	Mar 25, 1975
2 King Faisal II, Iraq *Murdered with his entire household; their bodies were paraded through Baghdad as part of a military coup.*	July 14, 1958
3 King Abdullah ibn al-Hussein, Jordan *Gunned down on a visit to his father's tomb in Jerusalem by Mustafa Ashu, a young Palestinian nationalist.*	July 20, 1951
4 King Ananda Mahidol, Rama VIII, Thailand *Assassinated in the palace, having been conspired against by his personal secretary and others.*	June 9, 1946
5 King Alexander I, Yugoslavia *Shot in Marseilles by an assassin sent by Croat leader Ante Pavelic.*	Oct 9, 1934
6 King Sardar Mohammad Nadir Khan, Afghanistan *Shot while giving out prizes at a school.*	Nov 8, 1933
7 King George I, Greece *Killed in Salonika by Schinas, a Greek revolutionary.*	Mar 18, 1913
8 King Carlos I, Portugal *Ambushed and murdered, together with Luis Philippe, the crown prince, by anti-royalists.*	Feb 1, 1908
9 King Alexander Obrenovich, Serbia *Shot to death and hacked with sabers, together with his wife, Draga, by military conspirators.*	July 11, 1903
10 King Umberto I, Italy *Murdered in Monza by anarchist Gaetano Bresci.*	July 29, 1900

TOP 10 ⭐
LONGEST-REIGNING MONARCHS

MONARCH/COUNTRY	REIGN	AGE AT ACCESSION	REIGN YEARS
1 King Louis XIV, France	1643–1715	5	72
2 King John II, Liechtenstein	1858–1929	18	71
3 Emperor Franz-Josef, Austria-Hungary	1848–1916	18	67
4 Queen Victoria, Great Britain	1837–1901	18	63
5 Emperor Hirohito, Japan	1926–89	25	62
6 Emperor Kangxi, China	1662–1722	8	61
7 Emperor Qianlong, China	1736–96	25	60
8 King Christian IV, Denmark	1588–1648	11	59*
9 King George III, Great Britain	1760–1820	22	59*
10 Prince Honore III, Monaco	1733–93	13	59*

* Those with the same number of reign years are ranked according to days.

Background image: **EMPEROR AND EMPRESS HIROHITO**

Did You Know? Despite being pregnant 17 times, British Queen Anne produced only one child – William, Duke of Gloucester – who survived infancy, although he died at the age of 11.

63

The Political World

FIRST COUNTRIES TO RATIFY THE UN CHARTER

	COUNTRY	DATE
1	Nicaragua	July 6, 1945
2	US	Aug 8, 1945
3	France	Aug 31, 1945
4	Dominican Republic	Sep 4, 1945
5	New Zealand	Sep 19, 1945
6	Brazil	Sep 21, 1945
7	Argentina	Sep 24, 1945
8	China	Sep 28, 1945
9	Denmark	Oct 9, 1945
10	Chile	Oct 11, 1945

In New York on June 26, 1945, barely weeks after the end of World War II in Europe (the Japanese did not surrender until September 3), 50 nations signed the World Security Charter, thereby establishing the United Nations as an international peacekeeping organization. The UN came into effect on October 24, which has since been celebrated as United Nations Day.

TOP 10 ★

US PRESIDENTS WITH THE MOST CHILDREN

	PRESIDENT	CHILDREN
1	John Tyler	14
2	William Henry Harrison	10
3	Rutherford Birchard Hayes	8
4	James Abram Garfield	7
5	=George Herbert Walker Bush	6
	=Thomas Jefferson	6
	=Franklin Delano Roosevelt	6*
	=Theodore Roosevelt	6
	=Zachary Taylor	6
10	=John Adams	5
	=Grover Cleveland	5
	=Andrew Johnson	5
	=Ronald Reagan	5

* Including one child deceased

KEEPING THE PEACE
Since its formation in 1945, the United Nations has deployed forces to maintain the peace in the world's troublespots. Here, peacekeeping troops enter East Timor in September 1999.

TOP 10 ★

LONGEST-LIVED US PRESIDENTS

	PRESIDENT	LIFESPAN YEARS	DAYS
1	John Adams	90	247
2	Herbert Clark Hoover	90	71
3	Ronald Reagan*	89	
4	Harry S. Truman	88	232
5	James Madison	85	104
6	Thomas Jefferson	83	82
7	Richard M. Nixon	81	104
8	John Quincy Adams	80	227
9	Martin Van Buren	79	231
10	Dwight D. Eisenhower	78	165

* At 89 on February 6, 2000, Ronald Reagan is the oldest living former president.

John Adams was the first president to have children, and lived long enough to see his son, John Quincy Adams, become president.

FIRST COUNTRIES TO GIVE WOMEN THE VOTE

	COUNTRY	YEAR
1	New Zealand	1893
2	Australia, (South Australia, 1894; Western Australia, 1898; Australia united, 1901)	1902
3	Finland (a Grand Duchy under the Russian Crown)	1906
4	Norway (restricted franchise; all women over 25 in 1913)	1907
5	Denmark and Iceland (a Danish dependency until 1918)	1915
6	=Netherlands	1917
	=USSR	1917
8	=Austria	1918
	=Canada	1918
	=Germany	1918
	=Great Britain and Ireland (Ireland part of the United Kingdom until 1921; women over 30 – lowered to 21 in 1928)	1918
	=Poland	1918

TOP 10 ⭐
LONGEST-SERVING PRESIDENTS TODAY

PRESIDENT	COUNTRY	TOOK OFFICE
1 General Gnassingbé Eyadéma	Togo	Apr 14, 1967
2 El Hadj Omar Bongo	Gabon	Dec 2, 1967
3 Colonel Mu'ammar Gadhafi*	Libya	Sep 1, 1969
4 Lt.-General Hafiz al-Asad	Syria	Feb 22, 1971
5 Zayid ibn Sultan al-Nuhayyan	United Arab Emirates	Dec 2, 1971
6 Fidel Castro	Cuba	Nov 2, 1976
7 France-Albert René	Seychelles	June 5, 1977
8 Daniel Teroitich arap Moi	Kenya	Oct 14, 1978
9 Saddam Hussein	Iraq	July 16, 1979
10 Teodoro Obiang Nguema Mbasogo	Equatorial Guinea	Aug 3, 1979

* Since a reorganization in 1979, Colonel Gadhafi has held no formal position but continues to rule under the ceremonial title of "Leader of the Revolution."

TOP 10 ⭐
YOUNGEST US PRESIDENTS

PRESIDENT	AGE ON TAKING OFFICE YEARS	DAYS
1 Theodore Roosevelt	42	322
2 John F. Kennedy	43	236
3 William J. Clinton	46	154
4 Ulysses S. Grant	46	236
5 Grover Cleveland	47	351
6 Franklin Pierce	48	101
7 James A. Garfield	49	105
8 James K. Polk	49	122
9 Millard Fillmore	50	184
10 Chester A. Arthur	50	350

The Constitution states that a president must be at least 35 years old on taking office. Vice-President Theodore Roosevelt assumed the office of president following the assassination of William McKinley. John F. Kennedy was the youngest president to be elected.

THE 10 ⭐
FIRST FEMALE PRIME MINISTERS AND PRESIDENTS

PRIME MINISTER OR PRESIDENT/COUNTRY	PERIOD IN OFFICE
1 Sirimavo Bandaranaike, (PM), Sri Lanka	1960–65/ 1970–77/ 1994–
2 Indira Gandhi (PM), India	1966–77/ 1980–84
3 Golda Meir (PM), Israel	1969–74
4 Maria Estela Perón (P), Argentina	1974–76
5 Elisabeth Domitien (PM), Central African Republic	1975–76
6 Margaret Thatcher (PM), UK	1979–90
7 Dr. Maria Lurdes Pintasilgo (PM), Portugal	1979–80
8 Vigdís Finnbogadóttir (P), Iceland	1980–
9 Mary Eugenia Charles (PM), Dominica	1980–95
10 Gro Harlem Brundtland (PM), Norway	Feb–Oct 1981/ 1986–89/ 1990–96

WOMEN IN POWER

The Swedish parliament has a high proportion of women members. Worldwide, women legislators today comprise 13 percent of all legislators.

TOP 10 ⭐
PARLIAMENTS WITH THE HIGHEST PERCENTAGE OF WOMEN MEMBERS*

PARLIAMENT/ ELECTION	WOMEN MEMBERS	TOTAL MEMBERS	% WOMEN
1 Sweden, 1998	149	349	42.7
2 Denmark, 1998	67	179	37.4
3 Finland, 1999	74	200	37.0
4 Norway, 1997	60	165	36.4
5 Netherlands, 1998	54	150	36.0
6 Iceland, 1999	22	63	34.9
7 Germany, 1998	207	669	30.9
8 South Africa, 1999	120	400	30.0
9 New Zealand, 1999	35	120	29.2
10 Cuba, 1998	166	601	27.6
US, 1998	58	435	13.3

* As at December 25, 1999

Source: *Inter-Parliamentary Union*

This information is based on the most recent general election results available for all democratic countries.

Did You Know? Félix Houhouët-Boigny, President of the Côte d'Ivoire until his death in 1993 at the age of 88, was the world's oldest president.

Human Achievements

THE 10 ★
NORTH POLE FIRSTS

1 First to reach the Pole?
American adventurer Frederick Albert Cook claimed that he had reached the Pole, accompanied by two Inuits, on April 21, 1908, but his claim is disputed. It is more likely that Robert Edwin Peary, Matthew Alexander Henson (both Americans), and four Inuits were first at the Pole on April 6, 1909.

2 First to fly over the Pole in an airship
A team of 16, led by Roald Amundsen, the Norwegian explorer who first reached the South Pole in 1911, flew across the North Pole on May 12, 1926 in the Italian-built airship Norge.

3 First to land at the Pole in an aircraft
Soviets Pavel Afanaseyevich Geordiyenko, Mikhail Yemel'yenovich Ostrekin, Pavel Kononovich Sen'ko, and Mikhail Mikhaylovich Somov arrived at and departed from the Pole by air on April 23, 1948.

4 First solo flight over the Pole in a single-engined aircraft
Capt. Charles Francis Blair, Jr. of the US flew a single-engined Mustang fighter, Excalibur III, on May 29, 1951, crossing from Bardufoss, Norway, to Fairbanks, Alaska.

5 First submarine to surface at the Pole
USS Skate surfaced at the Pole on March 17, 1959.

6 First confirmed overland journey to the Pole
American Ralph S. Plaisted, with companions Walter Pederson, Gerald Pitzel, and Jean Luc Bombardier, reached the Pole on April 18, 1968, using snowmobiles.

7 First solo overland journey to the Pole
Japanese explorer Naomi Uemura reached the Pole on May 1, 1978, traveling by dog sled, and was then picked up by an airplane.

8 First to reach the Pole on skis
A team of seven, led by Dimitry Shparo (USSR), was the first to reach the North Pole on May 31, 1979.

9 First crossing on a Pole-to-Pole expedition
Sir Ranulph Fiennes and Charles Burton walked over the North Pole on April 10, 1982, having crossed the South Pole on December 15, 1980.

10 First woman to walk to the Pole
Along with five male companions, American physical education teacher Ann Bancroft reached the Pole on May 1, 1986.

Lt.-Cdr. Richard Byrd and Floyd Bennett claimed to have traversed the Pole on May 9, 1926 in an aircraft, but recent analysis of Byrd's diary indicates that they turned back some 150 miles (241 km) short of the Pole, thereby disqualifying their entry.

POLE TO POLE
The 1979–82 Transglobe Expedition led by Sir Ranulph Fiennes, here at Scott Base, South Pole, was the first to traverse both Poles.

THE 10 ★
CIRCUMNAVIGATION FIRSTS

CIRCUMNAVIGATION/CRAFT	VOYAGER(S)	RETURN DATE
1 First, *Vittoria*	Juan Sebastian de Elcano*	Sep 6, 1522
2 First in less than 80 days, *various*	"Nellie Bly"#	Jan 25, 1890
3 First solo, *Spray*	Capt. Joshua Slocum	July 3, 1898
4 First by air, *Chicago, New Orleans*	Lt. Lowell Smith, Lt. Leslie P. Arnold	Sep 28, 1924
5 First nonstop by air, *Lucky Lady II*	Capt. James Gallagher	Mar 2, 1949
6 First underwater, *Triton*	Capt. Edward L. Beach	Apr 25, 1960
7 First nonstop solo, *Suhaili*	Robin Knox-Johnston	Apr 22, 1969
8 First helicopter, *Spirit of Texas*	H. Ross Perot, Jr. and Jay Coburn	Sep 30, 1982
9 First air without refueling, *Voyager*	Richard Rutan and Jeana Yeager	Dec 23, 1986
10 First by balloon, *Breitling Orbiter 3*	Brian Jones and Bertrand Piccard	Mar 21, 1999

* *The expedition was led by Ferdinand Magellan, but he did not survive the voyage.*

Real name Elizabeth Cochrane. This US journalist set out to beat the fictitious "record" established in Jules Verne's novel Around the World in 80 Days.

THE 10 FIRST MOUNTAINEERS TO CLIMB EVEREST
(Mountaineer/nationality/date)

1 Edmund Hillary, New Zealander, May 29, 1953 **2 Tenzing Norgay**, Nepalese, May 29, 1953 **3 Jürg Marmet**, Swiss, May 23, 1956 **4 Ernst Schmied**, Swiss, May 23, 1956 **5 Hans-Rudolf von Gunten**, Swiss, May 24, 1956 **6 Adolf Reist**, Swiss, May 24, 1956 **7 Wang Fu-chou**, Chinese, May 25, 1960 **8 Chu Ying-hua**, Chinese, May 25, 1960 **9 Konbu**, Tibetan, May 25, 1960 **10 = Nawang Gombu**, Indian, May 1, 1963; **= James Whittaker**, American, May 1, 1963

Nawang Gombu and James Whittaker are 10th equally because they ascended the last feet to the summit side by side.

The citizens of which country have won the most Nobel Prizes for Literature?
see p.69 for the answer

A US
B UK
C France

THE 10 ★
FIRST SUCCESSFUL HUMAN DESCENTS OVER NIAGARA FALLS

	NAME/METHOD	DATE
1	**Annie Edson Taylor**, Wooden barrel	Oct 24, 1901
2	**Bobby Leach**, Steel barrel	July 25, 1911
3	**Jean Lussier**, Steel and rubber ball fitted with oxygen cylinders	July 4, 1928
4	**William Fitzgerald** (a.k.a. Nathan Boya), Steel and rubber ball fitted with oxygen cylinders	July 15, 1961
5	**Karel Soucek**, Barrel	July 3, 1984
6	**Steven Trotter**, Barrel	Aug 18, 1985
7	**Dave Mundy**, Barrel	Oct 5, 1985
8 =	**Peter deBernardi**, Metal container	Sep 28, 1989
=	**Jeffrey Petkovich**, Metal container	Sep 28, 1989
10	**Dave Mundy**, Diving bell	Sep 26, 1993

Source: *Niagara Falls Museum*

TOP 10 ★
FASTEST CROSS-CHANNEL SWIMMERS

	SWIMMER/NATIONALITY	YEAR	TIME HRS:MINS
1	**Chad Hundeby**, American	1994	7:17
2	**Penny Lee Dean**, American	1978	7:40
3	**Tamara Bruce**, Australian	1994	7:53
4	**Philip Rush**, New Zealander	1987	7:55
5	**Hans van Goor**, Dutch	1995	8:02
6	**Richard Davey**, British	1988	8:05
7	**Irene van der Laan**, Dutch	1982	8:06
8	**Paul Asmuth**, American	1985	8:12
9	**Anita Sood**, Indian	1987	8:15
10	**John van Wisse**, Australian	1994	8:17

Source: *Channel Swimming Association*

The first person to swim the Channel was Matthew Webb (British), who on August 24–25, 1875 made the crossing in what now seems the rather leisurely time of 21 hours 45 minutes.

NIAGARA FALLS

Annie Edson Taylor, a Michigan schoolteacher, celebrated her 43rd birthday in 1901 by being the first to plunge over Niagara Falls and survive. She was followed in 1911 by 69-year-old Bobby Leach (who later died when he slipped on a piece of orange peel!). On July 4, 1928, watched by an excited crowd of 100,000, Jean Lussier (seen here), a circus acrobat from Springfield, Massachusetts, traveled over the Falls in a 758-lb (344-kg) steel-reinforced rubber sphere. In 1920, barber Charles Stephens became one of many killed in the attempt. Other failed efforts include those of George Stathakis (1930) and William Hill, Jr. (1951).

SNAP SHOTS ★

THE 10 LATEST WINNERS OF *TIME* MAGAZINE'S "PERSON OF THE YEAR" AWARD

(Year/recipient)

1 1999, **Jeffrey T. Bezos**, founder of Amazon.com **2** 1998, **Bill Clinton**, US President/**Kenneth Starr**, Independent Counsel **3** 1997, **Andrew S. Grove**, CEO of Intel, microchip company **4** 1996, **David Ho**, AIDS researcher **5** 1995, **Newt Gingrich**, US politician **6** 1994, **Pope John Paul II** **7** 1993, **Yasser Arafat**, F. W. de Klerk, Nelson Mandela, Yitzhak Rabin, "peacemakers" **8** 1992, **Bill Clinton**, US President **9** 1991, **George Bush**, US President **10** 1990, **Ted Turner**, US businessman

CHANNEL NO. 3

In 1994, 17-year-old Australian Tamara Bruce achieved the third-fastest Channel swim of all time, becoming the 487th person to swim from England to France.

The Nobel Century

LATEST WINNERS OF THE NOBEL PRIZE FOR PHYSICS

WINNER	COUNTRY	YEAR
1 = Gerardus 't Hooft	Netherlands	1999
= Martinus J. G. Veltman	Netherlands	1999
3 = Robert B. Laughlin	US	1998
= Horst L. Störmer	Germany	1998
= Daniel C. Tsui	US	1998
6 = Steven Chu	US	1997
= William D. Phillips	US	1997
= Professor Claude Cohen-Tannoudji	France	1997
9 = David M. Lee	US	1996
= Douglas D. Osheroff	US	1996
= Robert C. Richardson	US	1996

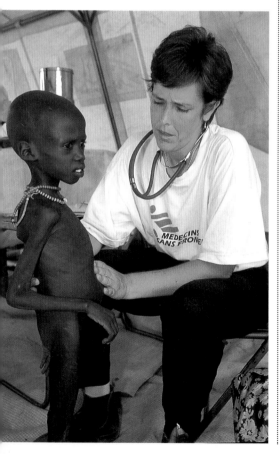

NOBEL PRIZE-WINNING COUNTRIES*

	COUNTRY	PHY	CHE	PH/MED	LIT	PCE	ECO	TOTAL
1	US	67	43	78	10	18	25	241
2	UK	21	25	24	8	13	7	98
3	Germany	20	27	16	7	4	1	75
4	France	12	7	7	12	9	1	48
5	Sweden	4	4	7	7	5	2	29
6	Switzerland	2	5	6	2	3	–	18
7	USSR	7	1	2	3	2	1	16
8	Netherlands	8	3	2	–	1	1	15
9	Italy	3	1	3	6	1	–	14
10	Denmark	3	–	5	3	1	–	12

Phy – Physics; Che – Chemistry; Ph/Med – Physiology or Medicine; Lit – Literature; Pce – Peace; Eco – Economic Sciences. Germany includes the united country before 1948, West Germany to 1990 and the united country since 1990

In addition, institutions including the Red Cross have been awarded 17 Nobel Peace Prizes

LATEST WINNERS OF THE NOBEL PEACE PRIZE

WINNER	COUNTRY	YEAR
1 Médecins Sans Frontières	Belgium	1999
2 = John Hume	UK	1998
= David Trimble	UK	1998
4 = International Campaign to Ban Landmines	–	1997
= Jody Williams	US	1997
6 = Carlos Filipe Ximenes Belo	East Timor	1996
= José Ramos-Horta	East Timor	1996
8 Joseph Rotblat	UK	1995
9 = Yasir Arafat	Palestine	1994
= Shimon Peres	Israel	1994
= Itzhak Rabin	Israel	1994

COMPASSION WITHOUT LIMITS

Brussels-based Médecins Sans Frontières, which has provided emergency medical aid worldwide since 1971, won the Peace Prize in 1999. International organizations have been awarded the prize 17 times.

TOP 10 NOBEL PHYSICS PRIZE-WINNING COUNTRIES

(Country/prizes)

1 US, 67 **2** UK, 21 **3** Germany, 20
4 France, 12 **5** Netherlands, 8
6 USSR, 7 **7** Sweden, 4
8 = Austria, 3; = Denmark, 3;
= Italy, 3; = Japan, 3

NOBEL PEACE PRIZE-WINNING COUNTRIES

	COUNTRY	PRIZES
1	US	18
2	International institutions	17
3	UK	13
4	France	9
5	Sweden	5
6 =	Belgium	4
=	Germany	4
=	South Africa	4
9 =	Israel	3
=	Switzerland	3

Who was the longest-reigning British king?
see p.62 for the answer
A Henry VIII
B Charles II
C George III

THE 10 ★
LATEST WINNERS OF THE NOBEL PRIZE FOR LITERATURE

	WINNER	COUNTRY	YEAR
1	Günter Grass	Germany	1999
2	José Saramago	Portugal	1998
3	Dario Fo	Italy	1997
4	Wislawa Szymborska	Poland	1996
5	Seamus Heaney	Ireland	1995
6	Kenzaburo Oe	Japan	1994
7	Toni Morrison	US	1993
8	Derek Walcott	Saint Lucia	1992
9	Nadine Gordimer	South Africa	1991
10	Octavio Paz	Mexico	1990

TOP 10 NOBEL LITERATURE PRIZE-WINNING COUNTRIES
(Country/prizes)

❶ France, 12 ❷ US, 10 ❸ UK, 8
❹ = Sweden, 7; = Germany, 7 ❻ Italy, 6
❼ Spain, 5 ❽ = Denmark, 3; = Ireland, 3;
= Norway, 3; = Poland, 3; = USSR, 3

LITERARY LAUREATE

German novelist Günter Grass, the most famous of whose darkly humorous stories is The Tin Drum, won the 1999 Nobel Prize for Literature.

THE 10 ★
LATEST WINNERS OF THE NOBEL PRIZE FOR PHYSIOLOGY OR MEDICINE

	WINNER	COUNTRY	YEAR
1	Günter Blobel	Germany	1999
2	=Robert F. Furchgott	US	1998
	=Louis J. Ignarro	US	1998
	=Ferid Murad	US	1998
5	Stanley B. Prusiner	US	1997
6	=Peter C. Doherty	Australia	1996
	=Rolf M. Zinkernagel	Switzerland	1996
8	=Christiane Nüsslein-Volhard	Germany	1995
	=Eric F. Wieschaus	US	1995
	=Edward B. Lewis	US	1995

THE 10 ★
LATEST WINNERS OF THE NOBEL PRIZE FOR CHEMISTRY

	WINNER/COUNTRY		YEAR
1	Ahmed Zewail,	Egypt	1999
2	=Walter Kohn,	US	1998
	=John A. Pople,	UK	1998
4	=Paul D. Boyer,	US	1997
	=John E. Walker,	UK	1997
	=Jens C. Skou,	Denmark	1997
7	=Sir Harold W. Kroto,	UK	1996
	=Richard E. Smalley,	US	1996
9	=Paul Crutzen,	Netherlands	1995
	=Mario Molina,	Mexico	1995
	=Frank Sherwood Rowland,	US	1995

TOP 10 NOBEL PHYSIOLOGY OR MEDICINE PRIZE-WINNING COUNTRIES

	COUNTRY	PRIZES
1	US	78
2	UK	24
3	Germany	16
4	=France	7
	=Sweden	7
6	Switzerland	6
7	Denmark	5
8	=Austria	4
	=Belgium	4
10	=Australia	3
	=Italy	3

TOP 10 NOBEL CHEMISTRY PRIZE-WINNING COUNTRIES
(Country/prizes)

❶ US, 43 ❷ Germany, 27 ❸ UK, 25 ❹ France, 17 ❺ Switzerland, 5
❻ Sweden, 4 ❼ = Canada, 3; = Netherlands, 3 ❾ = Argentina, 1; = Austria, 1;
= Belgium, 1; = Czechoslovakia, 1; = Egypt, 1; = Finland, 1; = Hungary, 1;
= Italy, 1; = Japan, 1; = Mexico, 1; = Norway, 1; = USSR, 1

Criminal Records

The US ranks second in the world for its total prison population, which rises annually. Here inmates move through the cell blocks of the Ellis II prison unit at Huntsville Prison, Texas.

TOP 10 ★
COUNTRIES WITH THE HIGHEST PRISON POPULATION RATES

COUNTRY	TOTAL PRISON POPULATION*	PRISONERS PER 100,000
1 Russia	1,009,863	685
2 US	1,725,842	645
3 Belarus	52,033	505
4 Kazakhstan	82,945	495
5 Belize	1,118	490
6 Bahamas	1,401	485
7 Singapore	15,746#	465
8 Kyrgyzstan	19,857	440
9 Ukraine	211,568	415
10 Latvia	10,070	410

* *Including pre-trial detainees*

\# *Almost half the detainees are held in drug rehabilitation centres*

Source: *Home Office*

THE 10 ★
STATES WITH THE MOST PRISONERS ON DEATH ROW

STATE	PRISONERS UNDER DEATH SENTENCE*
1 California	561
2 Texas	462
3 Florida	389
4 Pennsylvania	232
5 North Carolina	224
6 Ohio	199
7 Alabama	185
8 Illinois	160
9 Oklahoma	149
10 Georgia	134

* *As at January 1, 2000*

Source: *Death Penalty Information Center*

A total of 3,652 prisoners were on death row at the start of 2000, some having been sentenced in more than one state, causing a higher total to be arrived at by adding individual state figures together.

THE 10 ★
MOST COMMON REASONS FOR ARREST IN THE US

OFFENCE	RATE*	ARRESTS
1 Drug abuse violations	596.2	1,108,788
2 Driving while under the influence	521.0	968,868
3 Larceny/theft	505.6	940,243
4 Drunkenness	274.4	510,318
5 Disorderly conduct	269.9	501,866
6 Breaking liquor laws	241.0	448,187
7 Aggravated assault	193.5	359,892
8 Fraud	144.3	268,351
9 Burglary	125.5	233,435
10 Vandalism	114.8	213,495

* *Per 100,000 inhabitants*

Did You Know? Marie-Augustin, the 22-year-old Marquis de Pélier, was jailed in 1786 for whistling at Queen Marie Antoinette. Forgotten, he was not released unil 1832.

COUNTRIES WITH THE MOST POLICE OFFICERS

	COUNTRY	POPULATION PER POLICE OFFICER*
1	Russia	81
2	Singapore	93
3	Uruguay	120
4	Kazakhstan	128
5	Bahamas	134
6	Croatia	149
7	Saint Vincent and Grenadines	167
8	Lithuania	183
9	Cyprus	191
10	Malta	197

* In latest year for which figures available

Source: Fifth United Nations Survey of Crime Trends and Operation of Criminal Justice Systems

Police manpower figures generally include only full-time paid officials, and exclude clerical and volunteer staff.

COUNTRIES WITH THE FEWEST POLICE OFFICERS

	COUNTRY	POPULATION PER POLICE OFFICER*
1	Mexico	21,691
2	Madagascar	4,692
3	Costa Rica	2,751
4	Egypt	2,691
5	Morocco	996
6	Zambia	936
7	Spain	777
8	India	745
9	Nicaragua	688
10	Philippines	645
	US	333

* In latest year for which figures available

Source: Fifth United Nations Survey of Crime Trends and Operation of Criminal Justice Systems

FIRST COUNTRIES TO ABOLISH CAPITAL PUNISHMENT

	COUNTRY	DATE ABOLISHED
1	Russia	1826
2	Venezuela	1863
3	Portugal	1867
4 =	Brazil	1882
=	Costa Rica	1882
6	Ecuador	1897
7	Panama	1903
8	Norway	1905
9	Uruguay	1907
10	Colombia	1910

Some countries abolished capital punishment in peacetime only, or for all crimes except treason, generally abolishing it totally at a more recent date, although several later reinstated it. Some countries retained capital punishment on their statute books but effectively abolished it.

COUNTRIES WITH THE HIGHEST CRIME RATES

	COUNTRY	RATE*
1	Gibraltar	18,316
2	Surinam	17,819
3	St. Kitts and Nevis	15,468
4	Finland	14,799
5	Rwanda	14,550
6	New Zealand	13,854
7	Sweden	12,982
8	Denmark	10,525
9	Canada	10,451
10	US Virgin Islands	10,441
	US	5,374

* Reported crime per 100,000 population

MOUNTING GUARD

Canada is one of only a handful of countries with a crime rate of more than 10,000 reported crimes per 100,000 inhabitants.

Murder File

MOST COMMON MURDER WEAPONS AND METHODS IN ENGLAND AND WALES

WEAPON OR METHOD	VICTIMS (1998/99)
1 Sharp instrument	207
2 Hitting and kicking	101
3 Strangulation and asphyxiation	81
4 Blunt instrument	68
5 Poison or drugs	56
6 Shooting	47
7 Burning	30
8 Motor vehicle	15
9 Drowning	7
10 Explosion	2

MOST COMMON MURDER WEAPONS AND METHODS IN THE US

WEAPON OR METHOD	VICTIMS (1998)
1 Handguns	7,361
2 Knives or cutting instruments	1,877
3 Firearms (type not stated)	609
4 "Personal weapons" (hands, feet, fists, etc.)	949
5 Blunt objects (hammers, clubs, etc.)	741
6 Shotguns	619
7 Rifles	538
8 Strangulation	211
9 Fire	130
10 Asphyxiation	99

Source: FBI Uniform Crime Reports

RELATIONSHIPS OF MURDER VICTIMS TO PRINCIPAL SUSPECTS IN THE US

RELATIONSHIP	VICTIMS (1998)
1 Acquaintance	3,773
2 Stranger	1,839
3 Wife	649
4 Girlfriend	429
5 Friend	418
6 Son	259
7 Daughter	210
8 Husband	190
9 Boyfriend	182
10=Father	120
=Neighbor	120

Source: FBI Uniform Crime Reports

Nearly 27 percent of the 14,088 murders committed in the US in 1998 were committed by acquaintances, and another 13 percent by strangers. FBI statistics also recorded 5,393 murders where the victim's relationship to the suspect was unknown, 265 "other family members" (those not specified elsewhere), 88 brothers, 99 mothers, and 25 sisters.

MOST PROLIFIC SERIAL KILLERS OF THE 20TH CENTURY

NAME/COUNTRY/CRIMES AND PUNISHMENT	VICTIMS*
1 **Pedro Alonso López**, Colombia	300

Captured in 1980, López, nicknamed the "Monster of the Andes," led police to 53 graves, but probably murdered at least 300 in Colombia, Ecuador, and Peru. He was sentenced to life.

| 2 **Henry Lee Lucas**, US | 200 |

Lucas admitted in 1983 to 360 murders. He remains on Death Row in Huntsville Prison, Texas.

| 3 **Luis Alfredo Gavarito**, Colombia | 140 |

Gavarito confessed in 1999 to a spate of murders, which are still the subject of investigation.

| 4 **Dr. Harold Shipman**, UK | 131 |

In January 2000, Manchester doctor Shipman was found guilty of the murder of 15 women patients, but police believe his total number of victims to be at least 131, and perhaps over 150.

| 5=**Donald Henry "Pee Wee" Gaskins**, US | 100 |

Gaskins was executed in 1991 for a series of murders that may have reached 200.

| =**Javed Iqbal**, Pakistan | 100 |

Iqbal and two accomplices were found guilty in March 2000 of murdering boys in Lahore. He was sentenced to be publicly strangled, dismembered, and his body dissolved in acid.

| 7 **Delfina and Maria de Jesús Gonzales**, Mexico | 91 |

In 1964 the Gonzales sisters were sentenced to 40 years' imprisonment for killing 80 women and 11 men.

| 8 **Bruno Lüdke**, Germany | 86 |

Lüdke confessed to murdering 86 women in 1928–43. He died in a hospital after a lethal injection.

| 9 **Daniel Camargo Barbosa**, Ecuador | 71 |

Barbosa was sentenced to just 16 years in prison for a catalog of crimes.

| 10 **Kampatimar Shankariya**, India | 70 |

Caught after a two-year killing spree, Shankariya was hanged in Jaipur, India, in 1979.

* Estimated minimum; includes individual and partnership murderers; excludes mercy killings by doctors, murders by bandits and by groups, such as political and military atrocities, and gangland slayings.

WORST CITIES FOR MURDER IN THE US

CITY	MURDERS (1998)*
1 Chicago	703
2 New York	633
3 Detroit	430
4 Los Angeles	426
5 Philadelphia	338
6 Baltimore	312
7 Washington, D.C.	260
8 Houston	254
9 Dallas	252
10 New Orleans	230

* Murders and non-negligent manslaughter

Source: FBI Uniform Crime Reports

THE 10 ★
COUNTRIES WITH THE HIGHEST MURDER RATES

	COUNTRY	ANNUAL MURDERS PER 100,000 POPULATION
1	Swaziland	88.1
2	Colombia	81.9
3	Namibia	72.4
4	South Africa	56.9
5	Lesotho	33.9
6	Belize	33.2
7	Philippines	30.1
8	Jamaica	27.6
9	Guatemala	27.4
10	French Guiana	27.2
	US	7.3

TOP 10 ★
COUNTRIES WITH THE LOWEST MURDER RATES

	COUNTRY	ANNUAL MURDERS PER 100,000 POPULATION
1=	Argentina	0.1
=	Brunei	0.1
3=	Burkina Faso	0.2
=	Niger	0.2
5=	Guinea	0.5
=	Guinea-Bissau	0.5
=	Iran	0.5
8=	Finland	0.6
=	Saudi Arabia	0.6
10=	Cameroon	0.7
=	Ireland	0.7
=	Mongolia	0.7

Among countries that report to international monitoring organizations, some 18 record murder rates of fewer than one per 100,000. It should be borne in mind, however, that some countries do not report, and there are a number of places that, having had no murders in recent years, could claim a murder rate of zero.

FIREPOWER
While handguns are the most common murder weapons in the US and certain other countries, restrictions on their use elsewhere relegates them to a less significant position.

TOP 10 ★
CIRCUMSTANCES FOR MURDER IN THE US

	REASON	MURDERS (1998)
1	Argument (unspecified)	4,080
2	Robbery	1,232
3	Narcotic drug laws violation	679
4	Juvenile gang killing	627
5	Felony (unspecified)	268
6	Argument over money or property	240
7	Brawl due to influence of alcohol	206
8	Romantic triangle	184
9	Brawl due to influence of narcotics	116
10	Suspected felony	104

Source: FBI Uniform Crime Reports

A total of 14,088 murders were reported in 1998, including 1,560 without a specified reason, and 4,358 for which the reasons were unknown.

THE 10 ★
WORST STATES FOR MURDER IN THE US

	STATE	FIREARMS USED	TOTAL MURDERS (1998)
1	California	1,469	2,171
2	Texas	899	1,346
3	New York	521	898
4	Illinois*	537	701
5	Michigan	439	684
6	Pennsylvania	424	611
7	North Carolina	373	607
8	Louisiana	415	540
9	Georgia	329	519
10	Maryland	331	405

* Provisional figures

Source: FBI Uniform Crime Reports

Of the 8,482 murders committed in the Top 10 states in 1998, 5,737 (or 67 percent) involved firearms. New Hampshire had just four murders.

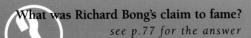

What was Richard Bong's claim to fame?
see p.77 for the answer

A He won the Nobel Prize for Physics
B He was the leading US air ace of World War II
C He held the Olympic long-jump record

Military Matters

"BAZOOKA"

American radio comedian Bob Burns (1893–1956) invented a bizarre trombone-like musical instrument to which he gave the name "bazooka." Bazoo was a slang word for the mouth, and Burns added the *ka* suffix to make it sound like an instrument, such as a harmonica. When the antitank rocket-launcher was demonstrated during World War II, a soldier commented that it "looks just like Bob Burns' bazooka."

WHY DO WE SAY?

THE 10 YEARS WITH THE MOST NUCLEAR EXPLOSIONS

(Year/explosions)

1. 1962, 178
2. 1958, 116
3. 1968, 79
4. 1966, 76
5. 1961, 71
6. 1969, 67
7. 1978, 66
8. = 1967, 64; = 1970, 64
10. 1964, 60

TOP 10 ★

COUNTRIES WITH THE LARGEST DEFENSE BUDGETS

	COUNTRY	BUDGET ($ MILLION)
1	US	270,200
2	Japan	41,100
3	UK	34,600
4	Russia	31,000
5	France	29,500
6	Germany	24,700
7	Saudi Arabia	18,400
8	Italy	16,200
9	China	12,600
10	South Korea	11,600

The so-called "peace dividend" – the savings made as a consequence of the end of the Cold War between the West and the former Soviet Union – means that both the numbers of personnel and the defense budgets of many countries have been cut.

TOP 10 LARGEST ARMED FORCES

	COUNTRY	ARMY	NAVY	AIR	TOTAL
			ESTIMATED ACTIVE FORCES		
1	China	1,830,000	230,000	420,000	2,480,000
2	US	469,300	369,800	361,400	1,371,500*
3	India	980,000	53,000	140,000	1,173,000
4	North Korea	950,000	46,000	86,000	1,082,000
4	Russia	348,000	171,500	184,600	1,004,100#
6	South Korea	560,000	60,000	52,000	672,000
7	Turkey	525,000	51,000	63,000	639,000
8	Pakistan	520,000	22,000	45,000	587,000
9	Iran	350,000	20,600	50,000	545,600+
10	Vietnam	412,000	42,000	30,000★	484,000

* Includes 171,000 Marine Corps personnel
\# Includes Strategic Deterrent Forces, Paramilitary, National Guard, etc.
\+ Includes 125,000 Revolutionary Guards
★ 15,000 air force/15,000 air defense

TOP 10 SMALLEST ARMED FORCES*
(Country/estimated total active forces)

1 Antigua and Barbuda, 150 **2** Seychelles, 450 **3** Barbados, 610
4 Luxembourg, 768 **5** The Gambia, 800 **6** Bahamas, 860 **7** Belize, 1,050
8 Cape Verde, 1,100 **9** Equatorial Guinea, 1,320 **10** Guyana, 1,600

* Excluding countries not declaring a defense budget

TOP 10 ★ COUNTRIES WITH THE MOST SUBMARINES

COUNTRY	SUBMARINES
1 US	76
2 China	71
3 Russia (and associated states)	over 70
4 North Korea	26
5 South Korea	19
6 =India	16
=Japan	16
8 =Turkey	15
=UK	15
10 Germany	14

TOP 10 ★ COUNTRIES WITH THE LARGEST NAVIES

COUNTRY	MANPOWER (1999)*
1 US	369,800
2 China	230,000
3 Russia	171,500
4 Taiwan	68,000
5 France	62,600
6 South Korea	60,000
7 India	53,000
8 Turkey	51,000
9 Indonesia	47,000
10 North Korea	46,000

* Including naval air forces and marines

CRUISE SHIP
The US Navy is the world's largest. Here, the destroyer USS Merrill *launches a Tomahawk cruise missile.*

THE 10 ★ 20TH-CENTURY WARS WITH THE MOST MILITARY FATALITIES

WAR	YEARS	MILITARY FATALITIES
1 World War II	1939–45	15,843,000
2 World War I	1914–18	8,545,800
3 Korean War	1950–53	1,893,100
4 =Sino-Japanese War	1937–41	1,000,000
=Biafra–Nigeria Civil War	1967–70	1,000,000
6 Spanish Civil War	1936–39	611,000
7 Vietnam War	1961–73	546,000
8 =India–Pakistan War	1947	200,000
=USSR invasion of Afghanistan	1979–89	200,000
=Iran–Iraq War	1980–88	200,000

The statistics of warfare have always been an imperfect science. Not only are battle deaths seldom recorded accurately, but figures are often deliberately inflated by both sides in a conflict. These figures thus represent military historians' "best guesses" – and fail to take into account civilian deaths.

TOP 10 COUNTRIES WITH THE MOST CONSCRIPTED PERSONNEL
(Country/conscripts)

1 China, 1,275,000 **2** Turkey, 528,000 **3** Russia, 330,000
4 Egypt, 320,000 **5** Iran, 250,000 **6** South Korea, 159,000
7 Germany, 142,000 **8** Poland, 141,600
9 Italy, 126,000 **10** Israel, 107,500

Most countries have abolished the peacetime draft (the UK did so in 1960 and the US in 1973), and now recruit their forces entirely on a voluntary basis.

TOP 10 COUNTRIES WITH THE HIGHEST MILITARY/CIVILIAN RATIO
(Country/ratio* in 1999)

1 North Korea, 503 **2** Israel, 289
3 United Arab Emirates, 243 **4** Singapore, 228
5 Jordan, 207 **6** Syria, 193 **7** Iraq, 180 **8** Bahrain, 176
9 = Taiwan, 173; = Qatar, 173
US, 50

* Military personnel per 10,000 population

Did You Know? The first submarine attack to destroy a warship took place on February 17, 1864, when the Confederate submarine *H.L. Hunley* sunk the Union sloop *Housatonic* off Charleston, South Carolina.

Air Wars

AREAS OF EUROPE MOST BOMBED BY ALLIED AIRCRAFT* IN WORLD WAR II

AREA	BOMBS DROPPED (IMPERIAL TONS)
1 Germany	1,350,321
2 France	583,318
3 Italy	366,524
4 Austria, Hungary, and the Balkans	180,828
5 Belgium and Netherlands	88,739
6 Southern Europe and Mediterranean	76,505
7 Czechoslovakia and Poland	21,419
8 Norway and Denmark	5,297
9 Sea targets	564
10 British Channel Islands	93

British and US

Between Aug 1942 and May 1945 alone, Allied air forces (Bomber Command plus 8 and 15 US Air Forces) flew 731,969 night sorties (and Bomber Command a further 67,598 day sorties), dropping a total of 1,850,919 imperial tons of bombs.

COUNTRIES SUFFERING THE GREATEST AIRCRAFT LOSSES IN WORLD WAR II

COUNTRY	AIRCRAFT LOST
1 Germany	116,584
2 USSR	106,652
3 US	59,296
4 Japan	49,485
5 UK	33,090
6 Australia	7,160
7 Italy	5,272
8 Canada	2,389
9 France	2,100
10 New Zealand	684

Reports of aircraft losses vary considerably from country to country, some of them including aircraft damaged, lost due to accidents, or scrapped, as well as those destroyed during combat. Very precise combat loss figures exist for the Battle of Britain: during the period July 10 to Oct 31, 1940, 1,065 RAF aircraft were destroyed, compared with 1,922 Luftwaffe fighters, bombers, and other aircraft.

CITIES MOST BOMBED BY THE RAF AND USAF IN WORLD WAR II

CITY	ESTIMATED CIVILIAN FATALITIES
1 Dresden	over 100,000
2 Hamburg	55,000
3 Berlin	49,000
4 Cologne	20,000
5 Magdeburg	15,000
6 Kassel	13,000
7 Darmstadt	12,300
8 = Heilbronn	7,500
= Essen	7,500
10 Dortmund	6,000
= Wuppertal	6,000

The high level of casualties in Dresden resulted principally from the saturation bombing and the firestorm that ensued after Allied raids on the lightly defended city. Although the main objective was to destroy the railway marshalling yards, the scale of the raids was massive: 775 British bombers took part in the first night's raid on Feb 13, 1945, followed the next day by 450 US bombers, with a final attack by 200 US bombers on Feb 15.

GERMAN AIR ACES OF WORLD WAR II

PILOT	KILLS CLAIMED
1 Major Eric Hartmann	352
2 Major Gerhard Barkhorn	301
3 Major Günther Rall	275
4 Oberlt. Otto Kittel	267
5 Major Walther Nowotny	258
6 Major Wilhelm Batz	237
7 Major Erich Rudorffer	222
8 Oberst. Heinz Bär	220
9 Oberst. Hermann Graf	212
10 Major Heinrich Ehrler	209

Many of these figures relate to kills on the Eastern Front, where the Luftwaffe was undoubtedly superior to its Soviet opponents.

JAPANESE AIR ACES OF WORLD WAR II

PILOT	KILLS CLAIMED
1 W. O. Hiroyoshi Nishizawa	87
2 Lt. Tetsuzo Iwamoto	80
3 Petty Officer 1st Class Shoichi Sugita	70
4 Lt. Saburo Sakai	64
5 Petty Officer 1st Class Takeo Okumura	54
6 Petty Officer 1st Class Toshio Ohta	34
7 W. O. Kazuo Sugino	32
8 Petty Officer 1st Class Shizuo Ishii	29
9 Ensign Kaeneyoshi Muto	28
10 = Lt. Sadaaki Akamatsu	27
= Lt. Junichi Sasai	27

US AIR ACES OF THE KOREAN WAR

PILOT	KILLS CLAIMED*
1 Capt. Joseph McConnell, Jr.	16
2 Major James Jabara	15
3 Capt. Manuel J. Fernandez	14.5
4 Major George A. Davis, Jr.	14
5 Col. Royal N. Baker	13
6 = Major Frederick C. Blesse	10
= Lt. Harold H. Fischer	10
= Lt. Col. Vermont Garrison	10
= Col. James K. Johnson	10
= Capt. Lonnie R. Moore	10
= Capt. Ralph S. Parr, Jr.	10

Decimals refer to kills shared across groups such as flying squadrons

Background image: **BOMB-DAMAGED DRESDEN**

TOP GUNS

Majors Richard I. Bong (left) and Thomas B. McGuire (right), the leading US air aces of World War II, are shown here in Leyte, the Philippines, in 1944. After achieving a total of 78 kills between them, they were both killed in crashes the following year.

TOP 10 US AIR ACES OF WORLD WAR II

(Pilot/kills claimed*)

1 Major Richard I. Bong, 40 **2** Major Thomas B. McGuire, 38 **3** Cdr. David S. McCampbell, 34 **4** = Col. Francis S. Gabreski#, 28; = Lt-Col. Gregory Boyington, 28 **6** = Major Robert S. Johnson, 27; = Col. Charles H. MacDonald, 27 **8** = Major George E. Preddy, 26; = Major Joseph J. Foss, 26 **10** Lt. Robert M. Hanson, 25

* Decimals refer to kills shared across groups such as flying squadrons
 # Also 6.5 kills in Korean War

TOP 10 COUNTRIES WITH THE MOST COMBAT AIRCRAFT*

(Country/combat aircraft)

1 Russia, 3,966 **2** China, 3,520 **3** US, 2,598 **4** India, 774 **5** Taiwan, 598 **6** North Korea, 593 **7** Egypt, 583 **8** France, 531 **9** Ukraine, 521 **10** South Korea, 488

* Air force only, exluding long-range strike/attack aircraft

TOP 10 ★ BRITISH AND COMMONWEALTH AIR ACES OF WORLD WAR II

PILOT/COUNTRY	KILLS CLAIMED*
1 Sqd. Ldr. Marmaduke Thomas St John Pattle, South Africa	over 40
2 Gp. Capt. James Edgar "Johnny" Johnson, Great Britain	33.91
3 Wing Cdr. Brendan "Paddy" Finucane, Ireland	32
4 Flt. Lt. George Frederick Beurling, Canada	31.33
5 Wing Cdr. John Randall Daniel Braham, Great Britain	29
6 Gp. Capt. Adolf Gysbert "Sailor" Malan, South Africa	28.66
7 Wing Cdr. Clive Robert Caldwell, Australia	28.5
8 Sqd. Ldr. James Harry "Ginger" Lacey, Great Britain	28
9 Sqd. Ldr. Neville Frederick Duke, Great Britain	27.83
10 Wing Cdr. Colin F. Gray, New Zealand	27.7

* Decimals refer to kills shared across groups such as flying squadrons

TOP COMBAT AIRCRAFT

Following its debut in 1976, the F-16 Fighting Falcon proved to be one of the most versatile fighter aircraft of the 20th century. Although designed for air-to-air fighting, it is equally valued for air-to-ground attack, and is available in both one- and two-seater versions. In military terms, it has a relatively low cost (some $20 million each), a considerable range of some 2,000 miles (3,220 km), and is strongly built. It is highly maneuverable, has a top speed of 1,350 mph (2,170 km/h), and is capable of achieving Mach 2.05 at 40,000 ft (12,190 m), with a ceiling of 50,000 ft (15,240 m). Its US makers, Lockheed Martin, have produced over 2,000 F-16s, while a similar number are on order, making it the world's most extensively flown combat aircraft.

SNAP SHOTS

TOP 10 ★ FASTEST FIGHTER AIRCRAFT OF WORLD WAR II

AIRCRAFT/COUNTRY	MAXIMUM SPEED MPH	KM/H
1 Messerschmitt Me 163, Germany	596	959
2 Messerschmitt Me 262, Germany	560	901
3 Heinkel He 162A, Germany	553	890
4 P-51-H Mustang, US	487	784
5 Lavochkin La-11, USSR	460	740
6 Spitfire XIV, UK	448	721
7 Yakovlev Yak-3, USSR	447	719
8 P-51-D Mustang, US	440	708
9 Tempest VI, UK	438	705
10 Focke-Wulf Fw 190D, Germany	435	700

Also known as the Komet, the Messerschmitt Me 163 was a short-range rocket-powered interceptor brought into service in 1944–45, during which time this aircraft scored a number of victories over its slower Allied rivals. The Messerschmitt Me 262 was the first jet in operational service. The jet engine of the Soviet Yakovlev Yak-3 was mounted centrally under the cockpit. To avoid the danger of setting the tail-wheel tire on fire, it was replaced with an all-steel wheel, making landings a somewhat noisy affair.

Did You Know? The highest "score" by a night-fighter pilot was the total of 121 kills credited to World War II pilot Major Heinz-Wolfgang Schnauffer.

77

World Religions

LARGEST JEWISH POPULATIONS

	COUNTRY	TOTAL JEWISH POPULATION
1	US	6,122,462
2	Israel	4,354,900
3	France	640,156
4	Russia	460,266
5	Ukraine	424,136
6	UK	345,054
7	Canada	342,096
8	Argentina	253,666
9	Brazil	107,692
10	Belarus	107,350
	World total	15,050,000

The Diaspora – the scattering of the Jewish people – has been in progress for nearly 2,000 years, and Jewish communities are found in virtually every country in the world. In 1939 the total world Jewish population was around 17 million. Some 6 million fell victim to Nazi persecution, but numbers have now topped 15 million.

JEWISH PRAYERS

The Wailing Wall, Jerusalem, was part of the temple erected by King Herod. Jews traditionally pray here, lamenting the destruction of the temple in AD 70.

LARGEST CHRISTIAN DENOMINATIONS

	DENOMINATION	MEMBERS
1	Roman Catholic	912,636,000
2	Orthodox	139,544,000
3	Pentecostal	105,756,000
4	Lutheran	84,521,000
5	Baptist	67,146,000
6	Anglican	53,217,000
7	Presbyterian	47,972,000
8	Methodist	25,599,000
9	Seventh Day Adventist	10,650,000
10	Churches of Christ	6,400,000

Source: *Christian Research*

Although Christian communities are found in almost every country in the world, it is difficult to put a precise figure on nominal membership (a declared religious persuasion) rather than active participation (regular attendance at a place of worship). In the US, Roman Catholicism is the largest single denomination in a total of 36 states, and the Southern Baptist Convention in 10 states. However, the latter has the most churches nationwide: a total of 37,893.

LARGEST HINDU POPULATIONS

	COUNTRY	TOTAL HINDU POPULATION
1	India	814,632,942
2	Nepal	21,136,118
3	Bangladesh	14,802,899
4	Indonesia	3,974,895
5	Sri Lanka	2,713,900
6	Pakistan	2,112,071
7	Malaysia	1,043,500
8	US	798,582
9	South Africa	649,980
10	Mauritius	587,884
	World total	865,000,000

More than 99 percent of the world's Hindu population lives in Asia, with 94 percent in India.

RELIGIOUS BELIEFS

	RELIGION	MEMBERS*
1	Christianity	2,015,743,000
2	Islam	1,215,693,000
3	Hinduism	865,000,000
4	Non-religions	774,693,000
5	Buddhism	362,245,000
6	Tribal religions	255,950,000
7	Atheism	151,430,000
8	New religions	102,174,000
9	Sikhism	23,102,000
10	Judaism	15,050,000

* *Estimated total projections to mid-1998*

Outside the Top 10, several other religions have members numbering in millions, among them some 7 million Baha'is, 6 million Confucians, 4 million Jains, and 3 million Shintoists.

LARGEST CHRISTIAN POPULATIONS

	COUNTRY	TOTAL CHRISTIAN POPULATION
1	US	182,674,000
2	Brazil	157,973,000
3	Mexico	88,380,000
4	China	73,300,000
5	Philippines	65,217,000
6	Germany	63,332,000
7	Italy	47,403,000
8	France	45,624,000
9	Nigeria	38,969,000
10	Dem. Rep. of Congo	37,922,000
	World total	2,015,743,000

Source: *Christian Research*

Did You Know? A Holocaust Memorial Museum in Washington, D.C. honors the millions of Jews killed during the Holocaust.

TOP 10 ★
LARGEST MUSLIM POPULATIONS

	COUNTRY	TOTAL MUSLIM POPULATION
1	Pakistan	157,349,290
2	Indonesia	156,213,374
3	Bangladesh	133,873,621
4	India	130,316,250
5	Iran	74,087,700
6	Turkey	66,462,107
7	Russia	64,624,770
8	Egypt	57,624,098
9	Nigeria	46,384,120
10	Morocco	33,542,780
	World total	1,215,693,000

Historically, Islam spread as a result of conquest, missionary activity, and through contacts with Muslim traders. In such countries as Indonesia, its appeal lay in part in its opposition to Western colonial influences, which, along with the concept of Islamic community and other tenets, has attracted followers worldwide.

BOWING TO MECCA

Islam places many strictures on its female members but is nonetheless the world's fastest-growing religion. Here, hundreds of Muslim women unite in prayer.

TOP 10 ★
LARGEST BUDDHIST POPULATIONS

	COUNTRY	TOTAL BUDDHIST POPULATION
1	China	104,000,000
2	Japan	90,510,000
3	Thailand	57,450,000
4	Vietnam	50,080,000
5	Myanmar (Burma)	41,880,000
6	Sri Lanka	12,540,000
7	South Korea	11,110,000
8	Cambodia	9,870,000
9	India	7,000,000
10	Malaysia	3,770,000
	World total	362,245,000

HEAD OF THE FAITH

Although India now features in ninth place among countries with high Buddhist populations, the religion originated there in the 6th century BC.

Town & Country

Countries of the World

TOP 10 ★

LARGEST COUNTRIES

| COUNTRY | AREA | |
	SQ MILES	SQ KM
1 Russia	6,590,876	17,070,289
2 Canada	3,849,670	9,970,599
3 China	3,705,408	9,596,961
4 US	3,540,321	9,169,389
5 Brazil	3,286,488	8,511,965
6 Australia	2,967,909	7,686,848
7 India	1,269,346	3,287,590
8 Argentina	1,073,512	2,780,400
9 Kazakhstan	1,049,156	2,717,300
10 Sudan	967,500	2,505,813
World total	52,435,381	135,807,000

TOP 10 COUNTRIES IN WHICH WOMEN MOST OUTNUMBER MEN

(Country/women per 100 men)

1 Latvia, 120 **2** = Cape Verdi, 115; = Ukraine, 115
4 Russia, 114 **5** = Belarus, 112; = Estonia, 112;
= Lithuania, 112 **8** = Hungary, 109; = Antigua and
Barbuda, 109; = Georgia, 109; = Moldova, 109
Source: *United Nations*

TOP 10 ★

SMALLEST COUNTRIES

| COUNTRY | AREA | |
	SQ MILES	SQ KM
1 Vatican City	0.17	0.44
2 Monaco	0.77	1.95
3 Gibraltar	2.50	6.47
4 Macao	6.20	16.06
5 Nauru	8.20	21.23
6 Tuvalu	10.00	25.90
7 Bermuda	20.60	53.35
8 San Marino	23.00	59.57
9 Liechtenstein	61.00	157.99
10 Antigua	108.00	279.72

The "country" status of several of these microstates is questionable, since their government, defense, currency, and other features are often intricately linked with those of larger countries, such as the Vatican City with Italy's.

TOP 10 ★

LONGEST BORDERS

| COUNTRY | BORDERS | |
	MILES	KM
1 China	13,759	22,143
2 Russia	12,514	20,139
3 Brazil	9,129	14,691
4 India	8,763	14,103
5 US	7,611	12,248
6 Dem. Rep. of Congo	6,382	10,271
7 Argentina	6,006	9,665
8 Canada	5,526	8,893
9 Mongolia	5,042	8,114
10 Sudan	4,783	7,697

This list represents the total length of borders, compiled by adding together the lengths of individual land borders.

RUSSIAN SURVIVORS

The disproportionately high number of women in Russia and other former Soviet countries is the result of high mortality rates among the region's men, caused in part by poor diet and excessive consumption of alcohol and tobacco.

TOP 10 COUNTRIES IN WHICH MEN MOST OUTNUMBER WOMEN

(Country/men per 100 women)

1 Qatar, 189 **2** United Arab Emirates, 174 **3** Bahrain, 133
4 Saudi Arabia, 124 **5** = Oman, 113; = Andorra, 113
7 = Guam, 112; = Hong Kong, 112 **9** Brunei, 110 **10** Kuwait, 109
Source: *United Nations*

Did You Know? The US's 3,987-mile (6,416-km) frontier with Canada is the longest continuous frontier in the world.

TOP 10 MOST DENSELY POPULATED COUNTRIES

	COUNTRY	AREA (SQ KM)	ESTIMATED POPULATION*	POPULATION PER SQ KM
1	Monaco	1.95	32,231	16,528.7
2	Singapore	618	3,571,710	5,779.5
3	Malta	316	383,285	1,212.9
4	Maldives	298	310,425	1,041.7
5	Bahrain	694	641,539	924.4
6	Bangladesh	143,998	129,146,695	896.9
7	Mauritius	1,865	1,196,172	641.4
8	Barbados	430	259,248	602.9
9	South Korea	99,274	47,350,529	476.9
10	San Marino	61	25,215	413.4
	US	9,169,389	274,943,496	30.0
	World	135,807,000	6,073,098,801	44.7

For the year 2000

Source: *US Bureau of the Census/United Nations*

TOP 10 ★
LARGEST COUNTRIES IN EUROPE

	COUNTRY	AREA SQ MILES	AREA SQ KM
1	**Russia** (in Europe)	1,818,629	4,710,227
2	**Ukraine**	233,090	603,700
3	**France**	211,208	547,026
4	**Spain***	194,897	504,781
5	**Sweden**	173,732	449,964
6	**Germany**	137,838	356,999
7	**Finland**	130,119	337,007
8	**Norway**	125,182	324,220
9	**Poland**	120,725	312,676
10	**Italy**	116,304	301,226

* Including offshore islands

The UK falls just outside the Top 10 at 94,247 sq miles (244,101 sq km). Excluding the Isle of Man and the Channel Islands, its area comprises England (50,351 sq miles/130,410 sq km), Scotland (30,420 sq miles/78,789 sq km), Wales (8,015 sq miles/20,758 sq km), and Northern Ireland (5,461 sq miles/14,144 sq km).

TOP 10 COUNTRIES WITH THE OLDEST POPULATIONS

(Country/percentage over 65)

1 Sweden, 17.3 **2** = Italy, 16.6; = Greece, 16.6 **4** Portugal, 16.1 **5** Belgium, 16.0 **6** Spain, 15.9 **7** UK, 15.8 **8** Norway, 15.7 **9** = Germany, 15.5; = Japan, 15.5

Source: *World Bank*

Nine of the ten countries with the oldest populations are in western Europe, implying that this region has lower death rates and a higher life expectancy than the rest of the world.

LOOKING TO THE FUTURE

Soaring birth rates in many African countries have created broad-based population pyramids, with up to half their populations aged under 15.

TOP 10 COUNTRIES WITH THE YOUNGEST POPULATIONS

(Country/percentage under 15)

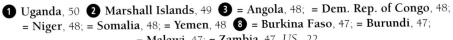

1 Uganda, 50 **2** Marshall Islands, 49 **3** = Angola, 48; = Dem. Rep. of Congo, 48; = Niger, 48; = Somalia, 48; = Yemen, 48 **8** = Burkina Faso, 47; = Burundi, 47; = Malawi, 47; = Zambia, 47 US, 22

Source: *United Nations*

Countries with high proportions of their people under the age of 15 are usually characterized by high birth rates and high death rates.

World Cities

TOP 10 ★
MOST DENSELY POPULATED CITIES*

	CITY/COUNTRY	POPULATION PER SQ MILE	SQ KM
1	Hong Kong, China	253,957	98,053
2	Lagos, Nigeria	174,982	67,561
3	Dhaka, Bangladesh	165,500	63,900
4	Jakarta, Indonesia	146,724	56,650
5	Bombay, India	142,442	54,997
6	Ahmadabad, India	131,250	50,676
7	Ho Chi Minh City (Saigon), Vietnam	131,097	50,617
8	Shenyang, China	114,282	44,125
9	Bangalore, India	112,880	43,583
10	Cairo, Egypt	107,260	41,413

Includes only cities with populations of over 2 million

Source: *US Bureau of the Census*

RUSH HOUR – NIGERIAN STYLE

Nigeria's former capital and still its most important city, Lagos, is also one of the world's densest and fastest-growing cities, as a result of which it suffers from traffic congestion, overcrowding, and slum dwellings.

TOP 10 ★
FASTEST-GROWING CITIES

	CITY/COUNTRY	EST. INCREASE, 1995–2010 (%)*
1	Hangzhou, China	171.1
2	Addis Ababa, Ethiopia	170.7
3	Kabul, Afghanistan	156.3
4	Handan, China	141.6
5	Isfahan, Iran	141.3
6	Maputo, Mozambique	139.9
7	Lagos, Nigeria	139.5
8	Luanda, Angola	138.8
9	Nairobi, Kenya	133.6
10	Qingdao, China	132.4

Urban agglomerations of over 1 million population only

Source: *United Nations*

TOP 10 ★
LARGEST CITIES IN NORTH AMERICA

	CITY/STATE/COUNTRY	EST. POPULATION, 2015*
1	Mexico City, Mexico	19,200,000
2	New York, US	17,600,000
3	Los Angeles, US	14,200,000
4	Chicago, US	7,500,000
5	Toronto, Canada	5,200,000
6	Philadelphia, US	4,800,000
7	Santo Domingo, Dominican Republic	4,700,000
8 =	Guadalajara, Mexico	4,500,000
=	San Francisco, US	4,500,000
10 =	Dallas, US	4,400,000
=	Washington, DC, US	4,400,000

Of urban agglomeration

Source: *United Nations*

TOP 10 ★
HIGHEST CITIES

	CITY/COUNTRY	HEIGHT FT	M
1	Wenchuan, China	16,730	5,099
2	Potosí, Bolivia	13,045	3,976
3	Oruro, Bolivia	12,146	3,702
4	Lhasa, Tibet	12,087	3,684
5	La Paz, Bolivia	11,916	3,632
6	Cuzco, Peru	11,152	3,399
7	Huancayo, Peru	10,660	3,249
8	Sucre, Bolivia	9,301	2,835
9	Tunja, Colombia	9,252	2,820
10	Quito, Ecuador	9,249	2,819

Lhasa was formerly the highest capital city in the world, a role now occupied by La Paz, capital of Bolivia. Wenchuan is situated at more than half the elevation of Everest, and even the cities at the foot of this list are more than one-third as high.

Did You Know? Ein Bokek, beside the Dead Sea, is the world's lowest inhabited place at 1,291 ft (393.5 m) below sea level.

TOP 10 ⭐
LARGEST CITIES

CITY/COUNTRY	EST. POPULATION, 2015*
1 **Tokyo**, Japan	28,900,000
2 **Bombay**, India	26,200,000
3 **Lagos**, Nigeria	24,600,000
4 **São Paulo**, Brazil	20,300,000
5 **Dhaka**, Bangladesh	19,500,000
6 **Karachi**, Pakistan	19,400,000
7 **Mexico City**, Mexico	19,200,000
8 **Shanghai**, China	18,000,000
9 **New York**, USA	17,600,000
10 **Calcutta**, India	17,300,000

* Of urban agglomeration

Source: *United Nations*

The definition taken in the above and other city lists is the United Nations definition of "urban agglomeration", which comprises the city or town proper and also the suburban fringe or thickly settled territory lying outside of, but adjacent to, the city boundaries.

TOP 10 ⭐
LARGEST CITIES IN THE US*

CITY/STATE	POPULATION
1 **New York**, New York	7,420,166
2 **Los Angeles**, California	3,597,556
3 **Chicago**, Illinois	2,802,079
4 **Houston**, Texas	1,786,691
5 **Philadelphia**, Pennsylvania	1,436,287
6 **San Diego**, California	1,220,666
7 **Phoenix**, Arizona	1,198,064
8 **San Antonio**, Texas	1,114,130
9 **Dallas**, Texas	1,075,894
10 **Detroit**, Michigan	970,196

* Estimated figures up to July 1, 1999

Source: *US Bureau of the Census*

These are estimates for central city areas only, not for the total metropolitan areas that surround them, which may be several times as large.

TOP 10 ⭐
LARGEST CITIES IN EUROPE

CITY/COUNTRY	EST. POPULATION, 2015*
1 **Paris**, France	9,700,000
2 **Moscow**, Russia	9,300,000
3 **London**, UK	7,600,000
4 **Essen**, Germany	6,600,000
5 **St. Petersburg**, Russia	5,100,000
6 **Milan**, Italy	4,300,000
7 **Madrid**, Spain	4,100,000
8 = **Frankfurt**, Germany	3,700,000
= **Katowice**, Poland	3,700,000
10 **Dusseldorf**, Germany	3,400,000

* Of urban agglomeration

Source: *United Nations*

PARISIAN GRANDEUR

A population of 9.5 million, a central location, and cultural and other attractions have led to the inexorable growth of Paris to its present rank as Europe's largest city.

TOP 10 ⭐
LARGEST NONCAPITAL CITIES

CITY/COUNTRY/CAPITAL CITY	POPULATION
1 **Shanghai**, China *Beijing*	13,584,000 *11,299,000*
2 **Bombay**, India *New Delhi*	15,138,000 *8,419,000*
3 **Calcutta***, India *New Delhi*	11,923,000 *8,419,000*
4 **Lagos**, Nigeria *Abuja*	10,287,000 *378,671*
5 **São Paulo**, Brazil *Brasília*	10,017,821 *1,864,000*
6 **Karachi***, Pakistan *Islamabad*	9,733,000 *350,000*
7 **Tianjin**, China *Beijing*	9,415,000 *11,299,000*
8 **Istanbul***, Turkey *Ankara*	8,274,921 *2,937,524*
9 **New York**, USA *Washington, DC*	7,420,166 *523,124*
10 **Madras**, India *New Delhi*	6,002,000 *8,419,000*

* Former capital

TOP 10 ⭐
MOST POPULATED FORMER CAPITAL CITIES

CITY/COUNTRY	CEASED TO BE CAPITAL	POPULATION*
1 **Calcutta**, India	1912	11,021,918
2 **Istanbul**, Turkey	1923	7,774,169
3 **Karachi**, Pakistan	1968	7,183,000
4 **Rio de Janeiro**, Brazil	1960	5,547,033
5 **St. Petersburg**, Russia	1980	4,273,001
6 **Berlin**, Germany	1949	3,472,009
7 **Alexandria**, Egypt	c.641	3,380,000
8 **Melbourne**, Australia	1927	3,189,200
9 **Nanjiang**, China	1949	2,610,594
10 **Philadelphia**, US	1800	1,524,249

* Within administrative boundaries

States of the US

TOP 10 LARGEST STATES IN THE US

	STATE	AREA* SQ MILES	AREA* SQ KM
1	Alaska	615,230	1,593,438
2	Texas	267,277	692,244
3	California	158,869	411,469
4	Montana	147,046	380,847
5	New Mexico	121,598	314,937
6	Arizona	114,006	295,274
7	Nevada	110,567	286,367
8	Colorado	104,100	269,618
9	Wyoming	97,818	253,349
10	Oregon	97,132	251,571

* Total, including water

Source: *US Bureau of the Census*

TOP 10 ★ SMALLEST STATES IN THE US

	STATE	AREA* SQ MILES	SQ KM
1	Rhode Island	1,231	3,189
2	Delaware	2,396	6,206
3	Connecticut	5,544	14,358
4	Hawaii	6,459	16,729
5	New Jersey	8,215	21,277
6	Massachusetts	9,241	23,934
7	New Hampshire	9,283	24,044
8	Vermont	9,615	24,903
9	Maryland	12,297	31,849
10	West Virginia	24,231	62,759

* Total, including water

The District of Columbia has a total area of 68 sq miles (177 sq km). It also has the smallest area of inland water, at just 7 sq miles (18 sq km). Of the States in this list, Maryland has the greatest area of inland water – 68 sq miles (1,761 sq km) – and Hawaii the least – 36 sq miles (93 sq km).

TOP 10 ★ MOST DENSELY POPULATED STATES IN THE US

	STATE	POPULATION PER SQ MILE OF LAND AREA*
1	New Jersey	1,093.8
2	Rhode Island	945.9
3	Massachusetts	784.3
4	Connecticut	675.7
5	Maryland	525.3
6	New York	384.9
7	Delaware	380.4
8	Florida	276.2
9	Ohio	273.7
10	Pennsylvania	267.8

* Estimated

Source: *US Bureau of the Census*

The district of Columbia accommodates 8,519 people per sq mile of land area. The least densely populated State is Alaska, with just 1.1 people per sq mile, with Wyoming (5.0 people per sq mile), and Montana (6.0 people per sq mile) in second and third places respectively.

THE 10 ★ FIRST STATES OF THE US

	STATE	ENTERED UNION
1	Delaware	Dec 7, 1787
2	Pennsylvania	Dec 12, 1787
3	New Jersey	Dec 18, 1787
4	Georgia	Jan 2, 1788
5	Connecticut	Jan 9, 1788
6	Massachusetts	Feb 6, 1788
7	Maryland	Apr 28, 1788
8	South Carolina	May 23, 1788
9	New Hampshire	June 21, 1788
10	Virginia	June 25, 1788

The names of two of the first 10 American states commemorate early colonists. Delaware Bay (and hence the river, and later the state) was named after Thomas West, Lord De La Warr, a governor of Virginia. Pennsylvania was called "Pensilvania," or "Penn's woodland," in its original charter, issued in 1681 to the Quaker leader William Penn by King Charles II. Two states were named after places with which their founders had associations: New Jersey was the subject of a deed issued in 1644 by the Duke of York to John Berkeley and Sir George Carteret, who came from Jersey in the Channel Islands, and New Hampshire was called after the English county by settler Captain John Mason.

THE 10 ★ LAST STATES OF THE US

	STATE	ENTERED UNION
1	Hawaii	Aug 21, 1959
2	Alaska	Jan 3, 1959
3	Arizona	Feb 14, 1912
4	New Mexico	Jan 6, 1912
5	Oklahoma	Nov 16, 1907
6	Utah	Jan 4, 1896
7	Wyoming	July 10, 1890
8	Idaho	July 3, 1890
9	Washington	Nov 11, 1889
10	Montana	Nov 8, 1889

TOP 10 ★
MOST HIGHLY POPULATED STATES IN THE US

	STATE	POPULATION 1900	1999*
1	California	1,485,053	33,145,121
2	Texas	3,048,710	20,044,141
3	New York	7,268,894	18,196,601
4	Florida	528,542	15,111,244
5	Illinois	4,821,550	12,128,370
6	Pennsylvania	6,302,115	11,994,016
7	Ohio	4,157,545	11,256,654
8	Michigan	2,420,982	9,863,775
9	New Jersey	1,883,669	8,143,412
10	Georgia	2,216,231	7,788,240

* Estimated

Source: *US Bureau of the Census*

The total population of the US according to the 1900 Census was 76,212,168, compared to the US Bureau of the Census's 1999 estimate of 272,690,813. The population has expanded more than 69-fold in the 210 years since 1790, when it was just 3,929,214. Some states continue to grow faster than others: Florida's population is now 28 times its 1900 figure, and in the 1980s alone increased by 30 percent.

TOP 10 ★
LEAST POPULATED STATES IN THE US

	STATE	POPULATION, 1999*
1	Wyoming	479,602
2	Vermont	593,740
3	Alaska	619,500
4	North Dakota	633,666
5	South Dakota	733,133
6	Delaware	753,538
7	Montana	882,779
8	Rhode Island	990,819
9	Hawaii	1,185,497
10	New Hampshire	1,201,134

* Estimated

Source: *US Bureau of the Census*

TOP 10 ★
US STATES WITH THE GREATEST AREA OF TRIBAL LAND

	STATE	ACRES
1	Arizona	20,087,538
2	New Mexico	7,882,619
3	Montana	5,574,835
4	South Dakota	4,520,719
5	Nevada	2,721,000
6	Washington	2,718,516
7	Utah	2,319,286
8	Wyoming	2,059,632
9	Alaska	1,352,205
10	Oklahoma	1,097,004

A total of 34 states contain 56,183,794 acres of tribal land. The remaining 16 states have no tribal land at all.

TOP 10 ★
LARGEST NATIVE AMERICAN RESERVATIONS

	RESERVATION/STATE	POPULATION
1	**Navajo**, Arizona/New Mexico/ Utah	143,405
2	**Pine Ridge**, Nebraska/ South Dakota	11,182
3	**Fort Apache**, Arizona	9,825
4	**Gila River**, Arizona	9,116
5	**Papago**, Arizona	8,480
6	**Rosebud**, South Dakota	8,043
7	**San Carlos**, Arizona	7,110
8	**Zuni Pueblo**, Arizona/ New Mexico	7,073
9	**Hopi**, Arizona	7,061
10	**Blackfeet**, Montana	7,025

This list is based on those reservations that contain 5,000 or more native American inhabitants. It should be noted that not all native Americans chose to live in these areas (only 26.5 percent of Blackfeet do so, for example), while other, nonnative, inhabitants also reside in these areas, placing natives in a minority in certain areas.

TOP 10 ★
LARGEST NATIVE AMERICAN TRIBES

	TRIBE	POPULATION
1	Cherokee	308,132
2	Navajo	219,198
3	Chippewa	103,826
4	Sioux	103,255
5	Choctaw	82,299
6	Pueblo	52,939
7	Apache	50,051
8	Iroquois	49,038
9	Lumbee	48,444
10	Creek	43,550

The total Native American population as assessed by the 1990 Census was 1,878,285. Different authorities have estimated that the total North American population at the time of the first European arrivals in 1492 was anything from 1 to 10 million. This declined to a low in 1890 of some 90,000, but has experienced a substantial resurgence in the past century: according to successive Censuses, it had risen to 357,000 in 1950, 793,000 in 1970, and 1,479,000 in 1980.

TOP 10 ★
US STATES WITH THE LONGEST SHORELINES

	STATE	SHORELINE MILES	KM
1	Alaska	33,904	54,904
2	Florida	8,426	13,560
3	Louisiana	7,721	12,426
4	Maine	3,478	5,597
5	California	3,427	5,515
6	North Carolina	3,375	5,432
7	Texas	3,359	5,406
8	Virginia	3,315	5,335
9	Maryland	3,190	5,134
10	Washington	3,026	4,870

Pennsylvania's 890-mile (143-km) shoreline is the shortest among the states that have one – 26 states, plus the District of Columbia, have no shoreline.

Did You Know? Triggered by the Gold Rush, in the 50 years from 1850 to 1900 the population of California rose 16-fold from 93,000 to 1,485,053.

Place Names

LONGEST PLACE NAMES IN THE US*

NAME/LOCATION	LETTERS
1 Chargoggagoggmanchauggagoggchaubunagungamaugg (see Top 10 Longest Place Names)	45
2 Nunathloogagamiutbingoi, Dunes, Alaska	23
3 Winchester-on-the-Severn, Maryland	21
4 Scraper-Moechereville, Illinois	20
5 Linstead-on-the-Severn, Maryland	19
6 =Kentwood-in-the-Pines, California	18
=Lauderdale-by-the-Sea, Florida	18
=Vermilion-on-the-Lake, Ohio	18
9 =Chippewa-on-the-Lake, Ohio	17
=Fairhaven-on-the-Bay, Maryland	17
=Highland-on-the-Lake, New York	17
=Kleinfeltersville, Pennsylvania	17
=Mooselookmeguntic, Maine	17
=Palermo-by-the-Lakes, Ohio	17
=Saybrook-on-the-Lake, Ohio	17

* Single and hyphenated names only   Source: US Geological Survey

COUNTRIES WITH THE LONGEST OFFICIAL NAMES

OFFICIAL NAME*	COMMON ENGLISH NAME	LETTERS
1 al-Jamāhīrīyah al-Arabīya al-Lībīyah ash-Sha bīyah al-Ishtirākīyah	Libya	56
2 al-Jumhūrīyah al-Jazā'irīyah ad-Dīmuqrātīyah ash-Sha bīyah	Algeria	49
3 United Kingdom of Great Britain and Northern Ireland	United Kingdom	45
4 Sri Lankā Prajathanthrika Samajavadi Janarajaya	Sri Lanka	43
5 Jumhurīyat al-Qumur al-Ittihādīyah al-Islāmīyah	The Comoros	41
6 =al-Jumhūrīyah al-Islāmīyah al-Mūrītānīyah	Mauritania	36
=The Federation of St. Christopher and Nevis	St. Kitts and Nevis	36
8 Jamhuuriyadda Dimuqraadiga Soomaaliya	Somalia	35
9 al-Mamlakah al-Urdunnīyah al-Hāshimīyah	Jordan	34
10 Repoblika Demokratika n'i Madagaskar	Madagascar	32

* Some official names have been transliterated from languages that do not use the Roman alphabet; their length may vary according to the method used.

TOP 10 MOST COMMON STREET NAMES IN THE US

1 2nd/Second Street **2** 3rd/Third Street **3** 1st/First Street **4** 4th/Fourth Street
5 Park Street **6** 5th/Fifth Street **7** Main Street **8** 6th/Sixth Street **9** Oak Street
10 7th/Seventh Street   Source: US Bureau of the Census

MOST COMMON PLACE NAMES IN THE US

NAME	OCCURRENCES
1 Fairview	287
2 Midway	252
3 Riverside	180
4 Oak Grove	179
5 Five Points	155
6 Oakland	149
7 Greenwood	145
8 =Bethel	141
=Franklin	141
10 Pleasant Hill	140

Source: US Geological Board

TREES AFTER WHICH US STREETS ARE NAMED

NAME	OCCURRENCES
1 Oak	6,946
2 Pine	6,170
3 Maple	6,103
4 Cedar	5,644
5 Elm	5,233
6 Walnut	4,799
7 Willow	4,017
8 Cherry	3,669
9 Hickory	3,297
10 Chestnut	2,994

Source: US Bureau of the Census

PEOPLE AFTER WHOM US STREETS ARE NAMED

NAME	OCCURRENCES
1 Washington	4,979
2 Lincoln	4,044
3 Jackson	3,725
4 Johnson	3,325
5 Jefferson	3,306
6 Smith	3,076
7 Franklin	2,882
8 Adams	2,856
9 Davis	2,769
10 Williams	2,682

Source: US Bureau of the Census

Did You Know? 1st/First Street is the third most common street name in the US only because many streets that would be so designated are instead called Main Street.

TOP 10 ★
LONGEST PLACE NAMES*

NAME	LETTERS

1 Krung thep mahanakhon bovorn ratanakosin mahintharayutthaya mahadilok pop noparatratchathani burirom udomratchanivetmahasathan amornpiman avatarnsathit sakkathattiyavisnukarmprasit   167

When the poetic name of Bangkok, capital of Thailand, is used, it is usually abbreviated to "Krung Thep" (city of angels).

2 Taumatawhakatangihangakoauauotamateaturipukakapikimaungahoronukupokaiw-henuakitanatahu   85

This is the longer version (the other has a mere 83 letters) of the Maori name of a hill in New Zealand. It translates as "The place where Tamatea, the man with the big knees, who slid, climbed and swallowed mountains, known as land-eater, played on the flute to his loved one."

3 Gorsafawddachaidraigddanheddogleddollônpenrhynareurdraethceredigion   67

A name contrived by the Fairbourne Steam Railway, Gwynedd, North Wales, for publicity purposes and in order to outdo its rival, No. 4. It means "The Mawddach station and its dragon teeth at the Northern Penrhyn Road on the golden beach of Cardigan Bay."

4 Llanfairpwllgwyngyllgogerychwyrndrobwllllantysiliogogogoch   58

This is the place in Gwynedd famed especially for the length of its train tickets. It means "St. Mary's Church in the hollow of the white hazel near to the rapid whirlpool of Llantysilio of the Red Cave." Questions have been raised about its authenticity, since its official name comprises only the first 20 letters, and the full name appears to have been invented as a hoax in the 19th century by a local poet, John Evans, known as Y Bardd Cocos. It also has Britain's longest Internet site name:
http://www.llanfairpwllgwyngyllgogerychwyrndrobwllllantysiliogogogoch.wales.com/llanfair

5 El Pueblo de Nuestra Señora la Reina de los Angeles de la Porciuncula   57

The site of a Franciscan mission and the full Spanish name of Los Angeles; it means "the town of Our Lady the Queen of the Angels of the Little Portion." Nowadays it is customarily known by its initial letters, "LA," making it also one of the shortest-named cities in the world.

6 Chargoggagoggmanchauggagoggchaubunagungamaugg   45

America's second longest place name, a lake near Webster, Massachusetts. Its Indian name, loosely translated, means "You fish on your side, I'll fish on mine, and no one fishes in the middle." It is said to be pronounced "Char-gogg-a-gogg (pause) man-chaugg-a-gogg (pause) chau-bun-a-gung-amaugg." It is, however, an invented extension of its real name (Chagungungamaug Pond, or "boundary fishing place"), devised in the 1920s by Larry Daly, the editor of the Webster Times.

7 = Lower North Branch Little Southwest Miramichi   40

Canada's longest place name – a short river in New Brunswick.

= Villa Real de la Santa Fe de San Francisco de Asis   40

The full Spanish name of Santa Fe, New Mexico, translates as, "Royal city of the holy faith of St. Francis of Assisi."

9 Te Whakatakanga-o-te-ngarehu-o-te-ahi-a-Tamatea   38

The Maori name of Hammer Springs, New Zealand; like the second name in this list, it refers to a legend of Tamatea, explaining how the springs were warmed by "the falling of the cinders of the fire of Tamatea." Its name is variously written either hyphenated or as a single word.

10 Meallan Liath Coire Mhic Dhubhghaill   32

The longest multiple name in Scotland, a place near Aultanrynie, Highland, this is alternatively spelled Meallan Liath Coire Mhic Dhughaill (30 letters).

* Including single-word, hyphenated, and multiple-word names

CITY OF ANGELS
The original 57-letter Spanish name of Los Angeles contrasts dramatically with its more common designation as "LA."

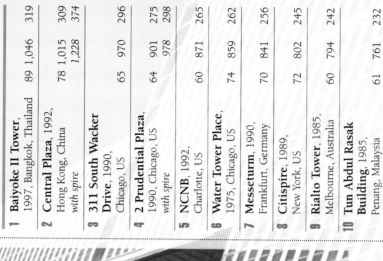

TOP 10 ★

TALLEST HABITABLE BUILDINGS

BUILDING/YEAR/ LOCATION	STOREYS	HEIGHT FT	M
1 Petronas Towers, 1996, Kuala Lumpur, Malaysia	96	1,482	452
2 Sears Tower, 1974, Chicago, US *with spires*	110	1,454 1,707	443 520
3 World Trade Center*, 1972, New York, US	110	1,368	417
4 World Finance Center, 2001, Hong Kong, China	88	1,312	400
5 Jin Mao Building, 1997, Shanghai, China *with spire*	93	1,255 1,378	382 420
6 Empire State Building, 1931, New York, US *with spire*	102	1,250 1,472	381 449
7 T & C Tower, 1997, Kao-hsiung, Taiwan	85	1,142	348
8 Amoco Building, 1973, Chicago, US	80	1,136	346
9 John Hancock Center, 1969, Chicago, US *with spires*	100	1,127 1,470	343 449
10 Shun Hing Square, 1996, Shenzen, China *with spires*	80	1,082 1,260	330 384

* Twin towers; the second tower, completed in 1973, has the same number of stories but is slightly smaller at 1,360 ft (415m), although its spire takes it up to 1,710 ft (521 m).

TOP 10 ★

TALLEST REINFORCED CONCRETE BUILDINGS

BUILDING/YEAR/ LOCATION	STOREYS	HEIGHT FT	M
1 Baiyoke II Tower, 1997, Bangkok, Thailand	89	1,046	319
2 Central Plaza, 1992, Hong Kong, China *with spire*	78	1,015 1,228	309 374
3 311 South Wacker Drive, 1990, Chicago, US	65	970	296
4 2 Prudential Plaza, 1990, Chicago, US *with spire*	64	901 978	275 298
5 NCNB, 1992, Charlotte, US	60	871	265
6 Water Tower Place, 1975, Chicago, US	74	859	262
7 Messeturm, 1990, Frankfurt, Germany	70	841	256
8 Citispire, 1989, New York, US	72	802	245
9 Rialto Tower, 1985, Melbourne, Australia	60	794	242
10 Tun Abdul Rasak Building, 1985, Penang, Malaysia	61	761	232

Reinforced concrete was patented in France on March 16, 1867 by Joseph Monier (1823–1906) and was later developed by another Frenchman, François Hennebique (1842–1921). The first American buildings constructed from it date from a century ago, and since then it has become one of the most important of all building materials. It is constructed from concrete slabs containing steel bars which expand and contract at the same rate as the concrete. This provides great tensile strength and fire resistance. These qualities make it the ideal construction material for bridge spans and skyscrapers.

CHICAGO GIANT

Chicago's tallest skyscraper weighs 222,500 tons (201,848 tonnes). It has 16,100 windows and contains 43,000 miles (69,000 km) of telephone cable.

TOP 10 CITIES
WITH THE MOST SKYSCRAPERS*

(City/country/skyscrapers)

❶ New York City, US, 162 ❷ Chicago, US, 72 ❸ Hong Kong, China, 41
❹ Shanghai, China, 38 ❺ Tokyo, Japan, 29 ❻ Houston, US, 27 ❼ Singapore, 25
❽ Los Angeles, US, 21 ❾ Dallas, US, 19 ❿ Sydney, Australia, 18
* Habitable buildings of more than 500 ft (152 m)

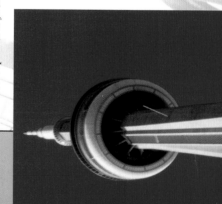

TOP 10 ★
TALLEST TELECOMMUNICATIONS TOWERS

	TOWER/YEAR/LOCATION	HEIGHT FT	M
1	CN Tower, 1975, Toronto, Canada	1,821	555
2	Ostankino Tower, 1967, Moscow, Russia	1,762	537
3	Oriental Pearl Broadcasting Tower, 1995, Shanghai, China	1,535	468
4	Menara Telecom Tower, 1996, Kuala Lumpur, Malaysia	1,381	421
5	Tianjin TV and Radio Tower, 1991, Tianjin, China	1,362	415
6	Central Radio and TV Tower, 1994, Beijing, China	1,328	405
7	TV Tower, 1983, Tashkent, Uzbekistan	1,230	375
8	Liberation Tower, 1998, Kuwait City, Kuwait	1,220	372
9	Alma-Ata Tower, 1983, Kazakhstan	1,214	370
10	TV Tower, 1969, Berlin, Germany	1,198	365

TOP 10 ★
TALLEST MASTS

	MAST/LOCATION	HEIGHT FT	M
1	KVLY Channel 11 TV Tower (formerly KTHI-TV), Blanchard/Fargo, North Dakota,	2,063	629
2	KSLA-TV Mast, Shreveport, Louisiana	1,898	579
3	=WBIR-TV Mast, Knoxville, Tennessee	1,749	533
	=WTVM & WRBL TV Mast, Columbus, Georgia	1,749	533
5	KFVS TV Mast, Cape Girardeau, Missouri	1,676	511
6	WPSD-TV Mast, Paducah, Kentucky	1,638	499
7	WGAN TV Mast, Portland, Maine	1,619	493
8	KWTV TV Mast, Oklahoma City, Oklahoma	1,572	479
9	BREN Tower, Area 25, Nevada Test Site, Nevada	1,530	465
10	Omega Base Navigational Mast, Gippsland, Victoria, Australia	1,400	426

TOP 10 HIGHEST PUBLIC OBSERVATORIES

	BUILDING/LOCATION	OBSERVATORY	YEAR	HEIGHT FT	M
1	CN Tower, Toronto, Canada	Space deck	1975	447	1,465
2	World Trade Center, New York, NY	Rooftop Tower B	1973	415	1,360
3	Sears Tower, Chicago, IL	103rd floor	1974	412	1,353
4	Empire State Building, New York, NY	102nd floor Outdoor observatory	1931	381 320	1,250 1,050
5	Ostankino Tower, Moscow, Russia	5th floor turret	1967	360	1,181
6	Oriental Pearl Broadcasting Tower, Shanghai, China	VIP observation level Public observation level	1995	350 263	1,148 863
7	Jin Mao Building, Shanghai, China	88th floor	1997	340	1,115
8	John Hancock Center, Chicago, IL	94th floor	1968	314	1,030
9	Sky Central Plaza, Guanghshou, China	90th floor	1996	310	1,016
10	KL Tower, Kuala Lumpur, Malaysia	Revolving restaurant Public observation level	1995	282 276	925 907

TALLEST BY FAR
The world's tallest free-standing structure, the CN Tower in Toronto, Canada, attracts almost 2 million visitors a year to its space deck level at 1,465 ft (447 m).

Bridges & Other Structures

TOP 10 ★
LONGEST ROAD TUNNELS

TUNNEL/YEAR	LOCATION	LENGTH MILES	KM
1 Laerdal, 2000	Norway	15.22	24.50
2 St. Gotthard, 1980	Switzerland	10.14	16.32
3 Arlberg, 1978	Austria	8.69	13.98
4 =Fréjus, 1980	France/Italy	8.02	12.90
=Pinglin Highway, U/C	Taiwan	8.02	12.90
6 Mont-Blanc, 1965	France/Italy	7.21	11.60
7 Gudvangen, 1992	Norway	7.08	11.43
8 Folgefonn, 2001	Norway	6.90	11.10
9 Kan-Etsu II, 1991	Japan	6.87	11.06
10 Kan-Etsu I, 1986	Japan	6.79	10.93

U/C = under construction

TOP 10 ★
LONGEST STEEL ARCH BRIDGES

BRIDGE/YEAR/LOCATION	LONGEST SPAN FT	M
1 New River Gorge, 1977, Fayetteville, West Virginia	1,700	518
2 Kill Van Kull, 1931, Bayonne, New Jersey/ Staten Island, New York	1,654	504
3 Sydney Harbour, 1932, Australia	1,650	503
4 Fremont, 1973, Portland, Oregon	1,257	383
5 Port Mann, 1964, Vancouver, Canada	1,200	366
6 Thatcher Ferry, 1962, Panama Canal	1,128	344
7 Laviolette, 1967, Quebec, Canada	1,100	335
8 =Runcorn–Widnes, 1961, UK	1,082	330
=Zdákov, 1967, Lake Orlik, Czech Republic	1,082	330
10 =Birchenough, 1935, Fort Victoria, Zimbabwe	1,080	329
=Roosevelt Lake, 1990, Arizona	1,080	329

SHANGHAI SURPRISE

One of the world's longest cable-stayed bridges, Shanghai's Yang Pu was built to ease traffic congestion on the city's busy inner ring road.

TOP 10 ★
LARGEST SPORTS STADIUMS

STADIUM/LOCATION	CAPACITY
1 Strahov Stadium, Prague, Czech Republic	240,000
2 Maracaña Municipal Stadium, Rio de Janeiro, Brazil	220,000
3 Rungnado Stadium, Pyongyang, South Korea	150,000
4 National Stadium of Iran, Azadi, Iran	128,000
5 Estádio Maghalaes Pinto, Belo Horizonte, Brazil	125,000
6 =Estádio Morumbi, São Paulo, Brazil	120,000
=Estádio da Luz, Lisbon, Portugal	120,000
=Senayan Main Stadium, Jakarta, Indonesia	120,000
=Yuba Bharati Krirangan, Nr. Calcutta, India	120,000
10 Estádio Castelão, Fortaleza, Brazil	119,000

These figures represent maximum capacities. In fact, new safety regulations introduced in many countries mean that actual audiences for most events are smaller. The Aztec Stadium, Mexico City, holds 107,000, with most of the seats under cover. The New Orleans Superdome is the largest indoor stadium, with a capacity of 97,365. The Michigan Football Stadium, Ann Arbor, MI, built in 1927, is the largest outdoor stadium in the US, with a seating capacity of 107,501. The largest stadium in the UK is Wembley Stadium, with a capacity of 80,000. This is being replaced with a new National Stadium, with a capacity of 90,000, scheduled for completion in 2003.

TOP 10 ★
LONGEST CABLE-STAYED BRIDGES

BRIDGE/YEAR/LOCATION	LENGTH OF MAIN SPAN FT	M
1 Tatara, 1999, Onomichi–Imabari, Japan	2,920	890
2 Pont de Normandie, 1994, Le Havre, France	2,808	856
3 Qinghzhou Minjiang, 1996, Fozhou, China	1,985	605
4 Yang Pu, 1993, Shanghai, China	1,975	602
5 =Meiko–Chuo, 1997, Nagoya, Japan	1,936	590
=Xu Pu, 1997, Shanghai, China	1,936	590
7 Skarnsundet, 1991, Trondheim Fjord, Norway	1,739	530
8 Tsurumi Tsubasa, Yokohama, Japan	1,673	510
9 =Ikuchi, 1994, Onomichi–Imabari, Japan	1,608	490
=Öresund, 2000, Copenhagen–Malmö, Denmark/Sweden)	1,608	490

TOP 10 ⭐
LONGEST CANTILEVER BRIDGES

BRIDGE/YEAR/LOCATION	LONGEST SPAN FT	M
1 **Pont de Québec**, 1917, Canada	1,800	549
2 **Firth of Forth**, 1890, Scotland	1,710	521
3 **Minato**, 1974, Osako, Japan	1,673	510
4 **Commodore John Barry**, 1974, New Jersey/Pennsylvania	1,622	494
5 =**Greater New Orleans 1**, 1958, Louisiana	1,575	480
=**Greater New Orleans 2**, 1988, Louisiana	1,575	480
7 **Howrah**, 1943, Calcutta, India	1,500	457
8 **Gramercy**, 1995, Louisiana	1,460	445
9 **Transbay**, 1936, San Francisco	1,400	427
10 **Baton Rouge**, 1969, Louisiana	1,235	376

TOP 10 ⭐
LONGEST UNDERWATER TUNNELS

TUNNEL/YEAR/LOCATION	LENGTH MILES	KM
1 **Seikan**, 1988, Japan	33.49	53.90
2 **Channel Tunnel**, 1994, France/England	31.03	49.94
3 **Dai–Shimizu**, 1982, Japan	13.78	22.17
4 **Shin–Kanmon**, 1975, Japan	11.61	18.68
5 **Great Belt Fixed Link** (Eastern Tunnel), 1997, Denmark	4.97	8.00
6 **Bømlafjord***, 2000, Norway	4.86	7.82
7 **Oslofjord***, 2000, Norway	4.59	7.39
8 **Severn**, 1886, UK	4.36	7.01
9 **Magerøysund***, 1999, Norway	4.27	6.87
10 **Haneda**, 1971, Japan	3.72	5.98

* Road; others rail

The need to connect the Japanese islands of Honshu, Kyushu, and Hokkaido has resulted in a wave of undersea tunnel building in recent years, with the Seikan the most ambitious project of all. Connecting Honshu and Hokkaido, 14.4 miles (23.3 km) of the tunnel is 328 ft (100 m) below the seabed. It took 24 years to complete.

TOP 10 ⭐
HIGHEST DAMS

DAM/RIVER/LOCATION	YEAR	HEIGHT FT	M
1 **Rogun**, Vakhsh, Tajikistan	U/C	1,099	335
2 **Nurek**, Vakhsh, Tajikistan	1980	984	300
3 **Grande Dixence**, Dixence, Switzerland	1961	935	285
4 **Inguri**, Inguri, Georgia	1980	892	272
5 **Vajont**, Vajont, Italy	1960	860	262
6 =**Manuel M. Torres (Chicoasén)**, Grijalva, Mexico	1980	856	261
=**Tehri**, Bhagirathi, India	U/C	856	261
8 **Alvaro Obregon (El Gallinero)**, Tenasco, Mexico	1946	853	260
9 **Mauvoisin**, Drance de Bagnes, Switzerland	1957	820	250
10 **Alberto Lleras C.**, Guavio, Colombia	1989	797	243

U/C = under construction

Source: *International Commission on Large Dams (ICOLD)*

TOP 10 ⭐
LONGEST SUSPENSION BRIDGES

BRIDGE/YEAR/LOCATION	LENGTH OF MAIN SPAN FT	M
1 **Akashi–Kaiko**, 1998, Kobe–Naruto, Japan	6,529	1,990
2 **Great Belt**, 1997, Denmark	5,328	1,624
3 **Humber Estuary**, 1981, UK	4,626	1,410
4 **Jiangyin**, 1998, China	4,544	1,385
5 **Tsing Ma**, 1997, Hong Kong, China	4,518	1,377
6 **Verrazano Narrows**, 1964, New York	4,260	1,298
7 **Golden Gate**, 1937, San Francisco	4,200	1,280
8 **Höga Kusten**, 1997, Veda, Sweden	3,970	1,210
9 **Mackinac Straits**, 1957, Michigan	3,800	1,158
10 **Minami Bisan-seto**, 1988, Kojima–Sakaide, Japan	3,609	1,100

The Messina Strait Bridge between Sicily and Calabria, Italy, remains a speculative project but, if constructed according to plan, it will have by far the longest center span of any bridge at 10,892 ft (3,320 m). However, at 12,828 ft (3,910 m), Japan's Akashi–Kaiko bridge, completed in 1998 and with a main span of 6,528 ft (1,990 m), is the world's longest overall.

DAM RECORD BUSTER

An incongruous mural depicting Lenin celebrates this Soviet engineering accomplishment, the building of the world's second highest dam, the Nurek in Tajikistan.

Background image: **PONT DE QUÉBEC CANADA**

Where is the tallest mast outside the US?
see p.91 for the answer
A Germany
B Australia
C China

青が散る　宮本輝　み

Culture & Learning

Word Power

LONGEST WORDS IN THE ENGLISH LANGUAGE*

WORD/MEANING   LETTERS

1 Ornicopytheobibliopsychocrystarroscioaerogenethliometeoroaustrohiero-
anthropoichthyopyrosiderochpnomyoalectryoophiobotanopegohydrorhab-
docrithoaleuroalphitohalomolybdoclerobeloaxinocoscinodactyliogeolitho-
pessopsephocatoptrotephraoneirochiroonychodactyloarithstichooxogelo-
scogastrogyrocerobletonooenoscapulinaniac   310

Medieval scribes used this word to refer to "A deluded human who practices divination or forecasting by means of phenomena, interpretation of acts, or other manifestations related to the following animate or inanimate objects and appearances: birds, oracles, Bible, ghosts, crystal gazing, shadows, air appearances, birth stars, meteors, winds, sacrificial appearances, entrails of humans and fishes, fire, red-hot irons, altar smoke, mice, grain picking by rooster, snakes, herbs, fountains, water, wands, dough, meal, barley, salt, lead, dice, arrows, hatchet balance, sieve, ring suspension, random dots, precious stones, pebbles, pebble heaps, mirrors, ash writing, dreams, palmistry, nail rays, finger rings, numbers, book passages, name letterings, laughing manners, ventriloquism, circle walking, wax, susceptibility to hidden springs, wine, and shoulder blades."

2 Lopadotemachoselachogaleokranioleipsanodrimhypotrimmatosilphioparao-
melitokatakechymenokichlepikossyphophattoperisteralektryonoptekephall-
iokigklopeleiolagoiosiraiobaphetraganopterygon   182

The English transliteration of a 170-letter Greek word that appears in The Ecclesiazusae (a comedy by the Greek playwright Aristophanes, c.448–380 BC). It is used as a description of a 17-ingredient dish.

3 Aequeosalinocalcalinosetaceoaluminosocupreovitriolic   52

Invented by a medical writer, Dr. Edward Strother (1675–1737), to describe the spa waters at Bath.

4 Osseocarnisanguineoviscericartilaginonervomedullary   51

Coined by writer and East India Company official Thomas Love Peacock (1785–1866), and used in his satire Headlong Hall (1816) as a description of the structure of the human body.

5 Pneumonoultramicroscopicsilicovolcanoconiosis   45

It first appeared in print (though ending in "-koniosis") in F. Scully's Bedside Manna [sic] (1936), then found its way into Webster's Dictionary and is now in the Oxford English Dictionary. It is said to mean a lung disease caused by breathing fine dust.

6 Hepaticocholecystostcholecystenterostomies   42

Surgical operations to create channels of communication between gall bladders and hepatic ducts or intestines.

7 Praetertranssubstantiationalistically   37

The adverb describing the act of surpassing the act of transubstantiation; the word is found in Mark McShane's novel Untimely Ripped (1963).

8= Pseudoantidisestablishmentarianism   34

A word meaning "false opposition to the withdrawal of state support from a Church," derived from that perennial favorite long word, antidisestablishmentarianism (a mere 28 letters).

= Supercalifragilisticexpialidocious   34

An invented word, but perhaps now eligible since it has appeared in the Oxford English Dictionary. It was popularized by the song of this title in the film Mary Poppins (1964), where it is used to mean "wonderful," but it was originally written in 1949 in an unpublished song by Parker and Young who spelled it "supercalafajalistickespialadojus" (32 letters).

10= Encephalomyeloradiculoneuritis   30

A syndrome caused by a virus associated with encephalitis.

= Hippopotomonstrosesquipedalian   30

Appropriately, the word that means "pertaining to an extremely long word."

= Pseudopseudohypoparathyroidism   30

First used (hyphenated) in the US in 1952 and (unhyphenated) in Great Britain in The Lancet in 1962 to describe a medical case in which a patient appeared to have symptoms of pseudohypoparathyroidism, but with "no manifestations suggesting hypoparathyroidism."

* Excluding names of chemical compounds

MOST USED LETTERS IN WRITTEN ENGLISH

SURVEY*		#MORSE
e	1	e
t	2	t
a	3	a
o	4	i
i	5	n
n	6	o
s	7	s
r	8	h
h	9	r
l	10	d

* The order as indicated by a survey across approximately 1 million words appearing in a wide variety of printed texts, ranging from newspapers to novels.

 # The order estimated by Samuel Morse, the inventor in the 1830s of Morse code, based on his calculations of the respective quantities of type used by a printer. The number of letters in the printer's type trays ranged from 12,000 for "e" to 4,400 for "d," with only 200 for "z."

MOST COMMON WORDS IN ENGLISH

SPOKEN ENGLISH		WRITTEN ENGLISH
the	1	the
and	2	of
I	3	to
to	4	in
of	5	and
a	6	a
you	7	for
that	8	was
in	9	is
it	10	that

Various surveys have been conducted to establish the most common words in spoken English of various types, from telephone conversations to broadcast commentaries. Beyond the Top 10, words such as "yes" and "well" appear.

Did You Know? Honorificabilitudinitatibus (27 letters), which means "honorably," is the longest word used by Shakespeare; it appears in *Love's Labour's Lost* (Act V, Scene i).

TOP 10 ★
COUNTRIES WITH THE MOST ENGLISH-LANGUAGE SPEAKERS*

	COUNTRY	APPROXIMATE NO. OF SPEAKERS
1	US	232,910,000
2	UK	57,520,000
3	Canada	18,655,000
4	Australia	15,204,000
5	South Africa	3,900,000
6	Ireland	3,590,000
7	New Zealand	3,309,000
8	Jamaica	2,400,000
9	Trinidad and Tobago	1,199,000
10	Guyana	749,000

Inhabitants for whom English is their mother tongue

The Top 10 represents the countries with the greatest numbers of inhabitants who speak English as their mother tongue. After the 10th entry, the figures dive to around or under 260,000, in the case of the Bahamas, Barbados, and Zimbabwe. In addition to these and others that make up a world total that is probably in excess of 500 million, there are perhaps as many as 1 billion who speak English as a second language: a large proportion of the population of the Philippines, for example, speaks English, and there are many countries, such as India, Nigeria, and other former British colonies in Africa, where English is either an official language or is widely understood.

THE ROSETTA STONE

Made in Egypt in around 200 BC and discovered in 1799 during the French occupation of Egypt, the Rosetta Stone was taken to England in 1801 and is now in the British Museum, London. It has the same inscription in three different alphabets – Egyptian hieroglyphics at the top, demotic Egyptian in the middle, and Greek below. After a painstaking study of the relationship between the different alphabets, French scholar Jean François Champollion (1790–1832) was able to decipher the hieroglyphics, all knowledge of which had previously been lost. The Rosetta Stone thus provided the key to our understanding of this ancient language.

SNAP SHOTS★

TOP 10 ★
MOST WIDELY SPOKEN LANGUAGES

	LANGUAGE	APPROXIMATE NO. OF SPEAKERS
1	Chinese (Mandarin)	1,075,000,000
2	English	514,000,000
3	Hindustani	496,000,000
4	Spanish	425,000,000
5	Russian	275,000,000
6	Arabic	256,000,000
7	Bengali	215,000,000
8	Portuguese	194,000,000
9	Malay-Indonesian	176,000,000
10	French	129,000,000

According to mid-1999 estimates by Emeritus Professor Sidney S. Culbert of the University of Washington, in addition to those languages appearing in the Top 10, there are three further languages that are spoken by more than 100 million individuals: German (128 million), Japanese (126 million), and Urdu (105 million). A further 13 languages are spoken by 50–100 million people: Punjabi (94), Korean (78), Telugu (76), Tamil (74), Marathi (71), Cantonese (71), Wu (70), Vietnamese (67), Javanese (64), Italian (63), Turkish (61), Tagalog (58), and Thai (52).

TOP 10 MOST STUDIED FOREIGN LANGUAGES IN THE US*

❶ Spanish ❷ French ❸ German
❹ Japanese ❺ Italian
❻ Chinese (Mandarin) ❼ Latin
❽ Russian
❾ Ancient Greek ❿ Hebrew

* In US institutions of higher education
Source: *Modern Language Association of America*
These rankings are from the most recent survey conducted every five years, from colleges and universities in the fall of 1995.

TOP 10 ★
LANGUAGES OFFICIALLY SPOKEN IN THE MOST COUNTRIES

	LANGUAGE	COUNTRIES
1	English	57
2	French	33
3	Arabic	23
4	Spanish	21
5	Portuguese	8
6	= Dutch	4
	= German	4
8	= Chinese (Mandarin)	3
	= Danish	3
	= Italian	3
	= Malay	3

There are many countries in the world with more than one official language – both English and French are recognized officially in Canada, for example. English is used in numerous countries as the lingua franca – the common language that enables people who speak mutually unintelligible languages to communicate with each other.

97

Children in School

China has the most children in school and the world's longest school year, but spends just 2 percent of its GNP on education – less than half that of Western countries.

TOP 10 ★
COUNTRIES SPENDING THE MOST ON EDUCATION

COUNTRY	EXPENDITURE AS PERCENTAGE OF GNP*
1 Kiribati	11.4
2 Moldova	9.4
3 Namibia	8.4
4 Botswana	7.8
5 Denmark	7.7
6 South Africa	7.5
7 Barbados	7.3
8 =Finland	7.2
=Zimbabwe	7.2
10 Sweden	7.1
US	4.7

* Gross National Product in latest year for which data available

Source: *UNESCO*

A number of other countries rank high in this list, but there are insufficient recent data to include them. In 1980, French Guiana spent 16.5 percent of its GNP on education, Martinique 14.5 percent, and Guadeloupe 13.6 percent. The US and UK do not make it into the Top 20.

TOP 10 COUNTRIES WITH THE LONGEST SCHOOL YEARS

(Country/school year in days)

1 China, 251 **2** Japan, 243 **3** Korea, 220 **4** Israel, 215 **5** = Germany, 210; = Russia, 210 **7** Switzerland, 207 **8** = Netherlands, 200; = Scotland, 200; = Thailand, 200

US, 180

THE 10 ★
COUNTRIES WITH THE MOST PRIMARY SCHOOL PUPILS PER TEACHER

COUNTRY	PRIMARY SCHOOL PUPILS PER TEACHER*
1 Central African Republic	77
2 Congo	70
3 Mali	70
4 Chad	67
5 Malawi	59
6 Bangladesh	63
7 =Afghanistan	58
=Mozambique	58
=Rwanda	58
=Senegal	58
US	16

* In latest year for which figures available

Source: *UNESCO*

TOP 10 ★
STATES WITH THE HIGHEST HIGH SCHOOL GRADUATION RATES

STATE	PERCENTAGE RATE
1 Washington	92.0
2 Alaska	90.6
3 Wyoming	90.0
4 Colorado	89.6
5 Minnesota	89.4
6 Utah	89.3
7 Kansas	89.2
8 =Montana	89.1
=Nevada	89.1
10 Wisconsin	88.0

Source: Statistical Abstract of the United States

The average graduation for the US was 82.8 percent. The state with the lowest rate was West Virginia, with 76.4 percent.

"ACADEMY"

Fabled queen Helen of Troy ("the face that launched a thousand ships") was kidnapped from Sparta by Theseus and later rescued by her brothers Castor and Pollux. They were assisted in their task by an Athenian named Academus. A grove or public garden called the Grove of Academus was planted in Athens to commemorate this event. It was here that the Greek philosopher Plato founded his school of philosphy, where like-minded scholars could gather to listen to his orations and discuss moral issues. This school was called the Academia, from which we have the word "academy."

WHY DO WE SAY?

EDUCATING THE MASSES
Indian culture places a high value on education, and consequently some 7 percent of the country's entire population attends secondary school.

COUNTRIES WITH THE MOST SECONDARY SCHOOL PUPILS

	COUNTRY	SECONDARY SCHOOL PUPILS
1	China	69,155,538
2	India	68,872,393
3	US	21,473,692
4	Russia	13,732,000
5	Indonesia	12,223,753
6	Japan	9,878,568
7	Iran	8,776,792
8	Germany	8,260,674
9	Mexico	7,589,414
10	Egypt	6,726,738

In the US, about 8 percent of the population attends secondary school – a figure that shows how impressive India's rate of 7 percent is.

Source: *UNESCO*

COUNTRIES WITH THE HIGHEST ILLITERACY RATES*

COUNTRY	FEMALE ILLITERACY RATE (%)		MALE ILLITERACY RATE (%)	COUNTRY
Niger	93.4	1	79.1	Niger
Burkina Faso	90.8	2	71.7	Nepal
Guinea-Bissau	85.5	3	70.5	Burkina Faso
Afghanistan	85.0	4	60.6	Mali
Yemen	82.8	5	59.3	Guinea-Bissau
Sierra Leone	81.8	6	57.0	Senegal
= Central African Republic	79.7	7	54.6	Sierra Leone
= Nepal	79.7	8	54.5	Ethiopia
Guinea	78.1	9	52.8	Afghanistan
Liberia	77.6	10	52.0	Central African Republic

* Age over 15; figures estimated where no recent data available Source: *UNESCO*

The United Nations defines an illiterate person as someone who cannot, with understanding, both read and write a short, simple statement on his or her daily life. Literacy is a good measure of educational achievement in developing regions, because it reflects successful schooling, not just attendance at school as is measured by enrolment figures. The Top 10 list shows that in some countries of the world, the majority of the population cannot read or write.

COUNTRIES WITH THE HIGHEST PERCENTAGE OF MALE SECONDARY SCHOOL TEACHERS

	COUNTRY	SECONDARY SCHOOL TEACHERS	MALE (%)*
1	Chad	2,598	96
2 =	Bangladesh	128,389	90
=	Dem. Rep. of Congo	59,325	90
=	Mauritania	1,600	90
5 =	Ethiopia	25,075	89
=	Togo	4,736	89
7 =	Burkina Faso	3,346	88
=	Equatorial Guinea	466	88
=	Guinea	4,690	88
=	Nepal	25,357	88
	US	1,394,080	56

* In latest year for which figures available

Whose notebooks are known as *The Codex Hammer*?
see p.102 for the answer

A Mozart
B Leonardo da Vinci
C Marco Polo

Higher Education

CRÈME DE LA CRÈME

Between the late 1960s and 1970, the University of Paris was split into 13 separate establishments, which comprise the world's largest higher education body.

TOP 10 ★ LARGEST UNIVERSITIES

	UNIVERSITY/LOCATION	STUDENTS
1	**University of Paris***, France	311,163
2	**University of Calcutta**, India	300,000
3	**University of Mexico**, Mexico	269,000
4	**University of Bombay**, India	262,350
5	**University of Guadalajara**, Mexico	214,986
6	**University of Rome**, Italy	189,000
7	**University of Buenos Aires**, Argentina	183,397
8	**University of Rajasthan**, India	175,000
9	**University of California**, US	157,331
10	**Gujarat University**, India	153,379

* *Divided into numerous separate centers; the figure is for the combined total of all the centers.*

The huge number of university institutions in India reflects not only the country's massive population and the high value placed on education in Indian culture, but also the inclusion of many "Affiliating and Teaching" colleges attached to universities.

TOP 10 ★ COUNTRIES WITH THE HIGHEST PERCENTAGE OF FEMALE UNIVERSITY STUDENTS

	COUNTRY	PERCENTAGE OF FEMALE STUDENTS*
1	**Cyprus**	75
2	**US Virgin Islands**	74
3	**Qatar**	73
4	**United Arab Emirates**	72
5	**Kuwait**	66
6	**Namibia**	65
7	**Myanmar**	64
8	**Barbados**	62
9	**Mongolia**	61
10=	**Bulgaria**	60
=	**Cuba**	60
=	**Panama**	60

* *In latest year for which data available*
Source: *UNESCO*

THE 10 ★ COUNTRIES WITH THE LOWEST PERCENTAGE OF FEMALE UNIVERSITY STUDENTS

	COUNTRY	PERCENTAGE OF FEMALE STUDENTS*
1	**Equatorial Guinea**	4
2=	**Central African Republic**	9
=	**Guinea**	9
4	**Chad**	12
5=	**Eritrea**	13
=	**Yemen**	13
7	**Mali**	14
8	**Mauritania**	15
9	**Cambodia**	16
10=	**Ethiopia**	17
=	**Tanzania**	17
=	**Togo**	17

* *In latest year for which data available*
Source: *UNESCO*

WOMAN'S WORK

Women study separately but in large numbers at the United Arab Emirates University in Al-Ain, which was founded in 1976.

TOP 10 COUNTRIES OF ORIGIN OF FOREIGN STUDENTS STUDYING IN THE US

(Country/students)

1 Japan, 45,531 **2** Rep. of Korea, 36,231
3 India, 31,743 **4** Canada, 23,005
5 Malaysia, 14,015 **6** Indonesia, 12,820
7 Hong Kong, 12,018 **8** Germany, 9,017
9 Mexico, 8,687 **10** Turkey, 7,678

Source: *Modern Language Association of America*

TOP 10 HOST COUNTRIES FOR US FOREIGN STUDENTS

(Country/students)

1 UK, 8,600 **2** Germany, 4,225
3 France, 3,392 **4** Canada, 2,687
5 China, 2,213 **6** Japan, 1,164
7 Philippines, 1,118 **8** Ireland, 937
9 Australia, 903 **10** Norway, 565

TOP 10 ★
COUNTRIES WITH THE MOST UNIVERSITY STUDENTS

	COUNTRY	PERCENTAGE FEMALE	UNIVERSITY STUDENTS*
1	US	53	8,529,132
2	India	32	4,425,247
3	China	36	3,170,936
4	Russia	53	2,587,510
5	Japan	29	2,311,618
6	Philippines	57	2,017,972
7	Indonesia	31	1,889,408
8	Germany	42	1,857,906
9	Brazil	53	1,716,263
10	Korea	32	1,556,949

* In latest year for which data available
Source: *UNESCO*

GRADUATION DAY

Decked in their traditional tasseled mortar boards and gowns, more students graduate from US universities than from those of any other country.

TOP 10 ★
EDUCATION AND CULTURE CHARITIES IN THE US

	ORGANIZATION	ANNUAL REVENUE ($)
1	Smithsonian Institution	389,769,714
2	The Metropolitan Museum of Art	345,871,722
3	Metropolitan Opera Association, Inc.	194,012,000
4	Art Institute of Chicago	188,387,076
5	Colonial Williamsburg Foundation	164,493,241
6	American Museum of Natural History	159,814,425
7	Museum of Modern Art	150,860,642
8	Museum of Fine Arts, Boston	133,990,465
9	National Gallery of Art	126,920,029
10	J. F. Kennedy Center for the Performing Arts	112,899,574

Source: *NonProfit Times*

TOP 10 ★
COUNTRIES WITH THE HIGHEST PROPORTION OF ADULTS IN HIGHER EDUCATION

	COUNTRY	TOTAL ADULT STUDENTS	ADULT STUDENTS PER 100,000*
1	Canada	1,763,105	5,997
2	Korea	2,541,659	5,609
3	Australia	1,002,476	5,552
4	US	14,261,778	5,339
5	New Zealand	162,350	4,508
6	Finland	213,995	4,190
7	Norway	180,383	4,164
8	Spain	1,591,863	4,017
9	Ireland	47,955	3,618
10	France	2,091,688	3,600

* In latest year for which data available
Source: *UNESCO*

Where would you find the 270-ft (82-m) tall statue of Motherland?

see p.110 for the answer

A Volgograd, Russia
B Kiev, Ukraine
C Prague, Czech Republic

Book Firsts & Records

TOP 10 MOST CITED AUTHORS OF ALL TIME
(Author/country/dates)

1 **William Shakespeare**, UK, 1564–1616 **2** **Charles Dickens**, UK, 1812–70
3 **Sir Walter Scott**, UK, 1771–1832 **4** **Johann Goethe**, Germany, 1749–1832
5 **Aristotle**, Greece, 384–322 BC **6** **Alexandre Dumas (père)**, France, 1802–70
7 **Robert Louis Stevenson**, UK, 1850–94 **8** **Mark Twain**, US, 1835–1910
9 **Marcus Tullius Cicero**, Italy, 106–43 BC **10** **Honoré de Balzac**, France, 1799–1850

This Top 10 is based on a search of a major US library computer database, Citations, which includes books both by and about the author, with a total of more than 15,000 for Shakespeare.

TOP 10 ★ LARGEST LIBRARIES

LIBRARY	LOCATION	FOUNDED	BOOKS
1 Library of Congress	Washington, DC	1800	23,994,965
2 National Library of China	Beijing, China	1909	20,000,000
3 National Library of Canada	Ottawa, Canada	1953	16,000,000
4 Deutsche Bibliothek*	Frankfurt, Germany	1990	15,997,000
5 British Library#	London, UK	1753	15,000,000
6 Harvard University Library	Cambridge, Massachusetts	1638	13,617,133
7 Vernadsky Central Scientific Library of the National Academy of Sciences	Kiev, Ukraine	1919	13,000,000
8 Russian State Library+	Moscow, Russia	1862	11,750,000
9 New York Public Library★	New York	1895	11,445,971
10 Bibliotheque Nationale de Paris	Paris, France	1400	11,000,000

* *Formed in 1990 through the unification of the Deutsche Bibliothek, Frankfurt (founded 1947) and the Deutsche Bucherei, Leipzig*

Founded as part of the British Museum, 1753; became an independent body in 1973

+ *Founded 1862 as Rumyantsev Library, formerly State V. I. Lenin Library*

★ *Astor Library founded 1848, consolidated with Lenox Library and Tilden Trust to form New York Public Library in 1895*

The figures for books in such vast collections as held by the libraries listed above represent only a fraction of the total collections, which include manuscripts, microfilms, maps, prints, and records. The Library of Congress has perhaps more than 100 million cataloged items and the New York Public Library more than 26 million manuscripts, maps, audio-visual, and other cataloged items in addition to books.

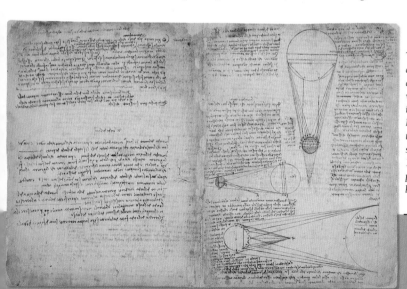

UNDER THE HAMMER
The Codex Hammer, a collection of Leonardo da Vinci's scientific writings, was compiled in the early 16th century. It has over 350 drawings that illustrate the artist's scientific theories. In 1994 it achieved a record price at auction when bought by Bill Gates.

TOP 10 ★ MOST EXPENSIVE BOOKS AND MANUSCRIPTS EVER SOLD AT AUCTION

BOOK OR MANUSCRIPT/SALE	PRICE ($)*

1 **The Codex Hammer**, c.1508–10, Christie's, New York, Nov 11, 1994 — 30,800,000
This Leonardo da Vinci notebook was bought by Bill Gates, the billionaire founder of Microsoft.

2 **The Gospels of Henry the Lion**, c.1173–75, Sotheby's, London, Dec 6, 1983 — 10,841,000
At the time of its sale, this became the most expensive manuscript or book ever sold.

3 **The Birds of America**, John James Audubon, 1827–38, Christie's, New York, Mar 10, 2000 — 8,000,000
This holds the record for any natural history book.

4 **The Canterbury Tales**, Geoffrey Chaucer, c.1476–77, Christie's, London, July 8, 1998 — 7,696,720
Printed by William Caxton and bought by Paul Getty.

5 **The Gutenberg Bible**, 1455, Christie's, New York, Oct 22, 1987 — 5,390,000
This is one of the first books ever printed, by Johann Gutenberg and Johann Fust in 1455.

6 **The Northumberland Bestiary**, c.1250–60, Sotheby's, London, Nov 29, 1990 — 5,049,000
This holds the record for an English manuscript.

7 **The Burdett Psalter and Hours**, 1282–86, Sotheby's, London, June 23, 1998 — 4,517,640
This is the third most expensive illustrated manuscript ever sold.

8 **Autograph manuscript of nine symphonies by Wolfgang Amadeus Mozart**, c.1773–74, Sotheby's, London, May 22, 1987 — 3,854,000
This holds the record for any music manuscript.

9 **The Birds of America**, John James Audubon, 1827–38, Sotheby's, New York, June 6, 1989 — 3,600,000

10 **The Hours of Saint-Lô**, 1470, Sotheby's, New York, Apr 21, 1998 — 3,300,000

* *Excluding premiums*

THE 10 ★
FIRST PUBLICATIONS PRINTED IN ENGLAND
AUTHOR/BOOK

1 *Propositio ad Carolum ducem Burgundiae**

2 Cato, *Disticha de Morbidus*

3 Geoffrey Chaucer, *The Canterbury Tales*

4 *Ordinale seu Pica ad usem Sarum* ("*Sarum Pie*")

5 John Lydgate, *The Temple of Glass*

6 John Lydgate, *Stans Puer Mensam*

7 John Lydgate, *The Horse, the Sheep and the Goose*

8 John Lydgate, *The Churl and the Bird*

9 *Infanta Salvatoris*

10 William Caxton, advertisement for "*Sarum Pie*"

* *This work was printed before September 1476; all the others were printed in either 1476 or 1477.*

THE 10 FIRST POCKET BOOKS*
(Author/title)

1 James Hilton, *Lost Horizon*
2 Dorothea Brande, *Wake Up and Live!*
3 William Shakespeare, *Five Great Tragedies* 4 Thorne Smith, *Topper*
5 Agatha Christie, *The Murder of Roger Ackroyd* 6 Dorothy Parker, *Enough Rope* 7 Emily Brontë, *Wuthering Heights* 8 Samuel Butler, *The Way of All Flesh* 9 Thornton Wilder, *The Bridge of San Luis Rey* 10 Felix Salten, *Bambi*

* *All published in 1939*

"BLURB"
American humorist Frank Gelett Burgess (1866–1951), best known as the author of the nonsense poem *I Never Saw a Purple Cow*, was also the inventor of the word "blurb" – the effusive text used on book jackets to describe the book within. In his book *Are You a Bromide?*, Burgess claimed that its author was Miss Belinda Blurb, whose work was said to be the sensation of the year.

WHY DO WE SAY?

BEST RED AUTHOR
During the Cultural Revolution, Chinese leader Mao Tse-tung (Zedong) became the subject of a personality cult, with his bestselling Quotations ... (Little Red Book) its most potent symbol.

TOP 10 ★
LARGEST LIBRARIES IN THE US

LIBRARY/LOCATION	BOOKS
1 **Library of Congress**, Washington, DC	23,994,965
2 **Harvard University**, Cambridge, MA	13,617,133
3 **New York Public Library**, New York	11,445,971
4 **Yale University**, New Haven, CT	9,932,080
5 **Queens Borough Public Library**, New York	9,237,300
6 **University of Illinois**, Urbana, IL	9,024,928
7 **University of California**, Berkeley, CA	8,628,028
8 **Cincinnati and Hamilton County Public Library**, Cincinnati, OH	8,582,637
9 **Chicago Public Library**, Chicago, OH	8,100,000
10 **Free Library of Philadelphia**, PA	7,891,532

Source: *American Library Association*

TOP 10 ★
BESTSELLING BOOKS OF ALL TIME

BOOK/AUTHOR	FIRST PUBLISHED	APPROX. SALES
1 *The Bible*	c.1451–55	over 6,000,000,000
2 *Quotations from the Works of Mao Tse-tung* (dubbed *Little Red Book* by the Western press)	1966	900,000,000
3 *American Spelling Book* by Noah Webster	1783	up to 100,000,000
4 *The Guinness Book of Records*	1955	over 85,000,000*
5 *World Almanac*	1868	73,500,000*
6 *The McGuffey Readers* by William Holmes McGuffey	1836	60,000,000
7 *The Common Sense Book of Baby and Child Care* by Benjamin Spock	1946	over 50,000,000
8 *A Message to Garcia* by Elbert Hubbard	1899	up to 40,000,000
9 = *In His Steps: "What Would Jesus Do?"* by Rev. Charles Monroe Sheldon	1896	over 30,000,000
= *Valley of the Dolls* by Jacqueline Susann	1966	over 30,000,000

* *Aggregate sales of annual publication*

Which language is not among the world's Top 10?
see p.97 for the answer
A Japanese
B Spanish
C French

103

Bestsellers & Literary Awards

TOP 10 HARDBACK NONFICTION TITLES OF 1999 IN THE US

(Title/author/sales)

1 *Tuesdays With Morrie*, Mitch Alborn, 2,500,000 **2** *The Greatest Generation*, Tom Brokaw, 1,968,597 **3** *Guinness World Records 2000 Millennium Edition*, Guinness Media, 1,908,770 **4** *'Tis*, Frank McCourt, 1,675,000 **5** *Who Moved My Chess?*, Spencer Johnson, 1,000,000 **6** *The Courage to Be Rich*, Suze Orman, 950,584 **7** *The Greatest Generation Speaks*, Tom Brokaw, 936,710 **8** *Sugar Busters!*, H. Leighton Steward, Morrison C. Bethea, Sam S. Andrews, and Luis A. Balart, 762,432 **9** *The Art of Happiness*, Dalai Lama and Howard C. Cutler, 750,744 **10** *The Century*, Peter Jennings and Todd Brewster, 700,000

Source: Publishers Weekly

THE WRITE STUFF

Michael Cunningham made his debut as a novelist in 1990 and rounded off the decade in 1999 by winning the Pulitzer Prize for Fiction.

THE 10 ★ LATEST WINNERS OF THE HUGO AWARDS FOR BEST SCIENCE FICTION NOVEL

YEAR	AUTHOR/TITLE
1999	Connie Willis, *To Say Nothing of the Dog*
1998	Joe Haldeman, *Forever Peace*
1997	Kim Stanley Robinson, *Blue Mars*
1996	Neal Stephenson, *The Diamond Age*
1995	Lois McMaster Bujold, *Mirror Dance*
1994	Kim Stanley Robinson, *Green Mars*
1993	Vernor Vinge, *A Fire Upon the Deep*
1992	Connie Willis, *Doomsday Book*
1991	Lois McMaster Bujold, *Barrayar*
1990	Lois McMaster Bujold, *The Vor Game*

Hugo Awards for science fiction novels, short stories, and other fiction and non fiction works are presented by the World Science Fiction Society. They were established in 1953 as "Science Fiction Achievement Awards for the best science fiction writing." The prize in the Awards' inaugural year was presented to Alfred Bester for *The Demolished Man*.

THE 10 ★ LATEST WINNERS OF THE PULITZER PRIZE FOR FICTION

YEAR	AUTHOR/TITLE
1999	Michael Cunningham, *The Hours*
1998	Philip Roth, *American Pastoral*
1997	Steven Millhauser, *Martin Dressler: The Tale of an American Dreamer*
1996	Richard Ford, *Independence Day*
1995	Carol Shields, *The Stone Diaries*
1994	E. Annie Proulx, *The Shipping News*
1993	Robert Olen Butler, *A Good Scent from a Strange Mountain: Stories*
1992	Jane Smiley, *A Thousand Acres*
1991	John Updike, *Rabbit at Rest*
1990	Oscar Hijuelos, *The Mambo Kings Play Song of Love*

THE 10 ★ LATEST WINNERS OF THE RANDOLPH CALDECOTT MEDAL

YEAR	AUTHOR/TITLE
2000	Simms Taback, *Joseph Had a Little Overcoat*
1999	Jacqueline Briggs Martin, *Snowflake Bentley*
1998	Paul O. Zelinsky, *Rapunzel*
1997	David Wisniewski, *Golem*
1996	Peggy Rathman, *Officer Buckle and Gloria*
1995	Eve Bunting, *Smoky Night*
1994	Allen Say, *Grandfather's Journey*
1993	Emily Arnold McCully, *Mirette on the High Wire*
1992	David Wiesner, *Tuesday*
1991	David Macauley, *Black and White*

THE 10 ★ LATEST WINNERS OF THE WHITBREAD "BOOK OF THE YEAR" AWARD

YEAR	AUTHOR/TITLE
1999	Seamus Heaney, *Beowulf*
1998	Ted Hughes, *Birthday Letters*
1997	Ted Hughes, *Tales from Ovid*
1996	Seamus Heaney, *The Spirit Level*
1995	Kate Atkinson, *Behind the Scenes at the Museum*
1994	William Trevor, *Felicia's Journey*
1993	Joan Brady, *Theory of War*
1992	Jeff Torrington, *Swing Hammer Swing!*
1991	John Richardson, *A Life of Picasso*
1990	Nicholas Mosley, *Hopeful Monsters*

Winning his second Whitbread Award, in 1999 for his translation of the Anglo Saxon poem *Beowulf*, Seamus Heaney controversially only narrowly defeated J. K. Rowling, whose *Harry Potter and the Prisoner of Azkaban* went on to win the "Children's Book of the Year" Award.

Did You Know? Before being filmed, *Gone With the Wind* was the bestselling US novel of both 1936 and 1937, in the latter year winning the Pulitzer prize for Fiction.

TOP 10
CHILDREN'S BOOKS OF 1999 IN THE US

	TITLE	SALES
1	*Harry Potter and the Prisoner of Azkaban*	3,600,000
2	*Harry Potter and the Chamber of Secrets*	3,400,000
3	*Harry Potter and the Sorcerer's Stone*	3,100,000
4	*Love You Forever*	559,865
5	*Goodnight Moon*	515,877
6	*The Cheerios Play Book*	488,962
7	*Green Eggs and Ham*	452,504
8	*Scholastic Children's Dictionary*	444,000
9	*Disney's Tarzan Read-Aloud Storybook*	428,902
10	*Guess How Much I Love You*	420,936

Source: Publishers' Weekly

THE 10 LATEST WINNERS OF THE BOOKER PRIZE
(Year/author/title)

1 1999 J. M. Coetzee, *Disgrace*
2 1998 Ian McEwan, *Amsterdam*
3 1997 Arundhati Roy, *The God of Small Things* **4** 1996 Graham Swift, *Last Orders* **5** 1995 Pat Barker, *The Ghost Road* **6** 1994 James Kelman, *How Late It Was, How Late* **7** 1993 Roddy Doyle, *Paddy Clarke Ha Ha Ha*
8 1992 = Michael Ondaatje, *The English Patient*; = Barry Unsworth, *Sacred Hunger* **10** 1991 Ben Okri, *Famished Road*

The South African writer J. M. Coetzee is the only person to have won the Booker prize twice (*Life and Times of Michael K* in 1983).

FIRST THINGS FIRST
Bengal-born Arundhati Roy achieved fame and fortune with her Booker prize-winning The God of Small Things.

TOP 10
HARDBACK FICTION TITLES OF 1999 IN THE US

	TITLE/AUTHOR	SALES
1	*The Testament*, John Grisham	2,475,000
2	*Hannibal*, Thomas Harris	1,550,000
3	*Assassins*, Jerry B. Jenkins and Tim LaHaye	1,484,752
4	*Star Wars: Episode 1 – The Phantom Menace*, Terry Brooks	1,419,852
5	*Timeline*, Michael Crichton	1,351,800
6	*Hearts in Atlantis*, Stephen King	1,325,000
7	*Apollyon*, Jerry B. Jenkins and Tim LaHaye	1,172,132
8	*The Girl Who Loved Tom Gordon*, Stephen King	1,075,000
9	*Irresistible Forces*, Danielle Steel	975,000
10	*Tara Road*, Maeve Binchy	950,000

Source: Publishers Weekly

THE 10
LATEST WINNERS OF THE NATIONAL BOOK AWARD FOR FICTION

YEAR	AUTHOR/TITLE
1999	Ha Jin, *Waiting*
1998	Alice McDermott, *Charming Billy*
1997	Charles Frazier, *Cold Mountain*
1996	Andrea Barrett, *Ship Fever and Other Stories*
1995	Philip Roth, *Sabbath's Theater*
1994	William Gaddis, *A Frolic of His Own*
1993	E. Annie Proulx, *The Shipping News*
1992	Cormac McCarthy, *All the Pretty Horses*
1991	Norman Rush, *Mating*
1990	Charles Johnson, *Middle Passage*

The National Book Award is presented by the National Book Foundation as part of its program to foster reading in the United States. Past recipients include William Styron's *Sophie's Choice* and John Irving's *The World According to Garp*.

THE 10
LATEST WINNERS OF THE JOHN NEWBERRY MEDAL

YEAR	AUTHOR/TITLE
2000	Christopher Paul Curtis, *Bud, Not Buddy*
1999	Louis Sachar, *Holes*
1998	Karen Hesse, *Out of the Dust*
1997	E. L. Konigsburg, *The View from Saturday*
1996	Karen Cushman, *The Midwife's Apprentice*
1995	Sharon Creech, *Walk Two Moons*
1994	Lois Lowry, *The Giver*
1993	Cynthia Rylant, *Missing May*
1992	Phyllis Reynolds Naylor, *Shiloh*
1991	Jerry Spinelli, *Maniac Magee*

The John Newbery Medal is awarded annually for "the most distinguished contribution to American literature for children." Its first winner in 1923 was Hugh Lofting's *The Voyages of Doctor Dolittle*. The medal is named after John Newbery (1713–67), a London bookseller and publisher who specialized in children's books.

The Press

TOP 10 LONGEST-RUNNING COMIC STRIPS IN THE US

(Comic strip/first published)

1 *Gasoline Alley*, 1918 **2** *Winnie Winkle*, 1920 **3** *Tarzan*, 1929 **4** *Blondie*, 1930 **5** *Dick Tracy*, 1931 **6** *Alley Oop*, 1933 **7** *L'il Abner*, 1934 **8** *The Phantom*, 1936 **9** *Prince Valliant*, 1937 **10** *Nancy*, 1938

Source: ©2000 Gemstone Publishing, Inc.
All rights reserved.

TOP 10 ★ LONGEST-RUNNING MAGAZINES IN THE US

MAGAZINE	FIRST PUBLISHED
1 *Scientific American*	1845
2 *Town & Country*	1846
3 *Harper's**	1850
4 *The Moravian*	1856
5 *The Atlantic#*	1857
6 *Armed Forces Journal+*	1863
7 *The Nation*	1865
8 *American Naturalist*	1867
9 *Harper's Bazaar*	1867
10 *Animals★*	1868

* *Originally* Harper's New Monthly Magazine
\# *Originally* The Atlantic Monthly
\+ *Originally* Army and Navy Journal
★ *Originally* Our Dumb Animals

Source: *Magazine Publishers of America*

TOP 10 ★ MAGAZINES IN THE US

MAGAZINE/NO. OF ISSUES A YEAR	CIRCULATION*
1 *NRTA/AARP Bulletin*, 10	20,444,791
2 *Modern Maturity*, 36	20,369,590
3 *Reader's Digest*, 12	13,368,327
4 *TV Guide*, 52	11,807,043
5 *National Geographic Magazine*, 12	8,618,632
6 *Better Homes and Gardens*, 12	7,600,667
7 *Family Circle*, 17	5,002,255
8 *Good Housekeeping* ,12	4,626,346
9 *Ladies Home Journal*, 12	4,500,404
10 *McCall's*, 12	4,202,995

* *Average for first six months of 1999*
Source: *Magazine Publishers of America*

TOP 10 WOMEN'S MAGAZINES IN THE US

(Magazine/no. of issues a year/circulation)*

1 *Better Homes and Gardens* (12), 7,600,667 **2** *Family Circle* (17), 5,002,255 **3** *Good Housekeeping* (12), 4,626,346 **4** *Ladies Home Journal* (12), 4,500,404 **5** *McCall's* (12), 4,202,995 **6** *Woman's Day* (17), 4,085,214 **7** *Cosmopolitan* (12), 2,879,076 **8** *Redbook* (12), 2,801,385 **9** *Glamour* (12), 2,207,241 **10** *First For Women* (17), 1,506,003

* *Average for first six months of 1999*
Source: *Magazine Publishers of America*

"TABLOID"

The British drug company Burroughs, Wellcome & Co. registered "tabloid" as a trade name on March 14, 1884. Derived from the word "tablet," it was applied to concentrated types of drugs marketed by the firm. By the end of the nineteenth century, "tabloid" was used to describe anything compressed and small. The phrase "tabloid journalism," which described the content of small-format newspapers, soon became so established in the language that the company could no longer claim the word as their trademark.

WHY DO WE SAY ?

TOP 10 ★ DAILY NEWSPAPERS IN THE US

NEWSPAPER	AVERAGE DAILY CIRCULATION*
1 *Wall Street Journal*	1,752,693
2 *USA Today*	1,671,539
3 *New York Times*	1,086,293
4 *Los Angeles Times*	1,078,186
5 *Washington Post*	763,305
6 *New York Daily News*	701,831
7 *Chicago Tribune*	657,690
8 *Long Island Newsday*	574,941
9 *Houston Chronicle*	542,414
10 *Dallas Morning News*	490,249

* *Through September 30, 1999*
Source: *Audit Bureau of Circulations*

Apart from the *Wall Street Journal*, which focuses mainly on financial news, *USA Today* remains the United States' only true national daily newspaper. Historically, America's press has been regionally based, and, in consequence, the top four listed are the only newspapers with million-plus circulations. This contrasts with, for example, the UK, where, despite its comparatively small population, nationwide newspapers dominate the market, five of them achieving sales in excess of 1 million.

SNAP HAPPY

Despite the growth of television, newspaper photographers continue to provide images to feed the insatiable demands of the world's press, often going to extraordinarily intrusive lengths to gain their shots.

RISING SUN

Launched in 1964 as a revamped Daily Herald, British tabloid The Sun has become the world's bestselling English-language daily newspaper.

TOP 10 ★

OLDEST NATIONAL NEWSPAPERS PUBLISHED IN THE US

NEWSPAPER/PUBLISHED	YEAR ESTABLISHED
1 *The Hartford Courant*, Hartford, CT	1764
2 =*Poughkeepsie Journal*, Poughkeepsie, NY	1785
=*The Augusta Chronicle*, Augusta, GA	1785
=*Register Star*, Hudson, NY	1785
5 =*Pittsburgh Post Gazette*, Pittsburgh, PA	1786
=*Daily Hampshire Gazette*, Northampton, MA	1786
7 *The Berkshire Eagle*, Pittsfield, MA	1789
8 *Norwich Bulletin*, Norwich, CT	1791
9 *The Recorder*, Greenfield, MA	1792
10 *Intelligencer Journal*, Lancaster, PA	1794

Source: Editor & Publisher Year Book

Among earlier newspapers no longer extant are the *Boston News-Letter*, first published in 1704 by New England postmaster John Campbell. It measured just 7½ x 12 in (19 x 30 cm) and had a circulation of 300 copies.

TOP 10 NEWSPAPER-READING COUNTRIES

(Country/daily newspapers per 1,000 people)

❶ Norway, 593   ❷ Japan, 580
❸ Finland, 455   ❹ Sweden, 446
❺ South Korea, 394   ❻ Kuwait, 376
❼ UK, 332   ❽ Switzerland, 330
❾ Singapore, 324   ❿ Denmark, 311
US, 212

Source: *World Bank*

TOP 10 ★

ENGLISH-LANGUAGE DAILY NEWSPAPERS

NEWSPAPER	COUNTRY	AVERAGE DAILY CIRCULATION
1 *The Sun*	UK	3,592,000
2 *Daily Mail*	UK	2,300,000
3 *The Mirror*	UK	2,290,000
4 *Wall Street Journal*	US	1,740,000
5 *USA Today*	US	1,653,000
6 *Times of India*	India	1,296,000
7 *The Express*	UK	1,096,000
8 *Los Angeles Times*	US	1,068,000
9 *The New York Times*	US	1,067,000
10 *The Daily Telegraph*	UK	1,026,000

TOP 10 ★

DAILY NEWSPAPERS

NEWSPAPER	COUNTRY	AVERAGE DAILY CIRCULATION
1 *Yomiuri Shimbun*	Japan	14,533,000
2 *Asahi Shimbun*	Japan	12,601,000
3 *Mainichi Shimbun*	Japan	5,846,000
4 *Chunichi Shimbun*	Japan	4,704,000
5 *Bild-Zeitung*	Germany	4,409,000
6 *The Sun*	UK	3,592,000
7 *Daily Mail*	UK	2,300,000
8 *The Mirror*	UK	2,290,000
9 *Wall Street Journal*	US	1,740,000
10 *USA Today*	US	1,653,000

Source: *World Association of Newspapers*

Which object has an area of 8,181 sq ft (760 sq m)?
see p.111 for the answer

A   The largest painting in the Louvre Museum, Paris
B   The robes of the Statue of Liberty
C   The pages of the world's biggest newspaper

Toys & Games

TOP 10 TOYS OF 1999 IN THE US*

1 Furbys **2** Hot Wheels basic cars
3 Star Wars Episode 1 figure #1
4 Barbie Millennium **5** Pokémon
booster packs **6** Furby Babies **7** Barbie
Sun Jamer 4x4 **8** Pokémon deck assistant
9 Sesame Street rock 'n' roll assistant
10 Pokémon Fossil booster packs

* By value of sales
Source: Toy Manufacturers of America, Inc.

TOP 10 ★
BOARD GAMES IN THE US, 1999

	GAME	MANUFACTURER
1	Pokémon Monopoly	Parker Brothers
2	Monopoly	Parker Brothers
3	Trouble	Milton Bradley
4	Pokémon Master Trainer	Milton Bradley
5	Operation	Milton Bradley
6	Connect Four	Milton Bradley
7	Twister	Milton Bradley
8	Disney Wonderful World of Trivia	Mattel
9	Standard Scrabble	Milton Bradley
10	The Game of Life	Milton Bradley

Source: NPD TRSTS Toys Tracking Service

TOP 10 INTERACTIVE ENTERTAINMENT SOFTWARE TITLES IN THE US, 1999*

(Game/format)

1 Pokémon Blue, Gameboy#
2 Pokémon Red, Gameboy# **3** Pokémon
Yellow, Gameboy# **4** Pokémon Pinball,
Gameboy# **5** Pokémon Snap, Nintendo 64#
6 Donkey Kong 64, Nintendo 64#
7 Gran Turismo Racing, Sony Playstation+
8 Super Smash Brothers, Nintendo 64#
9 Driver, Sony Platstation+ **10** Spyro the
Dragon, Sony Platstation+

* Ranked by units sold   # Published by Nintendo
+ Published by Sony
Source: NPD TRSTS Toys Tracking Service

THE 10 ★
TOYS INTRODUCED IN THE US IN 1999

	TOY	MANUFACTURER
1	Star Wars Episode 1 figure #1	Hasbro
2	Barbie Millennium	Mattel
3	Pokémon booster packs	Wizards of the Coast
4	Furby Babies	Tiger Electronics
5	Sesame Street rock 'n' roll assistant	Tyco Preschool
6	Pokémon Fossil booster packs	Wizards of the Coast
7	Disney Walk 'n' Wag Pluto	Mattel
8	Star Wars Episode 1 figure #2	Hasbro
9	Kawasaki new Ninja	Fisher-Price
10	Harley Davidson motorcycle	Fisher-Price

Source: Toy Manufacturers of America, Inc.

TOP 10 ★
MOST LANDED-ON SQUARES IN MONOPOLY®*

US GAME		UK GAME
Illinois Avenue	1	Trafalgar Square
Go	2	Go
B. & O. Railroad	3	Fenchurch Street Station
Free Parking	4	Free Parking
Tennessee Avenue	5	Marlborough Street
New York Avenue	6	Vine Street
Reading Railroad	7	King's Cross Station
St. James Place	8	Bow Street
Water Works	9	Water Works
Pennsylvania Railroad	5	Marylebone Station

* Based on a computer analysis of the probability of landing on each square

Monopoly® is a registered trade mark of Parker Brothers division of Tonka Corporation, US.

TOP 10 ★
HIGHEST-SCORING SCRABBLE® WORDS

	WORD/PLAY	SCORE
1	**QUARTZY**	164/162

(i) Play across a triple-word-score (red) square with the Z on a double-letter-score (light blue) square
(ii) Play across two double-word-score (pink) squares with Q and Y on pink squares

| **2** | **=BEZIQUE** | 161/158 |

(i) Play across a red square with either the Z or the Q on a light blue square
(ii) Play across two pink squares with the B and second E on two pink squares

| | **=CAZIQUE** | 161/158 |

(i) Play across a red square with either the Z or the Q on a light blue square
(ii) Play across two pink squares with the C and E on two pink squares

| **4** | **ZINKIFY** | 158 |

Play across a red square with the Z on a light blue square

| **5** | **=QUETZAL** | 155 |

Play across a red square with either the Q or the Z on a light blue square

| | **=JAZZILY** | 155 |

(Using a blank as one of the Zs) Play across a red square with the non-blank Z on a light blue square

| | **=QUIZZED** | 155 |

(Using a blank as one of the Zs) Play across a red square with the non-blank Z or the Q on a light blue square

| **8** | **=ZEPHYRS** | 152 |

Play across a red square with the Z on a light blue square

| | **=ZINCIFY** | 152 |

Play across a red square with the Z on a light blue square

| | **=ZYTHUMS** | 152 |

Play across a red square with the Z on a light blue square

All the Top 10 words contain seven letters and therefore earn the premium of 50 for using all the letters in the rack. Being able to play them depends on there already being suitable words on the board to which they can be added. In an actual game, the face values of the perpendicular words to which they are joined would also be counted, but these are discounted here as the total score variations would be infinite. Scrabble was invented in the US during the Depression by an unemployed architect, Alfred Butts, and developed in the 1940s by James Brunot.

TOP 10 ★
MOST EXPENSIVE TOYS EVER SOLD AT AUCTION BY CHRISTIE'S EAST, NY

TOY/SALE	PRICE ($)*
1 "The Charles," a fire-hose-reel made by American manufacturer George Brown and Co., c.1875, Dec 1991	231,000
2 Märklin fire station, Dec 1991	79,200
3 Horse-drawn double-decker tram, Dec 1991	71,500
4 Mikado mechanical bank, Dec 1993	63,000
5 Märklin ferris wheel, June 1994	55,200
6 Girl skipping rope mechanical bank, June 1994	48,300
7 Märklin battleship, June 1994	33,350
8 Märklin battleship, June 1994	32,200
9 =Bing keywind open phaeton tinplate automobile, Dec 1992	24,200
=Märklin fire pumper, Dec 1991	24,200

* Including 10 percent buyer's premium

Source: *Christie's East*

The fire-hose-reel at # 1 in this list is the record price paid at auction for a toy other than a doll. Models by the German tinplate maker Märklin, regarded by collectors as the Rolls-Royce of toys, similarly feature among the record prices of auction houses in the UK and other countries, where high prices have also been attained. On both sides of the Atlantic, pristine examples of high-quality mechanical toys (ideally in their original boxes, and unplayed with by the children for whom they were designed) command top dollar prices.

TOP 10 ★
MOST EXPENSIVE TEDDY BEARS SOLD AT AUCTION

BEAR/SALE	PRICE ($)*
1 "Teddy Girl," a 1904 Steiff bear, Christie's, London, Dec 5, 1994	169,928

This bear precisely doubled the previous world record for a teddy bear when it was acquired by Yoshiro Sekiguchi for a museum near Tokyo.

2 "Happy," a dual-plush Steiff teddy bear, 1926, Sotheby's, London, Sep 19, 1989	85,470

Although estimated at $1,000–$1,400, competitive bidding pushed the price up to the then world record, when it was acquired by collector Paul Volpp.

3 "Elliot," a blue Steiff bear, 1908, Christie's, London, Dec 6, 1993	74,275

Produced as a sample for Harrods.

4 "Teddy Edward," a golden mohair teddy bear, Christie's, London, Dec 9, 1996	60,176
5 Black Steiff teddy bear, c.1912, Sotheby's, London, May 18, 1990	45,327
6 Steiff, blank button, brown teddy bear, c.1905, Christie's, London, Dec 8, 1997	35,948
7 "Albert," a Steiff teddy bear, c.1910, Christie's, London, Dec 9, 1996	28,759
8 Steiff teddy bear, Christie's, London, Dec 9, 1996	26,962
9 "Theodore," a miniature Steiff teddy bear, 9 cm (3½ in) tall, c.1948, Christie's, London, Dec 11, 1995	22,705
10 ="Black Jack," black Steiff teddy bear, Christie's, London, May 22, 1997	21,569
=Cinnamon Steiff teddy bear, c.1905, Christie's, London, May 23, 1997	21,569

* Prices include buyer's premium

"TEDDY BEAR"

While on a hunting trip, US President Theodore ("Teddy") Roosevelt refused to shoot a young bear. This became the subject of a famous cartoon by Clifford K. Berryman, published in the *Washington Post*. Immediately afterward, Morris Michtom, a New York shopkeeper, made stuffed bears and, with Roosevelt's permission, advertised them as "Teddy's Bears". Margarete Steiff, a German toymaker, soon began making her toy bears, exporting them to the US to meet demand. **WHY DO WE SAY?**

TOP 10 ★
MOST EXPENSIVE DOLLS SOLD AT AUCTION

DOLL/SALE	PRICE ($)
1 Kämmer and Reinhardt doll, Sotheby's, London, Feb 8, 1994	282,750
2 Kämmer and Reinhardt bisque character doll, German, c.1909, Sotheby's, London, Oct 17, 1996	169,117

(Previously sold at Sotheby's, London, February 16, 1989, for $140,171)

3 Kämmer and Reinhardt bisque character doll, German, c.1909, Sotheby's, London, Oct 17, 1996	143,327
4 Albert Marque bisque character doll, Sotheby's, London, Oct 17, 1996	112,380
5 William and Mary wooden doll, English, c.1690, Sotheby's, London, Mar 24, 1987	110,396
6 Wooden doll, Charles II, 17th century, Christie's, London, May 18, 1989	103,850
7 Albert Marque bisque character doll, Sotheby's, London, Oct 17, 1996	91,748
8 =Albert Marque bisque character doll, Christie's, London, May 23, 1997	89,581
=Pressed bisque swivel-head Madagascar doll, Sotheby's, London, Oct 17, 1996	88,310
10 Shellacked pressed bisque swivel-head doll, Sotheby's, London, Oct 17, 1996	71,117

TOP 10 TOY RETAIL OUTLETS IN THE US, 1999*
(Outlet type/percentage of market share)

❶ **Discount stores**, 41.5 ❷ **National toy stores**, 21.7 ❸ **Other outlets (not toy stores)**, 12.8 ❹ **Mail order**, 5.3 ❺ **Department stores**, 4.1 ❻ **Other toy stores**, 3.7 ❼ **Food/drug stores**, 3.6 ❽ **Card/gift/stationery stores**, 3.1 ❾ **Hobby/craft stores**, 2.7 ❿ **Variety stores**, 1.5

* Ranked by dollar share perentage in 1998   Soure: *Toy Manufacturers of America Inc.*

Which comic book superhero first appeared in 1938?
see p.119 for the answer
A Batman
B Spider-Man
C Superman

TOP 10 ★

TALLEST FREESTANDING STATUES

STATUE/LOCATION	HEIGHT FT	M
1 Chief Crazy Horse, Thunderhead Mountain, South Dakota	563	172
2 Buddha, Tokyo, Japan	394	120
3 The Indian Rope Trick, Riddersberg Säteri, Jönköping, Sweden	337	103
4 Motherland, 1967, Volgograd (formerly Stalingrad), Russia	270	82
5 Buddha, Bamian, Afghanistan	173	53
6 Kannon, Otsubo-yama, near Tokyo, Japan	170	52
7 Statue of Liberty, New York	151	46
8 Christ, Rio de Janeiro, Brazil	125	38
9 Tian Tan (Temple of Heaven) Buddha, Po Lin Monastery, Lantau Island, Hong Kong	112	34
10 Quantum Cloud, Greenwich, London, UK	95	29

1 Chief Crazy Horse Started in 1948 by Polish-American sculptor Korczak Ziolkowski, and continued after his death in 1982 by his widow and eight of his children, this gigantic equestrian statue is even longer than it is high (641 ft/195 m). It is being carved out of the granite mountain by dynamiting and drilling.

2 Buddha This Japanese–Taiwanese project, unveiled in 1993, took seven years to complete and weighs 1,100 tons.

3 The Indian Rope Trick Sculptor Calle Örnemark's 159-ton wooden sculpture depicts a long strand of "rope" held by a fakir, while another figure ascends.

4 Motherland This concrete statue of a woman with a raised sword, designed by Yevgeniy Vuchetich, commemorates the Soviet victory at the Battle of Stalingrad (1942–43).

5 Buddha This dates from the 3rd–4th centuries AD.

6 Kannon The vast statue of the goddess of mercy was unveiled in 1961 in honor of the dead of World War II.

7 Statue of Liberty Designed by Auguste Bartholdi and presented to the US by the people of France, the statue was shipped in sections to Liberty (formerly Bedloes) Island, where it was assembled before being unveiled on October 28, 1886, and restored on July 4, 1986.

8 Christ The work of sculptor Paul Landowski and engineer Heitor da Silva Costa, the figure of Christ was unveiled in 1931.

9 Tian Tan (Temple of Heaven) Buddha This was completed after 20 years' work and was unveiled on December 29, 1993.

10 Quantum Cloud This gigantic steel human figure surrounded by a matrix of steel struts was created in 1999.

TOP 10 BEST-ATTENDED EXHIBITIONS AT THE FINE ARTS MUSEUM, BOSTON

(Exhibition/attendance)

1 *Monet in the 20th Century* (1998), 565,992   **2** *Monet in the Nineties* (1990), 537,502   **3** *Renoir* (1985–86), 515,795   **4** *John Singer Sargent* (1999), 318,707   **5** *Picasso: The Early Years, 1892–1906* (1997–98), 283,423   **6** *Winslow Homer* (1996), 276,922   **7** *A New World: Masterpieces of American Painting 1760–1910* (1983), 264,640   **8** *Herb Ritts: Work* (1996–97), 253,649   **9** *Mary Cassatt: Modern Woman* (1999), 230,750   **10** *Matisse, Picasso and Impressionist Masters from the Cone Collection* (1991–92), 221,886

Source: Museum of Fine Arts, Boston

HIGH AND MIGHTY

The statue of Christ the Redeemer, Rio de Janeiro, Brazil, is 100 ft (30 m) tall and stands on a 22-ft (7-m) pedestal with a chapel inside. It was unveiled in 1931 by the radio pioneer Guglielmo Marconi.

TOP 10 ★

LARGEST PAINTINGS
IN THE LOUVRE MUSEUM, PARIS

PAINTING/ARTIST	SIZE (HEIGHT X WIDTH)	
	FT	M
1 *Interior of Westminster Abbey*, Jean-Pierre Alaux	62 x 131	19.0 x 40.0
2 *Interior of St. Peter's, Rome*, Jean-Pierre Alaux	57 x 131	17.5 x 40.0
3 *Palace Ceiling*, Francesco Fontebasso	26 x 33	8.0 x 10.0
4 *The Marriage Feast at Cana*, Paolo Veronese	22 x 32	6.7 x 9.9
5 *The Coronation of Napoleon*, Jacques-Louis David	20 x 32	6.2 x 9.8
6 *The Battle of Arbela*, Charles Lebrun	15 x 42	4.7 x 12.7
7 *Alexander and Porus*, Charles Lebrun	15 x 41	4.7 x 12.6
8 *Crossing the Granicus*, Charles Lebrun	15 x 40	4.7 x 12.1
9 *The Battle of Eylau*, Antoine-Jean Gros	17 x 26	5.2 x 7.8
10 *Napoleon Visiting the Plague Victims of Jaffa*, Antoine-Jean Gros	17 x 24	5.2 x 7.2

TOP 10 ART EXHIBITIONS, 1999

(Exhibition/venue/total attendance)

① *Van Gogh's van Goghs*, Los Angeles County Museum, 821,004
② *Monet in the 20th Century*, The Royal Academy, London, 739,324
③ *The Maya*, Palazzo Grassi, Venice, 700,000 **④** *Richard Serra*, Bilbao Guggenheim, 675,071 **⑤** *Millet, van Gogh*, Musée d'Orsay, Paris, 661,568 **⑥** *Eduardo Chillida*, Bilbao Guggenheim, 542,770 **⑦** *Van Gogh's van Goghs*, National Gallery of Art, Washington, D.C. 480,496 **⑧** *Egyptian Art in the Age of Pyramids*, Metropolitan Museum of Fine Art, New York City, 473,234 **⑨** *John Singer Sargent*, National Gallery of Art, Washington, D.C. 453,937 **⑩** *Cézanne to van Gogh: Doctor Gachet Collection*, Metropolitan Museum of Fine Art, New York City, 429,024

Source: The Art Newspaper

Art on Sale

TOP 10 ★
MOST EXPENSIVE PAINTINGS EVER SOLD AT AUCTION

PAINTING/ARTIST/SALE	PRICE ($)
1 *Portrait of Dr. Gachet*, **Vincent van Gogh** (Dutch; 1853–90), Christie's, New York, May 15, 1990	75,000,000
2 *Au Moulin de la Galette*, **Pierre-Auguste Renoir** (French; 1841–1919), Sotheby's, New York, May 17, 1990	71,000,000
3 *Portrait de l'Artiste Sans Barbe*, **Vincent van Gogh**, Christie's, New York, Nov 19, 1998	65,000,000
4 *Rideau, Cruchon et Compotier*, **Paul Cézanne** (French; 1839–1906), Sotheby's, New York, May 10, 1999	55,000,000
5 *Les Noces de Pierrette, 1905*, **Pablo Picasso** (Spanish; 1881–1973), Binoche et Godeau, Paris, Nov 30, 1989	51,672,000
6 *Irises*, **Vincent van Gogh**, Sotheby's, New York, Nov 11, 1987	49,000,000
7 *Femme Assise Dans un Jardin*, **Pablo Picasso**, Sotheby's, New York, Nov 10, 1999	45,000,000
8 *Le Rêve*, **Pablo Picasso**, Christie's, New York, Nov 10, 1997	44,000,000
9 *Self Portrait: Yo Picasso*, **Pablo Picasso**, Sotheby's, New York, May 9, 1989	43,500,000
10 *Nu au Fauteuil Noir*, **Pablo Picasso**, Christie's, New York, Nov 9, 1999	41,000,000

TOP 10 ★
ARTISTS WITH MOST WORKS SOLD FOR MORE THAN ONE MILLION DOLLARS

ARTIST	TOTAL VALUE OF WORKS SOLD ($)	NO. OF WORKS SOLD
1 **Pablo Picasso** (Spanish; 1881–1973)	1,187,184,808	257
2 **Claude Monet** (French; 1888–1926)	828,576,015	196
3 **Pierre Auguste Renoir** (French; 1841–1919)	607,167,714	183
4 **Edgar Degas** (French; 1834–1917)	324,757,303	99
5 **Paul Cézanne** (French; 1839–1906)	387,426,172	74
6 **Marc Chagall** (Russian; 1887–1985)	160,935,200	70
7 = **Henri Matisse** (French; 1869–1954)	124,236,994	68
= **Camille Pissaro** (French; 1830–1903)	238,671,445	68
9 **Vincent van Gogh** (Dutch; 1853–90)	535,560,639	54
10 **Amedeo Modigliaini** (Italian; 1884–1920)	235,313,301	53

RAGS TO RICHES

The impoverished van Gogh painted this self-portrait, Portrait de l'Artist Sans Barbe, at Arles in September 1888. Just over a century later, it fetched $65 million at auction, making it the third most expensive painting sold at auction.

TOP 10 ★
MOST EXPENSIVE PAINTINGS BY 20TH-CENTURY ARTISTS*

PAINTING/ARTIST/SALE	PRICE ($)
1 *Paysage, Île de la Grane Jatte*, **George Seurat** (French; 1859–91) Sotheby's, New York, May 10, 1999	32,000,000
2 *Fugue*, **Wassily Kandinsky** (Russian; 1866–1944), Sotheby's, New York, May 17, 1990	19,000,000
3 *Interchange*, **Willem de Kooning** (American/Dutch; 1904–97), Sotheby's, New York, Nov 8, 1989	18,800,000
4 *Orange Marilyn*, **Andy Warhol** (American; 1928–87), Sotheby's, New York, May 14, 1998	15,750,000
5 *False Start*, **Jasper Johns** (American; b.1930), Sotheby's, New York, Nov 10, 1988	15,500,000
6 *Nu Assiss Sur un Divan*, **Amedeo Modigliani** (Italian; 1884–1920), Sotheby's, New York, Nov 11, 1999	15,250,000
7 *Woman*, **Willem de Kooning**, Christie's, New York, Nov 20, 1996	14,200,000
8 *Portrait de Jeanne Hebuterne*, **Amedeo Modigliani**, Sotheby's, New York, Nov 3, 1993	13,750,000
9 = *Anniversaire*, **Marc Chagall** (French/Russian; 1887–1985), Sotheby's, New York, May 17, 1990	13,500,000
= *La Pose Hindoue*, **Henri Matisse**, Sotheby's, New York, May 8 ,1995	13,500,000

* *Excluding Picasso, who would otherwise completely dominate the list*

Did You Know? Vincent van Gogh did not cut off his ear, as is popularly believed. He lopped off only part of his left ear lobe.

TOP 10 ⭐

MOST EXPENSIVE OLD MASTER PAINTINGS EVER SOLD AT AUCTION

PAINTING/ARTIST/SALE	PRICE ($)
1 *Portrait of Duke Cosimo I de Medici*, **Jacopo da Carucci (Pontormo)** (Italian; 1493–1558), Christie's, New York, May 31, 1989	32,000,000
2 *The Old Horse Guards, London, from St. James's Park*, **Canaletto** (Italian; 1697–1768), Christie's, London, Apr 15, 1992	16,008,000
3 *View of the Giudecca and the Zattere, Venice*, **Francesco Guardi** (Italian; 1712–93), Sotheby's, Monaco, Dec 1, 1989	13,943,000
4 *Venus and Adonis*, **Titian** (Italian; c.1488–1576), Christie's, London, Dec 13, 1991	12,376,000
5 *Tieleman Roosterman in Black Doublet, White Ruff*, **Frans Hals** (elder, Dutch; c.1580–1666), Christie's, London, July 8, 1999	11,625,000
6 *Le Retour du Bucentaure le Jour de l'Ascension*, **Canaletto**, Ader Tajan, Paris, Dec 15, 1993	11,316,000
7 *View of Molo from Bacino di San Marco, Venice* and *View of the Grand Canal Facing East from Campo di Santi, Venice* (pair), **Canaletto**, Sotheby's, New York, June 1, 1990	10,000,000
8 *Adoration of the Magi*, **Andrea Mantegna** (Italian; 1431–1506), Christie's, London, Apr 18, 1985	9,525,000
9 *Portrait of a Girl Wearing a Gold-trimmed Cloak*, **Rembrandt** (Dutch; 1606–69), Sotheby's, London, Dec 10, 1986	9,372,000
10 *Portrait of Bearded Man in Red Coat*, **Rembrandt**, Sotheby's, New York, Jan 30, 1998	8,250,000

THERE'S SOMETHING ABOUT MARY

Six paintings by Mary Cassatt, such as her Mother, Sara and the Baby, *are numbered among the 10 highest priced paintings by a woman.*

TOP 10 ⭐

MOST EXPENSIVE PAINTINGS BY WOMEN ARTISTS EVER SOLD AT AUCTION

PAINTING/ARTIST/SALE	PRICE ($)
1 *The Conversation*, **Mary Cassatt** (American; 1844–1926), Christie's, New York, May 11, 1988	4,100,000
2 *In the Box*, **Mary Cassatt**, Christie's, New York, May 23, 1996	3,700,000
3 = *Cache-cache*, **Berthe Morisot** (French; 1841–95), Sotheby's, New York, May 10, 1999	3,500,000
= *Mother, Sara and the Baby*, **Mary Cassatt**, Christie's, New York, May 10, 1989	3,500,000
5 *From the Plains*, **Georgia O'Keeffe** (American; 1887–1986), Sotheby's, New York, Dec 3, 1997	3,300,000
6 *Après le Déjeuner*, **Berthe Morisot**, Christie's, New York, May 14, 1997	3,250,000
7 *Autoretrato con Chango y Loro*, **Frida Kahlo** (Mexican; 1907–54), Sotheby's, New York, May 17, 1995	2,900,000
8 *Augusta Reading to Her Daughter*, **Mary Cassatt**, Sotheby's, New York, May 9, 1989	2,800,000
9 *Children Playing with Cat*, **Mary Cassatt**, Sotheby's, New York, Dec 3, 1998	2,700,000
10 *Sarah Holding Her Dog*, **Mary Cassatt**, Sotheby's, New York, Nov 11, 1999	2,500,000

113

TOP 10 ★
MOST EXPENSIVE PAINTINGS BY ANDY WARHOL

	PAINTING*/SALE	PRICE ($)
1	*Orange Marilyn*, Sotheby's, New York, May 14, 1998	15,750,000
2	*Shot Red Marilyn*, Sotheby's, New York, May 3, 1989	3,700,000
3	*Marilyn Monroe, Twenty Times*, Sotheby's, New York, Nov 10, 1988	3,600,000
4	*Marilyn X 100*, Sotheby's, New York, Nov 17, 1992	3,400,000
5	*Shot Red Marilyn*, Sotheby's, New York, Nov 2, 1994	3,300,000
6	*Big Torn Campbell's Soup Can*, Christie's, New York, May 7, 1997	3,200,000
7	*Orange Marilyn*, Christie's, New York, Nov 19, 1998	2,500,000
8	*Marion,* Sotheby's, New York, May 18, 1999	2,400,000
9	*Big Electric Chair*, Christie's, London, June 30, 1999	2,370,000
10	*Self Portrait*, Christie's, New York, May 12, 1998	2,200,000

* Including silkscreen works

"FAMOUS FOR 15 MINUTES"

Andy Warhol's own fame has outlived his famous phrase. His works continuing to attain considerable prices at auction.

HIGH FIGURES
The distinctive elongated figures created by Swiss sculptor Alberto Giacometti (1901–66), shown at work in his studio in 1958, command high prices at auction.

TOP 10 ★
MOST EXPENSIVE SCULPTURES BY ALBERTO GIACOMETTI

	SCULPTURE/SALE	PRICE ($)		SCULPTURE/SALE	PRICE ($)
1	*La Forêt – Sept Figures et Une Tête*, Sotheby's, New York, Nov 16, 1998	6,800,000	6	*Trois Hommes Qui Marchent*, Christie's, New York, May 11, 1988	3,500,000
2	*L'Homme Qui Marche I*, Christie's, London Nov 28, 1988	6,358,000	7	*Grande Femme Debout II*, Christie's, New York, May 12, 1987	3,300,000
3	*Trois Hommes Qui Marchent I*, Sotheby's, New York, Nov 11, 1999	5,200,000	8	*Trois Hommes Qui Marchent II*, Christie's, New York, May 14, 1997	3,200,000
4	*Grande Femme Debout I*, Christie's, New York, Nov 14, 1989	4,500,000	9	*Grande Femme Debout I*, Christie's, New York, May 12, 1987	2,800,000
5	*Grande Femme Debout I*, Christie's, New York, Nov 14, 1990	3,600,000	10	*L'Homme Qui Marche III – Walking Man III*, Christie's, New York, May 12, 1998	2,700,000

Did You Know? Between October 18 and December 4, 1961, Henri Matisse's painting *Le Bateau* hung upside down in the Museum of Modern Art, New York. An estimated 116,000 people passed through the gallery before anyone noticed.

TOP 10 ★
MOST EXPENSIVE SCULPTURES BY HENRY MOORE

SCULPTURE/SALE	PRICE ($)
1 =*Reclining Figure*, Christies, New York, May 13, 1999	3,700,000
=*Two-piece Reclining Figure, Points*, Christie's, New York, Nov 9, 1999	3,700,000
=*Working Model for UNESCO Reclining Figure*, Christie's, New York, May 15, 1990	3,700,000
4 *Reclining Figure, Angles*, Christie's, New York, Nov 13, 1996	2,400,000
5 *Draped Reclining Woman*, Sotheby's, New York, Nov 13, 1997	2,350,000
6 *Reclining Connected Forms*, Sotheby's, New York, May 17, 1990	2,200,000
7 =*Reclining Figure, Bone Skirt*, Sotheby's, New York, May 13, 1997	2,000,000
=*Working Model for Three Way Piece No. 3 Vertebrae*, Sotheby's, New York, May 17, 1990	2,000,000
9 =*Festival Reclining Figure*, Sotheby's, New York, May 11, 1994	1,850,000
=*Reclining Figure*, Sotheby's, New York, Nov 11, 1988	1,850,000

British sculptor Henry Spencer Moore (1898–1986) was a war artist before achieving international fame for his sculptures. Many of these were commissioned for public buildings, but those that have entered the marketplace have achieved consistently high prices.

SECOND KISS

Kiss II by pop artist Roy Lichtenstein (1923–97) gained a record $5.5 million at auction, followed closely at $5 million by Torpedo...Los. His work was partly inspired by images from comic strips.

TOP 10 ★
MOST EXPENSIVE PAINTINGS BY ROY LICHTENSTEIN

PAINTING/SALE	PRICE ($)
1 *Kiss II*, Christie's, New York, May 7, 1990	5,500,000
2 *Torpedo...Los*, Christie's, New York, Nov 7, 1989	5,000,000
3 *Tex!*, Christie's, New York, Nov 20, 1996	3,600,000
4 *Blang!*, Christie's, New York, May 7, 1997	2,600,000
5 *Kiss II*, Christie's, New York, May 3, 1995	2,300,000
6 *I...I'm Sorry!*, Sotheby's, New York, Nov 1, 1994	2,250,000
7 *The Ring*, Sotheby's, New York, Nov 19, 1997	2,000,000
8 =*I Can See the Whole Room... And There's Nobody in It*, Christie's, New York, Nov 9, 1988	1,900,000
=*Forest Scene*, Sotheby's, New York, Nov 19, 1996	1,900,000
10 *Girl With Piano*, Sotheby's, New York, Nov 17, 1992	1,650,000

TOP 10 ★
MOST EXPENSIVE PAINTINGS BY JACKSON POLLOCK

PAINTING*/SALE	PRICE ($)
1 *Number 8, 1950*, Sotheby's, New York, May 2, 1989	10,500,000
2 *Frieze*, Christie's, New York, Nov 9, 1988	5,200,000
3 *Search*, Sotheby's, New York, May 2, 1988	4,400,000
4 *Number 19, 1949*, Sotheby's, New York, May 2, 1989	3,600,000
5 *Number 31, 1949*, Christie's, New York, May 3, 1988	3,200,000
6 *Number 13*, Christie's, New York, Nov 7, 1990	2,800,000
7 *Number 26, 1950*, Sotheby's, New York, May 4, 1987	2,500,000
8 =*Number 20*, Sotheby's, New York, May 8, 1990	2,200,000
=*Number 19, 1948*, Christies, New York, May 4, 1993	2,200,000
=*Something of the Past*, Christie's, New York, May 7, 1996	2,200,000

* Includes mixed media compositions

Objects of Desire 1

MOST EXPENSIVE WATERCOLORS

WATERCOLOR/ARTIST/SALE	PRICE ($)
1 *La Moisson en Provence*, **Vincent van Gogh**, (Dutch; 1853–90), Sotheby's, London, June 24, 1997	13,280,000
2 *Les Toits – 1882*, **Vincent van Gogh**, Ader Picard & Tajan, Paris, Mar 20, 1990	4,669,000
3 *Nature Morte au Melon Vert*, **Paul Cézanne**, (French; 1839–1906), Sotheby's, London, Apr 4, 1989	3,933,000
4 *Die Sangerin L. Ais Fiordiligi*, **Paul Klee**, (Swiss; 1879–1940), Sotheby's, London, Nov 28, 1989	3,744,000
5 *John Biglin in Single Scull*, **Thomas Eakins**, (American; 1844–1916), Christie's, New York, May 23, 1990	3,200,000
6 *Au Moulin Rouge, La Fille du Roi d'Egypte*, **Pablo Picasso**, (Spanish; 1881–1973), Sotheby's, London, Nov 29, 1994	2,557,500
7 *Coral Divers*, **Winslow Homer** (American; 1836–1910), Christie's, New York, Dec 2, 1998	2,400,000
8 *Two Girls in Boat, Tynemouth, England*, **Winslow Homer**, Christie's, New York, Dec 2, 1998	2,300,000
9 *La Montagne Sainte-Victoire Vue des Lauves*, **Paul Cézanne**, Christie's, London, Nov 30, 1992	2,054,000
10 *Selbstbildnis. Skizze eines mannlichen aktes*, **Egon Schiele**, (Austrian; 1890–1918), Christie's, New York, Nov 19, 1998	2,000,000

MOST EXPENSIVE PRINTS

PRINT/ARTIST/SALE	PRICE ($)
1 *Diehard*, **Robert Rauschenberg** (American; b.1925), Sotheby's, New York, May 2, 1989	1,600,000
2 *Mao*, **Andy Warhol** (American; 1928–87), Sothebys, London, June 26, 1996	939,400
3 *Famille Tahitienne*, **Paul Gauguin** (French; 1848–1903), Francis Briest, Paris, Dec 4, 1998	806,900
4 *Elles*, **Henri de Toulouse-Lautrec** (French; 1864–1901), Sotheby's, New York, May 10, 1999	800,000
5 *Glider*, **Robert Rauschenberg**, Christie's, New York, Nov 14, 1995	750,000
6 *Elles*, **Henri de Toulouse-Lautrec**, Sotheby's, New York, Nov 7, 1997	695,000
7 = *La Suite Vollard*, **Pablo Picasso** (Spanish;1881–1973), Christie's, New York, Nov 2, 1999	650,000
= *Suicide*, **Andy Warhol**, Sotheby's, New York, May 18, 1999	650,000
9 *Head of Marilyn Monroe*, **Andy Warhol**, Beijers, Stockholm, May 21, 1990	640,500
10 *Les Saltimbanques*, **Pablo Picasso**, Sotheby's, New York, May 3, 1996	600,000

Included within the classification of prints are silkscreens, lithographs, monotypes, aquatints, woodcuts, engravings, and etchings.

TOP 10 ★
MOST EXPENSIVE DRAWINGS*

TITLE/ARTIST/SALE	PRICE ($)
1 *Famille de l'Arlequin,* **Pablo Picasso** (Spanish; 1881–1973), Christie's, New York, Nov 14, 1989	14,000,000
2 *Study for Head and Hand of an Apostle,* **Raphael** (Italian; 1483–1520), Christie's, London, Dec 13, 1996	7,920,000
3 *Oliviers avec les Alpilles au Fond,* **Vincent van Gogh** (Dutch; 1853–90), Sotheby's, London, Dec 7, 1999	7,776,000
4 =*Corpse and Mirror,* **Jasper Johns** (American: b.1930), Christie's, New York, Nov 10, 1997	7,600,000
=*Jardin de Fleurs,* **Vincent van Gogh,** Christie's, New York, Nov 14, 1990	7,600,000
6 *Rebus,* **Robert Rauschenberg** (American, b.1925), Sotheby's, New York, Apr 30, 1991	6,600,000
7 *Rebus,* **Robert Rauschenberg,** Sotheby's, New York, Nov 10, 1988	5,750,000
8 **Untitled oil crayon canvas, Cy Twombly** (American; b.1929), Sotheby's, New York, May 8, 1990	5,000,000
9 *Bateaux de Pêches sur la Plage à Saintes Marie de la Mer, Mediterranée,* **Vincent van Gogh** , Christie's, New York, May 5, 1998	4,600,000
10 *La Toilette de Venus,* **Pablo Picasso,** Sotheby's, New York, Nov 12, 1997	4,500,000

* Media include pencil, pen, ink, drawing, crayon

AHEAD OF THE FIELD

Van Gogh's harvest scene, La Moisson en Provence *(1888), sold for £8 million in 1997, making it the world's most expensive watercolor.*

TRIBAL RECORD

Edward S. Curtis's magnficent 20-volume set of photographs recording the life of North American Indians in the early twentieth century is the costliest ever sold at auction.

TOP 10 ★
MOST EXPENSIVE PHOTOGRAPHS

PHOTOGRAPH/PHOTOGRAPHER/SALE	PRICE ($)
1 *Egypte et Nubie: Sites et monuments les plus intéressants pour l'étude de l'art et de l'histoire** (1858), **Félix Teynard** (French; 1817–92), Laurin Guilloux Buffetaud Tailleur, Paris, Dec 21, 1990	707,000
2 *Noir et Blanche* (1926), **Man Ray** (American; 1890–1976), Christie's, New York, Oct 4, 1998	607,500
3 *The North American Indian** (1907–30), **Edward S. Curtis** (American; 1868–1952), Sotheby's, New York, Oct 7, 1993	662,500
4 *The North American Indian** (1907–30), **Edward S. Curtis,** Christie's, New York, Apr 6, 1995	464,500
5 *Georgia O'Keeffe: A Portrait – Hands with Thimble* (1930), **Alfred Stieglitz** (American; 1864–1946), Christie's, New York, Oct 8, 1993	398,500
6 =*Equivalents (21)** (1920s), **Alfred Stieglitz,** Christie's, New York, Oct 30, 1989	396,000
=*The North American Indian** (1907–30), **Edward S. Curtis,** Christie's, New York, Oct 13, 1992	396,000
8 *Mondrian's Pipe and Glasses* (1926), **André Kertész** (Hungarian-American; 1894–1985), Christie's, New York, Apr 17, 1997	376,500
9 *Noir et Blanche* (1926), **Man Ray,** Christie's, New York, Apr 21, 1994	354,500
10 *Chez Mondrian, Paris* (1926), **André Kertész,** Christie's, New York, Apr 17, 1997	299,500

* Collections; all others are single prints

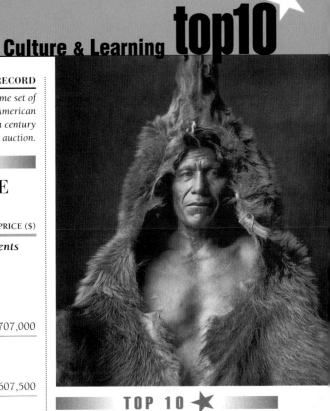

TOP 10 ★
MOST COLLECTED BEANIE BABIES*

BEANIE BABY
1 Bear
2 2000 Signature Bear#
3 Billionaire Bear
4 Billionaire Bear 2
5 Britannia
6 1998 Holiday Teddy Bear
7 1997 Holiday Teddy Bear
8 Chilly
9 Groovy#
10 Germania

* In April 2000

 # Beanie Buddy

Source: *Ty Inc.*

Beanie Babies were invented by Chicago toy designer H. Ty Warner, who introduced his first nine at a toy fair in 1993. They went on sale in Chicago the following year, and by 1995 – largely through word-of-mouth recommendation – had become one of the country's most popular and sought-after toys. The company's policy of constantly "retiring" selected lines and introducing new products has kept them at the forefront of collectables. (Bronty the Brontosaurus, for example, was retired on April 6, 2000.)

Objects of Desire 2

TOP 10 ★

MOST EXPENSIVE ITEMS OF ENGLISH FURNITURE

ITEM/SALE	PRICE ($)
1 The Dundas Armchairs, pair of George III giltwood armchairs, designed by Robert Adam and made by Thomas Chippendale, Christie's, London, July 3, 1997	2,855,000
2 The Warwick Tables, supplied to Queen Anne for St. James's Palace in 1704–05, by Gerrit Jensen, probably in association with Thomas Pelletier, Sotheby's, London, July 10, 1998	2,692,000
3 The Anglesey Desk, Regency bronze-mounted and brass-inlaid ebony and mahogany library desk, attributed to Marsh & Tatbam, Christie's, London, July 8, 1993	2,625,000
4 The Dundas Sofas, pair of George III giltwood sofas designed by Robert Adam and made by Thomas Chippendale, Christie's, London, July 3, 1997	2,579,000
5 The Lonsdale Langlois Commode, a George III ormolu-mounted rosewood, fruitwood, and marquetry bombe commode, Christie's, New York, Nov 24, 1998	2,532,500
6 The St. Giles's Dining-Chairs, set of 17 George II mahogany dining-chairs, attributed to William Hallett Senior, Christie's, London, July 8, 1999	1,890,000
7 A George II ormolu-mounted mahogany dressing and writing-commode, attributed to John Channon, Christie's, London, July 6, 1989	1,782,000
8 A George III mahogany commode, attributed to Thomas Chippendale, Christie's, London, Dec 5, 1991	1,655,000
9 The Stowe Apollo Tables, pair of George II gilt-gesso side tables, attributed to Benjamin Goodison, Christie's, London, July 9, 1998	1,531,000
10 The Raynham Commode, a George II ormolu-mounted mahogany commode, Christie's, New York, Nov 24, 1998	1,487,500

TOP 10 ★

MOST EXPENSIVE ITEMS OF AMERICAN FURNITURE

ITEM/SALE	PRICE ($)
1 The Nicholas Brown Chippendale mahogany block and shell desk and bookcase, c.1760–70, attributed to John Goddard, Christie's, New York, June 3, 1989	12,100,000
2 Richard Edwards Chippendale carved mahogany pier table, by Thomas Tufft, c.1775–76, Christie's, New York, Jan 20, 1990	4,620,000
3 The Samuel Whitehorne Queen Anne block-and-shell carved mahogany kneehole desk, attributed to Edmund Townsend, c.1780, Sotheby's, New York, Jan 20, 1996	3,632,500
4 Chippendale carved mahogany tea-table, c.1760–80, Christie's, New York, May 28, 1987	2,422,500
5 The Edwards-Harrison family Chippendale carved mahogany high chest-of-drawers, dressing table and pair of side chairs, by Thomas Tufft, c.1775–76, Christie's, New York, May 28, 1987	1,760,000
6 The Edward Jackson parcel gilt inlaid and figured mahogany mirrored bonnet-top secretary bookcase, c.1738–48, Sotheby's, New York, Jan 20, 1996	1,432,500
7 Chippendale carved mahogany tea-table, c.1760–80, Christie's, New York, Jan 25, 1986	1,045,000
8 Cornelius Stevenson Chippendale carved mahogany tea-table, attributed to Thomas Affleck, carving attributed to Nicholas Bernard & Martin Jugiez, c.1760–80, Christie's, New York, Jan 20, 1990	1,210,000
9 Chipppendale carved mahogany tea-table, c.1770, Christie's, New York, Jan 26, 1995	695,500
10 Chippendale mahogany block front and shell-carved kneehole desk, c.1760–85, Christie's, New York, June 2, 1983	627,000

TOP 10 ★

MOST EXPENSIVE MINIATURES

MINIATURE/ARTIST/SALE	PRICE ($)
1 *Two Orientals*, Francisco José de Goya y Lucientes (Spanish; 1746–1828), Christie's, London, Dec 3, 1997	580,000
2 *Maja and Celestina*, Francisco José de Goya y Lucientes, Sotheby's, New York, May 30, 1991	500,000
3 *Portrait of George Villiers, Duke of Buckingham*, Jean Petitot (French; 1607–91), Christie's, London, Apr 30, 1996	375,000
4 *Man Clasping Hand from Cloud*, possibly Lord Thomas Howard, Nicholas Hilliard, (British; 1547–1619), Christie's, London, Mar 3, 1993	230,400
5 *King George III when Prince of Wales Wearing Order of Garter*, Jean-Etienne Liotard, (Swiss; 1702–89), Christie's, London, Oct 21, 1997	187,450
6 *Portrait of Henry Stuart, Earl of Ross and 1st Duke of Albany*, attributed to Lievine Teerling-Bening (Flemish; 16th century), Bonhams, London, Nov 20, 1997	184,800
7 *Landscape with Saint Jerome*, Hans Bol (Dutch; 1534–93), Sotheby's, London, Feb 11, 1999	146,700
8 *Bacchic Scenes*, Jean Jacques de Gault (French; c.1738–1812), Sotheby's, Geneva, Nov 13, 1995	140,900
9 *Portrait of Tsar Nicholas II in Uniform with Orders*, Russian School (Russian; 20th century), Christie's, New York, Dec 1, 1995	140,000
10 *Lady Wearing Rust Coloured Dress with Lace Collar and Jewels*, Samuel Cooper (British; 1609–72), Sotheby's, London, Oct 11, 1994	127,000

Background image: **JIMI HENDRIX'S FENDER STRATOCASTER ELECTRIC GUITAR**

SUPER HERO

Created by writer Jerry Siegel (American, 1914–96) and artist Joe Shuster (Canadian, 1914–92), Superman made his debut in the June 1938 first issue of Action Comics, now the most prized of all comic books.

TOP 10 ★
MOST VALUABLE AMERICAN COMICS

COMIC	VALUE ($)
1 Action Comics No. 1	185,000

Published in June 1938, the first issue of Action Comics marked the original appearance of Superman.

| **2 Detective Comics No. 27** | 165,000 |

Issued in May 1939, it is prized as the first comic book to feature Batman.

| **3 Superman No. 1** | 130,000 |

The first comic book devoted to Superman, reprinting the original Action Comics story, was published in summer 1939.

| **4 Marvel Comics No. 1** | 115,000 |

The Human Torch and other heroes were first introduced in the issue dated October 1939.

| **5 All American Comics No. 16** | 65,000 |

The Green Lantern made his debut in the issue dated July 1940.

| **6 =Batman No. 1** | 63,000 |

Published in spring 1940, this was the first comic book devoted to Batman.

| **=Whizz Comics No. 2** | 63,000 |

Published in February 1940 – and confusingly numbered "2" when it was in fact the first issue – it was the first comic book to feature Captain Marvel.

| **8 Flash Comics No. 1** | 57,000 |

Dated January 1940, and featuring The Flash, it is rare because it was produced in small numbers for promotional purposes, and was unique since issue 2 was retitled Whizz Comics.

| **9 Captain America Comics No. 1** | 56,000 |

Published in March 1941, this was the original comic book in which Captain America appeared.

| **10 Detective Comics No. 1** | 50,000 |

Published in March 1937, it was the first in a long-running series.

Source: The Overstreet Comic Book Price Guide, #30, 2000. ©2000 Gemstone Publishing, Inc. All rights reserved.

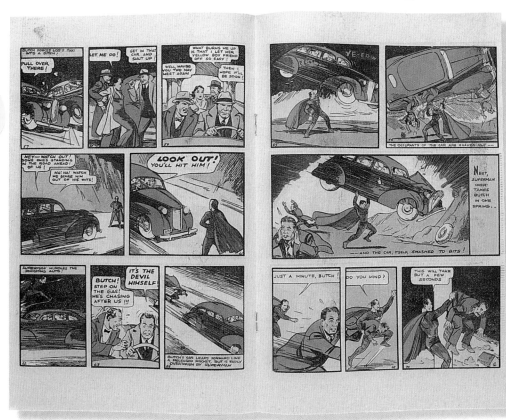

TOP 10 ★
MOST EXPENSIVE MUSICAL INSTRUMENTS

INSTRUMENT*/SALE	PRICE ($)	INSTRUMENT*/SALE	PRICE ($)
1 "Kreutzer" violin by Antonio Stradivari, Christies, London, Apr 1, 1998	1,582,800	**6 Double bass by Domenico Montagnana**, Sotheby's, London, Mar 16, 1999	250,300
2 "Cholmondeley" violoncello by Antonio Stradivari, Sotheby's, London, June 22, 1998	1,141,100	**7 Verne Powell's platinum flute**, Christie's, New York, Oct 18, 1986	187,000
3 Steinway grand piano, decorated by Lawrence Alma-Tadema and Edward Poynter for Henry Marquand, 1884–87, Sotheby Parke Bernet, New York, Mar 26, 1980	390,000	**8 English double-manual harpsichord by Burkat Shudi and John Broadwood**, Sotheby's, London, Oct 27, 1999	170,600
4 Jimi Hendrix's Fender Stratocaster electric guitar, Sotheby's, London, Apr 25, 1990	370,800	**9 Viola by Giovanni Paolo Maggini**, Christie's, London, Nov 20, 1984	161,100
5 Accoustic guitar owned by David Bowie, Paul McCartney, and George Michael, Christie's, London, May 18, 1994	339,800	**10 Seven-keyed bugle by Charles-Joseph Sax**, Brussels, 1842, Sotheby's, London, Nov 18, 1993	7,800

* Most expensive example only given per category of instrument

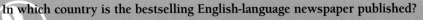

In which country is the bestselling English-language newspaper published? A US
see p.107 for the answer B India C UK

TOP 10 ★
Music

Chart Hits

TOP 10 ALBUMS OF ALL TIME
(Title/artist or group)

❶ Thriller, Michael Jackson **❷ Dark Side of the Moon**, Pink Floyd
❸ Their Greatest Hits 1971–1975, Eagles **❹ The Bodyguard**, Soundtrack
❺ Rumours, Fleetwood Mac **❻ Sgt. Pepper's Lonely Hearts Club Band**, The Beatles
❼ Led Zeppelin IV, Led Zeppelin **❽ Greatest Hits**, Elton John **❾ Jagged Little Pill**,
Alanis Morissette **❿ Bat Out of Hell**, Meat Loaf

Total worldwide sales of albums have traditionally been notoriously hard to gauge, but even with the huge expansion of the album market during the 1980s, and multiple million sales of many major releases, this Top 10 is still élite territory.

TOP 10 ALBUMS OF ALL TIME IN THE US
(Title/artist or group/sales)

❶ Their Greatest Hits 1971–75, Eagles, 26,000,000 **❷ Thriller**, Michael Jackson, 25,000,000 **❸ Led Zeppelin IV**, Led Zeppelin, 22,000,000 **❹ Rumours**, Fleetwood Mac, 18,000,000 **❺ = The Beatles**, The Beatles, 17,000,000; **= The Bodyguard**, Soundtrack, 17,000,000 **❼ = Boston**, Boston, 16,000,000; **= Back in Black**, AC/DC, 16,000,000; **= No Fences**, Garth Brooks, 16,000,000; **= Jagged Little Pill**, Alanis Morissette, 16,000,000; **= Cracked Rear View**, Hootie & the Blowfish, 16,000,000

Source: *RIAA*

SOARING LIKE EAGLES

One of the world's bestselling albums, the Eagles' Their Greatest Hits 1971–1975, was also the first to be certified platinum.

TOP 10 ★ ARTISTS WITH THE MOST CONSECUTIVE US TOP 10 HITS

	ARTIST OR GROUP/PERIOD	HITS
1	Elvis Presley, Mar 1956–62	30
2	The Beatles, Dec 1964–76	20
3	Janet Jackson, Sep 1989–98	18
4	=Michael Jackson, July 1979–1988	17
	=Madonna, Mar 1984–Oct 1989	17
6	Pat Boone, Feb 1956–58	14
7	=Whitney Houston, May 1985–91	13
	=Phil Collins, Feb 1984–90	13
	=Lionel Richie, July 1981–Feb 1987	13
10	Mariah Carey, June 1990–94	11

Source: *The Popular Music Database*

TOP 10 ★ SINGLES THAT STAYED LONGEST IN THE US CHARTS

	TITLE/ARTIST OR GROUP/ FIRST CHART ENTRY	WEEKS IN CHART
1	*How Do I Live*, LeAnn Rimes, 1997	69
2	*Foolish Games/You Were Meant for Me*, Jewel, 1996	65
3	*Macarena (Bayside Boys Mix)*, Los Del Rio, 1996	60
4	*I Don't Want to Wait*, Paula Cole, 1997	56
5	=*Missing*, Everything But The Girl, 1996	55
	=*Barely Breathing*, Duncan Sheik, 1996	55
7	*December 1963 (Oh, What a Night)*, Four Seasons, 1976*	54
8	*Too Close*, Next, 1998	53
9	=*Truly Madly Deeply*, Savage Garden, 1997	52
	=*How's it Going to Be*, Third Eye Blind, 1997	52

* Re-charted in 1994

Source: *The Popular Music Database*

TOP 10 ★ ARTISTS WITH THE MOST WEEKS ON THE US SINGLES CHART*

	ARTIST OR GROUP	TOTAL WEEKS
1	Elvis Presley	1,586
2	Elton John	1,006
3	Stevie Wonder	766
4	Madonna	740
5	Rod Stewart	731
6	James Brown	706
7	Pat Boone	697
8	Michael Jackson	661
9	The Beatles	629
10	Fats Domino	605

* Up to January 1, 2000

Source: *The Popular Music Database*

TOP 10 ★
SINGLES OF ALL TIME

TITLE/ARTIST OR GROUP/YEAR	SALES EXCEED
1 *Candle in the Wind (1997)/ Something About the Way You Look Tonight*, Elton John, 1997	37,000,000
2 *White Christmas*, Bing Crosby, 1943	30,000,000
3 *Rock Around the Clock*, Bill Haley and His Comets, 1954	17,000,000
4 *I Want to Hold Your Hand*, The Beatles, 1963	12,000,000
5 =*Hey Jude*, The Beatles, 1968	10,000,000
=*It's Now or Never*, Elvis Presley, 1960	10,000,000
=*I Will Always Love You*, Whitney Houston, 1993	10,000,000
8 =*Hound Dog/Don't Be Cruel*, Elvis Presley, 1956	9,000,000
=*Diana*, Paul Anka, 1957	9,000,000
10 =*I'm a Believer,* The Monkees, 1966	8,000,000
=*(Everything I Do) I Do it for You*, Bryan Adams, 1991	8,000,000

TOP 10 ★
SINGLES OF ALL TIME IN THE US

TITLE/ARTIST OR GROUP	APPROX. US SALES
1 *Candle in the Wind (1997)/ Something About the Way You Look Tonight*, Elton John	11,000,000
2 =*Hey Jude*, The Beatles	4,000,000
=*We Are the World*, USA for Africa	4,000,000
=*I Will Always Love You*, Whitney Houston	4,000,000
=*Whoomp! (There it Is)*, Tag Team	4,000,000
=*Hound Dog/Don't Be Cruel*, Elvis Presley	4,000,000
7 =*Love Me Tender/Any Way You Want Me*, Elvis Presley	3,000,000
=*Everything I Do (I Do it for You)*, Bryan Adams	3,000,000
=*Macarena*, Los Del Rio	3,000,000
=*I'll Be Missing You*, Puff Daddy and Faith Evans (featuring 112)	3,000,000
=*How Do I Live*, LeAnn Rimes	3,000,000

Source: *RIAA*

The USA for Africa's 1985 charity single *We Are the World* had a host of special circumstances surrounding it and launching it into the elite 4-million mega-seller league. It took the remarkable global response to the death of Diana, Princess of Wales, to generate sales capable of overtaking it, which Elton John's specially penned tribute did – and by a considerable margin.

TEEN TRIUMPH
Paul Anka's song Diana, released when he was just 16 years old, remains one of the bestselling singles of all time.

OLD BLUE EYES
Frank Sinatra is one of only two septuagenarians to achieve a Top 10 hit in the UK. His single, New York, New York, *remains a highly popular classic.*

TOP 10 ★
OLDEST SINGERS TO HAVE A TOP 10 HIT IN THE UK

ARTIST/TITLE	AGE YRS	MTHS
1 **Frank Sinatra**, *New York, New York*	70	4
2 **Andy Williams**, *Music to Watch Girls By*	70	3
3 **Louis Armstrong**, *What a Wonderful World*	68	0
4 **Honor Blackman**, *Kinky Boots*	64	0
5 **Tom Jones***, *Mama Told Me Not to Come*	59	10
6 **Cliff Richard**, *The Millennium Prayer*	59	2
7 **James Brown**, *Living in America*	56	10
8 **Ted Heath**, *Swingin' Shepherd Blues*	56	2
9 **Petula Clark**, *Downtown '88 Remix*	56	0
10 **Diana Ross**, *Not Over You Yet*	55	7

* *With Stereophonics*

The ages listed are those of the artists at the end of the Top 10 run of their most recent (to date) Top 10 hit. Posthumous Top 10 entries – such as two by Bing Crosby – are not counted. With several of the artists here still actively and successfully recording, some may have further Top 10 hits yet to deliver.

123

Record Firsts

FIRST BRITISH SOLO ARTISTS TO HAVE A NO. 1 SINGLE IN THE US

	ARTIST/SINGLE	DATE AT NO. 1
1	**Mr. Acker Bilk**, *Stranger on the Shore*	May 26, 1962
2	**Petula Clark**, *Downtown*	Jan 23, 1965
3	**Donovan**, *Sunshine Superman*	Sep 3, 1966
4	**Lulu**, *To Sir With Love*	Oct 21, 1967
5	**George Harrison**, *My Sweet Lord*	Dec 26, 1970
6	**Rod Stewart**, *Maggie May*	Oct 2, 1971
7	**Gilbert O'Sullivan**, *Alone Again Naturally*	July 29, 1972
8	**Elton John**, *Crocodile Rock*	Feb 3, 1973
9	**Ringo Starr**, *Photograph*	Nov 24, 1973
10	**Eric Clapton**, *I Shot the Sheriff*	Sep 14, 1974

Source: *The Popular Music Database*

FIRST AMERICAN SOLO ARTISTS TO HAVE A NO. 1 SINGLE IN THE UK

	ARTIST/SINGLE	DATE AT NO. 1
1	**Al Martino**, *Here in My Heart*	Nov 14, 1952
2	**Jo Stafford**, *You Belong to Me*	Jan 16, 1953
3	**Kay Starr**, *Comes A-Long A-Love*	Jan 23, 1953
4	**Eddie Fisher**, *Outside of Heaven*	Jan 30, 1953
5	**Perry Como**, *Don't Let the Stars Get in Your Eyes*	Feb 6, 1953
6	**Guy Mitchell**, *She Wears Red Feathers*	Mar 13, 1953
7	**Frankie Laine**, *I Believe*	Apr 24, 1953
8	**Doris Day**, *Secret Love*	Apr 16, 1954
9	**Johnnie Ray**, *Such a Night*	Apr 30, 1954
10	**Kitty Kallen**, *Little Things Mean a Lot*	Sep 10, 1954

Source: *The Popular Music Database*

THE 10 FIRST US CHART SINGLES

(Single/artist)

1 *I'll Never Smile Again*, Tommy Dorsey **2** *The Breeze and I*, Jimmy Dorsey **3** *Imagination*, Glenn Miller **4** *Playmates*, Kay Kyser **5** *Fools Rush in*, Glenn Miller **6** *Where Was I*, Charlie Barnet **7** *Pennsylvania 6-5000*, Glenn Miller **8** *Imagination*, Tommy Dorsey **9** *Sierra Sue*, Bing Crosby **10** *Make-believe Island*, Mitchell Ayres

Source: Billboard

FIRST AMERICAN GROUPS TO HAVE A NO. 1 SINGLE IN THE UK

	GROUP/SINGLE	DATE AT NO. 1
1	**Bill Haley and His Comets**, *Rock Around the Clock*	Nov 25, 1955
2	**Dream Weavers**, *It's Almost Tomorrow*	Mar 16, 1956
3	**Teenagers featuring Frankie Lymon**, *Why Do Fools Fall in Love?*	July 20, 1956
4	**The Crickets**, *That'll Be the Day*	Nov 1, 1957
5	**Platters**, *Smoke Gets in your Eyes*	Mar 20, 1959
6	**Marcels**, *Blue Moon*	May 4, 1961
7	**Highwaymen**, *Michael*	Oct 12, 1961
8	**B. Bumble and the Stingers**, *Rocker*	May 17, 1962
9	**Supremes**, *Baby Love*	Nov 19, 1964
10	**Byrds**, *Mr. Tambourine Man*	July 22, 1965

Source: *The Popular Music Database*

SUPREME SUPREMES

Nine years after their first US No. 1, the Supremes became only the ninth US group to top the UK charts – the song was Baby Love.

THE 10 ★

FIRST BRITISH GROUPS TO HAVE A NO. 1 SINGLE IN THE US

	GROUP/SINGLE	DATE AT NO. 1
1	**Tornados**, *Telstar*	Dec 22, 1962
2	**The Beatles**, *I Want to Hold Your Hand*	Feb 1, 1964
3	**The Animals**, *House of the Rising Sun*	Sep 5, 1964
4	**Manfred Mann**, *Do Wah Diddy Diddy*	Oct 17, 1964
5	**Freddie and the Dreamers**, *I'm Telling You Now*	Apr 10,1965
6	**Wayne Fontana and the Mindbenders**, *The Game of Love*	Apr 24, 1965
7	**Herman's Hermits**, *Mrs. Brown You've Got a Lovely Daughter*	May 1, 1965
8	**The Rolling Stones**, *(I Can't Get No) Satisfaction*	July 10, 1965
9	**Dave Clark Five**, *Over and Over*	Dec 25, 1965
10	**Troggs**, *Wild Thing*	July 30, 1966

Source: *The Popular Music Database*

HIT MANN
Do Wah Diddy Diddy, a cover version of a US-written song, became British group Manfred Mann's debut No. 1 US chart hit.

THE 10 ★

FIRST US CHART ALBUMS

	ALBUM	ARTIST OR GROUP
1	*Al Jolson (Volume III)*	Al Jolson
2	*A Presentation of Progressive Jazz*	Stan Kenton
3	*Emperor's Waltz*	Bing Crosby
4	*Songs of Our Times*	Carmen Cavallaro
5	*Wizard at the Organ*	Ken Griffin
6	*Glenn Miller Masterpieces*	Glenn Miller
7	*Busy Fingers*	Three Suns
8	*Songs of Our Times*	B. Grant Orchestra
9	*Glenn Miller*	Glenn Miller
10	*Theme Song*	Various artists

Source: Billboard

This was the first albums Top 10 compiled by *Billboard* magazine, for its issue dated Sep 3, 1948.

THE 10 ★

FIRST MILLION-SELLING US SINGLES

	SINGLE/ARTIST	CERTIFICATION DATE
1	*Catch a Falling Star*, Perry Como	Mar 14, 1958
2	*He's Got the Whole World in in His Hands*, Laurie London	July 18, 1958
3	*Hard Headed Woman*, Elvis Presley	Aug 11, 1958
4	*Patricia*, Perez Prado	Aug 18, 1958
5	*Tom Dooley*, Kingston Trio	Jan 21, 1959
6	*Calcutta*, Lawrence Welk	Feb 14, 1961
7	*Big Bad John*, Jimmy Dean	Dec 14, 1961
8	*The Lion Sleeps Tonight*, The Tokens	Jan 19, 1962
9	*Can't Help Falling in Love*, Elvis Presley	Mar 30, 1962
10	*I Can't Stop Loving You*, Ray Charles	July 19, 1962

Source: *RIAA*

THE 10 ★

FIRST FEMALE SINGERS TO HAVE A NO. 1 HIT IN THE US

	ARTIST/SINGLE	DATE AT NO. 1
1	**Joan Weber**, *Let Me Go Lover*	Jan 1, 1955
2	**Georgia Gibbs**, *Dance With Me Henry (Wallflower)*	May 14, 1955
3	**Kay Starr**, *Rock and Roll Waltz*	Feb 18, 1956
4	**Gogi Grant**, *The Wayward Wind*	June 16, 1956
5	**Debbie Reynolds**, *Tammy*	Aug 19, 1957
6	**Connie Francis**, *Everybody's Somebody's Fool*	June 27, 1960
7	**Brenda Lee**, *I'm Sorry*	July 18, 1960
8	**Shelley Fabares**, *Johnny Angel*	Apr 7, 1962
9	**Little Eva**, *The Loco-motion*	Aug 25, 1962
10	**Little Peggy March**, *I Will Follow Him*	Apr 27, 1963

Source: *The Popular Music Database*

Did You Know? The Tornados' *Telstar*, the first ever US No. 1 by a British group, was inspired by the July 10, 1962 launch of the first satellite to transmit TV signals between Europe and the US. It sold over 5 million copies worldwide.

Chart Toppers

CHILD'S PLAY
Thirteen-year-old Donny Osmond's recording of *Go Away Little Girl* held the US No. 1 slot for three weeks in September 1971.

TOP 10
YOUNGEST SOLO ARTISTS TO HAVE A NO. 1 SINGLE IN THE US*

	ARTIST/TITLE/YEAR	AGE# YRS	MTHS
1	**Jimmy Boyd**, *I Saw Mommy Kissing Santa Claus*, 1952	12	11
2	**Stevie Wonder** *Fingertips*, 1963	13	1
3	**Donny Osmond**, *Go Away Little Girl*, 1971	13	7
4	**Michael Jackson**, *Ben*, 1972	13	11
5	**Laurie London**, *He's Got the Whole World in His Hands*, 1958	14	2
6	**Little Peggy March**, *I Will Follow Him*, 1963	15	0
7	**Brenda Lee**, *I'm Sorry*, 1960	15	5
8	**Paul Anka**, *Diana*, 1957	16	0
9	**Tiffany**, *I Think We're Alone Now*, 1987	16	10
10	**Lesley Gore**, *It's My Party*, 1963	17	0

* To December 1999
\# During first week of debut No. 1 US single
Source: *The Popular Music Database*

TOP 10 ARTISTS WITH THE MOST CONSECUTIVE NO. 1 SINGLES IN THE US*
(Artist or group/period/consecutive weeks at No. 1)

1 **Elvis Presley**, 1956–58, 10
2 **Whitney Houston**, 1985–88, 7
3 = **The Beatles**, 1964–66, 6;
= Bee Gees, 1977–79, 6; = Paula Abdul, 1988–91, 6 **6** = Michael Jackson, 1987–88, 5; = Supremes, 1964–65, 5; = Mariah Carey, 1990–91, 5; = Mariah Carey, 1995–98, 5 **10** Jackson 5, 1970, 4; = George Michael, 1987–88, 4

* To December 1999
Source: *The Popular Music Database*

TOP 10
ALBUMS WITH THE MOST CONSECUTIVE WEEKS AT NO. 1 IN THE US

	TITLE/ARTIST OR GROUP	WEEKS AT NO. 1
1	*Love Me or Leave Me* (Soundtrack), Doris Day	25
2	=*Calypso*, Harry Belafonte	24
	=*Saturday Night Fever*, Soundtrack	24
	=*Purple Rain* (Soundtrack), Prince	24
5	*Blue Hawaii* (Soundtrack), Elvis Presley	20
6	*Rumours*, Fleetwood Mac	19
7	=*More of the Monkees*, The Monkees	18
	=*Please Hammer Don't Hurt 'Em*, MC Hammer	18
9	=*Thriller*, Michael Jackson (1st entry)	17
	=*Thriller*, Michael Jackson (2nd entry)	17
	=*Some Gave All*, Billy Ray Cyrus	17

* Based on Billboard *charts, up to January 1, 2000*

TOP 10
LONGEST GAPS BETWEEN NO. 1 HIT SINGLES IN THE US

	ARTIST OR GROUP/PERIOD	GAP YRS	MTHS
1	**Cher**, Mar 23, 1974–Mar 19, 1999	24	11
2	**Elton John**, Nov 11, 1975–Oct 11, 1997	21	11
3	**Beach Boys**, Dec 10, 1966–Nov 5, 1988	21	11
4	**Paul Anka**, July 13, 1959–Aug 24, 1974	15	1
5	**George Harrison**, June 30, 1973–Jan 16, 1988	14	7
6	**Neil Sedaka**, Aug 11, 1962–Feb 1, 1975	12	6
7	**Four Seasons**, July 18, 1964–Mar 13, 1976	11	8
8	**Herb Alpert**, June 22, 1968–Oct 20, 1979	11	4
9	**Frank Sinatra**, July 9, 1955–July 2, 1966	11	0
10	**Stevie Wonder**, Aug 10, 1963–Jan 27, 1973	10	5

Source: *The Popular Music Database*

TOP 10
ARTISTS WITH THE MOST NO. 1 SINGLES IN THE US

	ARTIST OR GROUP	NO. 1 SINGLES
1	The Beatles	20
2	Elvis Presley	18
3	Mariah Carey	14*
4	Michael Jackson	13
5	The Supremes	12
6	=Whitney Houston	11
	=Madonna	11
8	Stevie Wonder	10
9	=Paul McCartney/Wings	9
	=Bee Gees	9
	=Elton John	9

* Includes a duet with Boyz II Men
Source: *The Popular Music Database*

SATCHMO SINGS

Four years after his chart-topping success in the US, Louis Armstrong topped the UK charts at the age of 67. His hit, What a Wonderful World, *sold over 1 million copies worldwide.*

TOP 10 ★

OLDEST ARTISTS TO HAVE A NO. 1 SINGLE IN THE US*

ARTIST OR GROUP/TITLE	AGE# YRS	MTHS
1 **Louis Armstrong**, *Hello Dolly!*	63	10
2 **Lawrence Welk**, *Calcutta*	57	11
3 **Morris Stoloff**, *Moonglow and Theme from Picnic*	57	10
4 **Cher**, *Believe*	52	9
5 **Frank Sinatra+**, *Somethin' Stupid*	51	4
6 **Elton John**, *Candle in the Wind (1997)/ Something About the Way You Look Tonight*	50	6
7 **Lorne Greene**, *Ringo*	49	9
8 **Dean Martin**, *Everybody Loves Somebody*	47	2
9 **Bill Medley★**, *(I've Had) The Time of My Life*	47	2
10 **Sammy Davis, Jr.**, *The Candy Man*	46	6

* To December 1999

During first week of No. 1 single

+ Duet with Nancy Sinatra

★ Duet with Jennifer Warnes

Source: *The Popular Music Database*

TOP 10 ★

SINGLES THAT STAYED LONGEST AT NO. 1 IN THE US*

TITLE/ARTIST OR GROUP/YEAR	WEEKS AT NO. 1
1 *One Sweet Day*, Mariah Carey and Boyz II Men, 1995	16
2 =*I Will Always Love You*, Whitney Houston, 1992	14
=*I'll Make Love to You*, Boyz II Men, 1994	14
=*Macarena (Bayside Boys Mix)*, Los Del Rio, 1995	14
=*Candle in the Wind (1997)/ Something About the Way You Look Tonight*, Elton John, 1997	14
6 =*End of the Road*, Boyz II Men, 1992	13
=*The Boy Is Mine*, Brandy & Monica, 1998	13
8 =*Don't Be Cruel/Hound Dog*, Elvis Presley, 1956	11
=*I Swear*, All-4-One, 1994	11
=*Un-break My Heart*, Toni Braxton, 1996	11

* Based on Billboard *charts*

Source: *The Popular Music Database*

TOP 10 SLOWEST US ALBUM CHART RISES TO NO. 1

(Title/artist or group/weeks to reach No. 1)

1 *First Take*, Roberta Flack, 118   **2** *You Don't Mess Around With Jim*, Jim Croce, 81
3 *Forever Your Girl*, Paula Abdul, 64   **4** *Film Encores*, Mantovani & His Orchestra, 59
5 *Fleetwood Mac*, Fleetwood Mac, 58   **6** *Hangin' Tough*, New Kids on the Block, 55
7 *Nick of Time*, Bonnie Raitt, 52;   = *Throwing Copper*, Live, 52   **9** *Appetite for Destruction*, Guns 'N Roses, 50;   = *Whitney Houston*, Whitney Houston, 50

Source: *The Popular Music Database*

BROTHERS IN WAITING

A gap of almost a decade separates the Bee Gees' No. 1 hits: I've Gotta Get a Message to You *in September 1968 and* Tragedy *in April 1978.*

TOP 10 ★

SINGLES OF THE 1990s IN THE US

SINGLE/ARTIST OR GROUP	YEAR RELEASED
1 *Candle in the Wind (1997)/Something About the Way You Look Tonight*, Elton John	1997
2 *I Will Always Love You*, Whitney Houston	1992
3 *Whoomp! (There It Is)*, Tag Team	1993
4 *Macarena*, Los Del Rio	1995
5 *(Everything I Do) I Do It for You*, Bryan Adams	1991
6 *I'll Be Missing You*, Puff Daddy and Faith Evans (featuring 112)	1997
7 *How Do I Live*, LeAnn Rimes	1997
8 *Gangsta's Paradise*, Coolio (featuring L.V.)	1995
9 *Dazzey Duks*, Duice	1993
10 *Fantasy*, Mariah Carey	1995

TOP 10 ★

SINGLES OF THE 1990s IN THE US, MALE

SINGLE/ARTIST	YEAR RELEASED
1 *Candle in the Wind (1997)/Something About the Way You Look Tonight*, Elton John	1997
2 *(Everything I Do) I Do It for You*, Bryan Adams	1991
3 *Gangsta's Paradise*, Coolio featuring L.V.	1995
4 *How Do U Want It*, 2 Pac	1996
5 *I Believe I Can Fly*, R. Kelly	1996
6 *You Make Me Wanna ...*, Usher	1997
7 *Livin' La Vida Loca*, Ricky Martin	1999
8 *Here Comes the Hotstepper*, Ini Kamoze	1994
9 *Ice Ice Baby*, Vanilla Ice	1990
10 *This Is How We Do It*, Montell Jordan	1995

TOP 10 SINGLES OF THE 1990s IN THE US, FEMALE

(Single/artist/year released)

1 *I Will Always Love You,* Whitney Houston, 1992 **2** *How Do I Live*, LeAnn Rimes, 1997 **3** *The Boy Is Mine*, Brandy & Monica, 1998 **4** *Fantasy*, Mariah Carey, 1995 **5** *Vogue*, Madonna, 1990 **6** *You Were Meant for Me/Foolish Games*, Jewel, 1996 **7** *The Power of Love*, Celine Dion, 1993 **8** *Believe*, Cher, 1999 **9** *Hero*, Mariah Carey, 1993 **10** *You're Still the One*, Shania Twain, 1998

FANTASY FIGURE

Mariah Carey's 1995 single Fantasy became the first ever by a female artist to debut at US No. 1, becoming one of the top sellers of the decade.

TOP 10 ★
SINGLES OF EACH YEAR IN THE 1990s IN THE US

YEAR	SINGLE/ARTIST OR GROUP
1990	*Vogue*, Madonna
1991	*(Everything I Do) I Do It for You*, Bryan Adams
1992	*I Will Always Love You*, Whitney Houston
1993	*Rump Shaker*, Wreckx 'N' Effect
1994	*Whoomp! There It Is*, Tag Team
1995	*Gangsta's Paradise*, Coolio featuring L.V.
1996	*Macarena (Bayside Boys Mix)*, Los Del Rio
1997	*Candle in the Wind (1997)/ Something About the Way You Look Tonight*, Elton John
1998	*The Boy Is Mine*, Brandy & Monica
1999	*Believe*, Cher

Source: *RIAA*

TOP 10 ★
SINGLES OF EACH YEAR IN THE 1980s IN THE US

YEAR	SINGLE/ARTIST OR GROUP
1980	*Another One Bites the Dust*, Queen
1981	*Endless Love*, Diana Ross and Lionel Richie
1982	*Eye of the Tiger*, Survivor
1983	*Islands in the Stream*, Kenny Rogers and Dolly Parton
1984	*When Doves Cry*, Prince
1985	*We Are the World*, USA for Africa
1986	*That's What Friends Are For*, Dionne Warwick and Friends
1987	*I Wanna Dance With Somebody (Who Loves Me)*, Whitney Houston
1988	*Kokomo*, The Beach Boys
1989	*Wild Thing*, Tone Loc

TOP 10 ★
SINGLES OF THE 1980s IN THE US

	SINGLE/ARTIST OR GROUP	YEAR RELEASED
1	*We Are the World*, USA for Africa	1985
2	*Physical*, Olivia Newton-John	1981
3	*Endless Love*, Diana Ross and Lionel Richie	1981
4	*Eye of the Tiger*, Survivor	1982
5	*I Love Rock 'n' Roll*, Joan Jett and The Blackhearts	1982
6	*When Doves Cry*, Prince	1984
7	*Celebration*, Cool and The Gang	1981
8	*Another One Bites the Dust*, Queen	1980
9	*Wild Thing*, Tone Loc	1989
10	*Islands in the Stream*, Kenny Rogers and Dolly Parton	1983

America's top-selling single of the 1980s was, rather fittingly, a record that included contributions from many of those artists who had become the recording élite during the decade – the charity single for Africa's famine victims, *We Are the World*.

TOP 10 ★
SINGLES OF THE 1970s IN THE US

	SINGLE/ARTIST OR GROUP	YEAR RELEASED
1	*You Light up My Life*, Debby Boone	1977
2	*Le Freak*, Chic	1978
3	*Night Fever*, Bee Gees	1978
4	*Stayin' Alive*, Bee Gees	1978
5	*Shadow Dancing*, Andy Gibb	1978
6	*Disco Lady*, Johnnie Taylor	1976
7	*I'll Be There*, Jackson 5	1970
8	*Star Wars Theme/Cantina Band*, Meco	1977
9	*Car Wash*, Rose Royce	1976
10	*Joy to the World*, Three Dog Night	1971

During the last four years of the 1970s, singles sales in the United States rose to their highest-ever level, and chart-topping records were almost routinely selling over 2 million copies.

QUEEN RULES
Queen's Bohemian Rhapsody was one of the UK's top sellers of the 1970s, while Another One Bites the Dust *was a US smash of the 1980s.*

TOP 10 ★
SINGLES OF THE 1960s IN THE US

	SINGLE/ARTIST OR GROUP	YEAR RELEASED
1	*I Want to Hold Your Hand*, The Beatles	1964
2	*It's Now or Never*, Elvis Presley	1960
3	*Hey Jude*, The Beatles	1968
4	*The Ballad of the Green Berets*, Sgt. Barry Sadler	1966
5	*Love is Blue*, Paul Mauriat	1968
6	*I'm a Believer*, The Monkees	1966
7	*Can't Buy Me Love*, The Beatles	1964
8	*She Loves You*, The Beatles	1964
9	*Sugar Sugar*, The Archies	1969
10	*The Twist*, Chubby Checker	1960

Which female group has had the most US and UK hits?
see p.134 for the answer

A Spice Girls
B The Supremes
C Bangles

BRIDGING THE ATLANTIC

Simon and Garfunkel's single and album Bridge over Troubled Water *topped the UK and US charts simultaneously in March 1970.*

TOP 10 ★
ALBUMS OF THE 1960s IN THE US

ALBUM/ARTIST OR GROUP	YEAR RELEASED
1 **West Side Story** (Original Soundtrack), Various	1961
2 **Blue Hawaii** (Original Soundtrack), Elvis Presley	1961
3 **The Sound of Music** (Original Soundtrack), Various	1965
4 **Sgt. Pepper's Lonely Hearts Club Band**, The Beatles	1967
5 **More of the Monkees**, The Monkees	1967
6 **Days of Wine and Roses**, Andy Williams	1963
7 **G.I. Blues**, Elvis Presley	1960
8 **The Button-Down Mind Of Bob Newhart**, Bob Newhart	1960
9 **Whipped Cream & Other Delights**, Herb Alpert & The Tijuana Brass	1965
10 **A Hard Day's Night** (Original Soundtrack), The Beatles	1964

TOP 10 ALBUMS OF EACH YEAR IN THE 1960s IN THE US
(Year/album/artist or group)

1 1960 *The Sound of Music*, Original Cast **2** 1961 *Judy at Carnegie Hall*, Judy Garland, **3** 1962 *West Side Story*, Soundtrack **4** 1963 *John Fitzgerald Kennedy: A Memorial Album*, Documentary **5** 1964 *Meet The Beatles*, The Beatles **6** 1965 *Mary Poppins*, Soundtrack **7** 1966 *Whipped Cream & Other Delights*, Herb Alpert & The Tijuana Brass **8** 1967 *Sgt. Pepper's Lonely Hearts Club Band*, The Beatles **9** 1968 *The Beatles* (*"White Album"*), The Beatles **10** 1969 *Hair*, Broadway Cast

TOP 10 ★
ALBUMS OF THE 1970s IN THE US

ALBUM/ARTIST OR GROUP	YEAR RELEASED
1 **Rumours**, Fleetwood Mac	1977
2 **Their Greatest Hits, 1971–1975**, The Eagles	1976
3 **The Dark Side of the Moon**, Pink Floyd	1973
4 **Tapestry**, Carole King	1971
5 **Saturday Night Fever** (Original Soundtrack), Various	1977
6 **Led Zeppelin IV** (Untitled), Led Zeppelin	1971
7 **Boston**, Boston	1976
8 **Grease** (Original Soundtrack), Various	1978
9 **Frampton Comes Alive!**, Peter Frampton	1976
10 **Songs in the Key of Life**, Stevie Wonder	1976

TOP 10 ★
ALBUMS OF EACH YEAR IN THE 1970s IN THE US

YEAR	ALBUM/ARTIST OR GROUP
1970	**Bridge Over Troubled Water**, Simon and Garfunkel
1971	**Tapestry**, Carole King
1972	**American Pie**, Don McLean
1973	**Dark Side of the Moon**, Pink Floyd
1974	**John Denver's Greatest Hits**, John Denver
1975	**Captain Fantastic and the Brown Dirt Cowboy**, Elton John
1976	**Frampton Comes Alive**, Peter Frampton
1977	**Rumours**, Fleetwood Mac
1978	**Saturday Night Fever**, Soundtrack
1979	**Breakfast in America**, Supertramp

THRILLS GALORE

It has been estimated that Michael Jackson's Thriller *album has sold 25 million copies in the US and more than 45 million worldwide.*

TOP 10 ★
ALBUMS OF EACH YEAR IN THE 1990s IN THE US

YEAR	ALBUM/ARTIST OR GROUP
1990	*Please Hammer Don't Hurt 'Em*, MC Hammer
1991	*Ropin' the Wind*, Garth Brooks
1992	*Some Gave All*, Billy Ray Cyrus
1993	*The Bodyguard*, Whitney Houston/Soundtrack
1994	*The Sign*, Ace of Base
1995	*Cracked Rear View*, Hootie & the Blowfish
1996	*Jagged Little Pill*, Alanis Morissette
1997	*Spice*, Spice Girls
1998	*Titanic*, Soundtrack
1999	*Millennium*, Backstreet Boys

TOP 10 ★
ALBUMS OF THE 1980s IN THE US

	ALBUM/ARTIST OR GROUP	YEAR RELEASED
1	*Thriller*, Michael Jackson	1982
2	*Born in the USA*, Bruce Springsteen	1984
3	*Dirty Dancing* (Original Soundtrack), Various	1987
4	*Purple Rain* (Original Soundtrack), Prince & The Revolution	1984
5	*Can't Slow Down*, Lionel Richie	1983
6	*Whitney Houston*, Whitney Houston	1985
7	*Hysteria*, Def Leppard	1987
8	*Slippery When Wet*, Bon Jovi	1986
9	*Appetite For Destruction*, Guns N' Roses	1988
10	*The Wall*, Pink Floyd	1979

TOP 10 ALBUMS OF EACH YEAR IN THE 1980s IN THE US
(Year/album/artist or group)

1 1980 *The Wall*, Pink Floyd **2** 1981 *Hi Infidelity*, REO Speedwagon **3** 1982 *Asia*, Asia **4** 1983 *Thriller*, Michael Jackson **5** 1984 *Purple Rain*, Prince & The Revolution **6** 1985 *Like a Virgin*, Madonna **7** 1986 *Whitney Houston*, Whitney Houston **8** 1987 *Slippery When Wet*, Bon Jovi **9** 1988 *Faith*, George Michael **10** 1989 *Girl You Know It's True*, Milli Vanilli

MADONNA V HAMMER

While Madonna's The Immaculate Collection was the UK's top selling album of 1990, with nine weeks at No. 1, it was held off the top slot in the US by MC Hammer with Please Hammer Don't Hurt 'Em.

TOP 10 ALBUMS OF THE 1990s IN THE US
(Album/artist or group/year released)

1 *The Bodyguard*, Soundtrack, 1992 **2** *No Fences*, Garth Brooks, 1990 **3** *Jagged Little Pill*, Alanis Morissette, 1995 **4** *Cracked Rear View*, Hootie & the Blowfish, 1994 **5** *Ropin' the Wind*, Garth Brooks, 1991 **6** *Come on Over*, Shania Twain, 1997 **7** *Breathless*, Kenny G, 1992 **8** *II*, Boyz II Men, 1994 **9** *The Woman in Me*, Shania Twain, 1995 **10** *Pieces of You*, Jewel, 1997

Source: *RIAA*

Did You Know? The album from the 1992 film *The Bodyguard* became a worldwide bestseller, its 16 million-plus sales in the US making it the country's bestselling soundtrack album ever.

Female Singers

TOP 10 ★
YOUNGEST FEMALE SINGERS TO HAVE A NO. 1 SINGLE IN THE US

			AGE	
	SINGER/TITLE/YEAR	YEARS	MONTHS	DAYS
1	**Little Peggy March**, *I Will Follow Him*, 1963	15	1	20
2	**Brenda Lee**, *I'm Sorry*, 1960	15	7	7
3	**Tiffany**, *I Think We're Alone*, 1987	16	1	5
4	**Lesley Gore**, *It's My Party*, 1963	17	0	30
5	**Little Eva**, *The Loco-Motion*, 1962	17	1	27
6	**Britney Spears**, *...Baby One More Time*, 1999	17	2	25
7	**Monica**, *The First Night*, 1998	17	11	9
8	**Shelley Fabares**, *Johnny Angel*, 1962	18	2	19
9	**Debbie Gibson**, *Foolish Beat*, 1988	18	6	4
10	**Christina Aguilera**, *Genie in a Bottle*, 1999	18	7	13

Source: *The Popular Music Database*

The ages shown are those of each artist on the publication date of the chart in which she achieved her first No. 1 single.

TOP 10 ★
OLDEST FEMALE SINGERS TO HAVE A NO. 1 SINGLE IN THE US

			AGE	
	SINGER/TITLE/YEAR	YEARS	MONTHS	DAYS
1	**Cher**, *Believe*, 1999	52	9	15
2	**Tina Turner**, *What's Love Got to Do With It*, 1984	45	9	5
3	**Bette Midler**, *The Wind Beneath My Wings*, 1989	44	8	24
4	**Kim Carnes**, *Bette Davis Eyes*, 1981	35	9	26
5	**Dolly Parton**, *9 to 5*, 1981	35	1	2
6	**Georgia Gibbs**, *Dance With Me Henry*, 1955	34	8	18
7	**Deniece Williams**, *Let's Hear If for the Boy*, 1985	33	11	23
8	**Kay Starr**, *Rock and Roll Waltz*, 1956	33	6	15
9	**Anne Murray**, *You Needed Me*, 1978	33	4	15
10	**Roberta Flack**, *The First Time Ever I Saw Your Face*, 1972	33	2	5

Source: *The Popular Music Database*

The ages shown are those of each artist on the publication date of the chart in which her first No. 1 single reached the top.

BRITNEY'S BEST

Her debut single ...Baby One More Time was a No. 1 hit for Louisiana-born Britney Spears, a former performer on Disney Channel's Mickey Mouse Club.

TOP 10 SINGLES BY FEMALE SINGERS IN THE US

(Title/artist/year)

1 *I Will Always Love You*, Whitney Houston, 1992 **2** *How Do I Live*, LeAnn Rimes, 1997 **3** *The Boy Is Mine*, Brandy & Monica, 1998 **4** *Fantasy*, Mariah Carey, 1995 **5** *Vogue*, Madonna, 1990 **6** *Mr. Big Stuff*, Jean Knight, 1971 **7** *You Were Meant for Me/Foolish Games*, Jewel, 1996 **8** *You Light Up My Life*, Debby Boone, 1977 **9** *The Power of Love*, Celine Dion, 1993 **10** *Believe*, Cher, 1999

Source: *The Popular Music Database*

Among these blockbusters, all platinum sellers, it is fitting that Whitney Houston's multiplatinum success from *The Bodyguard Original Soundtrack* was also written by a woman – Dolly Parton.

SINGING PHENOMENON

Born Cherilyn Sarkasian La Pier in El Centro, California, on May 20, 1946, Cher formed the singing double act of Sonny and Cher with her husband Sonny Bono. Their single *I Got You Babe* topped the charts in both the US and UK in 1965, and Cher went on to achieve her first solo million-seller, *Bang Bang (My Baby Shot Me Down)* the following year. Televison work with Sonny (from whom she was divorced in 1974) and later movie acting, for which she won an Oscar in 1988 (for *Moonstruck*), have since served as the backdrop to a quite phenomenal singing career that saw her score a No. 1 hit at the age of 52.

SNAP SHOTS

TOP 10 ★ ALBUMS BY FEMALE SINGERS IN THE US

	TITLE/ARTIST	YEAR
1	*The Bodyguard* (Soundtrack), Whitney Houston	1992
2	*Jagged Little Pill*, Alanis Morissette	1995
3	*Whitney Houston*, Whitney Houston	1985
4	*Come on Over*, Shania Twain	1997
5 =	*The Woman in Me*, Shania Twain	1995
=	*Pieces of You*, Jewel	1997
7 =	*Tapestry*, Carole King	1971
=	*Let's Talk About Love*, Celion Dion	1997
=	*Falling into You*, Celine Dion	1996
=	*Music Box*, Maria Carey	1993
=	*Like a Virgin*, Madonna	1984

Source: *The Popular Music Database*

SAILING TO FAME

One of Canada's most successful singers, Celine Dion achieved worldwide fame with My Heart Will Go On from the movie Titanic.

TOP 10 ★ FEMALE SINGERS WITH THE MOST TOP 10 HITS IN THE US

	SINGER	TOP 10 HITS*
1	Madonna	32
2	Janet Jackson (including duets with Michael Jackson and Busta Rhymes)	24
3	Whitney Houston (including duets with CeCe Winans and Faith Evans)	20
4	Mariah Carey (including duets with Boyz II Men, Luther Vandross, and Jay-Z)	19
5	Aretha Franklin (including a duet with George Michael)	17
6	Connie Francis	16
7	Olivia Newton-John (including duets with John Travolta and Electric Light Orchestra)	15
8	Donna Summer	14
9 =	Brenda Lee	12
=	Diana Ross (including duets with Marvin Gaye and Lionel Richie)	12
=	Dionne Warwick (including a duet with the Detroit Spinners and one with "Friends" Stevie Wonder, Gladys Knight, and Elton John)	12

* To January 1, 2000

Did You Know? Released in 1915, Romanian soprano Alma Gluck's *Carry Me Back to Old Virginny* was the first recording by a woman to sell over a million copies.

Female Groups

TOP 10 ★
FEMALE GROUPS OF ALL TIME IN THE US

	GROUP	SINGLES AT NO. 1	SINGLES IN TOP 10	TOP 20
1	The Supremes	12	20	24
2	The Pointer Sisters	–	7	13
3	TLC	2	9	11
4 =	Expose	1	8	9
=	The McGuire Sisters	2	4	9
6	The Fontane Sisters	2	2	8

	GROUP	SINGLES AT NO. 1	SINGLES IN TOP 10	TOP 20
7 =	The Shirelles	2	6	7
=	Martha & the Vandellas	–	6	7
=	En Vogue	–	5	7
=	Spice Girls	–	4	7

Source: *The Popular Music Database*

TOP TRIO

The initial letters of the singers' nicknames – "T-Boz," "Left Eye," and "Chilli" – provided the name for the 1990s' singing sensation TLC.

TOP 10 ★
FEMALE GROUPS OF ALL TIME IN THE UK*

	GROUP	SINGLES AT NO. 1	SINGLES IN TOP 10	TOP 20
1	The Supremes	1	13	18
2 =	Eternal	1	13	15
=	Bananarama	–	10	15
4	Spice Girls	8	9	9
5 =	The Three Degrees	1	5	7
=	Sister Sledge	1	4	7
=	The Nolans	–	3	7
8	All Saints	3	6	6
9 =	The Bangles	1	3	5
=	Salt-n-Pepa	–	4	5

* To 1 January 2000

The Supremes also had three other Top 20 hits, not included here, in partnership with Motown male groups the Four Tops and the Temptations. However, Bananarama's charity revival of *Help!*, shared with Dawn French and Jennifer Saunders, has been included because all the participants are female. The only two groups to have had more than one chart-topper – the Spice Girls and All Saints – had their success in the late '90s.

WORTH THEIR SALT

Formed as a duo in 1985 and joined by Spinderella in 1987, rap girl group Salt-n-Pepa have achieved huge success on both sides of the Atlantic.

TOP 10 ★
SINGLES BY FEMALE GROUPS IN THE US

TITLE/GROUP	YEAR
1 *Don't Let Go*, En Vogue	1996
2 *Hold On*, En Vogue	1990
3 *Wannabe*, Spice Girls	1997
4 *Whatta Man*, Salt-n-Pepa	1994
5 *Expressions*, Salt-n-Pepa	1990
6 *Push It*, Salt-n-Pepa	1987
7 *Waterfall*, TLC	1995
8 *Creep*, TLC	1994
9 *Weak*, SWV	1993
10 *Baby, Baby, Baby*, TLC	1992

Source: *The Popular Music Database*

TOP 10 ★
ALBUMS BY FEMALE GROUPS IN THE US

TITLE/GROUP	YEAR
1 *Crazysexycool*, TLC	1994
2 *Wide Open Spaces*, Dixie Chicks	1998
3 *Spice*, Spice Girls	1997
4 *Wilson Phillips*, Wilson Phillips	1990
5 *Very Necessary*, Salt-n-Pepa	1993
6 *Ooooooohhh ... On the TLC Tip*, TLC	1992
7 *Fanmail*, TLC	1999
8 *Spiceworld*, Spice Girls	1997
9 *Funky Divas*, En Vogue	1992
10 *It's That Time*, SWV	1993

Source: *The Popular Music Database*

As this list exemplifies, the 1990s saw a huge surge in the popularity of all-girl groups, with sales eclipsing those of such predecessors as The Supremes and Bangles.

TOP 10 ★
SINGLES BY FEMALE GROUPS IN THE UK

TITLE/GROUP	YEAR
1 *Wannabe*, Spice Girls	1996
2 *Say You'll Be There*, Spice Girls	1996
3 *2 Become 1*, Spice Girls	1996
4 *Never Ever*, All Saints	1997
5 *C'Est La Vie*, B*Witched	1998
6 *Goodbye*, Spice Girls	1998
7 *Viva Forever*, Spice Girls	1998
8 *Spice up Your Life*, Spice Girls	1997
9 *Too Much*, Spice Girls	1997
10 *Mama/Who Do You Think You Are*, Spice Girls	1997

Such has been the Spice Girls' impact on popular music that they have totally rewritten the record book as far as successful girl-group singles are concerned, snatching eight of the all-time bestsellers in the UK.

GIRL POWER
The original lineup of five Spice Girls achieved unprecedented dominance of the singles charts during the late 1990s.

Which classical composer is considered the most prolific?
see p.153 for the answer
A Beethoven
B Mozart
C Haydn

Star Singles & Albums

TOP 10 ★
BEATLES SINGLES IN THE US

	SINGLE	YEAR
1	Hey Jude	1968
2	Get Back	1969
3	Something	1969
4	Let It Be	1970
5	The Long and Winding Road	1970
6	I Want to Hold Your Hand	1964
7	Can't Buy Me Love	1964
8	She Loves You	1964
9	I Feel Fine	1964
10	Help!	1965

Source: *The Popular Music Database*

The top four titles here were all certified with 2 million-plus sales in 1999.

BEAT ALL

In a lifespan of little over 10 years (1960–70), the Beatles revolutionized rock music, achieving 20 US and 17 UK No. 1 singles and worldwide sales of more than 1 billion recordings.

TOP 10 ★
ARTISTS WITH THE MOST ALBUM SALES IN THE US

	ARTIST OR GROUP	TOTAL ALBUM SALES*
1	The Beatles	106,530,000
2	Garth Brooks	92,000,000
3	Led Zeppelin	83,620,000
4	Elvis Presley	77,280,000
5	Eagles	65,000,000
6	Billy Joel	63,250,000
7	Barbra Streisand	62,750,000
8	Elton John	61,620,000
9	Aerosmith	54,370,000
10	Pink Floyd	52,600,000

* To 1 January 2000

Source: *RIAA*

The RIAA, which certifies US record sales, has logged over 70 artists who have achieved total album sales of more than 20 million each.

TOP 10 ★
ELVIS PRESLEY SINGLES IN THE US

	SINGLE	YEAR
1	Don't Be Cruel/Hound Dog	1956
2	It's Now or Never	1960
3	Love Me Tender	1956
4	Heartbreak Hotel	1956
5	Jailhouse Rock	1957
6	All Shook Up	1957
7	(Let Me Be Your) Teddy Bear	1957
8	Are You Lonesome Tonight?	1960
9	Don't	1958
10	Too Much	1957

Source: *MRIB*

Elvis had dozens of million-selling singles, scattered throughout his career, but most of his monster hits were during his 1950s heyday when he was the spearhead of rock 'n' roll music.

KING OF ROCK

Elvis Presley's first singles were released in 1954, when he was 19. Baby, Let's Play House, released in 1955, became his first chart hit in the US.

TOP 10 JOHN LENNON SINGLES IN THE US
(Single/year)

1 *(Just Like) Starting Over*, 1980
2 *Woman*, 1981 **3** *Instant Karma*, 1970
4 *Whatever Gets You Thru the Night*, 1974 **5** *Imagine*, 1971 **6** *#9 Dream*, 1974 **7** *Nobody Told Me*, 1984
8 *Watching the Wheels*, 1981 **9** *Power to the People*, 1971 **10** *Mind Games*, 1973

Source: *MRIB*

TOP 10 ★
MADONNA ALBUMS IN THE US

	ALBUM	YEAR
1	*Like a Virgin*	1984
2	*True Blue*	1986
3	*The Immaculate Collection*	1990
4	*Like a Prayer*	1989
5	*Ray of Light*	1998
6	*Madonna*	1983
7	*Erotica*	1992
8	*Bedtime Stories*	1994
9	*Something to Remember*	1990
10	*I'm Breathless*	1987

Source: *The Popular Music Database*

Madonna's second album, *Like a Virgin*, was released in December 1984 and rocketed to No. 1. Two singles from it – the title song and *Angel* – both achieved gold status, while the album itself became the first by a female artist since Carole King's 1971 *Tapestry* to sell more than 10 million.

TOP 10 ★
ELTON JOHN SINGLES IN THE US

	SINGLE	YEAR
1	*Candle in the Wind (1997)/ Something About the Way You Look Tonight*	1997
2	*Crocodile Rock*	1972
3	*Goodbye Yellow Brick Road*	1973
4	*Island Girl*	1975
5	*Philadelphia Freedom*	1975
6	*Can You Feel the Love Tonight*	1994
7	*Lucy in the Sky With Diamonds*	1974
8	*Little Jeannie*	1980
9	*Daniel*	1973
10	*The Bitch Is Back*	1974

Source: *The Popular Music Database*

During the 1970s, Elton John's popularity in America exceeded that in his native UK, so that US million-sellers like *Island Girl* and *Philadelphia Freedom* do not appear in his UK Top 10. His 1997 version of *Candle in the Wind* broke records on both sides of the Atlantic.

TOP 10 ★
ROLLING STONES ALBUMS IN THE US

	ALBUM	YEAR
1	*Hot Rocks 1964–1971*	1972
2	*Some Girls*	1978
3	*Tattoo You*	1981
4	*Big Hits (High Tide and Green Grass)*	1966
5	*Let it Bleed*	1969
6	*Steel Wheels*	1989
7	*Voodoo Lounge*	1994
8	*Bridges to Babylon*	1997
9	*Out of Our Heads*	1965
10	*Emotional Rescue*	1980

Source: *The Popular Music Database*

ROLLING ON

The Rolling Stones' greatest album successes come from the decades 1960s to 1980s, but they continued to perform live throughout the 1990s.

Did You Know? *Come On*, the Rolling Stones' first single (1963), had to be re-recorded, altering the word "jerk" to "guy" in order to avoid a radio ban.

137

Pop Stars of the 90s

TOP 10 ★ BOYZ II MEN SINGLES IN THE US

	TITLE	YEAR
1	I'll Make Love to You	1994
2	End of the Road	1992
3	On Bended Knee	1994
4	4 Seasons of Loneliness	1997
5	Motownphilly	1991
6	In the Still of the Nite	1992
7	A Song for Mama	1997
8	It's so Hard to Say Goodbye to Yesterday	1991
9	Water Runs Dry	1995
10	I Will Get There	1999

TOP 10 ★ MICHAEL BOLTON SINGLES IN THE US

	TITLE	YEAR
1	Said I Loved You ... But I Lied	1993
2	When a Man Loves a Woman	1991
3	Time, Love and Tenderness	1991
4	To Love Somebody	1992
5	Love is a Wonderful Thing	1991
6	How Can We Be Lovers	1990
7	When I'm Back on My Feet Again	1990
8	Missing You Now	1992
9	Go the Distance	1997
10	Can I Touch You ... There?	1995

TOP 10 ★ CELINE DION SINGLES IN THE US

	TITLE	YEAR
1	The Power of Love	1993
2	Because You Loved Me	1996
3	It's All Coming Back to Me Now	1996
4	My Heart Will Go On	1998
5	All By Myself	1997
6	Beauty and the Beast	1992
7	Where Does My Heart Beat Now	1990
8	That's the Way It Is	1999
9	If You Asked Me To	1992
10	When I Fall in Love	1993

TOP 10 ★ JANET JACKSON SINGLES IN THE US

	TITLE	YEAR
1	Again	1993
2	That's the Way Love Goes	1993
3	Together Again	1997
4	Love Will Never do Without You	1990
5	Escapade	1990
6	Black Cat	1990
7	Runaway	1995
8	If	1993
9	You Want This	1994
10	Any Time, Any Place	1994

TOP 10 ★ MARIAH CAREY SINGLES IN THE US

	TITLE	YEAR
1	Hero	1993
2	Always be My Baby	1996
3	Fantasy	1995
4	My All	1997
5	Honey	1997
6	Dreamlover	1993
7	I Still Believe	1999
8	Love Takes Time	1990
9	Vision of Love	1990
10	Heartbreaker	1999

TOP 10 MADONNA SINGLES IN THE US

(Single/year)

❶ Vogue, 1990 ❷ Justify My Love, 1990 ❸ Take a Bow, 1994 ❹ This Used to be My Playground, 1992 ❺ Erotica, 1992 ❻ Secret, 1994 ❼ I'll Remember, 1994 ❽ You'll See, 1995 ❾ Ray of Light, 1998 ❿ Frozen, 1998

Source: MRIB

TOP 10 ★ PRINCE SINGLES IN THE US

	TITLE	YEAR
1	Cream	1991
2	The Most Beautiful Girl in the World	1994
3	7	1992
4	Thieves in the Temple	1990
5	Gett Off	1991
6	Diamonds and Pearls	1991
7	1999	1992
8	I Hate U	1995
9	Money Don't Matter 2 Night	1992
10	Letitgo	1994

TOP 10 TLC SINGLES IN THE US

(Title/year)

❶ Waterfalls, 1995 ❷ Creep, 1995 ❸ Baby-Baby-Baby, 1992 ❹ Ain't 2 Proud 2 Beg, 1992 ❺ Unpretty, 1999 ❻ No Scrubs, 1999 ❼ Red Light Special, 1995 ❽ Diggin' on You, 1996 ❾ What About Your Friends, 1992 ❿ Hat 2 Da Back, 1993

TOP 10 ★
WHITNEY HOUSTON SINGLES IN THE US

	TITLE	YEAR
1	I Will Always Love You	1992
2	Exhale (Shoop Shoop)	1995
3	I Believe in You and Me	1996
4	Heartbreak Hotel*	1999
5	My Love Is Your Love	1999
6	I'm Your Baby Tonight	1990
7	All the Man That I Need	1990
8	I'm Every Woman	1993
9	It's Not Right but It's Okay	1999
10	I Have Nothing	1993

* With Faith Evans & Kelly Price

TOP 10 ★
JODECI SINGLES IN THE US

	TITLE	YEAR
1	Lately	1993
2	Cry for You	1994
3	Come and Talk to Me	1992
4	Freek 'N You	1995
5	Forever My Lady	1991
6	Get On Up	1996
7	Feenin'	1994
8	Love U 4 Life	1996
9	Stay	1992
10	Let's Go Through the Motions	1993

TOP 10 R. KELLY SINGLES IN THE US
(Single/year)

1. Bump and Grind, 1994 2. I Believe I Can Fly, 1997
3. I'm Your Angel*, 1998 4. Down Low (Nobody Has to Know)#, 1996 5. You Remind Me of Something, 1996
6. I Can't Sleep Baby (If I), 1996 7. You Body's Callin', 1994
8. Sex Me, Parts 1 & 2, 1993 9. Gotham City, 1997
10. If I Could Turn Back the Hands of Time, 1999

* With Celanie Dion # Featuring Ronald Isley

GORGEOUS GEORGE
George Michael has achieved bestselling albums across two decades in both the UK and the US.

TOP 10 GEORGE MICHAEL SINGLES OF THE 1990s IN THE US
(Title/year)

1. I Want Your Sex, 1987 2. Faith, 1987
3. Don't Let the Sun Go Down on Me*, 1992
4. One More Try, 1988 5. Freedom, 1991
6. Fastlove, 1996 7. Jesus to a Child, 1996
8. Too Funky, 1992 9. Father Figure, 1988
10. Praying for Time, 1990

*With Elton John

Did You Know? Whitney Houston's mother, Cissy Houston, née Drinkard, began her musical career in a group called The Drinkard Sisters, with her nieces Dionne and Dee Dee Warwick.

TOP 10 ★ HEAVY METAL ALBUMS IN THE US

	TITLE/ARTIST	APPROX. SALES
1 =	*Back in Black*, AC/DC	16,000,000
=	*Boston*, Boston	16,000,000
3	*Bat Out of Hell*, Meat Loaf	13,000,000
4 =	*Slippery When Wet*, Bon Jovi	12,000,000
=	*Hysteria*, Def Leppard	12,000,000
=	*Metallica*, Metallica	12,000,000
7 =	*Van Halen*, Van Halen	10,000,000
=	*Eliminator*, ZZ Top	10,000,000
=	*1984*, Van Halen	10,000,000
10 =	*Pyromania*, Def Leppard	9,000,000
=	*Aerosmith's Greatest Hits*, Aerosmith	9,000,000

Source: RIAA

TOP 10 ★ REGGAE ALBUMS IN THE US, 1999

	TITLE	ARTIST
1	Reggae Gold 1999	Various
2	Strictly the Best 21	Various
3	Reggae Gold 1998	Various
4	Pure Reggae	Various
5	The Doctor	Beenie Man
6	Reggae Party	Various
7	DJ Reggae Mix	Various
8	Best of Bob Marley	Bob Marley
9	Everyone Falls in Love	Tantro Metro & Devonte
10	Labour of Love III	UB40

Source: Billboard

DIAMOND FOR HEAVY METAL

In 1999, Joe Elliot, Def Leppard's vocalist, received an RIAA Diamond award (for albums that have sold more than 10 million copies) for the band's 1987 Hysteria.

▶ TOP 10 ★
REGGAE ALBUMS IN THE UK

	TITLE/ARTIST OR GROUP	YEAR
1	*Legend*, Bob Marley and the Wailers	1984
2	*The Best of UB40 Vol. 1*, UB40	1987
3	*Labour of Love II*, UB40	1989
4	*Labour of Love*, UB40	1983
5	*Promises and Lies*, UB40	1993
6	*Present Arms*, UB40	1981
7	*Signing Off*, UB40	1980
8	*Tease Me*, Chaka Demus and Pliers	1993
9	*Labour of Love III*, UB40	1998
10	*Exodus*, Bob Marley and the Wailers	1977

Source: *The Popular Music Database*

▶ TOP 10 ★
INSTRUMENTAL SINGLES IN THE US

	TITLE/ARTIST OR GROUP	YEAR
1	*Star Wars Theme/Cantina Band*, Meco	1977
2	*Love Is Blue*, Paul Mauriat	1968
3	*Theme from A Summer Place*, Percy Faith	1960
4	*Rise*, Herb Alpert	1979
5	*Tequila*, Champs	1958
6	*Cherry Pink and Apple Blossom White*, Perez Prado	1955
7	*Stranger on the Shore*, Acker Bilk	1962
8	*Telstar*, Tornados	1963
9	*Patricia*, Perez Prado	1958
10	*Wonderland by Night*, Bert Kaempfert	1961

Source: *The Popular Music Database*

Meco (Meco Monardo) is the arranger responsible for such hits as Gloria Gaynor's *Never Can Say Goodbye*. Upon the release of *Star Wars*, he issued his own version of the theme tune, which overtook the official London Symphony Orchestra recording to reach No. 1 in the US charts. British jazz musician Acker Bilk's *Stranger on the Shore* represents a particular achievement, reaching No. 1 in both the UK and US charts.

▶ TOP 10 ★
LATIN POP ALBUMS IN THE US, 1999

	TITLE	ARTIST
1	*Vuelve*	Ricky Martin
2	*Bailamos*	Enrique Iglesias
3	*Donde Estan los Ladrones?*	Shakira
4	*Cosas del Amor*	Enrique Iglesias
5	*MTV Unplugged*	Maná
6	*Trozos de Mi Alma*	Marco Antonio Solís
7	*Marte es Un Placer*	Luis Miguel
8	*Atado a Tu Amor*	Chayanne
9	*Amor, Familia y Respeto*	A. B. Quintanilla y Los Kumbia Kings
10	*Latin Mix USA Vol. 2*	Various Artists

Source: Billboard

Music Genres 2

TOP 10 ★
IRISH ALBUMS IN THE UK

	TITLE/ARTIST	YEAR
1	*Talk on Corners*, Corrs	1997
2	*By Request*, Boyzone	1999
3	*The Joshua Tree*, U2	1987
4	*Where We Belong*, Boyzone	1998
5	*Watermark*, Enya	1988
6	*Shepherd Moons*, Enya	1991
7	*Rattle and Hum*, U2	1988
8	*Said and Done*, Boyzone	1995
9	*A Different Beat*, Boyzone	1996
10	*Achtung Baby!*, U2	1991

Source: *The Popular Music Database*

THE BOYS IN THE BAND

A string of UK No. 1 albums has secured Boyzone four of the Top 10 Irish albums of all time. The band was formed in Dublin in 1993 as Ireland's answer to Take That.

TOP 10 ★
WORLD MUSIC ALBUMS IN THE US, 1999

	TITLE	ARTIST
1	*Sogno*	Andrea Bocelli
2	*Romanza*	Andrea Bocelli
3	*Buena Vista Social Club*	Buena Vista Social Club
4	*Tears of Stone*	Chieftains
5	*The Book of Secrets*	Loreena McKennitt
6	*Buena Vista Social Club*	Buena Vista Social Club Presents Ibrahim Ferrer
7	*The Irish Tenors*	John McDermott/ Anthony Kearns/Ronan Tynan
8	*Sueno* (with Spanish tracks)	Andrea Bocelli
9	*Romanza* (with Spanish tracks)	Andrea Bocelli
10	*Return To Pride Rock – Songs Inspired by Disney's The Lion King II*	Various Artists

Source: Billboard

TOP 10 ★
JAZZ ALBUMS IN THE US

	ALBUM/ARTIST OR GROUP	YEAR
1	*Time Out Featuring Take Five*, Dave Brubeck Quartet	1960
2	*Hello Dolly*, Louis Armstrong	1964
3	*Getz & Gilberto*, Stan Getz and Joao Gilberto	1964
4	*Sun Goddess*, Ramsey Lewis	1975
5	*Jazz Samba*, Stan Getz and Charlie Byrd	1962
6	*Bitches Brew*, Miles Davies	1970
7	*The In Crowd*, Ramsey Lewis Trio	1965
8	*Time Further Out*, Dave Brubeck Quartet	1961
9	*Mack the Knife – Ella in Berlin*, Ella Fitzgerald	1960
10	*Exodus to Jazz*, Eddie Harris	1961

Did You Know? The first-ever rap album to reach a mass audience and achieve gold status was *Run-D.M.C.*, by the group of that name, on December 17, 1984.

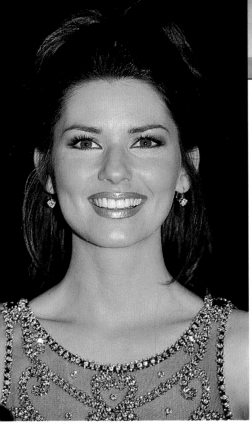

TWAIN MAKES HER MARK

Although it combines rock, pop, and country genres, Canadian-born Shania Twain's Come on Over *ranks as the bestselling country album in the US.*

TOP 10 ★
RAP SINGLES IN THE US

TITLE/ARTIST	APPROX. SALES
1 *Whoomp! (There It Is)*, Tag Team	4,000,000
2 *I'll be Missing You*, Puff Daddy & Faith Evans (featuring 112)	3,000,000
3 = *How Do U Want It*, 2Pac	2,000,000
= *Tha Crossroads*, Bone Thugs-N-Harmony	2,000,000
= *Gangsta's Paradise*, Coolio featuring L. V.	2,000,000
= *Dazzey Duks*, Duice	2,000,000
= *O.P.P.*, Naughty By Nature	2,000,000
= *Baby Got Back*, Sir Mix-A-Lot	2,000,000
= *Wild Thing*, Tone Loc	2,000,000
= *Jump*, Kris Kross	2,000,000
= *Rump Shaker*, Wreckx-N-Effect	2,000,000
= *Can't Nobody Hold Me Down*, Puff Daddy	2,000,000

Source: *RIAA*

TOP 10 ★
COUNTRY ALBUMS IN THE US

TITLE/ARTIST	APPROX. SALES
1 *Come on Over*, Shania Twain	17,000,000
2 *No Fences*, Garth Brooks	16,000,000
3 *Ropin' the Wind*, Garth Brooks	14,000,000
4 *Greatest Hits*, Kenny Rogers	12,000,000
5 *The Woman in Me*, Shania Twain	11,000,000
6 *The Hits*, Garth Brooks	10,000,000
7 = *Some Gave All*, Billy Ray Cyrus	9,000,000
= *Garth Brooks*, Garth Brooks	9,000,000
9 = *Greatest Hits*, Patsy Cline	8,000,000
= *In Pieces*, Garth Brooks	8,000,000
= *The Chase*, Garth Brooks	8,000,000
= *Wide Open Spaces*, Dixie Chicks	8,000,000

Source: *RIAA*

COOL GUY

Coolio (born Artis Ivey, 1963) sold over a million copies of his debut album, It Takes a Thief, *achieving even greater success with his bestselling 1995 album,* Gangsta's Paradise.

COUNTRY GOLD

In a recording career of over 30 years, Kenny Rogers has gained an impressive 28 gold and 44 platinum albums in the US.

TOP 10 ★
MALE ARTISTS WITH THE MOST PLATINUM ALBUMS IN THE US

	ARTIST	PLATINUM ALBUMS
1	Garth Brooks	97
2	Elvis Presley	75
3	Billy Joel	74
4	Elton John	58
5=	Michael Jackson	53
=	Bruce Springsteen	53
7	George Strait	46
8	Kenny Rogers	44
9	Kenny G	41
10	Neil Diamond	35

Source: *RIAA*

Platinum singles and albums in the US are those that have achieved sales of 1 million units. The award has been made by the Recording Industry Association of America (RIAA) since 1976, when it was introduced in response to escalating music sales, as a result of which many discs were outselling the 500,000 required to achieve a gold award. In 1984 the RIAA introduced multiplatinum awards for certified sales of 2 million or more.

TOP 10 ★
GROUPS WITH THE MOST PLATINUM ALBUMS IN THE US

	GROUP	PLATINUM ALBUMS
1	The Beatles	90
2	Led Zeppelin	80
3	Pink Floyd	66
4	The Eagles	62
5	Aerosmith	51
6	Van Halen	50
7	Fleetwood Mac	46
8	Alabama	44
9=	AC/DC	42
=	U2	42

Source: *The Popular Music Database*

TOP 10 ★
GROUPS WITH THE MOST GOLD ALBUMS IN THE US

	GROUP	GOLD ALBUMS
1	The Beatles	40
2	The Rolling Stones	37
3	Kiss	23
4	Rush	22
5=	Aerosmith	21
=	Alabama	21
=	Chicago	21
8	Jefferson Airplane/Starship	20
9	The Beach Boys	19
10	Santana	18

Source: *RIAA*

The RIAA's gold awards have been presented since 1958 to artists who have sold 500,000 of a single, album, or multidisc set. The first single to be so honored was Perry Como's *Catch a Falling Star*, and the first album was the soundtrack to *Oklahoma*. To date, more than 8,000 titles have been certified gold. Three further groups – AC/DC, Queen, and the Temptations – have each received 17 gold awards.

TOP 10 ★
MALE ARTISTS WITH THE MOST GOLD ALBUMS IN THE US

	ARTIST	GOLD ALBUMS
1	Elvis Presley	62
2	Neil Diamond	35
3	Elton John	32
4	Kenny Rogers	28
5	Frank Sinatra	26
6	Bob Dylan	24
7=	George Strait	23
=	Willie Nelson	23
9	Hank Williams, Jr.	21
10=	Paul McCartney/Wings	20
=	Rod Stewart	20

Source: *RIAA*

TOP 10 ★
MALE ARTISTS WITH THE MOST GOLD ALBUMS IN THE UK

	ARTIST	GOLD ALBUMS
1=	Elton John	20
=	Cliff Richard	20
3	Rod Stewart	19
4=	Neil Diamond	17
=	James Last	17
=	Paul McCartney*	17
7	Mike Oldfield	16
8=	David Bowie	15
=	Elvis Presley	15
10	Prince	13

* *Including gold albums with Wings*

Source: *BPI*

Did You Know? In the US, gold discs are those that have sold 500,000, while platinum are for sales of 1 million. The newer diamond award is for sales of 10 million.

FEMALE ARTISTS WITH THE MOST PLATINUM ALBUMS IN THE US

	ARTIST	PLATINUM ALBUMS
1	Barbra Streisand	49
2	Madonna	47
3 =	Whitney Houston	45
=	Mariah Carey	45
5	Celine Dion	34
6	Reba McEntire	24
7	Linda Ronstadt	23
8 =	Janet Jackson	19
=	Shania Twain	19
9 =	Sade	18
=	Gloria Estefan	18

Source: *RIAA*

FEMALE ARTISTS WITH THE MOST GOLD ALBUMS IN THE US

	ARTIST	GOLD ALBUMS
1	Barbra Streisand	40
2	Reba McEntire	19
3	Linda Ronstadt	17
4	Olivia Newton-John	15
5 =	Aretha Franklin	13
=	Madonna	13
=	Dolly Parton	13
8 =	Gloria Estefan*	12
=	Anne Murray	12
=	Tanya Tucker	12

* Includes hits with Miami Sound Machine

Source: *RIAA*

ONE OF THE BEST

With eight gold and 17 platinum albums to her name, Tina Turner has secured a place in the top echelons of music.

FEMALE ARTISTS WITH THE MOST PLATINUM ALBUMS IN THE UK

	ARTIST	PLATINUM ALBUMS
1	Madonna	35
2	Celine Dion	21
3	Whitney Houston	19
4	Tina Turner	17
5 =	Enya	12
=	Gloria Estefan	12
7 =	Kylie Minogue	10
=	Mariah Carey	10
=	Alanis Morissette	10
10	Kate Bush	9

Source: *BPI*

FEMALE ARTISTS WITH THE MOST GOLD ALBUMS IN THE UK

	ARTIST	GOLD ALBUMS
1	Diana Ross	17
2 =	Barbra Streisand	12
=	Madonna	12
4	Donna Summer	9
5 =	Mariah Carey	8
=	Tina Turner	8
7 =	Kate Bush	7
=	Cher	7
=	Celine Dion	7
10 =	Joan Armatrading	6
=	Janet Jackson	6

Source: *BPI*

GOLDEN SUMMER

Donna Summer has been making hit records for almost 30 years, during which time she has scored nine gold albums in the UK.

Oscar-winning Movie Music

THE 10 ★
"BEST SONG" OSCAR WINNERS OF THE 1940s

YEAR	TITLE/MOVIE
1940	*When You Wish Upon a Star*, Pinocchio
1941	*The Last Time I Saw Paris*, Lady Be Good
1942	*White Christmas*, Holiday Inn
1943	*You'll Never Know*, Hello, Frisco, Hello
1944	*Swinging on a Star*, Going My Way
1945	*It Might as Well Be Spring*, State Fair
1946	*On the Atchison, Topeka and Santa Fe*, The Harvey Girls
1947	*Zip-A-Dee-Doo-Dah*, Song of the South
1948	*Buttons and Bows*, The Pale Face
1949	*Baby, It's Cold Outside*, Neptune's Daughter

THE 10 ★
"BEST SONG" OSCAR WINNERS OF THE 1950s

YEAR	TITLE/MOVIE
1950	*Mona Lisa*, Captain Carey
1951	*In the Cool, Cool, Cool of the Evening*, Here Comes the Groom
1952	*High Noon (Do Not Forsake Me, Oh My Darling)*, High Noon
1953	*Secret Love*, Calamity Jane
1954	*Three Coins in the Fountain*, Three Coins in the Fountain
1955	*Love Is a Many-Splendored Thing*, Love Is a Many-Splendored Thing
1956	*Whatever Will Be, Will Be (Que Sera, Sera)*, The Man Who Knew Too Much
1957	*All the Way*, The Joker Is Wild
1958	*Gigi*, Gigi
1959	*High Hopes*, A Hole in the Head

Doris Day benefited strongly from these Oscars, scoring million-selling singles with *Secret Love* and *Whatever Will Be, Will Be*.

THE 10 ★
"BEST SONG" OSCAR WINNERS OF THE 1960s

YEAR	TITLE/MOVIE
1960	*Never on Sunday*, Never on Sunday
1961	*Moon River*, Breakfast at Tiffany's
1962	*Days of Wine and Roses*, Days of Wine and Roses
1963	*Call Me Irresponsible*, Papa's Delicate Condition
1964	*Chim Chim Cheree*, Mary Poppins
1965	*The Shadow of Your Smile*, The Sandpiper
1966	*Born Free*, Born Free
1967	*Talk to the Animals*, Dr. Dolittle
1968	*The Windmills of Your Mind*, The Thomas Crown Affair
1969	*Raindrops Keep Fallin' on My Head*, Butch Cassidy and the Sundance Kid

Both *The Windmills of Your Mind* and *Raindrops Keep Fallin' on My Head* hit the US Top 10. Sacha Distel's cover version of the 1969 Oscar winner charted five times in the UK in 1970.

TOP 10 ★
"BEST SONG" OSCAR-WINNING SINGLES IN THE US

	TITLE/ARTIST OR GROUP	YEAR
1	*You Light up My Life*, Debby Boone	1977
2	*Up Where We Belong*, Joe Cocker and Jennifer Warnes	1982
3	*Evergreen*, Barbra Streisand	1976
4	*My Heart Will Go On*, Celine Dion	1997
5	*I Just Called to Say I Love You*, Stevie Wonder	1984
6	*Arthur's Theme (Best That You Can Do)*, Christopher Cross	1981
7	*The Way We Were*, Barbra Streisand	1973
8	*A Whole New World*, Peabo Bryson and Regina Belle	1992
9	*Raindrops Keep Fallin' on My Head*, B. J. Thomas	1969
10	*(I've Had) The Time of My Life*, Bill Medley and Jennifer Warnes	1987

Source: *The Popular Music Database*

ALL IN A DAY'S WORK

Songs by Doris Day (real name Doris Kappelhoff), from films in which she also starred, produced a duo of Oscar winners in the 1950s.

OSCAR-WINNING PRINCE
A new phenomenon is that half the Oscar-winning songs of the past decade are from animated movies, such as the 1998 winner The Prince of Egypt.

THE 10 ★
"BEST SONG" OSCAR WINNERS OF THE 1970s

YEAR	TITLE/MOVIE
1970	*For All We Know*, Lovers and Other Strangers
1971	*Theme from "Shaft,"* Shaft
1972	*The Morning After*, The Poseidon Adventure
1973	*The Way We Were*, The Way We Were
1974	*We May Never Love Like This Again*, The Towering Inferno
1975	*I'm Easy*, Nashville
1976	*Evergreen*, A Star is Born
1977	*You Light up My Life*, You Light up My Life
1978	*Last Dance*, Thank God It's Friday
1979	*It Goes Like It Goes*, Norma Rae

THE 10 ★
"BEST SONG" OSCAR WINNERS OF THE 1980s

YEAR	TITLE/MOVIE
1980	*Fame*, Fame
1981	*Up Where We Belong*, An Officer and a Gentleman
1982	*Arthur's Theme (Best That You Can Do)*, Arthur
1983	*Flashdance... What a Feeling*, Flashdance
1984	*I Just Called to Say I Love You*, The Woman in Red
1985	*Say You, Say Me*, White Nights
1986	*Take My Breath Away*, Top Gun
1987	*(I've Had) The Time of My Life*, Dirty Dancing
1988	*Let the River Run*, Working Girl
1989	*Under the Sea*, The Little Mermaid

THE 10 ★
"BEST SONG" OSCAR WINNERS OF THE 1990s

YEAR	TITLE/MOVIE
1990	*Sooner or Later (I Always Get My Man)*, Dick Tracy
1991	*Beauty and the Beast*, Beauty and the Beast
1992	*Whole New World*, Aladdin
1993	*Streets of Philadelphia*, Philadelphia
1994	*Can You Feel the Love Tonight*, The Lion King
1995	*Colors of the Wind*, Pocahontas
1996	*You Must Love Me*, Evita
1997	*My Heart Will Go On*, Titanic
1998	*When You Believe*, The Prince of Egypt
1999	*You'll Be in My Heart*, Tarzan

What is the most popular pop music movie?
see p.149 for the answer

A *Purple Rain*
B *La Bamba*
C *The Blues Brothers*

Soundtrack Smashes

TOP 10 ★

MUSICAL MOVIES*

	TITLE	YEAR
1	*Grease*	1978
2	*Saturday Night Fever*	1977
3	*The Sound of Music*	1965
4	*Footloose*	1984
5	*American Graffiti*	1973
6	*Mary Poppins*	1964
7	*Flashdance*	1983
8	*The Rocky Horror Picture Show*	1975
9	*Coal Miner's Daughter*	1980
10	*My Fair Lady*	1964

* Traditional musicals (in which the cast actually sing) and movies in which a musical soundtrack is a major component of the movie are included

MUSIC TO THE EARS

Despite being made over 35 years ago, The Sound of Music, starring British actress Julie Andrews, remains among the Top 10 highest-earning musicals of all time.

TOP 10 ★

JAMES BOND MOVIE THEMES IN THE US

	TITLE/ARTIST OR GROUP	YEAR
1	*A View to a Kill*, Duran Duran	1985
2	*Nobody Does It Better* (from *The Spy Who Loved Me*), Carly Simon	1977
3	*Live and Let Die*, Paul McCartney and Wings	1973
4	*For Your Eyes Only*, Sheena Easton	1981
5	*Goldfinger*, Shirley Bassey	1965
6	*Thunderball*, Tom Jones	1966
7	*All Time High* (from *Octopussy*), Rita Coolidge	1983
8	*You Only Live Twice*, Nancy Sinatra	1967
9	*Diamonds Are Forever*, Shirley Bassey	1972
10	*Goldfinger*, John Barry	1965

TOP 10 ORIGINAL SOUNDTRACK ALBUMS OF ALL TIME IN THE US
(Album/sales)

❶ *The Bodyguard*, 17,000,000 ❷ *Saturday Night Fever*, 15,000,000 ❸ *Purple Rain*, 13,000,000 ❹ *Dirty Dancing*, 11,000,000 ❺ = *The Lion King*, 10,000,000; = *Titanic*, 10,000,000 ❼ = *Grease*, 8,000,000; = *Footloose*, 8,000,000 ❾ = *Top Gun*, 7,000,000; = *Waiting to Exhale*, 7,000,000

Source: *RIAA*

NOBODY DOES IT BETTER

Written by Marvin Hamlisch and Carole Bayer Sager, Carly Simon's song from The Spy Who Loved Me *was a US and UK hit.*

TOP 10 ★
ARTISTS WITH THE MOST "BEST SONG" OSCAR NOMINATIONS

	ARTIST/WINS/YEARS	NOMINATIONS
1	**Sammy Cahn**, 4, 1942–75	26
2	**Johnny Mercer**, 4, 1938–71	18
3	=**Paul Francis Webster**, 3, 1944–76	16
	=**Alan and Marilyn Bergman**, 2, 1968–95	16
5	**James Van Heusen**, 4, 1944–68	14
6	=**Henry Warren**, 3, 1935–57	11
	=**Henry Mancini**, 2, 1961–86	11
	=**Ned Washington**, 1, 1940–61	11
9	=**Alan Menken**, 4, 1986–97	10
	=**Sammy Fain**, 2, 1937–77	10
	=**Leo Robin**, 1, 1934–53	10
	=**Jule Styne**, 1, 1940–68	10

It was not until 1934 that the category of "Best Song" was added to the many accolades bestowed on movies. The awards are often multiple, including the writers of the music and the lyrics.

THE 10 ★
FIRST DISNEY "BEST SONG" OSCAR WINNERS

YEAR	TITLE/MOVIE
1940	*When You Wish Upon a Star*, Pinocchio
1947	*Zip-a-Dee-Doo-Dah*, Song of the South
1964	*Chim Chim Cher-ee*, Mary Poppins
1989	*Under the Sea*, The Little Mermaid
1990	*Sooner or Later (I Always Get My Man)*, Dick Tracy
1991	*Beauty and the Beast*, Beauty and The Beast
1992	*Whole New World*, Aladdin
1994	*Can You Feel the Love Tonight*, The Lion King
1995	*Colors of the Wind*, Pocahontas
1996	*You Must Love Me*, Evita

TOP 10 ★
POP MUSIC MOVIES

	TITLE	YEAR
1	*The Blues Brothers*	1980
2	*Purple Rain*	1984
3	*La Bamba*	1987
4	*The Doors*	1991
5	*What's Love Got to Do With It?*	1993
6	*Xanadu*	1980
7	*The Jazz Singer*	1980
8	*Sgt. Pepper's Lonely Hearts Club Band*	1978
9	*Lady Sings the Blues*	1972
10	*Pink Floyd – The Wall*	1982

RAINING PRINCE
Produced in 1984, Prince's semi-autobiographical movie Purple Rain is one of the most successful pop music movies ever released.

Music Awards

LATEST GRAMMY RECORDS OF THE YEAR

YEAR	RECORD/ARTIST
1999	*Smooth*, Santana featuring Rob Thomas
1998	*My Heart Will Go On*, Celine Dion
1997	*Sunny Came Home*, Shawn Colvin
1996	*Change the World*, Eric Clapton
1995	*Kiss from a Rose*, Seal
1994	*All I Wanna Do*, Sheryl Crow
1993	*I Will Always Love You*, Whitney Houston
1992	*Tears in Heaven*, Eric Clapton
1991	*Unforgettable*, Natalie Cole with Nat "King" Cole
1990	*Another Day in Paradise*, Phil Collins

THE 10 LATEST RECIPIENTS OF THE GRAMMY LIFETIME ACHIEVEMENT AWARD

(Year/artist*)

1 2000 Harry Belafonte **2** 2000 Woody Guthrie **3** 2000 John Lee Hooker **4** 2000 Mitch Miller **5** 2000 Willie Nelson **6** 1999 Johnny Cash **7** 2000 Sam Cooke **8** 1999 Otis Redding **9** 1999 William "Smokey" Robinson **10** 1999 Mel Tormé

* Listed alphabetically by year
Source: *NARAS*

ARTISTS WITH THE MOST GRAMMY AWARDS

	ARTIST	AWARDS
1	Sir Georg Solti	31
2	Quincy Jones	26
3	Vladimir Horowitz	25
4	Pierre Boulez	23
5	Stevie Wonder	21
6	Henry Mancini	20
7=	John T. Williams	17
=	Leonard Bernstein	17
9=	Aretha Franklin	15
=	Itzhak Perlman	15

The Grammy Awards ceremony has been held annually in the United States since its inauguration on May 4, 1959, and the awards are considered to be the most prestigious in the music industry.

FIRST GRAMMY RECORDS OF THE YEAR

YEAR	RECORD/ARTIST OR GROUP
1958	*Nel Blu Dipinto di Blu (Volare)*, Domenico Modugno
1959	*Mack the Knife*, Bobby Darin
1960	*Theme From a Summer Place*, Percy Faith
1961	*Moon River*, Henry Mancini
1962	*I Left My Heart in San Francisco*, Tony Bennett
1963	*The Days of Wine and Roses*, Henry Mancini
1964	*The Girl from Ipanema*, Stan Getz and Astrud Gilberto
1965	*A Taste of Honey*, Herb Alpert and the Tijuana Brass
1966	*Strangers in the Night*, Frank Sinatra
1967	*Up Up and Away*, 5th Dimension

CASHBACK

Johnny Cash was awarded the accolade of a Grammy Lifetime Achievement Award in 1999, 44 years after releasing his first single, Hey Porter/Cry Cry Cry.

TOP 10 ★
COUNTRY MUSIC AWARDS WINNERS

	ARTIST	AWARDS
1	Vince Gill	15
2	George Strait	12
3	Garth Brooks	11
4 =	Roy Clark	10
=	Brooks & Dunn	10
6 =	Alabama	9
=	Chet Atkins	9
=	Judds	9
9 =	Loretta Lynn	8
=	Ronnie Milsap	8
=	Willie Nelson	8
=	Dolly Parton	8
=	Ricky Skaggs	8

The Country Music Awards are the most prestigious Country awards, held as an annual ceremony since 1967. Veteran Country instrumentalist Roy Clark netted the Instrumentalist of the Year award for seven consecutive years between 1974 and 1980.

THE 10 ★
LATEST GRAMMY SONGS OF THE YEAR

YEAR	SINGLE/SONGWRITER(S)
1999	*Smooth*, Itaal Shur and Rob Thomas
1998	*My Heart Will Go On*, James Horner and Will Jennings
1997	*Sunny Came Home*, Shawn Colvin
1996	*Change the World*, Gordon Kennedy, Wayne Kirkpatrick, and Tommy Sims
1995	*Kiss From a Rose*, Seal
1994	*Streets of Philadelphia*, Bruce Springsteen
1993	*A Whole New World*, Alan Menken and Tim Rice
1992	*Tears in Heaven*, Eric Clapton
1991	*Unforgettable*, Irving Gordon
1990	*From a Distance*, Julie Gold

THE 10 ★
LATEST GRAMMY NEW ARTISTS OF THE YEAR

YEARS	NEW ARTIST
1999	Christina Aguilera
1998	Lauryn Hill
1997	Paula Cole
1996	LeeAnn Rimes
1995	Hootie & The Blowfish
1994	Sheryl Crow
1993	Toni Braxton
1992	Arrested Development
1991	Mark Cohn
1990	Mariah Carey

THE 10 ★
LATEST RECIPIENTS OF THE SONGWRITERS HALL OF FAME SAMMY CAHN LIFETIME ACHIEVEMENT AWARD

YEAR	RECIPIENT
1999	Kenny Rogers
1998	Berry Gordy
1997	Vic Damone
1996	Frankie Laine
1995	Steve Lawrence and Eydie Gorme
1994	Lena Horne
1993	Ray Charles
1992	Nat "King" Cole
1991	Gene Autry
1990	B. B. King

THE 10 LATEST INDUCTEES INTO THE ROCK 'N' ROLL HALL OF FAME

1 Eric Clapton 2 Earth, Wind & Fire 3 Lovin' Spoonful 4 Moonglows 5 Bonnie Raitt 6 James Taylor 7 Nat King Cole (Early influence category) 8 Billie Holiday (Early influence category) 9 King Curtis (Sideman) 10 = James Jamerson (Sideman); = Earl Palmer (Sideman); = Hal Blaine (Sideman); = Scotty Moore (Sideman)

THE 10 ★
LATEST INDUCTEES INTO THE COUNTRY MUSIC HALL OF FAME

YEAR	ARTIST*
1999	Johnny Bond
1999	Dolly Parton
1999	Conway Twitty
1998	George Morgan
1998	Elvis Presley
1998	E. W. "Bud" Wendell
1998	Tammy Wynette
1997	Harlan Howard
1997	Cindy Walker
1997	Brenda Lee

Listed alphabetically by year

Source: *Country Music Association*

Founded in 1961 by the Country Music Association in Nashville, the Country Music Hall of Fame recognizes outstanding contributions to the world of Country. It inducted 72 members between 1961 and 1999.

THE 10 LATEST GRAMMY POP VOCAL PERFORMANCES OF THE YEAR, MALE

1 1999 Sting, *Brand New Day* 2 1998 Eric Clapton, *My Father's Eyes* 3 1997 Elton John, *Candle in the Wind 1997* 4 1996 Eric Clapton, *Change the World* 5 1995 Seal, *Kiss from a Rose* 6 1994 Elton John, *Can You Feel the Love Tonight* 7 1993 Sting, *If I Ever Lose My Faith in You* 8 1992 Eric Clapton, *Tears in Heaven* 9 1991 Michael Bolton, *When a Man Loves a Woman* 10 1990 Roy Orbison, *Oh, Pretty Woman*

Did You Know? The first-ever Grammy Record of the Year, *Nel Blu Dipinto di Blu (Volare)*, was revived by David Bowie in the 1986 film *Absolute Beginners*.

Classical & Opera

LONGEST OPERAS PERFORMED AT THE METROPOLITAN OPERA HOUSE, NEW YORK CITY*

	OPERA	COMPOSER	RUNNING TIME HR:MIN
1	Götterdämmerung	Richard Wagner	4:27
2	Die Meistersinger von Nürnberg	Richard Wagner	4:21
3	Parsifal	Richard Wagner	4:17
4 =	Les Troyens	Hector Berlioz	4:02
=	Siegfried	Richard Wagner	4:02
6	Tristan und Isolde	Richard Wagner	4:00
7	Die Walküre	Richard Wagner	3:41
8	Don Carlo	Giuseppe Verdi	3:33
9	Semiramide	Gioachino Rossini	3:30
10	Lohengrin	Richard Wagner	3:28

* In current repertory
\# Excluding intervals

Source: Metropolitan Opera House

CLASSICAL ALBUMS OF ALL TIME IN THE US

	TITLE	PERFORMER/ORCHESTRA
1	The Three Tenors In Concert	Carreras, Domingo, Pavarotti
2	Romanza	Andrea Bocelli
3	Sogno	Andrea Bocelli
4	Chant	Benedictine Monks of Santo Domingo De Silos
5	The Three Tenors in Concert 1994	Carreras, Domingo, Pavarotti
6	Sacred Arias	Andrea Bocelli
7	Tchaikovsky: Piano Concerto No. 1	Van Cliburn
8	Fantasia (50th Anniversary Edition)	Soundtrack (Philadelphia Orchestra)
9	Perhaps Love	Placido Domingo
10	O Holy Night	Luciano Pavarotti

Classical recordings held far greater sway in the early years of the US album chart, and most notably during the 1950s, than they have in subsequent decades, and this is partly reflected in the vintage nature of much of the Top 10. The two film soundtracks contained short pieces or excerpts by a number of composers, including Bach, Beethoven, and Stravinsky in *Fantasia*, and Richard Strauss and Johann Strauss in *2001: A Space Odyssey*. According to some criteria, the soundtrack album of *Titanic* is regarded as a "classical" album; if accepted as such, it would appear at No. 1 in this Top 10.

LATEST WINNERS OF THE "BEST CLASSICAL ALBUM" GRAMMY AWARD

YEAR	COMPOSER/TITLE	CONDUCTOR/SOLOIST/ORCHESTRA
1999	Stravinsky, Firebird; The Right of Spring; Perséphone	Michael Tilson Thomas, Stuart Neill, San Francisco Symphony Orchestra
1998	Barber, Prayers of Kierkegaard/ Vaughan Williams, Dona Nobis Pacem/ Bartok, Cantata Profana	Robert Shaw, Richard Clement, Nathan Gunn, Atlanta Symphony Orchestra and chorus
1997	Danielpour, Kirchner, Rouse, Premières – Cello Concertos	Yo-Yo Ma, David Zinman, Philadelphia Orchestra
1996	Corigliano, Of Rage and Remembrance	Leonard Slatkin, National Symphony Orchestra
1995	Claude Debussy, La Mer	Pierre Boulez, Cleveland Orchestra
1994	Béla Bartók, Concerto for Orchestra; Four Orchestral Pieces, Op. 12	Pierre Boulez, Chicago Symphony Orchestra
1993	Béla Bartók, The Wooden Prince	Pierre Boulez, Chicago Symphony Orchestra and Chorus
1992	Gustav Mahler, Symphony No. 9	Leonard Bernstein, Berlin Philharmonic Orchestra
1991	Leonard Bernstein, Candide	Leonard Bernstein, London Symphony Orchestra
1990	Charles Ives, Symphony No. 2 (and Three Short Works)	Leonard Bernstein, New York Philharmonic Orchestra

Source: NARAS

LATEST WINNERS OF THE "BEST CLASSICAL CONTEMPORARY COMPOSITION" GRAMMY AWARD

YEAR	COMPOSER	TITLE
1999	Pierre Boulez	Répons
1998	Krzysztof Penderecki	Metamorphosen
1997	John Adams	El Dorado
1996	John Corigliano	String Quartet
1995	Olivier Messiaen	Concert à Quatre
1994	Stephen Albert	Cello Concerto
1993	Elliott Carter	Violin Concerto
1992	Samuel Barber	The Lovers
1991	John Corigliano	Symphony No. 1
1990	Leonard Bernstein	Arias and Barcarolles

NORMAN CONQUEST
One of the world's leading opera divas, Georgia-born Jessye Norman's role on a recording of Bluebeard's Castle *contributed to its gaining the 1999 Grammy "Best Opera Recording" award.*

TOP 10 MOST PROLIFIC CLASSICAL COMPOSERS

(Composer/nationality/hours of music)

❶ Joseph Haydn (1732–1809), Austrian, 340 **❷ George Handel** (1685–1759), German–English, 303 **❸ Wolfgang Amadeus Mozart** (1756–91), Austrian, 202 **❹ Johann Sebastian Bach** (1685–1750), German, 175 **❺ Franz Schubert** (1797–1828), German, 134 **❻ Ludwig van Beethoven** (1770–1827), German, 120 **❼ Henry Purcell** (1659–95), English, 116 **❽ Giuseppe Verdi** (1813–1901), Italian, 87 **❾ Anton Dvořák** (1841–1904), Czech, 79 **❿ = Franz Liszt** (1811–86), Hungarian, 76; **= Peter Tchaikovsky** (1840–93), Russian, 76

This list is based on a survey conducted by *Classical Music*, which ranked classical composers by the total number of hours of music each composed.

THE 10 ★
LATEST WINNERS OF THE "BEST OPERA RECORDING" GRAMMY AWARD

YEAR	COMPOSER/TITLE	SOLOISTS/ORCHESTRA
1999	Stravinsky, *The Rake's Progress*	Ian Bostridge, Bryn Terfel, Anne Sofie van Otter, Deborah York, Monteverdi Choir, London Symphony Orchestra
1998	Bartok, *Bluebeard's Castle*	Jessye Norman, Laszlo Polgar, Karl-August Naegler, Chicago Symphony Orchestra
1997	Richard Wagner, *Die Meistersinger von Nürnberg*	Ben Heppner, Herbert Lippert, Karita Mattila, Alan Opie, Rene Pape, Jose van Dam, Iris Vermillion, Chicago Symphony Chorus, Chicago Symphony Orchestra
1996	Benjamin Britten, *Peter Grimes*	Philip Langridge, Alan Opie, Janice Watson, Opera London, London Symphony Chorus, City of London Sinfonia
1995	Hector Berlioz, *Les Troyens*	Charles Dutoit, Orchestra Symphonie de Montreal
1994	Carlisle Floyd, *Susannah*	Jerry Hadley, Samuel Ramey, Cheryl Studer, Kenn Chester
1993	George Handel, *Semele*	Kathleen Battle, Marilyn Horne, Samuel Ramey, Sylvia McNair, Michael Chance
1992	Richard Strauss, *Die Frau Ohne Schatten*	Placido Domingo, Jose Van Dam, Hildegard Behrens
1991	Richard Wagner, *Götterdämmerung*	Hildegard Behrens, Ekkehard Wlashiha
1990	Richard Wagner, *Das Rheingold*	James Morris, Kurt Moll, Christa Ludwig

Source: *NARAS*

TOP 10 LARGEST OPERA HOUSES

(Opera house/location/capacity*)

❶ Arena di Verona,# Verona, Italy, 16,663 **❷ Municipal Opera Theater**,# St. Louis, MO, 11,745 **❸ Music Hall**, Cincinnati, OH, 3,417 **❹ Teatro alla Scala**, Milan, Italy, 3,600 **❺ Civic Opera House**, Chicago, IL, 3,563 **❻ The Metropolitan**, Lincoln Center, NY, 3,500; **= Teatro San Carlo**, Naples, Italy, 3,500 **❽ = Teatro Massimo**, Palermo, Italy, 3,200; **= The Hummingbird Center**, Toronto, Canada, 3,200 **❿ Halle aux Grains**, Toulouse, France, 3,000

* For indoor venues, seating capacity given; numbers may be increased by standing capacity   # Open-air venue
Although there are many more venues where opera is regularly performed, this list is limited to those venues where the principal performances are opera.

Did You Know? After performing *Otello* at the Vienna Staatsoper on July 30, 1991, Placido Domingo received 101 curtain calls and was applauded for 1 hour 20 minutes.

153

Stage & Screen

MONEY FOR NOTHING

MONEY FOR NOTHING

Much Ado About Nothing, *starring Emma Thompson and Kenneth Branagh (who also directed it), achieved both critical and commercial success.*

THE 10 ★
LATEST WINNERS OF TONY AWARDS FOR A PLAY

YEAR	PLAY
1999	Side Man
1998	Art
1997	The Last Night of Ballyhoo
1996	Master Class
1995	Love! Valour! Compassion!
1994	Angels in America Part II: Perestroika
1993	Angels in America Part I: Millennium Approaches
1992	Dancing at Lughnasa
1991	Lost in Yonkers
1990	The Grapes of Wrath

The Tony Awards, established by the American Theater Wing, honor outstanding Broadway plays and musicals, actors and actresses, music, costume and other contributions. They are named after the actress and director Antoinette Perry (1988–46), who headed the American Theater Wing during World War II.

THE 10 ★
LATEST WINNERS OF TONY AWARDS FOR A MUSICAL

YEAR	PLAY
1999	Fosse
1998	The Lion King
1997	Titanic
1996	Rent
1995	Sunset Boulevard
1994	Passion
1993	Kiss of the Spider Woman
1992	Crazy for You
1991	The Will Rogers Follies
1990	City of Angels

TOP 10 ★
FILMS OF SHAKESPEARE PLAYS

	FILM	YEAR
1	William Shakespeare's Romeo + Juliet	1996
2	Romeo and Juliet	1968
3	Much Ado About Nothing	1993
4	Hamlet	1990
5	Henry V	1989
6	Hamlet	1996
7	Richard III	1995
8	Othello	1995
9	The Taming of the Shrew	1967
10	Hamlet	1948

TOP 10 ★
MOST PRODUCED PLAYS BY SHAKESPEARE, 1961–99

	PLAY	PRODUCTIONS
1	A Midsummer Night's Dream	30
2 =	Macbeth	26
=	Twelfth Night	26
4	Romeo and Juliet	25
5	The Taming of the Shrew	24
6 =	As You Like It	23
=	Richard III	23
8	King Lear	22
9 =	Hamlet	21
=	Much Ado About Nothing	21

TOP 10 MOST-FILMED PLAYS BY SHAKESPEARE

❶ Hamlet **❷** Romeo and Juliet **❸** Macbeth **❹** A Midsummer Night's Dream
❺ Julius Caesar **❻** Othello **❼** Richard III **❽** Henry V **❾** The Merchant of Venice
❿ Antony and Cleopatra

Counting modern versions, including those in foreign languages, but discounting made-for-TV films, parodies, and stories derived from the plays, it appears that *Hamlet* is the most-filmed of all Shakespeare's works, with some 70 releases to date, while *Romeo and Juliet* has been remade on at least 40 occasions.

Which 1950s movie won the most "Best Picture" Oscars?
see p.166 for the answer

A *All About Eve*
B *Ben-Hur*
C *From Here to Eternity*

TOP 10 ★
LONGEST-RUNNING COMEDIES ON BROADWAY

COMEDY/YEARS	PERFORMANCES
1 *Life With Father*, 1939–47	3,224
2 *Abie's Irish Rose*, 1922–27	2,327
3 *Gemini*, 1977–81	1,819
4 *Harvey*, 1944–49	1,775
5 *Born Yesterday*, 1946–49	1,642
6 *Mary, Mary*, 1961–64	1,572
7 *The Voice of the Turtle*, 1943–48	1,557
8 *Barefoot in the Park*, 1963–67	1,530
9 *Same Time Next Year*, 1975–78	1,454
10 *Brighton Beach Memoirs*, 1983–86	1,299

Source: *The League of American Theaters and Producers*

TOP 10 ★
LATEST PULITZER DRAMA AWARDS

YEAR*	AUTHOR/PLAY
2000	Jhumpa Lahiri, *Dinner With Friends*
1999	Margaret Edson, *Wit*
1998	Paula Vogel, *How I Learned to Drive*
1996	Jonathan Larson, *Rent*
1995	Horton Foote, *The Young Man from Atlanta*
1994	Edward Albee, *Three Tall Women*
1993	Tony Kushner, *Angels in America: Millennium Approaches*
1992	Robert Schenkkan, *The Kentucky Cycle*
1991	Neil Simon, *Lost in Yonkers*
1990	August Wilson, *The Piano Lesson*

* *No award was made in 1997*

The Pulitzer Drama Award is made for "an American play, preferably original and dealing with American life."

TOP 10 ★
LONGEST-RUNNING SHOWS ON BROADWAY

SHOW/YEARS	PERFORMANCES
1 *Cats*, 1982–	7,200*
2 *A Chorus Line*, 1975–90	6,137
3 *Oh! Calcutta!*, 1976–89	5,962
4 *Les Misérables*, 1987–	5,378#
5 *The Phantom of the Opera*, 1988–	5,008#
6 *Miss Saigon*, 1991–	3,619#
7 *42nd Street*, 1980–89	3,486
8 *Grease*, 1972–80	3,388
9 *Fiddler on the Roof*, 1964–72	3,242
10 *Life With Father*, 1939–47	3,224

* *Total as at January 1, 2000; closed June 25, 2000 after record 7,397 performances*

Total as at January 1, 2000; still running

Source: *The League of American Theaters and Producers*

Cats became the longest-running Broadway show of all time on June 19, 1997, when it notched up its 6,138th performance. *Les Misérables* celebrated its 13th anniversary on March 12, 2000 with its 5,351st performance. By that date, it had been seen by 7.5 million people in New York and 42 million worldwide. *Life With Father*, the earliest show to be listed here, was a roaring success from the moment it opened. Its popularity had not been predicted, and after the lead parts were refused by major actors and actresses, the author, Howard Lindsay, and his wife, Dorothy Stickney, decided to play the roles themselves. They continued to do so, to rave reviews, for the following five years.

OUT OF THEIR MISERY
Les Misérables *has achieved the dual feat of being one of the longest-running musicals both in London and on Broadway.*

TOP 10 ★
LONGEST-RUNNING MUSICALS ON BROADWAY

MUSICAL/YEARS	PERFORMANCES
1 *Cats*, 1982–2000	7,200*
2 *A Chorus Line*, 1975–90	6,137
3 *Les Misérables*, 1987–	5,278#
4 *The Phantom of the Opera*, 1988–	5,008#
5 *Miss Saigon*, 1901–	3,619#
6 *42nd Street*, 1980–89	3,486
7 *Grease*, 1972–80	3,388
8 *Fiddler on the Roof*, 1964–72	3,242
9 *Hello Dolly!*, 1964–71	2,844
10 *My Fair Lady*, 1956–62	2,717

* *Total as at January 1, 2000; closed June 25, 2000 after record 7,397 performances*

Total as at January 1, 2000; still running

Source: *The League of American Theaters and Producers*

Box-Office Winners

TOP 10 HIGHEST-GROSSING MOVIES OF ALL TIME

	MOVIE	YEAR	GROSS INCOME ($) US	WORLD
1	*Titanic*	1997	600,800,000	1,835,100,000
2	*Star Wars: Episode I – The Phantom Menace*	1999	431,100,000	922,600,000
3	*Jurassic Park*	1993	357,100,000	920,100,000
4	*Independence Day*	1996	306,200,000	811,200,000
5	*Star Wars*	1977/97	461,000,000	798,000,000
6	*The Lion King*	1994	312,900,000	767,900,000
7	*E.T.: The Extra-Terrestrial*	1982	399,800,000	704,800,000
8	*Forrest Gump*	1994	329,700,000	679,700,000
9	*The Lost World: Jurassic Park*	1997	229,100,000	614,400,000
10	*Men in Black*	1997	250,100,000	586,100,000

TOP 10 ★
MOVIE OPENINGS OF ALL TIME IN THE US

	MOVIE/RELEASE DATE	OPENING WEEKEND GROSS ($)
1	*The Lost World: Jurassic Park*, May 23, 1997	72,132,785
2	*Star Wars: Episode I – The Phantom Menace*, May 21, 1999	64,820,970
3	*Toy Story 2*, Nov 24, 1999	57,388,839
4	*Austin Powers: The Spy Who Shagged Me*, June 11, 1999	54,917,604
5	*Batman Forever*, June 16, 1995	52,784,433
6	*Men in Black*, July 2, 1997	51,068,455
7	*Independence Day*, July 3, 1996	50,228,264
8	*Jurassic Park*, June 11, 1993	47,059,560
9	*Batman Returns*, June 19, 1992	45,687,711
10	*Mission: Impossible*, May 22, 1996	45,436,830

MONSTER MOVIE
Jurassic Park *set new standards for animatronic action and reigned as the world's highest-earning movie for five years, before being toppled by* Titanic.

Did You Know? On May 19, 1999, *Star Wars: Episode I – The Phantom Menace* became the highest-earning movie in a single day, taking a total of $28,540,000 at 2,970 box offices across the US.

TOP 10 ★
HIGHEST-GROSSING MOVIES OF ALL TIME IN THE UK

	MOVIE	YEAR	UK GROSS (£)
1	Titanic	1998	68,532,000
2	The Full Monty	1997	51,992,000
4	Star Wars: Episode I – The Phantom Menace	1999	50,735,000
4	Jurassic Park	1993	47,140,000
5	Toy Story 2	2000	40,169,000
6	Independence Day	1996	36,800,000
7	Men In Black	1997	35,400,000
8	Notting Hill	1999	30,404,000
9	The World is Not Enough	1999	28,367,000
10	Four Weddings and a Funeral	1994	27,800,000

Inevitably, because of inflation, the top-grossing movies of all time are releases from the 1990s.

BEST OF BRITISH

The highest-earning British-made movie, The Full Monty, was successful both in the UK and worldwide, grossing in excess of $250 million.

BACK FROM THE FUTURE

In the second of the two Terminator movies, Arnold Schwarzenegger is a caring cyborg who protects a boy and his mother from a near-indestructible rival.

TOP 10 ★
HIGHEST-GROSSING MOVIES OF ALL TIME IN THE US

	MOVIE	YEAR	US GROSS ($)
1	Titanic	1997	600,800,000
2	Star Wars	1977/97	461,000,000
3	Star Wars: Episode I – The Phantom Menace	1999	431,100,000
4	E.T.: The Extra-Terrestrial	1982	399,800,000
5	Jurassic Park	1993	357,100,000
6	Forrest Gump	1994	329,700,000
7	The Lion King	1994	312,900,000
8	Return of the Jedi	1983/97	309,100,000
9	Independence Day	1996	306,200,000
10	The Empire Strikes Back	1980/97	290,200,000

Star Wars: Episode I – The Phantom Menace was the fastest-earning movie ever, taking over $100 million in its first five days. Box-office revenue reached $102.7 million

TOP 10 ★
MOVIE SEQUELS THAT EARNED THE GREATEST AMOUNT MORE THAN THE ORIGINAL*

	ORIGINAL	OUTEARNED BY
1	The Terminator	Terminator 2: Judgment Day
2	First Blood	Rambo: First Blood Part II / Rambo III
3	Lethal Weapon	Lethal Weapon 2 / Lethal Weapon 3 / Lethal Weapon 4
4	Austin Powers: International Man of Mystery	Austin Powers: The Spy Who Shagged Me
5	Die Hard	Die Hard 2 / Die Hard With a Vengeance
6	Rocky	Rocky III / Rocky IV
7	Raiders of the Lost Ark	Indiana Jones and the Last Crusade
8	Ace Ventura: Pet Detective	Ace Ventura: When Nature Calls
9	48 HRS	Another 48 HRS
10	Patriot Games	Clear and Present Danger

* Ranked by greatest differential between original and highest-earning sequel

Movie Hits

TOP 10 ★

MOST EXPENSIVE MOVIES EVER MADE

	MOVIE	YEAR	BUDGET ($)
1	Titanic	1997	200,000,000
2 =	Waterworld	1995	175,000,000
=	Wild Wild West	1999	175,000,000
4 =	Speed 2: Cruise Control	1997	150,000,000
=	Armageddon	1998	150,000,000
6	Lethal Weapon 4	1998	140,000,000
7 =	Batman and Robin	1997	125,000,000
=	Godzilla	1998	125,000,000
9 =	Dante's Peak	1997	115,000,000
=	Star Wars: Episode I – The Phantom Menace	1999	115,000,000
=	The 13th Warrior	1999	115,000,000

It is coincidental that several of the most expensive movies ever made, including the first two in this Top 10, along with *Speed 2: Cruise Control*, are water-based. Large casts and large-scale special effects, such as those featured in *Titanic*, are major factors in escalating budgets.

HIGH WATER

Produced by and starring Kevin Costner, Waterworld *was one of the most expensive movies ever made, being topped only by* Titanic.

TOP 10 ★

BEST-ATTENDED MOVIES

	MOVIE	YEAR	ATTENDANCE
1	Gone With the Wind	1939	208,100,000
2	Star Wars	1977	198,600,000
3	The Sound of Music	1965	170,600,000
4	E.T.: The Extraterrestrial	1982	151,600,000
5	The Ten Commandments	1956	132,800,000
6	The Jungle Book	1967	126,300,000
7	Titanic	1997	124,300,000
8	Jaws	1975	123,300,000
9	Doctor Zhivago	1965	122,700,000
10	101 Dalmations	1961	119,600,000

This list is based on the actual number of people purchasing tickets at the US box office. Because it takes account of the relatively greater numbers of tickets sold to children and other discounted sales (such as matinees for certain movies), it differs both from lists that present total box-office receipts (which, as ticket prices increase, tend to feature more recent movies) and from those that are adjusted for inflation. However, it is interesting to observe that if inflation were factored in, *Gone With the Wind* would also top the all-time list, outearning even mega-blockbuster *Titanic* – the only movie from the 1990s to feature in this list. The 1960s stand out from other decades, contributing four movies to this list.

TOP 10 ★

MOVIE SERIES OF ALL TIME

	FILM SERIES	DATES
1	Star Wars / The Empire Strikes Back / Return of the Jedi / Star Wars Episode I: The Phantom Menace	1977–99
2	Jurassic Park / The Lost World: Jurassic Park	1993–97
3	Batman / Batman Returns / Batman Forever / Batman & Robin	1989–97
4	Raiders of the Lost Ark / Indiana Jones and the Temple of Doom / Indiana Jones and the Last Crusade	1981–89
5	Star Trek: The Motion Picture / II : The Wrath of Khan / III: The Search for Spock / IV: The Voyage Home / V: The Final Frontier / VI: The Undiscovered Country / Generations / First Contact / Insurrection	1979–98
6	Back to the Future / II / III	1985–90
7	Lethal Weapon / II / III / IV	1987–98
8	Home Alone / Home Alone 2: Lost in New York	1990–92
9	Jaws / 2 / 3(-D) /: The Revenge	1975–87
10	Die Hard / 2 / Die Hard With a Vengeance	1988–95

Based on total earnings of the original movie and all its sequels up to 1998, George Lucas's *Star Wars* series just beats Steven Spielberg's *Jurassic Park* and its sequel *The Lost World: Jurassic Park*, which have grossed $2,806,400,000 and $1,534,500,000 respectively around the world. Each of the other movie series in the Top 10 have achieved cumulative global earnings of more than $700 million.

"BLOCKBUSTER"

During World War II, "blockbuster" was air force slang for a bomb heavy enough to flatten an entire city block. Once the word had become widely used in military reports, it was adopted by journalists to describe a book or film that had a great impact. "Blockbuster" has since acquired the specific meaning of a film that has made more than $100 million on its North American release. This was once a rare phenomenon, but now some 200 films have gained this sobriquet.

WHY DO WE SAY?

TOP 10 MOVIES OF 1999

MOVIE	GROSS INCOME ($) US	WORLD TOTAL
1 *Star Wars: Episode I – The Phantom Menace*	430,500,000	977,900,000
2 *The Sixth Sense*	276,400,000	470,400,000
3 *The Matrix*	171,400,000	456,400,000
4 *The Mummy*	155,200,000	401,700,000
5 *Tarzan*	170,800,000	391,800,000
6 *Notting Hill*	116,000,000	354,800,000
7 *Austin Powers: The Spy Who Shagged Me*	205,400,000	308,400,000
8 *Runaway Bride*	152,100,000	281,600,000
9 *The World Is Not Enough*	118,600,000	265,200,000
10 *Toy Story 2*	211,200,000	234,700,000

TOP 10 ★ MOVIES OF 1999 IN THE US

MOVIE	US GROSS ($)
1 *Star Wars: Episode I – The Phantom Menace*	430,443,350
2 *The Sixth Sense*	276,386,495
3 *Toy Story 2*	208,851,257
4 *Austin Powers: The Spy Who Shagged Me*	205,887,913
5 *The Matrix*	171,383,253
6 *Tarzan*	170,904,824
7 *Big Daddy*	163,479,795
8 *The Mummy*	155,247,825
9 *Runaway Bride*	152,054,428
10 *The Blair Witch Project*	140,530,114

This list features only movies released in the US during 1999. Certain films released late in 1998, such as Patch Adams and Shakespeare in Love, continued to earn at the box office well into 1999, giving both these a place in the latter year's Top 20.

NEO CLASSIC

Keanu Reeves as Neo/Thomas A. Anderson shoots to thrill in The Matrix, one of the sci-fi movies that led the world's box office in 1999.

What do the top four highest-earning films of the 1940s have in common?

see p.162 for the answer

A They are all Disney cartoons
B They all star Humphrey Bogart
C They are all black-and-white

Movies of the Decades

MOVIES OF THE 1930s

1	Gone With the Wind*	1939
2	Snow White and the Seven Dwarfs	1937
3	The Wizard of Oz	1939
4	The Woman in Red	1935
5	King Kong	1933
6	San Francisco	1936
7 =	Hell's Angels	1930
=	Lost Horizon	1937
=	Mr. Smith Goes to Washington	1939
10	Maytime	1937

* Winner of "Best Picture" Academy Award

Gone With the Wind and Snow White and the Seven Dwarfs have generated more income than any other prewar movie. However, if the income of Gone With the Wind is adjusted to allow for inflation in the period since its release, it could be regarded as the most successful movie ever, earning some $885 million in the US alone.

MOVIES OF THE 1940s

1	Bambi	1942
2	Pinocchio	1940
3	Fantasia	1940
4	Cinderella	1949
5	Song of the South	1946
6	The Best Years of Our Lives*	1946
7	The Bells of St. Mary's	1945
8	Duel in the Sun	1946
9	Mom and Dad	1948
10	Samson and Delilah	1949

* Winner of "Best Picture" Academy Award

With the top four movies of the decade classic Disney cartoons, the 1940s may be regarded as the "golden age" of the animated movie.

TALL STORY

In one of movie history's most famous scenes, King Kong fights off his attackers atop the newly opened Empire State Building. The movie was one of the 1930s' highest earners.

MOVIES OF THE 1950s

1	Lady and the Tramp	1955
2	Peter Pan	1953
3	Ben-Hur*	1959
4	The Ten Commandments	1956
5	Sleeping Beauty	1959
6	Around the World in 80 Days*	1956
7 =	The Robe	1953
=	The Greatest Show on Earth*	1952
9	The Bridge on the River Kwai*	1957
10	Peyton Place	1957

* Winner of "Best Picture" Academy Award

While the popularity of animated movies continued, the 1950s was outstanding as the decade of the "big" picture (in cast and scale).

TOP 10 MOVIES OF THE 1960s

1 One Hundred and One Dalmatians, 1961 **2** The Jungle Book, 1967 **3** The Sound of Music*, 1965 **4** Thunderball, 1965 **5** Goldfinger, 1964 **6** Doctor Zhivago, 1965 **7** You Only Live Twice, 1967 **8** The Graduate, 1968 **9** Mary Poppins, 1964 **10** Butch Cassidy and the Sundance Kid, 1969

* Winner of "Best Picture" Academy Award

TOP 10 ★
MOVIES OF THE 1990s

1	Titanic*	1997
2	Star Wars: Episode I – The Phantom Menace	1999
3	Jurassic Park	1993
4	Independence Day	1996
5	The Lion King	1994
6	Forrest Gump*	1994
7	The Lost World: Jurassic Park	1997
8	Men in Black	1997
9	The Sixth Sense	1999
10	Armageddon	1998

* Winner of "Best Picture" Academy Award

Each of the Top 10 movies of the 1990s has earned more than $550 million around the world.

BRINGING THE HOUSE DOWN

The White House sustains a direct hit from the invading spacecraft in a scene from Independence Day, *one of the top movies of the 1990s.*

TOP 10 MOVIES OF THE 1980s

1 *E.T.: The Extra-Terrestrial*, 1982 **2** *Indiana Jones and the Last Crusade*, 1989 **3** *Batman*, 1989 **4** *Rain Man*, 1988 **5** *Return of the Jedi*, 1983 **6** *Raiders of the Lost Ark*, 1981 **7** *The Empire Strikes Back*, 1980 **8** *Who Framed Roger Rabbit*, 1988 **9** *Back to the Future*, 1985 **10** *Top Gun*, 1986

TOP 10 ★
MOVIES OF THE 1970s

1	Star Wars	1977/97
2	Jaws	1975
3	Close Encounters of the Third Kind	1977/80
4	The Exorcist	1973/98
5	Moonraker	1979
6	The Spy Who Loved Me	1977
7	The Sting*	1973
8	Grease	1978
9	The Godfather*	1972
10	Saturday Night Fever	1977

* Winner of "Best Picture" Academy Award

In the 1970s, the arrival of Steven Spielberg and George Lucas set the scene for the high-adventure blockbusters whose domination has continued ever since. Lucas wrote and directed *Star Wars*, formerly the highest-earning movie of all time.

JAWS OF DEATH

Although it once held the record as the world's highest-earning movie, Jaws *was eventually beaten by* Star Wars, *directed by George Lucas.*

Which actress provided the voice of Tzipporah in *The Prince of Egypt*?

see p.176 for the answer

A Julia Roberts
B Demi Moore
C Michelle Pfeiffer

Movie Genres

HORROR MOVIES

1	Jurassic Park	1993
2	The Lost World: Jurassic Park	1997
3	The Sixth Sense	1999
4	Jaws	1975
5	The Mummy	1999
6	Godzilla	1998
7	The Exorcist	1973
8	The Blair Witch Project	1999
9	Interview With the Vampire	1994
10	Jaws II	1978

VAMPIRE MOVIES

1	Interview With the Vampire	1994
2	Bram Stoker's Dracula	1992
3	From Dusk Till Dawn	1996
4	Love at First Bite	1979
5	The Lost Boys	1987
6	Vampires	1998
7	Dracula	1979
8	Fright Night	1985
9	Vampire in Brooklyn	1995
10	Buffy the Vampire Slayer	1992

WESTERNS

1	Dances With Wolves	1990
2	Wild Wild West	1999
3	Maverick	1994
4	Unforgiven	1992
5	Butch Cassidy and the Sundance Kid	1969
6	Jeremiah Johnson	1972
7	How the West Was Won	1962
8	Young Guns	1988
9	Young Guns II	1990
10	Pale Rider	1985

GHOST MOVIES

1	The Sixth Sense	1999
2	Ghost	1990
3	Ghostbusters	1984
4	Casper	1995
5	Ghostbusters II	1989
6	The Haunting	1999
7	Sleepy Hollow	1999
8	Beetlejuice	1988
9	Scrooged	1988
10	The House on Haunted Hill	1999

SCIENCE-FICTION MOVIES

1	Star Wars: Episode I – The Phantom Menace	1999
2	Jurassic Park	1993
3	Independence Day	1996
4	Star Wars	1977/97
5	E.T.: The Extra-Terrestrial	1982
6	The Lost World: Jurassic Park	1997
7	Men in Black	1997
8	Return of the Jedi	1983/97
9	Armageddon	1998
10	Terminator 2: Judgment Day	1991

WAR MOVIES

1	Saving Private Ryan	1998
2	Platoon	1986
3	Good Morning, Vietnam	1987
4	Apocalypse Now	1979
5	The Thin Red Line	1998
6	M*A*S*H	1970
7	Patton	1970
8	The Deer Hunter	1978
9	Full Metal Jacket	1987
10	Midway	1976

This list excludes successful movies that are not technically "war" films but that have military themes, such as *A Few Good Men* (1992), *The Hunt for Red October* (1990), *Crimson Tide* (1995), and *An Officer and a Gentleman* (1982), which would otherwise be placed in the top five, and *Top Gun* (1986), which would feature prominently in the list.

WHO YOU GONNA CALL?

Ghostbusters *starred Bill Murray alongside Dan Aykroyd and Harold Ramis, both of whom also co-wrote the first movie and its sequel.*

MOVIES STARRING ANIMALS

	MOVIE/YEAR	ANIMAL
1	*Jaws*, 1975	Shark
2	*101 Dalmatians*, 1996	Dogs
3	*Babe*, 1995	Pig
4	*Jaws II*, 1978	Shark
5	*Free Willy*, 1993	Orca whale
6	*Turner & Hooch*, 1989	Dog
7	*Jaws 3-D*, 1983	Shark
8	*Babe: Pig in the City*, 1998	Pig
9	*Beethoven*, 1992	Dog
10	*Homeward Bound II: Lost in San Francisco*, 1996	Dogs

This list is of films where real animals are acknowledged as central rather than secondary characters. Man-eating sharks, dogs, and pigs stand out as the most popular subjects!

FUTURE PERFECT

Schoolkid Marty McFly (Michael J. Fox) and scientist Dr. Emmett "Doc" L. Brown (Christopher Lloyd) are dazzled as the Doc's DeLorean zips back to 1955. The first Back to the Future *film earned $350 million.*

TOP 10 ★

TIME TRAVEL MOVIES

1	*Terminator 2: Judgment Day*	1991
2	*Back to the Future*	1985
3	*Back to the Future Part III*	1990
4	*Back to the Future Part II*	1989
5	*Timecop*	1994
6	*The Terminator*	1984
7	*Pleasantville*	1998
8	*Time Bandits*	1981
9	*Bill and Ted's Excellent Adventure*	1989
10	*Highlander III: The Sorcerer*	1994

TOP 10 COMEDY MOVIES

1 *Forrest Gump*, 1994 **2** *Home Alone*, 1990 **3** *Ghost*, 1990 **4** *Pretty Woman*, 1990 **5** *Mrs. Doubtfire*, 1993 **6** *The Flintstones*, 1994 **7** *Notting Hill*, 1999 **8** *Who Framed Roger Rabbit*, 1988 **9** *There's Something About Mary*, 1998 **10** *The Mask*, 1994

TOP 10 ★

DISASTER MOVIES

1	*Titanic*	1997
2	*Armageddon*	1998
3	*Twister*	1996
4	*Die Hard With a Vengeance*	1995
5	*Deep Imapct*	1998
6	*Apollo 13*	1995
7	*Outbreak*	1995
8	*Dante's Peak*	1997
9	*Daylight*	1996
10	*Die Hard*	1988

TOP 10 ★

COP MOVIES

1	*Die Hard With a Vengeance*	1995
2	*The Fugitive*	1993
3	*Basic Instinct*	1992
4	*Se7en*	1995
5	*Lethal Weapon 3*	1992
6	*Beverly Hills Cop*	1984
7	*Beverly Hills Cop II*	1987
8	*Lethal Weapon 4*	1998
9	*Speed*	1994
10	*Lethal Weapon 2*	1989

Although movies in which one of the central characters is a police officer have never been among the most successful movies of all time, many have earned respectable amounts at the box office. They are divided between those with a comic slant, such as all three *Beverly Hills Cop* movies, and darker police thrillers, such as *Basic Instinct*. Movies featuring FBI and CIA agents have been excluded here, thus eliminating blockbusters such as *Mission: Impossible* and *The Silence of the Lambs*.

"LIFE IS LIKE A BOX OF CHOCOLATES …"

As Forrest Gump, Tom Hanks plays a man whose simple homespun philosophy enables him to succeed against all odds.

Did You Know? The 1980 British movie *Raise the Titanic!* itself became a disaster movie, losing over $30 million of the $40 million it had cost to make, as it sank without trace at the box office.

Oscar-Winning Movies

TOP 10 ★
HIGHEST-EARNING "BEST PICTURE" OSCAR WINNERS

MOVIE	YEAR
1 Titanic	1997
2 Forrest Gump	1994
3 Dances With Wolves	1990
4 Rain Man	1988
5 Schindler's List	1993
6 Shakespeare in Love	1999
7 The English Patient	1996
8 American Beauty	1999
9 Braveheart	1995
10 Gone With the Wind	1939

THE 10 "BEST PICTURE" OSCAR WINNERS OF THE 1950s

(Year/movie)

1 1950 *All About Eve* **2** 1951 *An American in Paris* **3** 1952 *The Greatest Show on Earth* **4** 1953 *From Here to Eternity* **5** 1954 *On the Waterfront* **6** 1955 *Marty* **7** 1956 *Around the World in 80 Days* **8** 1957 *The Bridge on the River Kwai* **9** 1958 *Gigi* **10** 1959 *Ben-Hur*

The first winning film of the 1950s, *All About Eve*, received the most Oscar nominations (14), while the last, *Ben-Hur*, won the most (11).

THE 10 "BEST PICTURE" OSCAR WINNERS OF THE 1960s

(Year/film)

1 1960 *The Apartment* **2** 1961 *West Side Story* **3** 1962 *Lawrence of Arabia* **4** 1963 *Tom Jones* **5** 1964 *My Fair Lady* **6** 1965 *The Sound of Music* **7** 1966 *A Man for All Seasons* **8** 1967 *In the Heat of the Night* **9** 1968 *Oliver!* **10** 1969 *Midnight Cowboy*

The 1960 winner, *The Apartment*, was the last black-and-white winner until *Schindler's List* in 1993.

HEALTHY PATIENT
Nominated for 12 and winner of nine Oscars, The English Patient is also among the highest-earning of all "Best Picture" winners.

TOP 10 MOVIES NOMINATED FOR THE MOST OSCARS*
(Movie/year/awards/nominations)

1 = *All About Eve*, 1950, 6, 14; = *Titanic*, 1997, 11, 14 **3** = *Gone With the Wind*, 1939 ,8#, 13; = *From Here to Eternity*, 1953, 8, 13; = *Mary Poppins*, 1964, 5, 13; = *Who's Afraid of Virginia Woolf?*, 1966, 5, 13; = *Forrest Gump*, 1994, 6, 13; = *Shakespeare in Love*, 1998, 7, 13 **9** = *Mrs. Miniver*, 1942, 6, 12; = *The Song of Bernadette*, 1943, 4, 12; = *Johnny Belinda*, 1948, 1, 12; = *A Streetcar Named Desire*, 1951, 4, 12; = *On the Waterfront*, 1954, 8, 12; = *Ben-Hur*, 1959, 11, 12; = *Becket*, 1964, 1, 12; = *My Fair Lady*, 1964, 8, 12; = *Reds*, 1981, 3, 12; = *Dances With Wolves*, 1990, 7, 12; = *Schindler's List*, 1993, 7, 12; = *The English Patient*, 1996 , 9, 12

* Oscar® is a Registered Trademark
 # Plus two special awards

THE 10 ★
"BEST PICTURE" OSCAR WINNERS OF THE 1970s

YEAR	MOVIE
1970	Patton
1971	The French Connection
1972	The Godfather
1973	The Sting
1974	The Godfather Part II
1975	One Flew Over the Cuckoo's Nest
1976	Rocky
1977	Annie Hall
1978	The Deer Hunter
1979	Kramer vs. Kramer

THE 10 ★
"BEST PICTURE" OSCAR WINNERS OF THE 1980s

YEAR	MOVIE
1980	Ordinary People
1981	Chariots of Fire
1982	Gandhi
1983	Terms of Endearment
1984	Amadeus
1985	Out of Africa
1986	Platoon
1987	The Last Emperor
1988	Rain Man
1989	Driving Miss Daisy

Did You Know? *Who's Afraid of Virginia Woolf?* (1966) was the first film in which the entire cast was nominated for Oscars, with wins for both Elizabeth Taylor and Sandy Dennis.

DRAMATIC ENTRANCE
Career woman (Annette Benning) confronts drop-out husband (Kevin Spacey) in the suburban satire American Beauty, winner of the 1999 "Best Picture" Oscar.

THE 10 ⭐
LATEST "BEST PICTURE" OSCAR WINNERS

YEAR	MOVIE
1999	American Beauty
1998	Shakespeare in Love
1997	Titanic
1996	The English Patient
1995	Braveheart
1994	Forrest Gump
1993	Schindler's List
1992	Unforgiven
1991	The Silence of the Lambs
1990	Dances With Wolves

TOP 10 ⭐
MOVIES TO WIN THE MOST OSCARS

	MOVIE	YEAR	NOMINATIONS	AWARDS
1 =	Ben-Hur	1959	12	11
=	Titanic	1997	14	11
3	West Side Story	1961	11	10
4 =	Gigi	1958	9	9
=	The Last Emperor	1987	9	9
=	The English Patient	1996	12	9
7 =	Gone With the Wind	1939	13	8*
=	From Here to Eternity	1953	13	8
=	On the Waterfront	1954	12	8
=	My Fair Lady	1964	12	8
=	Cabaret	1972	10	8
=	Gandhi	1982	11	8
=	Amadeus	1984	11	8

* Plus two special awards

TOP 10 STUDIOS WITH THE MOST "BEST PICTURE" OSCARS
(Studio/awards)

1 United Artists, 13 **2** Columbia, 12
3 Paramount, 11 **4** MGM, 9
5 Twentieth Century Fox, 7 **6** Warner Bros, 6
7 Universal, 5 **8** Orion, 4 **9** = Miramax, 2; = RKO, 2

HEART'S CONTENT
In addition to its financial success, Mel Gibson's 1995 film Braveheart won five Oscars, including "Best Director" and "Best Actor."

ACTING HIS AGE

Septuagenarian actor John Gielgud secured a "Best Supporting Actor" Oscar for his role as Hobson, the acerbic valet to the lead character star of Arthur.

"OSCAR"

Founded on May 4, 1927, the Hollywood-based Academy of Motion Picture Arts and Sciences proposed improving the image of the movie industry by issuing "awards for merit or distinction" in various categories. The award itself, a statuette designed by Cedric Gibbons, was modeled by a young artist, George Stanley. The gold-plated naked male figure holds a sword and stands on a reel of film. It was simply called "the statuette" until 1931, when Academy librarian Margaret Herrick commented, "It looks like my Uncle Oscar!" – and the name stuck.

WHY DO WE SAY?

THE 10 "BEST ACTRESS" OSCAR WINNERS OF THE 1950s

(Year/actress/movie)

1. 1950 Judy Holiday, *Born Yesterday*
2. 1951 Vivien Leigh, *A Streetcar Named Desire*
3. 1952 Shirley Booth, *Come Back, Little Sheba*
4. 1953 Audrey Hepburn, *Roman Holiday*
5. 1954 Grace Kelly, *The Country Girl*
6. 1955 Anna Magnani, *The Rose Tattoo*
7. 1956 Ingrid Bergman, *Anastasia*
8. 1957 Joanne Woodward, *The Three Faces of Eve*
9. 1958 Susan Hayward, *I Want to Live*
10. 1959 Simone Signoret, *Room at the Top*

THE 10 ★ "BEST ACTOR" OSCAR WINNERS OF THE 1950s

YEAR	ACTOR/MOVIE
1950	Jose Ferrer, *Cyrano de Bergerac*
1951	Humphrey Bogart, *The African Queen*
1952	Gary Cooper, *High Noon*
1953	William Holden, *Stalag 17*
1954	Marlon Brando, *On the Waterfront**
1955	Ernest Borgnine, *Marty**
1956	Yul Brynner, *The King and I*
1957	Alec Guinness, *The Bridge on the River Kwai**
1958	David Niven, *Separate Tables*
1959	Charlton Heston, *Ben-Hur**

* Winner of "Best Picture" Oscar

THE 10 ★ "BEST ACTRESS" OSCAR WINNERS OF THE 1960s

YEAR	ACTRESS/MOVIE
1960	Elizabeth Taylor, *Butterfield 8*
1961	Sophia Loren, *Two Women*
1962	Anne Bancroft, *The Miracle Worker*
1963	Patricia Neal, *Hud*
1964	Julie Andrews, *Mary Poppins*
1965	Julie Christie, *Darling*
1966	Elizabeth Taylor, *Who's Afraid of Virginia Woolf?*
1967	Katharine Hepburn, *Guess Who's Coming to Dinner*
1968 =	Katharine Hepburn*, *The Lion in Winter*
=	Barbra Streisand*, *Funny Girl*
1969	Maggie Smith, *The Prime of Miss Jean Brodie*

* The only tie for "Best Actress"

TOP 10 ★ OLDEST OSCAR-WINNING ACTORS AND ACTRESSES

	ACTOR OR ACTRESS	AWARD/MOVIE	YEAR	AGE*
1	Jessica Tandy	"Best Actress" (*Driving Miss Daisy*)	1989	80
2	George Burns	"Best Supporting Actor" (*The Sunshine Boys*)	1975	80
3	Melvyn Douglas	"Best Supporting Actor" (*Being There*)	1979	79
4	John Gielgud	"Best Supporting Actor" (*Arthur*)	1981	77
5	Don Ameche	"Best Supporting Actor" (*Cocoon*)	1985	77
6	Peggy Ashcroft	"Best Supporting Actress" (*A Passage to India*)	1984	77
7	Henry Fonda	"Best Actor" (*On Golden Pond*)	1981	76
8	Katharine Hepburn	"Best Actress" (*On Golden Pond*)	1981	74
9	Edmund Gwenn	"Best Supporting Actor" (*Miracle on 34th Street*)	1947	72
10	Ruth Gordon	"Best Supporting Actress" (*Rosemary's Baby*)	1968	72

* At the time of the Award ceremony; those of apparently identical age have been ranked according to their precise age in days at the time of the ceremony

THE 10 ★
"BEST ACTOR" OSCAR WINNERS OF THE 1960s

YEAR	ACTOR/MOVIE
1960	Burt Lancaster, *Elmer Gantry*
1961	Maximilian Schell, *Judgement at Nuremberg*
1962	Gregory Peck, *To Kill a Mockingbird*
1963	Sidney Poitier, *Lilies of the Field*
1964	Rex Harrison, *My Fair Lady* *
1965	Lee Marvin, *Cat Ballou*
1966	Paul Scofield, *A Man for All Seasons* *
1967	Rod Steiger, *In the Heat of the Night* *
1968	Cliff Robertson, *Charly*
1969	John Wayne, *True Grit*

* *Winner of "Best Picture" Oscar*

THE 10 ★
"BEST ACTOR" OSCAR WINNERS OF THE 1970s

YEAR	ACTOR/MOVIE
1970	George C. Scott, *Patton* *
1971	Gene Hackman, *The French Connection* *
1972	Marlon Brando, *The Godfather* *
1973	Jack Lemmon, *Save the Tiger*
1974	Art Carney, *Harry and Tonto*
1975	Jack Nicholson, *One Flew Over the Cuckoo's Nest* *#
1976	Peter Finch, *Network*
1977	Richard Dreyfuss, *The Goodbye Girl*
1978	John Voight, *Coming Home*
1979	Dustin Hoffman, *Kramer vs. Kramer* *

* *Winner of "Best Picture" Oscar*

\# *Winner of "Best Director," "Best Actress," and "Best Screenplay" Oscars*

CABARET STAR

Liza Minnelli won "Best Actress" Oscar for her role as Sally Bowles in Cabaret. The movie itself received 10 nominations and eight wins, but lost "Best Picture" to The Godfather.

THE 10 "BEST ACTRESS" OSCAR WINNERS OF THE 1970s
(Year/actress/movie)

1 1970 Glenda Jackson, *Women in Love* **2** 1971 Jane Fonda, *Klute*
3 1972 Liza Minnelli, *Cabaret* **4** 1973 Glenda Jackson, *A Touch of Class*
5 1974 Ellen Burstyn, *Alice Doesn't Live Here Any More* **6** 1975 Louise Fletcher, *One Flew Over the Cuckoo's Nest* *# **7** 1976 Faye Dunaway, *Network* **8** 1977 Diane Keaton, *Annie Hall* *
9 1978 Jane Fonda, *Coming Home* **10** 1979 Sally Field, *Norma Rae*
* *Winner of "Best Picture" Oscar*
\# *Winner of "Best Director," "Best Actor," and "Best Screenplay" Oscars*

In which of these movies did Leonardo DiCaprio star? **A** *Peggy Sue Got Married*
see p.174 for the answer **B** *What's Eating Gilbert Grape*
  C *Raging Bull*

Oscar-Winning Stars 2

THE 10 ★
"BEST ACTRESS" OSCAR WINNERS OF THE 1980s

YEAR	ACTRESS/MOVIE
1980	Sissy Spacek, *Coal Miner's Daughter*
1981	Katharine Hepburn, *On Golden Pond**
1982	Meryl Streep, *Sophie's Choice*
1983	Shirley MacLaine, *Terms of Endearment*#
1984	Sally Field, *Places in the Heart*
1985	Geraldine Page, *The Trip to Bountiful*
1986	Marlee Matlin, *Children of a Lesser God*
1987	Cher, *Moonstruck*
1988	Jodie Foster, *The Accused*
1989	Jessica Tandy, *Driving Miss Daisy*#

* *Winner of "Best Actor" Oscar*
\# *Winner of "Best Picture" Oscar*

THE 10 ★
"BEST ACTOR" OSCAR WINNERS OF THE 1980s

YEAR	ACTOR/MOVIE
1980	Robert De Niro, *Raging Bull*
1981	Henry Fonda, *On Golden Pond**
1982	Ben Kingsley, *Gandhi*#
1983	Robert Duvall, *Tender Mercies*
1984	F. Murray Abraham, *Amadeus*#
1985	William Hurt, *Kiss of the Spider Woman*
1986	Paul Newman, *The Color of Money*
1987	Michael Douglas, *Wall Street*
1988	Dustin Hoffman, *Rain Man*#
1989	Daniel Day-Lewis, *My Left Foot*

* *Winner of "Best Actress" Oscar*
\# *Winner of "Best Picture" Oscar*

GETTING IN ON THE ACT

Jack Nicholson, winner of "Best Actor" Oscar for As Good As It Gets, *confronts Jill, a Brussels Griffon performing the part of Verdell.*

THE 10 ★
LATEST "BEST ACTOR" OSCAR WINNERS

YEAR	ACTOR/MOVIE
1999	Kevin Spacey, *American Beauty**
1998	Roberto Benigni, *La Vita è Bella (Life Is Beautiful)*
1997	Jack Nicholson, *As Good as It Gets*#
1996	Geoffrey Rush, *Shine*
1995	Nicolas Cage, *Leaving Las Vegas*
1994	Tom Hanks, *Forrest Gump**
1993	Tom Hanks, *Philadelphia*
1992	Al Pacino, *Scent of a Woman*
1991	Anthony Hopkins, *The Silence of the Lambs**#
1990	Jeremy Irons, *Reversal of Fortune*

* *Winner of "Best Picture" Oscar*
\# *Winner of "Best Actress" Oscar*

Tom Hanks shares the honor of two consecutive wins with Spencer Tracy (1937: *Captains Courageous* and 1938: *Boys Town*). Only four other actors have won twice: Marlon Brando (1954; 1972), Gary Cooper (1941; 1952), Dustin Hoffman (1977; 1988), and Jack Nicholson (1975; 1997),

GOLDEN DOUBLE

Katharine Hepburn and Henry Fonda won "Best Actress" and "Best Actor" Academy Awards for On Golden Pond. *It was Hepburn's fourth but Fonda's only Oscar, awarded just four months before his death.*

ROLE REVERSAL

Former television actress Hilary Swank (right) won the 1999 "Best Actress" Oscar for her demanding role as a girl who adopts the persona of a boy.

THE 10 ★
LATEST "BEST ACTRESS" OSCAR WINNERS

YEAR	ACTRESS/MOVIE
1999	Hilary Swank, *Boys Don't Cry*
1998	Gwyneth Paltrow, *Shakespeare in Love*
1997	Helen Hunt, *As Good as It Gets*
1996	Frances McDormand, *Fargo*
1995	Susan Sarandon, *Dead Man Walking*
1994	Jessica Lange, *Blue Sky*
1993	Holly Hunter, *The Piano*
1992	Emma Thompson, *Howard's End*
1991	Jodie Foster, *The Silence of the Lambs**
1990	Kathy Bates, *Misery*

* Winner of "Best Picture" and "Best Actor" Oscars

TOP 10 ★
YOUNGEST OSCAR-WINNING ACTORS AND ACTRESSES

	ACTOR OR ACTRESS	AWARD/MOVIE (WHERE SPECIFIED)	YEAR	AGE*
1	Shirley Temple	Special Award – outstanding contribution during 1934	1934	6
2	Margaret O' Brien	Special Award (*Meet Me in St Louis*)	1944	8
3	Vincent Winter	Special Award (*The Little Kidnappers*)	1954	8
4	Ivan Jandl	Special Award (*The Search*)	1948	9
5	Jon Whiteley	Special Award (*The Little Kidnappers*)	1954	10
6	Tatum O'Neal	"Best Supporting Actress" (*Paper Moon*)	1973	10
7	Anna Paquin	"Best Supporting Actress" (*The Piano*)	1993	11
8	Claude Jarman, Jr.	Special Award (*The Yearling*)	1946	12
9	Bobby Driscoll	Special Award (*The Window*)	1949	13
10	Hayley Mills	Special Award (*Pollyanna*)	1960	13

* At the time of the Award ceremony; those of apparently identical age have been ranked according to their precise age in days at the time of the ceremony

The Academy Awards ceremony usually takes place at the end of March in the year following that in which the film was released in the US, so the winners are generally at least a year older when they receive their Oscars than when they acted in their award-winning movies.

Who provided the voice of Woody in *Toy Story* and *Toy Story 2*?
see p.175 for the answer

A Jack Nicholson
B Dustin Hoffman
C Tom Hanks

THE 10 ★
LATEST WINNERS OF THE CANNES PALME D'OR FOR "BEST FILM"

YEAR	FILM/COUNTRY
1999	*Rosetta*, France
1998	*Eternity and a Day*, Greece
1997	*The Eel*, Japan/ *The Taste of Cherries*, Iran
1996	*Secrets and Lies*, UK
1995	*Underground*, Yugoslavia
1994	*Pulp Fiction*, US
1993	*Farewell My Concubine*, China/ *The Piano*, Australia
1992	*Best Intentions*, Denmark
1991	*Barton Fink*, US
1990	*Wild at Heart*, US

THE 10 ★
LATEST GOLDEN GLOBE AWARDS FOR "BEST PERFORMANCE BY AN ACTOR IN A MOTION PICTURE – MUSICAL OR COMEDY"

YEAR	ACTOR/MOVIE
2000	Jim Carrey, *Man on the Moon*
1999	Michael Caine, *Little Voice*
1998	Jack Nicholson, *As Good As It Gets*
1997	Tom Cruise, *Jerry Maguire*
1996	John Travolta, *Get Shorty*
1995	Hugh Grant, *Four Weddings and a Funeral*
1994	Robin Williams, *Mrs. Doubtfire*
1993	Tim Robbins, *The Player*
1992	Robin Williams, *The Fisher King*
1991	Gerard Depardieu, *Green Card*

During the past 10 years, more than half the Golden Globe awards in this category went to the stars of movies that earned in excess of $100 million apiece. *Four Weddings and a Funeral* was the all-time highest-earning British film until overtaken in 1998 by *The Full Monty*.

THE 10 ★
LATEST GOLDEN GLOBE AWARDS FOR "BEST PERFORMANCE BY AN ACTRESS IN A MOTION PICTURE – MUSICAL OR COMEDY"

YEAR	ACTRESS/MOVIE
2000	Janet McTeer, *Tumbleweeds*
1999	Gwyneth Paltrow, *Shakespeare in Love*
1998	Helen Hunt, *As Good As It Gets*
1997	Madonna, *Evita*
1996	Nicole Kidman, *To Die For*
1995	Jamie Lee Curtis, *True Lies*
1994	Angela Bassett, *What's Love Got to Do With It*
1993	Miranda Richardson, *Enchanted April*
1992	Bette Midler, *For the Boys*
1991	Julia Roberts, *Pretty Woman*

Although romantic comedies feature predominantly among the winners, a number of the successful actresses in this category received their awards for roles in movies that are either traditional musicals, or have a high musical content.

THE 10 ★
LATEST GOLDEN GLOBE AWARDS FOR "BEST MOTION PICTURE – MUSICAL OR COMEDY"

YEAR	MOVIE
2000	*Toy Story 2*
1999	*Shakespeare in Love*
1998	*As Good As It Gets*
1997	*Evita*
1996	*Babe*
1995	*The Lion King*
1994	*Mrs. Doubtfire*
1993	*The Player*
1992	*Beauty and the Beast*
1991	*Green Card*

The Golden Globes are awarded retrospectively, the 2000 award being presented for productions during 1999, and so on.

THE 10 ⭐
LATEST GOLDEN GLOBE AWARDS FOR "BEST PERFORMANCE BY AN ACTOR IN A MOTION PICTURE – DRAMA"

YEAR	ACTOR/MOVIE
2000	Denzel Washington, *The Hurricane*
1999	Jim Carrey, *The Truman Show*
1998	Peter Fonda, *Ulee's Gold*
1997	Geoffrey Rush, *Shine*
1996	Nicolas Cage, *Leaving Las Vegas*
1995	Tom Hanks, *Forrest Gump*
1994	Tom Hanks, *Philadelphia*
1993	Al Pacino, *Scent of a Woman*
1992	Nick Nolte, *The Prince of Tides*
1991	Jeremy Irons, *Reversal of Fortune*

No fewer than six of the 10 most recent Golden Globe Awards won by leading actors – those in 1990, and 1992–96 – were subsequently mirrored by the same actors' Oscar wins.

THE 10 ⭐
LATEST GOLDEN GLOBE AWARDS FOR "BEST DIRECTOR"

YEAR	DIRECTOR/MOVIE
2000	Sam Mendes, *American Beauty*
1999	Steven Spielberg, *Saving Private Ryan*
1998	James Cameron, *Titanic*
1997	Milos Foreman, *The People vs. Larry Flynt*
1996	Mel Gibson, *Braveheart*
1995	Robert Zemeckis, *Forrest Gump*
1994	Steven Spielberg, *Schindler's List*
1993	Clint Eastwood, *Unforgiven*
1992	Oliver Stone, *JFK*
1991	Kevin Costner, *Dances With Wolves*

TRUE TO FORM

Jim Carrey gained a Golden Globe for his part in The Truman Show, *a satire in which every detail of his life is secretly filmed for public broadcast.*

THE 10 ⭐
LATEST GOLDEN GLOBE AWARDS FOR "BEST PERFORMANCE BY AN ACTRESS IN A MOTION PICTURE – DRAMA"

YEAR	ACTRESS/MOVIE
2000	Hilary Swank, *Boys Don't Cry*
1999	Cate Blanchett, *Elizabeth*
1998	Judi Dench, *Mrs. Brown*
1997	Brenda Blethyn, *Secrets and Lies*
1996	Sharon Stone, *Casino*
1995	Jessica Lange, *Blue Sky*
1994	Holly Hunter, *The Piano*
1993	Emma Thompson, *Howard's End*
1992	Jodie Foster, *The Silence of the Lambs*
1991	Kathy Bates, *Misery*

THE 10 ⭐
LATEST RECIPIENTS OF THE AMERICAN FILM INSTITUTE LIFETIME ACHIEVEMENT WARDS

2000	Harrison Ford
1999	Dustin Hoffman
1998	Robert Wise
1997	Martin Scorsese
1996	Clint Eastwood
1995	Steven Spielberg
1994	Jack Nicholson
1993	Elizabeth Taylor
1992	Sidney Poitier
1991	Kirk Douglas

The Lifetime Achievement winners in the intervening years between the first and last 10 are: 1983: John Huston; 1984: Lillian Gish; 1985: Gene Kelly; 1986: Billy Wilder; 1987: Barbara Stanwyck; 1988: Jack Lemmon; 1989: Gregory Peck; and 1990: David Lean.

Which actress provides the voice of Marge on *The Simpsons*?
see p.184 for the answer
A Julie Kavner
B Catherine Keener
C Marie-Louise Parker

Leading Men

TOP 10 ★
LEONARDO DiCAPRIO MOVIES

1	Titanic	1997
2	The Man in the Iron Mask	1998
3	Romeo + Juliet	1996
4	The Beach	2000
5	The Quick and the Dead	1995
6	Marvin's Room	1996
7	What's Eating Gilbert Grape	1993
8	Celebrity	1998
9	This Boy's Life	1993
10	The Basketball Diaries	1995

TOP 10 ★
NICOLAS CAGE MOVIES

1	The Rock	1996
2	Face/Off	1997
3	Con Air	1997
4	City of Angels	1998
5	Snake Eyes	1998
6	8MM	1999
7	Moonstruck	1987
8	Leaving Las Vegas	1995
9	Peggy Sue Got Married	1986
10	It Could Happen to You	1994

RATTLING THE CAGE

Nicolas Cage stars as FBI biochemist Dr. Stanley Godspeed in the 1996 movie The Rock, *which is his highest-earning movie to date.*

TOP 10 ★
PIERCE BROSNAN MOVIES

1	Mrs. Doubtfire	1993
2	GoldenEye	1995
3	Tomorrow Never Dies	1997
4	The World Is Not Enough	1999
5	Dante's Peak	1997
6	The Thomas Crown Affair	1999
7	Mars Attacks!	1996
8	The Mirror Has Two Faces	1996
9	The Lawnmower Man	1992
10	Love Affair	1994

Pierce Brosnan, now best known as James Bond, provided the voice of King Arthur in *Quest for Camelot* (1998). If included, it would be ranked ninth. *The World Is Not Enough*, and six other movies in which Brosnan starred, have each earned well over $100 million apiece. His Top 10 total now approaches $2 billion.

PIERCING LOOK

Irish-born Pierce Brosnan took over the role of James Bond with GoldenEye. This, along with Tomorrow Never Dies *and* The World Is Not Enough, *are the highest earning of all the Bond series.*

TOP 10 ★
ARNOLD SCHWARZENEGGER MOVIES

1	Terminator 2: Judgment Day	1991
2	True Lies	1994
3	Total Recall	1990
4	Eraser	1996
5	Twins	1988
6	Kindergarten Cop	1990
7	End of Days	1999
8	Jingle All the Way	1996
9	Last Action Hero	1993
10	Junior	1994

TOP 10 ★
TOM CRUISE MOVIES

1	Mission: Impossible	1996
2	Rain Man	1988
3	Top Gun	1986
4	Jerry Maguire	1996
5	The Firm	1993
6	A Few Good Men	1992
7	Interview With the Vampire	1994
8	Days of Thunder	1990
9	Eyes Wide Shut	1999
10	Cocktail	1988

TOP 10 ★
MEL GIBSON MOVIES

1	Lethal Weapon 4	1998
2	Lethal Weapon 2	1989
3	Lethal Weapon 3	1992
4	Braveheart*	1995
5	Ransom	1996
6	Payback	1999
7	Conspiracy Theory	1997
8	Forever Young	1992
9	Maverick	1994
10	Bird on a Wire	1990

* Academy Award for "Best Director"

Mel Gibson also provided the voice of John Smith in *Pocahontas* (1995) and appeared uncredited as himself in *Casper* (1995). If included, these would enter in first and third positions respectively. Nine out of Gibson's Top 10 movies have earned more than $100 million each at the worldwide box office.

TOP 10 ★
BRAD PITT MOVIES

1	Se7en	1995
2	Interview With the Vampire	1994
3	Sleepers	1996
4	Legends of the Fall	1994
5	Twelve Monkeys	1995
6	The Devil's Own	1997
7	Seven Years in Tibet	1997
8	Meet Joe Black	1998
9	Fight Club	1999
10	Thelma & Louise	1991

PITT STOPPER

Brad (William Bradley) Pitt plays Detective David Mills in Se7en, *his most successful movie to date. Pitt appeared in more than 20 films during the 1990s.*

TOP 10 ★
JACK NICHOLSON MOVIES

1	Batman	1989
2	A Few Good Men	1992
3	As Good As It Gets*	1997
4	Terms of Endearment#	1983
5	Wolf	1994
6	One Flew Over the Cuckoo's Nest*	1975
7	Mars Attacks!	1996
8	The Witches of Eastwick	1987
9	The Shining	1980
10	Broadcast News	1987

* Academy Award for "Best Actor"
# Academy Award for "Best Supporting Actor"

TOP 10 ★
TOM HANKS MOVIES

1	Forrest Gump*	1994
2	Saving Private Ryan	1998
3	Apollo 13	1995
4	Sleepless in Seattle	1993
5	Philadelphia*	1993
6	You've Got M@il	1998
7	The Green Mile	1999
8	Big	1988
9	A League of Their Own	1992
10	Turner & Hooch	1989

* Academy Award for "Best Actor"

Tom Hanks also appeared in a voice-only part as Woody in *Toy Story* (1995) and *Toy Story 2* (1999). If included, these would be ranked third and fourth.

TOP 10 ★
JOHN TRAVOLTA MOVIES

1	Look Who's Talking	1989
2	Face/Off	1997
3	Pulp Fiction	1994
4	Grease	1978
5	The General's Daughter	1999
6	Phenomenon	1996
7	Saturday Night Fever*	1977
8	The Thin Red Line	1998
9	Get Shorty	1995
10	Broken Arrow	1996

* Nominated for Academy Award for "Best Actor"

TOP 10 DENZEL WASHINGTON MOVIES

❶ *Philadelphia*, 1993 ❷ *The Pelican Brief*, 1993 ❸ *Crimson Tide*, 1995 ❹ *The Siege*, 1998 ❺ *Courage Under Fire*, 1996 ❻ *The Bone Collector*, 1999 ❼ *The Preacher's Wife*, 1996 ❽ *Malcolm X*, 1992 ❾ *The Hurricane*, 1999 ❿ *Virtuosity*, 1995

TOP 10 JOHNNY DEPP MOVIES

❶ *Platoon*, 1986 ❷ *Donnie Brasco*, 1997 ❸ *Sleepy Hollow*, 1999 ❹ *Edward Scissorhands*, 1990 ❺ *Don Juan DeMarco*, 1995 ❻ *Freddy's Dead: The Final Nightmare**, 1991 ❼ *A Nightmare on Elm Street*, 1984 ❽ *The Astronaut's Wife*, 1999 ❾ *Fear and Loathing in Las Vegas*, 1998 ❿ *What's Eating Gilbert Grape*, 1993

* Uncredited appearance

What are the characters in *Reservoir Dogs* named after?
see p.179 for the answer
A Dogs
B Colors
C Planets

Leading Ladies

RYAN'S DAUGHTER

Born Margaret Mary Emily Anne Hyra, Meg Ryan took her mother's maiden name before her movie debut in 1981. She has gone on to enjoy huge success in a range of romantic comedies.

TOP 10 ★

MICHELLE PFEIFFER MOVIES

1	Batman Returns	1992
2	Dangerous Minds	1995
3	Wolf	1994
4	Up Close & Personal	1996
5	One Fine Day	1996
6	The Witches of Eastwick	1987
7	Tequila Sunrise	1988
8	Scarface	1983
9	Dangerous Liaisons	1988
10	The Age of Innocence	1993

Michelle Pfeiffer also provided the voice of Tzipporah in the animated movie *The Prince of Egypt* (1998). If this was included in her Top 10, it would feature in second place.

CATWOMAN

Batman Returns is Michelle Pfeiffer's most successful movie to date, but half the movies in her Top 10 have earned a healthy $100 million-plus.

TOP 10 ★

MEG RYAN MOVIES

1	Top Gun	1986
2	You've Got M@il	1998
4	Sleepless in Seattle	1993
5	City of Angels	1998
5	French Kiss	1995
6	Courage Under Fire	1996
7	When Harry Met Sally	1989
8	Addicted to Love	1997
9	When a Man Loves a Woman	1994
10	Joe Versus the Volcano	1990

Meg Ryan provided the voice of Anastasia in the 1997 movie of that title. If included, it would appear in ninth place.

TOP 10 ★

RENE RUSSO MOVIES

1	Lethal Weapon 3	1992
2	Ransom	1996
3	Lethal Weapon 4	1998
4	Outbreak	1995
5	In the Line of Fire	1993
6	The Thomas Crown Affair	1999
7	Get Shorty	1995
8	Tin Cup	1996
9	Major League II	1994
10	Major League	1989

TOP 10 NICOLE KIDMAN MOVIES

1 *Batman Forever*, 1995 **2** *Days of Thunder*, 1990 **3** *Eyes Wide Shut*, 1999 **4** *The Peacemaker*, 1997 **5** *Practical Magic*, 1998 **6** *Far and Away*, 1992 **7** *Malice*, 1993 **8** *To Die For*, 1995 **9** *My Life*, 1993 **10** *Portrait of a Lady*, 1996

TOP 10 ★

SHARON STONE MOVIES

1	Basic Instinct	1992
2	Total Recall	1990
3	The Specialist	1995
4	Last Action Hero	1993
5	Sliver	1993
6	Sphere	1998
7	Casino*	1995
8	Diabolique	1996
9	Police Academy 4: Citizens on Patrol	1987
10	Intersection	1994

* Academy Award nomination for "Best Actress"

Sharon Stone's part in *Last Action Hero* amounted to no more than a brief cameo. If it was discounted, *Action Jackson* (1988) would occupy 10th place.

PRETTY WOMAN

Former model Julia Roberts, shown here in My Best Friend's Wedding, became the first Hollywood actress to be paid $10 million (for her role in the 1996 movie Mary Reilly). She now commands almost $20 million.

TOP 10
WINONA RYDER MOVIES

1	Bram Stoker's Dracula	1992
2	Alien: Resurrection	1997
3	Edward Scissorhands	1990
4	Beetlejuice	1988
5	Little Women	1994
6	Mermaids	1990
7	The Age of Innocence	1993
8	How to Make an American Quilt	1995
9	Reality Bites	1994
10	The Crucible	1996

TOP 10 GWYNETH PALTROW MOVIES

1 *Se7en*, 1995 **2** *Hook*, 1991
3 *Shakespeare in Love**, 1998
4 *A Perfect Murder*, 1998
5 *The Talented Mr. Ripley*, 1999
6 *Sliding Doors*, 1998 **7** *Great Expectations*, 1998 **8** *Malice*, 1993
9 *Emma*, 1996 **10** *Hush*, 1998

* Academy Award for "Best Actress"

TOP 10
DEMI MOORE MOVIES

1	Ghost	1990
2	Indecent Proposal	1993
3	A Few Good Men	1992
4	Disclosure	1995
5	Striptease	1996
6	G.I. Jane	1997
7	The Juror	1996
8	About Last Night...	1986
9	St. Elmo's Fire	1985
10	Young Doctors in Love	1982

Demi Moore provided the voice of Esmeralda in *The Hunchback of Notre Dame* (1996). If included in her Top 10, it would be in second place.

TOP 10
JULIA ROBERTS MOVIES

1	Pretty Woman*	1990
2	Notting Hill	1999
3	Hook	1991
4	My Best Friend's Wedding	1997
5	Runaway Bride	1999
6	The Pelican Brief	1993
7	Sleeping with the Enemy	1991
8	Stepmom	1998
9	Conspiracy Theory	1997
10	Steel Magnolias#	1989

* Academy Award nomination for "Best Actress"

 # Academy Award nomination for "Best Supporting Actress"

Julia Roberts also appeared in a cameo role as herself in *The Player* (1992), which just failed to make her personal Top 10.

TOP 10
DREW BARRYMORE MOVIES

1	E.T.: The Extra-Terrestrial	1982
2	Batman Forever	1995
3	Scream	1996
4	The Wedding Singer	1998
5	Never Been Kissed	1999
6	Ever After	1998
7	Wayne's World 2	1993
8	Everyone Says I Love You	1996
9	Boys on the Side	1995
10	Mad Love	1995

TOP 10
GEENA DAVIS MOVIES

1	Tootsie	1982
2	Stuart Little	1999
3	A League of Their Own	1992
4	The Long Kiss Goodnight	1996
5	Beetlejuice	1988
6	Hero	1992
7	Fletch	1985
8	Thelma & Louise	1991
9	The Fly	1986
10	The Accidental Tourist	1988

TOP 10
UMA THURMAN MOVIES

1	Batman & Robin	1997
2	Pulp Fiction	1994
3	The Truth About Cats & Dogs	1996
4	The Avengers	1998
5	Dangerous Liaisons	1988
6	Final Analysis	1992
7	Beautiful Girls	1996
8	Les Misérables	1988
9	Johnny Be Good	1997
10	Gattaca	1998

In which movie remake did Pierce Brosnan star in the title role?   **A** *Bullitt*
see p.174 for the answer   **B** *The Thomas Crown Affair*
C *Papillon*

Character Actors

TOP 10 ★
KEVIN SPACEY MOVIES

1	Se7en	1995
2	Outbreak	1995
3	A Time to Kill	1996
4	American Beauty	1999
5	L.A. Confidential	1997
6	The Negotiator	1998
7	The Usual Suspects	1995
8	See No Evil, Hear No Evil	1989
9	Heartburn	1986
10	Midnight in the Garden of Good and Evil	1997

TOP 10
JAMES CAAN MOVIES

1 The Godfather, 1972 **2** Eraser, 1996 **3** Dick Tracy, 1990 **4** The Godfather Part III, 1990 **5** The Godfather Part II, 1974 **6** Misery, 1990 **7** Mickey Blue Eyes, 1999 **8** Honeymoon in Vegas, 1992 **9** Alien Nation, 1988 **10** The Program, 1993

TOP 10 MORGAN FREEMAN MOVIES

1 Robin Hood: Prince of Thieves, 1991 **2** Deep Impact, 1998 **3** Se7en, 1995 **4** Outbreak, 1995 **5** Unforgiven, 1992 **6** Driving Miss Daisy, 1989 **7** Kiss the Girls, 1997 **8** Amistad, 1997 **9** The Shawshank Redemption, 1994 **10** Chain Reaction, 1996

TOP 10 ★
KEVIN BACON MOVIES

1	Apollo 13	1995
2	A Few Good Men	1992
3	JFK	1991
4	Sleepers	1996
5	Animal House	1978
6	The River Wild	1994
7	Footloose	1984
8	Wild Things	1998
9	Flatliners	1990
10	Planes, Trains & Automobiles	1987

STRANGE STEVE

Steve Buscemi has carved out a movie career playing quirky roles, such as that of Carl Showalter in the Coen Brothers' Fargo.

TOP 10 STEVE BUSCEMI MOVIES

1 Armageddon, 1998 **2** Big Daddy, 1999 **3** Con Air, 1997 **4** Pulp Fiction, 1994 **5** The Wedding Singer*, 1998 **6** Rising Sun, 1993 **7** Desperado, 1995 **8** Fargo, 1996 **9** Escape from L.A., 1996 **10** The Big Lebowski, 1998

* Uncredited

TOP 10 ★
SAMUEL L. JACKSON MOVIES

1	Star Wars: Episode I – The Phantom Menace	1999
2	Jurassic Park	1993
3	Die Hard With a Vengeance	1995
4	Coming to America	1988
5	Pulp Fiction	1994
6	Patriot Games	1992
7	Deep Blue Sea	1999
8	A Time to Kill	1996
9	Sea of Love	1989
10	Jackie Brown	1997

ACTION JACKSON

Samuel Jackson received a Silver Bear award at the Berlin Film Festival for his role in Jackie Brown, one of a series of bad-guy roles.

TOP 10
TIM ROTH MOVIES

1 *Pulp Fiction*, 1994 **2** *Rob Roy*, 1995
3 *Everyone Says I Love You*, 1996
4 *Hoodlum*, 1997 **5** *Reservoir Dogs*,
1992 **5** *The Cook, the Thief, His Wife &*
Her Lover, 1989 **6** *Gridlock'd*, 1997
7 *Four Rooms*, 1995 **8** *A World Apart*,
1988 **10** *Vincent & Theo*, 1990

"LET'S GO TO WORK ..."
*British actor Tim Roth (second from right) appeared
as Mr. Orange in writer–director Quentin Tarantino's
cult debut, the violent gangster movie Reservoir Dogs.*

TOP 10 ★
JOHN MALKOVICH
MOVIES

1	In the Line of Fire	1993
2	The Man in the Iron Mask	1998
3	The Messenger: The Story of Joan of Arc	1999
4	Dangerous Liaisons	1988
5	Places in the Heart	1984
6	The Killing Fields	1984
7	Rounders	1998
8	Being John Malkovich	1999
9	Con Air	1997
10	Empire of the Sun	1987

Although uncredited, John Malkovich was the
narrator of the movie *Alive* (1993). If included, this
would be in fourth place. *Being John Malkovich*
(1999), in which a puppeteer enters the mind of
the actor, is a newcomer to his personal Top 10.

TOP 10 HARVEY KEITEL MOVIES

1 *Sister Act*, 1992 **2** *Pulp Fiction*, 1994 **3** *Get Shorty**, 1995 **4** *Cop Land*, 1997
5 *Rising Sun*, 1993 **6** *From Dusk Till Dawn*, 1996 **7** *Bugsy*, 1991
8 *Thelma & Louise*, 1991 **9** *The Piano*, 1993 **10** *Point of No Return*, 1993

* Uncredited cameo

TOP 10 ★
JOE PESCI MOVIES

1	Home Alone	1990
2	Lethal Weapon 3	1992
3	Lethal Weapon 4	1998
4	Home Alone 2: Lost in New York	1992
5	Lethal Weapon 2	1989
6	JFK	1991
7	Casino	1995
8	My Cousin Vinny	1992
9	GoodFellas	1990
10	Raging Bull	1980

TOP 10 ★
GARY BUSEY MOVIES

1	The Firm	1993
2	Under Siege	1992
3	Lethal Weapon	1987
4	Rookie of the Year	1993
5	Point Break	1991
6	Black Sheep	1996
7	Predator 2	1990
8	Drop Zone	1994
9	The Player	1992
10	Soldier	1998

Did You Know? *Reservoir Dogs* (1992) is not the first movie in which the
gangsters use colors as names: *The Taking of Pelham 123*
(1974) has characters called Blue, Green, Gray, and Brown.

Character Actresses

FAMILY JEWEL

A member of the Fonda movie family (daughter of Peter, granddaughter of Henry, niece of Jane) Bridget Fonda – shown here in Jackie Brown – has built a successful movie career since her 1982 debut.

TOP 10 ★
BRIDGET FONDA MOVIES

1	The Godfather Part III	1990
2	Jackie Brown	1997
3	The Road to Wellville	1994
4	Doc Hollywood	1991
5	Single White Female	1992
6	It Could Happen to You	1994
7	City Hall	1996
8	Lake Placid	1999
9	Point of No Return	1993
10	Singles	1992

TOP 10 ★
ALFRE WOODARD MOVIES

1	Star Trek: First Contact	1996
2	Primal Fear	1996
3	Scrooged	1988
4	Grand Canyon	1991
5	How to Make an American Quilt	1995
6	Blue Chips	1994
7	Heart and Souls	1993
8	Crooklyn	1994
9	Extremities	1986
10	Down in the Delta	1998

TOP 10 ★
CATHERINE KEENER MOVIES

1	8MM	1999
2	Out of Sight	1998
3	About Last Night...	1986
4	Being John Malkovich	1999
5	Switch	1991
6	Your Friends & Neighbors	1998
7	The Gun in Betty Lou's Handbag	1992
8	Walking and Talking	1996
9	Living in Oblivion	1995
10	Box of Moonlight	1996

TOP 10 ★
FRANCES McDORMAND MOVIES

1	Primal Fear	1996
2	Fargo*	1996
3	Madeline	1998
4	Mississippi Burning	1988
5	Darkman	1990
6	Raising Arizona	1987
7	Lone Star	1996
8	Beyond Rangoon	1995
9	The Butcher's Wife	1991
10	Short Cuts	1993

* Academy Award for "Best Actress"

TOP 10 JENNIFER JASON LEIGH MOVIES

1 *Backdraft*, 1991 **2** *Single White Female*, 1992 **3** *Dolores Claiborne*, 1995
4 *Miami Blues*, 1990 **5** *A Thousand Acres*, 1997 **6** *Rush*, 1991 **7** *Short Cuts*, 1993
8 *Georgia*, 1995 **9** *The Hudsucker Proxy*, 1994 **10** *eXistenZ*, 1999

TOP 10 ★ JULIE KAVNER MOVIES

1	Forget Paris	1995
2	Awakenings	1990
3	Hannah and Her Sisters	1986
4	Radio Days	1987
5	Deconstructing Harry	1997
6	New York Stories	1989
7	I'll Do Anything	1994
8	Alice	1990
9	Surrender	1987
10	This Is My Life	1992

Although an actress with a number of movies to her credit, Julie Kavner is best known for providing the voice of Marge Simpson and other characters in the TV series *The Simpsons*. She was also the voice of a pigeon in *Doctor Dolittle* (1998).

TOP 10 ★ EMMA THOMPSON MOVIES

1	Sense and Sensibility	1995
2	Junior	1994
3	Primary Colors	1998
4	Dead Again	1991
5	Howards End*	1992
6	In the Name of the Father #	1993
7	The Remains of the Day #	1993
8	Much Ado About Nothing	1993
9	Henry V	1989
10=	Impromptu	1991
=	Peter's Friends	1992

* *Academy Award for "Best Actress"*
\# *Academy Award nomination*

FIRM FAVORITE
Star of mainstream movies including The Firm, *Holly Hunter has also taken on offbeat parts such as those in* The Piano *and* Crash.

TOP 10 ★ HOLLY HUNTER MOVIES

1	The Firm*	1993
2	Copycat	1995
3	Always	1989
4	Broadcast News	1987
5	The Piano #	1993
6	Raising Arizona	1987
7	Crash	1996
8	Home for the Holidays	1995
9	Once Around	1991
10	Living Out Loud	1998

* *Academy Award nomination*
\# *Academy Award for "Best Actress"*

TOP 10 MARY-LOUISE PARKER MOVIES

1 *The Client*, 1994 **2** *Fried Green Tomatoes*, 1991
3 *Boys on the Side*, 1995 **4** *Grand Canyon*, 1991 **5** *Portrait of a Lady*, 1996
6 *Bullets Over Broadway*, 1994 **7** *Longtime Companion*, 1990 **8** *Mr. Wonderful*, 1993
9 *Goodbye Lover*, 1999 **10** *Naked in New York*, 1994

DRIVEN MAD
Kathy Bates has appeared in diverse roles, from the psychotic Annie Wilkes in Stephen King's Misery *to "Unsinkable" Molly Brown in* Titanic – *her most successful movie.*

TOP 10 ★ KATHY BATES MOVIES

1	Titanic	1997
2	The Waterboy	1998
3	Dick Tracy	1990
4	Fried Green Tomatoes	1991
5	A Civil Action*	1998
6	Misery	1990
7	Diabolique	1996
8	Dolores Claiborne	1995
9	Primary Colors	1998
10	The Morning After	1986

* *Uncredited*

Which cartoon character made his movie debut in 1938?
see p.187 for the answer
A Bugs Bunny
B Popeye
C Yogi Bear

The Directors

TOP 10 ★
MOVIES DIRECTED BY ACTORS

MOVIE/YEAR	DIRECTOR
1 *Pretty Woman*, 1990	Garry Marshall
2 *Dances With Wolves*, 1990	Kevin Costner
3 *The Bodyguard*, 1992	Kevin Costner
4 *Apollo 13*, 1995	Ron Howard
5 *Ransom*, 1996	Ron Howard
6 *Rocky IV*, 1985	Sylvester Stallone
7 *Doctor Dolittle*, 1998	Betty Thomas
8 *Runaway Bride*, 1999	Garry Marshall
9 *Waterworld*, 1995	Kevin Costner
10 *A Few Good Men*, 1992	Rob Reiner

The role of actor–director has a long cinema tradition, numbering such luminaries as Charlie Chaplin, Buster Keaton, Orson Welles, and John Huston among its ranks. Heading this list, *Pretty Woman* director Garry Marshall is the brother of actress–director Penny Marshall.

WOMAN'S WORLD
The rock 'n' roll comedy *Wayne's World* was directed by Penelope Spheeris, who also directed The Beverly Hillbillies (1993) and The Little Rascals (1994).

TOP 10 ★
MOVIES DIRECTED BY WOMEN

MOVIE/YEAR	DIRECTOR
1 *Look Who's Talking*, 1989	Amy Heckerling
2 *Doctor Dolittle*, 1998	Betty Thomas
3 *Sleepless in Seattle*, 1993	Nora Ephron
4 *The birdcage*, 1996	Elaine May
5 *You've Got M@il*, 1998	Nora Ephron
6 *Wayne's World*, 1992	Penelope Spheeris
7 *Big*, 1988	Penny Marshall
8 *Michael*, 1996	Nora Ephron
9 *A League of Their Own*, 1992	Penny Marshall
10 *Father of the Bride*, 1991	Nancy Meyers

TOP 10 ★
MOVIES DIRECTED BY MARTIN SCORSESE

1 *Cape Fear*		1991
2 *Casino*		1995
3 *The Color of Money*		1986
4 *GoodFellas*		1990
5 *The Age of Innocence*		1993
6 *Taxi Driver*		1976
7 *Raging Bull*		1980
8 *Bringing Out the Dead*		1999
9 *Alice Doesn't Live Here Anymore*	1975
10 *New York, New York*		1977

RUNAWAY SUCCESS
Actor–director Garry Marshall has achieved outstanding directorial triumphs with box-office smash hits such as Runaway Bride, in which he appears in an uncredited role.

TOP 10 ★
MOVIES DIRECTED BY STEVEN SPIELBERG

1 *Jurassic Park*		1993
2 *E.T.: The Extra-Terrestrial*		1982
3 *The Lost World: Jurassic Park*		1997
4 *Indiana Jones and the Last Crusade*		1989
5 *Saving Private Ryan*		1998
6 *Jaws*		1975
7 *Raiders of the Lost Ark*		1981
8 *Indiana Jones and the Temple of Doom*		1984
9 *Schindler's List*		1993
10 *Hook*		1991

Steven Spielberg has directed some of the most successful movies of all time: the top five in this list appear among the top 20 movie of all time, while the cumulative world box-office gross of his Top 10 amounts to over $5 billion. If his credits as producer are included, further blockbusters, such as *Deep Impact*, *The Mask of Zorro*, *Men in Black*, *The Flintstones*, *Casper*, *Twister*, the *Back to the Future* trilogy, *Gremlins*, *Poltergeist* (which he also wrote), the animated movie *An American Tail*, and the part-animated *Who Framed Roger Rabbit*, would all score highly.

Did You Know? Hollywood director D. W. Griffith (1875–1948) is considered the most prolific director of all time, with a remarkable 545 movies credited to him in the period 1908–36, spanning both the silent and talkie eras.

TOP 10 ★
MOVIES DIRECTED BY FRANCIS FORD COPPOLA

1	*The Godfather*	1972
2	*Bram Stoker's Dracula*	1992
3	*The Godfather Part III*	1990
4	*The Godfather Part II*	1974
5	*Jack*	1996
6	*Apocalypse Now*	1979
7	*The Rainmaker*	1997
8	*Peggy Sue Got Married*	1986
9	*The Cotton Club*	1984
10	*The Outsiders*	1983

TOP 10 ★
MOVIES DIRECTED BY STANLEY KUBRICK

1	*Eyes Wide Shut*	1999
2	*The Shining*	1980
3	*2001: A Space Odyssey*	1968
4	*Full Metal Jacket*	1987
5	*A Clockwork Orange*	1971
6	*Spartacus*	1960
7	*Barry Lyndon*	1975
8	*Dr. Strangelove or: How I Learned to Stop Worrying and Love the Bomb*	1964
9	*Lolita*	1962
10	*Paths of Glory*	1957

TOP 10 ★
MOVIES DIRECTED OR PRODUCED BY GEORGE LUCAS

1	*Star Wars: Episode I – The Phantom Menace* (D/P)	1999
2	*Star Wars* (D)	1977/97
3	*Return of the Jedi* (P)	1983/97
4	*The Empire Strikes Back* (P)	1980/97
5	*Indiana Jones and the Last Crusade* (P)	1989
6	*Raiders of the Lost Ark* (P)	1981
7	*Indiana Jones and the Temple of Doom* (P)	1984
8	*American Graffiti* (D)	1973
9	*Willow* (P)	1988
10	*The Land Before Time* (P)	1988

D = Director; P = Producer

George Lucas made the move from directing to producing after the phenomenal success of *Star Wars*. The first five movies on this list rank among the 20 highest-earning movies of all time.

TOP 10 MOVIES DIRECTED BY ROBERT ZEMECKIS

1 *Forrest Gump*, 1994 **2** *Who Framed Roger Rabbit*, 1988 **3** *Back to the Future*, 1985
4 *Back to the Future Part III*, 1990 **5** *Back to the Future Part II*, 1989 **6** *Contact*, 1997
7 *Death Becomes Her*, 1992 **8** *Romancing the Stone*, 1984 **9** *The House on Haunted Hill*, 1999 **10** *Used Cars*, 1980

TOP 10 ★
MOVIES DIRECTED BY JOHN CARPENTER

1	*Halloween*	1978
2	*Escape from L.A.*	1996
3	*Starman*	1984
4	*Escape from New York*	1981
5	*Vampires*	1998
6	*The Fog*	1980
7	*Christine*	1983
8	*Memoirs of an Invisible Man*	1992
9	*Prince of Darkness*	1987
10	*They Live*	1988

GREAT ESCAPES

Kurt Russell stars in Escape from L.A., *the futuristic sequel to* Escape from New York, *both movies directed by John Carpenter*

Movie Outtakes

TOP 10 ★
MOVIES WITH THE MOST EXTRAS

MOVIE/COUNTRY/YEAR	EXTRAS	MOVIE/COUNTRY/YEAR	EXTRAS
1 *Gandhi*, UK, 1982	300,000	6 *Tonko*, Japan, 1988	100,000
2 *Kolberg*, Germany, 1945	187,000	7 *The War of Independence*, Romania, 1912	80,000
3 *Monster Wang-magwi*, South Korea, 1967	157,000	8 *Around the World in 80 Days*, US, 1956	68,894
4 *War and Peace*, USSR, 1967	120,000	9 =*Intolerance*, US, 1916	60,000
5 *Ilya Muromets*, USSR, 1956	106,000	=*Dny Zrady*, Czechoslovakia, 1972	60,000

TOP 10 COUNTRIES WITH THE MOST MOVIE THEATERS
(Country/movie theaters)

1 China, 65,000   2 US, 34,186
3 India, 12,900   4 France, 4,762
5 Germany, 4,244   6 Spain, 2,968
7 UK, 2,638   8 Italy, 2,500
9 Canada, 2,486   10 Indonesia, 2,100

Source: Screen Digest

TOP 10 ★
MOVIE COUNTRIES

	COUNTRY	NO. OF MOVIE SCREENS PER MILLION INHABITANTS
1	Iceland	165.2
2	Sweden	131.3
3	US	128.3
4	Norway	89.2
5	Australia	86.1
6	Azerbaijan	85.8
7	France	81.1
8	Canada	81.0
9	New Zealand	78.1
10	Switzerland	75.8

Source: Screen Digest

A CAST OF THOUSANDS

Some 300,000 Delhi residents were drafted in as extras on Gandhi for a sequence that occupied just 125 seconds of screen time.

TOP 10 ★
MOST PROLIFIC MOVIE-PRODUCING COUNTRIES

	COUNTRY	AVERAGE NO. OF FILMS PRODUCED PER ANNUM, 1989–98
1	India	787
2	US	591
3	Japan	255
4	Philippines	160
5	France	148
6	China	127
7	Russia	124
8	=South Korea	73
	=Thailand	73
10	UK	67

Source: Screen Digest

CHINESE MOVIE-GOERS

Although in relation to its vast population it remains a minor player, China is steadily joining the ranks of the world's foremost makers and watchers of movies.

TOP 10 MOVIE-GOING COUNTRIES
(Country/total annual attendance)

1 India, 2,860,000,000 **2** US, 1,480,700,000 **3** Indonesia, 222,200,000 **4** France, 170,110,000 **5** Japan, 153,100,000 **6** Germany, 148,880,000 **7** Brazil, 137,160,000 **8** UK, 136,500,000 **9** China, 121,000,000 **10** Italy, 117,900,000

Source: Screen Digest

TOP 10 COUNTRIES SPENDING THE MOST ON MOVIE PRODUCTION
(Country/average investment per movie in $)

1 US, 14,000,000 **2** UK, 8,250,000 **3** France, 5,260,000 **4** Ireland, 5,140,000 **5** Australia, 4,370,000 **6** Italy, 3,930,000 **7** Argentina, 3,800,000 **8** Japan, 3,570,000 **9** Spain, 3,180,000 **10** Canada, 3,160,000

Source: Screen Digest

TOP 10 COUNTRIES WITH THE BIGGEST INCREASE IN MOVIE PRODUCTION
(Country/percentage increase in production, 1989–98)

1 Ireland, 400.0 **2** Luxembourg, 200.0 **3** UK, 117.5 **4** Iceland, 100.0 **5** New Zealand, 75.0 **6** Australia, 72.7 **7** Norway, 55.6 **8** Venezuela, 42.9 **9** France, 33.6 **10** = Austria, 33.3; = Brazil, 33.3

Source: Screen Digest

MOST EXPENSIVE ITEMS OF MOVIE MEMORABILIA EVER SOLD AT AUCTION

ITEM/SALE	PRICE ($)*
1 Clark Gable's Oscar for *It Happened One Night*, Christie's, Los Angeles, Dec 15, 1996	607,500
2 Vivien Leigh's Oscar for *Gone With the Wind*, Sotheby's, New York, Dec 15, 1993	562,500
3 Poster for *The Mummy, 1932*, Sotheby's, New York, Mar 1, 1997	453,500
4 James Bond's Aston Martin DB5 from *Goldfinger*, Sotheby's, New York, June 28, 1986	275,000
5 Clark Gable's personal script for *Gone With the Wind*, Christie's, Los Angeles, Dec 15, 1996	244,500
6 "Rosebud" sled from *Citizen Kane*, Christie's, Los Angeles, Dec 15, 1996	233,500
7 Herman J. Mankiewicz's scripts for *Citizen Kane* and *The American*, Christie's, New York, June 21, 1989	231,000
8 Judy Garland's ruby slippers from *The Wizard of Oz*, Christie's, New York, June 21, 1988	165,000
9 Piano from the Paris scene in *Casablanca*, Sotheby's, New York, Dec 16, 1988	154,000
10 Charlie Chaplin's hat and cane, Christie's, London, Dec 11, 1987 (resold at Christie's, London, Dec 17, 1993, for $86,900)	130,350

* $/£ conversion at rate then prevailing

LONGEST MOVIES EVER SCREENED

			DURATION	
MOVIE/COUNTRY		YEAR	HRS	MINS
1 *The Longest and Most Meaningless Movie in the World*, UK		1970	48	0
2 *The Burning of the Red Lotus Temple*, China		1928–31	27	0
3 ****, US		1967	25	0
4 *Heimat*, West Germany		1984	15	40
5 *Berlin Alexanderplatz*, West Germany/Italy		1980	15	21
6 *The Journey*, Sweden		1987	14	33
7 *The Old Testament*, Italy		1922	13	0
8 *Comment Yukong déplace les montagnes*, France		1976	12	43
9 *Out 1: Noli me Tangere*, France		1971	12	40
10 *Ningen No Joken* (*The Human Condition*), Japan		1958–60	9	29

The list includes commercially screened movies, but not "stunt" movies created solely to break endurance records (particularly those of their audiences), among which is the 85-hour *The Cure for Insomnia*.

	EPISODE	FIRST SCREENED
1	Simpsons Roasting on an Open Fire*	Dec 17, 1989
2	Bart the Genius	Jan 14, 1990
3	Homer's Odyssey	Jan 21, 1990
4	There's No Disgrace Like Homer	Jan 28, 1990
5	Bart the General	Feb 4, 1990
6	Moaning Lisa	Feb 11, 1990
7	The Call of the Simpsons	Feb 18, 1990
8	The Telltale Head	Feb 25, 1990
9	Life on the Fast Lane#	Mar 18, 1990
10	Homer's Night Out	Mar 25, 1990

* aka The Simpsons Christmas Special
\# aka Jacques to Be Wild

ON THE COUCH

The infinitely changing couch gag has been an enduring feature of the opening sequence of The Simpsons *– one of the most popular cartoons currently being screened on television.*

TOP 10 ★
ANIMATED MOVIES

1	The Lion King	1994
2	Aladdin	1992
3	Toy Story 2	1999
4	Tarzan	1999
5	A Bug's Life	1998
6	Toy Story	1995
7	Beauty and the Beast	1991
8	Who Framed Roger Rabbit*	1988
9	Pocahontas	1995
10	The Hunchback of Notre Dame	1996

* Part animated, part live action

The 1990s provided nine of the 10 most successful animated movies of all time, which, in turn, ejected a number of their high-earning predecessors from this Top 10. Animated movies stand out among the leading money-makers of each decade: in the 1930s, *Snow White* was the second highest-earning movie after *Gone With the Wind*.

THE 10 ★
LATEST OSCAR-WINNING ANIMATED MOVIES*

YEAR	FILM	DIRECTOR/COUNTRY
1999	The Old Man and the Sea	Aleksandr Petrov, USA
1998	Bunny	Chris Wedge, US
1997	Geri's Game	Jan Pinkava, US
1996	Quest	Tyron Montgomery, UK
1995	A Close Shave	Nick Park, UK
1994	Bob's Birthday	David Fine and Alison Snowden, UK
1993	The Wrong Trousers	Nick Park, UK
1992	Mona Lisa Descending a Staircase	Joan C. Gratz, US
1991	Manipulation	Daniel Greaves, UK
1990	Creature Comforts	Nick Park, UK

* In the category "Short Subjects (Animated Films)"

THE 10 ★
FIRST OSCAR-WINNING ANIMATED MOVIES*

YEAR	FILM	DIRECTOR#
1932	Flowers and Trees	Walt Disney
1934	The Three Little Pigs	Walt Disney
1935	The Tortoise and the Hare	Walt Disney
1936	Three Orphan Kittens	Walt Disney
1937	The Country Cousin	Walt Disney
1938	The Old Mill	Walt Disney
1939	Ferdinand the Bull	Walt Disney
1940	The Ugly Duckling	Walt Disney
1941	The Milky Way	Rudolf Ising
1942	Lend a Paw	Walt Disney

* In the category "Short Subjects (Cartoons)"
\# All from the US

Oscars were awarded in the category "Short Subjects (Cartoons)" until 1971, when it was altered to "Short Subjects (Animated Films)."

Did You Know? Walt Disney (1901–66) won an unequaled individual total of 26 Oscars and six special Academy Awards for his animated movies.

THE 10 ★
FIRST DISNEY ANIMATED FEATURES

1	*Snow White and the Seven Dwarfs*	1937
2	*Pinocchio*	1940
3	*Fantasia*	1940
4	*Dumbo*	1941
5	*Bambi*	1942
6	*Victory Through Air Power*	1943
7	*The Three Caballeros*	1945
8	*Make Mine Music*	1946
9	*Fun and Fancy Free*	1947
10	*Melody Time*	1948

Excluding part-animated movies such as *Song of the South* and *Mary Poppins*, and movies made specially for television serialization, Disney has made a total of 40 full-length animated feature movies up to the end of 1999, when *Fantasia 2000* was released.

TOP 10 ★
PART ANIMATION/PART LIVE-ACTION MOVIES

1	*Who Framed Roger Rabbit*	1988
2	*Casper*	1995
3	*Space Jam*	1996
4	*9 to 5*	1980
5	*Mary Poppins*	1964
6	*Small Soldiers*	1999
7	*Song of the South*	1946
8	*James and the Giant Peach*	1976
9	*Pete's Dragon*	1977
10	*Fletch Lives*	1989

With the increasing use of computer animation, the distinction between animation and live action is becoming blurred: even long-dead actors and actresses are now capable of being resurrected on film through sophisticated computer techniques.

THE 10 ★
FIRST BUGS BUNNY CARTOONS

	TITLE	RELEASED
1	*Porky's Hare Hunt*	Apr 30, 1938
2	*Hare-um Scare-um*	Aug 12, 1939
3	*Elmer's Candid Camera*	Mar 2, 1940
4	*A Wild Hare*	July 27, 1940
5	*Elmer's Pet Rabbit*	Jan 4, 1941
6	*Tortoise Beats Hare*	Mar 15, 1941
7	*Hiawatha's Rabbit Hunt*	June 7, 1941
8	*The Heckling Hare*	July 5, 1941
9	*All This and Rabbit Stew*	Sep 13,. 1941
10	*Wabbit Twouble*	Dec 20, 1941

Bugs Bunny's debut was as a co-star alongside Porky Pig in *Porky's Hare Hunt*. *A Wild Hare* was the first film in which he said the line that became his trademark: "Eh, what's up, Doc?"

TOP 10 ★
NON-DISNEY ANIMATED FEATURE MOVIES

1	*The Prince of Egypt*	1998
2	*Antz*	1998
3	*Pokémon the First Movie: Mewtwo Strikes Back*	1999
4	*The Rugrats Movie*	1998
5	*South Park: Bigger, Longer and Uncut*	1999
6	*Pocket Monsters: Revelation Lugia*	1999
7	*The Land Before Time*	1988
8	*An American Tail*	1986
9	*The Lord of the Rings*	1978
10	*All Dogs Go to Heaven*	1989

Such was the success of *Pocket Monsters: Revelation Lugia* in Japan that it earned a place in this list before being released elsewhere.

CAT AND MOUSE

Tom and Jerry, and their occasional accomplices, have been battling on celluloid for over 60 years. Despite current concern by the politically correct about the level of violence, the cartoons remain firm favorites with children of all ages.

TOP 10 ★
FIRST TOM AND JERRY CARTOONS

	CARTOON	RELEASE DATE		CARTOON	RELEASE DATE
1	*Puss Gets the Boot**	Feb 20, 1940	6	*Puss 'N' Toots*	May 30, 1942
2	*The Midnight Snack*	July 19, 1941	7	*The Bowling Alley-Cat*	July 18, 1942
3	*The Night Before Christmas**	Dec 6, 1941	8	*Fine Feathered Friend*	Oct 10, 1942
4	*Fraidy Cat*	Jan 17, 1942	9	*Sufferin' Cats!*	Jan 16, 1943
5	*Dog Trouble*	Apr 18, 1942	10	*The Lonesome Mouse*	May 22, 1943

* Academy Award nomination

On the Radio

TOP 10 ★
RADIO FORMATS IN THE US BY NO. OF STATIONS

	FORMAT	NO. OF STATIONS
1	Country	2,320
2	News/Talk	1,695
3	Adult Contemporary	784
4	Oldies	771
5	Religion (teaching and variety)	703
6	Adult Standards	602
7	Spanish	600
8	Contemporary Christian	529
9	CHR (Top 40)	439
10	Variety	436

Source: M Street

TOP 10 ★
LONGEST-RUNNING PROGRAMS ON NPR

	PROGRAM	FIRST BROADCAST
1	All Things Considered	1971
2	Weekend All Things Considered	1974
3	Fresh Air with Terry Gross	1977
4	Marian McPartland's Piano Jazz	1978
5	Morning Edition	1979
6	Weekend Edition/ Saturday with Scott Simon	1985
7	Performance Today	1987
8	Weekend Edition/ Sunday with Liane Hansen	1987
9	Car Talk	1987
10	Talk of the Nation	1991

All Things Considered, the longest-running NPR program, was first broadcast on May 3, 1971.

Source: National Public Radio

TOP 10 ★
STATES WITH THE MOST NPR MEMBER STATIONS

	STATE	NPR STATIONS
1	New York	40
2	California	34
3	Michigan	28
4	Ohio	26
5	Wisconsin	22
6	Alaska	21
7	Texas	18
8	=Colorado	17
	=Florida	17
	=North Carolina	17

Source: National Public Radio

TOP 10 ★
LAST NAB HALL OF FAME INDUCTEES

YEAR	INDUCTEE/OCCUPATION
2000	Tom Joyner, radio personality
1999	Wolfman Jack, radio personality
1998	Rush Limbaugh, radio personality
1997	Wally Phillips, radio personality
1996	Don Imus, radio personality
1995	Gary Owens, radio personality
1994	Harry Caray, radio sportscaster
1993	Grand Ole Opry, radio program
1992	Larry King, radio personality
1991	Douglas Edwards, radio correspondent

THE 10 ★
LAST GEORGE FOSTER PEABODY AWARDS FOR BROADCASTING WON BY NPR*

YEAR	AWARD WINNER
1999	Lost & Found Sound
1999	Morning Edition With Bob Edwards
1998	Coverage of Africa
1998	I Must Keep Fightin': The Art of Paul Robeson
1998	Performance Today
1997	Jazz from Lincoln Center
1996	Remorse: The 14 Stories of Eric Morse
1995	Wynton Marsalis: Making the Music/ Marsalis on Music
1994	Tobacco Stories and Wade in the Water: African American Sacred Music Traditions (NPR/Smithsonian Institution)
1993	Health Reform Coverage 1993

* Includes only programs made or co-produced by NPR

Source: Peabody Awards

In 1938, the National Association of Broadcasters formed a committee to establish a "Pulitzer Prize" for radio. These were inaugurated the following year under the sponsorship of the Henry W. Grady School of Journalism at the University of Georgia, and named in honor of George Foster Peabody, a native Georgian and noted philanthropist. The first awards, for radio programs broadcast in 1940, were presented at a banquet at the Commodore Hotel in New York on March 31, 1941. The ceremony was broadcast live nationwide on CBS and included addresses by CBS founder and chairman William S. Paley and noted reporter Elmer David, the recipient of the first personal Peabody Award. The awards are now regarded as the most prestigious in American broadcasting.

Background image: EKCO RADIO MODEL AD 65, 1932–34

TOP 10 ★ RADIO STATIONS OF THE 1990s*

	STATION	MARKET
1999	WQHT-FM	New York
1998	WSKQ-FM	New York
1997	WQHT-FM	New York
1996	WKTU-FM	New York
1995	WRKS-FM	New York
1994	WLTW-FM	New York
1993	WRKS-FM	New York
1992	WRKS-FM	New York
1991	WCBS-FM	New York
1990	WRKS-FM	New York

* Of all radio listening during an average week, 6 am to midnight, for listeners aged 12+

Source: Duncan's American Radio

THE 10 ★ LAST NAB NETWORK/ SYNDICATED PERSONALITIES OF THE YEAR

YEAR	WINNER/NETWORK OR SYNDICATION
1999	Bob Kevoian and Tom Griswold, AMFM Radio Networks
1998	Paul Harvey, ABC Radio Networks
1997	Dr. Laura Schlessinger, Synergy Broadcasting
1996	Paul Harvey, ABC Radio Networks
1995	Rush Limbaugh, EFM Media Management
1994	Don Imus, Westwood One Radio Networks
1993	Charles Osgood, CBS Radio Networks
1992	Rush Limbaugh, EFM Media Management
1991	Paul Harvey, ABC Radio Networks
1990	Larry King, Mutual Broadcasting System

★ SNAP SHOTS

RADIO FOR ALL

London inventor Trevor Bayliss, a former international swimmer and swimming-pool salesman, was inspired to develop his clockwork radio after seeing a television program about communication problems in Africa. After the necessary financial backing had been secured, his Freeplay® wind-up radio went into production in Cape Town, South Africa, in 1994, and is now available worldwide. Its simple operating mechanism – a coil spring that drives a dynamo, providing 40 minutes of play time, with optional solar cells – is a perfect solution for radio communication in communities without electricity and where batteries are expensive.

Top TV

TOP 10 ★
PRIMETIME PROGRAMS ON US TV, 1998–99

PROGRAM	VIEWERS
1 ER	14,492,000
2 NFL Monday Night Football	14,013,000
3 Frasier	13,243.000
4 Friends	13,188,000
5 60 Minutes	11,946,000
6 Touched by an Angel	11,587,000
7 Veronica's Closet	11,386,000
8 Jesse	10,902,000
9 CBS Sunday Movie	10,624,000
10 20/20 (Wednesday)	10,173,000

© Copyright 2000 Nielsen Media Research

TOP 10 ★
DAYTIME DRAMAS ON US TV, 1998–99

PROGRAM	VIEWERS
1 The Young and the Restless	6,598,000
2 The Bold and the Beautiful	4,673,000
3 The Days of Our Lives	4,439,000
4 General Hospital	4,242,000
5 As the World Turns	3,981,000
6 All My Children	3,893,000
7 Guiding Light	3,779,000
8 One Life to Live	3,477,000
9 Another World	2,409,000
10 Port Charles	2,169,000

© Copyright 2000 Nielsen Media Research

TOP 10 CABLE TELEVISION COUNTRIES
(Country/subscribers)

❶ US, 67,011,180 ❷ Germany, 18,740,260 ❸ Netherlands, 6,227,472 ❹ Russia, 5,784,432 ❺ Belgium, 3,945,342 ❻ Poland, 3,830,788 ❼ Romania, 3,000,000 ❽ UK, 2,666,783 ❾ France, 2,478,630 ❿ Switzerland, 2,156,120

Source: The Phillips Group

TOP 10 ★
SYNDICATED PROGRAMS ON US TV, 1998–99

PROGRAM	VIEWERS
1 WCW Wrestling	6,828,000
2 Judge Judy	6,675,000
3 Friends	6,328,000
4 Jerry Springer	6,185,000
5 Seinfeld	6,017,000
6 Entertainment Tonight	5,656,000
7 Frasier	4,932,000
8 =X-Files	4,860,000
=Home Improvement	4,860,000
10 ER	4,065,000

© Copyright 2000 Nielsen Media Research

TOP 10 ★
TELEVISION-WATCHING COUNTRIES

COUNTRY	AVERAGE DAILY VIEWING TIME HOURS	MINS
1 US	3	58
2 Greece	3	39
3 =Italy	3	36
=UK	3	36
5 Spain	3	31
6 =Canada	3	14
=Ireland	3	14
8 Germany	3	8
9 France	3	7
10 Belgium	2	57

Source: Screen Digest

A survey of television-viewing habits in Western Europe and North America showed that the number of channels, including new digital channels, is proliferating at a much faster rate than the time spent actually watching them, thus creating, in the jargon of the industry, "audience fragmentation." Viewers in the US watch, on average, 23 percent more than those in Europe, but this figure is decreasing by about half a percent per annum.

TOP 10 ★
PROGRAMS OF ALL TIME ON PBS TV*

PROGRAM/BROADCAST	AVERAGE AUDIENCE
1 The Civil War, Sep 1990	8,800,000
2 Life on Earth, Jan 1982	7,900,000
3 The Living Planet: A Portrait of the Earth, Feb 1985	7,800,000
4 The American Experience: The Kennedys, Sep 1992	7,000,000
5 Nature: Kingdom of the Ice Bear, Feb 1986	6,900,000
6 Cosmos, Sep 1980	6,500,000
7 =Planet Earth, Jan 1986	6,300,000
=Lewis & Clark: The Journey of the Corps of Discovery, Nov 1997	6,300,000
9 The Scarlet Letter, Sep 1979	5,700,000
10 Baseball, Sep 1994	5,000,000

* As of January 2000

Source: PBS

THE 10 ★
LATEST WINNERS OF THE DAYTIME EMMY AWARD FOR A CHILDREN'S PROGRAM

YEAR	PROGRAM
1998/99	The Island on Bird Street
1997/98	In His Father's Shoes
1996/97	Elmo Saves Christmas
1995/96	Stand Up
1994/95	A Child Betrayed: The Calvin Mire Story
1993/94	Dead Drunk: The Kevin Tunnel Story
1992/93	ABC Afterschool Special: Shades of a Single Protein
1991/92	Vincent and Me
1990/91	Lost in the Barrens
1989/90	CBS Schoolbreak Special: A Matter of Conscience

Did You Know? The funeral of Diana, Princess of Wales, on September 6, 1997, attracted the biggest television audience of all time, with an estimated 2.5 billion viewers worldwide.

TOP 10 ★
TV AUDIENCES OF ALL TIME IN THE US

	PROGRAM	DATE	HOUSEHOLDS VIEWING TOTAL	%
1	M*A*S*H Farewell Special	Feb 28, 1983	50,150,000	60.2
2	*Dallas*	Nov 21, 1980	41,470,000	53.3
3	*Roots* Part 8	Jan 30, 1977	36,380,000	51.1
4	Super Bowl XVI	Jan 24, 1982	40,020,000	49.1
5	Super Bowl XVII	Jan 30, 1983	40,480,000	48.6
6	XVII Winter Olympics	Feb 23, 1994	45,690,000	48.5
7	Super Bowl XX	Jan 26, 1986	41,490,000	48.3
8	*Gone with the Wind* Pt. 1	Nov 7, 1976	33,960,000	47.7
9	*Gone with the Wind* Pt. 2	Nov 8, 1976	33,750,000	47.4
10	Super Bowl XII	Jan 15, 1978	34,410,000	47.2

© Copyright 2000 Nielsen Media Research

TOP 10 ★
MOVIES OF ALL TIME ON PRIMETIME NETWORK TV

	MOVIE/YEAR RELEASED	BROADCAST	RATING (%)*
1	*Gone with the Wind* Pt. 1, 1939	Nov 7, 1976	47.7
2	*Gone with the Wind* Pt. 2, 1939	Nov 8, 1976	47.4
3	=*Love Story*, 1970	Oct, 1 1972	42.3
	=*Airport*, 1970	Nov 11, 1973	42.3
5	*The Godfather, Part II*, 1974	Nov 18, 1974	39.4
6	*Jaws*, 1975	Nov 4, 1979	39.1
7	*The Poseidon Adventure*, 1972	Oct 27, 1974	39.0
8	=*True Grit*, 1969	Nov 12, 1972	38.9
	=*The Birds*, 1963	Jan 6, 1968	38.9
10	*Patton*, 1970	Nov 19, 1972	38.5

* Of households viewing

© Copyright 2000 Nielsen Media Research

All the movies listed are dramas made for theatrical release, but if made-for-TV productions were included, then the controversial 1983 post-nuclear war movie, *The Day After* (screened on Nov 20, 1983), would rank in third place with a rating of 46.0 percent. It is significant that all the most watched movies on TV were broadcast before the dawn of the video era.

RAT RACE

After attracting a huge following as a television series, Rugrats was developed into a film – The Rugrats Movie – by Nickelodeon Pictures; it became a box-office smash.

Music on TV

LATEST RECIPIENTS OF THE MTV US "VIEWER'S CHOICE" AWARD

YEAR	ARTIST OR GROUP/TITLE
1999	Backstreet Boys, *I Want It That Way*
1998	Puff Daddy & the Family, featuring the Lox, Lil' Kim, the Notorious B.I.G. and fuzzbubble, *It's All About the Benjamins* (Rock Remix)
1997	Prodigy, *Breathe*
1996	Bush, *Glycerine*
1995	TLC, *Waterfalls*
1994	Aerosmith, *Cryin'*
1993	Aerosmith, *Livin' on the Edge*
1992	Red Hot Chili Peppers, *Under the Bridge*
1991	Queensryche, *Silent Lucidity*
1990	Aerosmith, *Janie's Got a Gun*

LATEST RECIPIENTS OF THE MTV "BEST VIDEO" AWARD

YEAR	ARTIST OR GROUP/TITLE
1999	Lauryn Hill, *Doo Wop (That Thing)*
1998	Madonna, *Ray of Light*
1997	Jamiroquai, *Virtual Insanity*
1996	The Smashing Pumpkins, *Tonight, Tonight*
1995	TLC, *Waterfalls*
1994	Aerosmith, *Cryin'*
1993	Pearl Jam, *Jeremy*
1992	Van Halen, *Right Now*
1991	R.E.M., *Losing My Religion*
1990	Sinead O'Connor, *Nothing Compares 2 U*

LATEST RECIPIENTS OF THE MTV "BEST GROUP VIDEO" AWARD

YEAR	ARTIST OR GROUP/TITLE
1999	TLC, *No Scrubs*
1998	Backstreet Boys, *Everybody (Backstreet's Back)*
1997	No Doubt, *Don't Speak*
1996	Foo Fighters, *Big Me*
1995	TLC, *Waterfalls*
1994	Aerosmith, *Cryin'*
1993	Pearl Jam, *Jeremy*
1992	U2, *Even Better Than the Real Thing*
1991	R.E.M., *Losing My Religion*
1990	The B-52s, *Love Shack*

TOP 10 MUSIC VIDEOS OF THE 20TH CENTURY ON MTV

(Artist or group/title)

1 Michael Jackson, *Thriller* **2** Madonna, *Vogue* **3** Nirvana, *Smells Like Teen Spirit* **4** Peter Gabriel, *Sledgehammer* **5** Run DMC with Aerosmith, *Walk This Way* **6** Guns N' Roses, *Sweet Child O' Mine* **7** Beastie Boys, *Sabotage* **8** Robert Palmer, *Addicted to Love* **9** 2Pac and Dr. Dre, *California Love* **10** Madonna, *Express Yourself*

PRODIGIOUS SUCCESS

Prodigy, featuring lead singer Keith Flint, won MTV US's "Viewer's Choice" award as well as three MTV Europe Music awards in 1997 for their single Breathe.

LATEST RECIPIENTS OF THE MTV "BEST FEMALE VIDEO" AWARD

YEAR	ARTIST/TITLE
1999	Lauryn Hill, *Doo Wop (That Thing)*
1998	Madonna, *Ray of Light*
1997	Jewel, *You Were Meant for Me*
1996	Alanis Morissette, *Ironic*
1995	Madonna, *Take a Bow*
1994	Janet Jackson, *If*
1993	k.d. lang, *Constant Craving*
1992	Annie Lennox, *Why*
1991	Janet Jackson, *Love Will Never Do Without You*
1990	Sinead O'Connor, *Nothing Compares 2 U*

THE 10 ★
LATEST RECIPIENTS OF THE MTV "BEST RAP VIDEO" AWARD

YEAR	ARTIST/TITLE
1999	Jay-Z featuring Ja Rule/Amil-lion, *Can I Get a…*
1998	Will Smith, *Gettin' Jiggy Wit it*
1997	The Notorious B.I.G., *Hypnotize*
1996	Coolio featuring LV, *Gangsta's Paradise*
1995	Dr. Dre, *Keep Their Heads Ringin'*
1994	Snoop Doggy Dogg, *Doggy Dogg World*
1993	Arrested Development, *People Everyday*
1992	Arrested Development, *Tennessee*
1991	L. L. Cool J, *Mama Said Knock You Out*
1990	MC Hammer, *U Can't Touch This*

Launched in 1981, MTV introduced its video awards three years later. The "Best Rap Video" category was added in 1989, when the winner was DJ Jazzy Jeff and the Fresh Prince for *Parents Just Don't Understand*.

THE 10 FIRST ARTISTS TO APPEAR IN PEPSI-COLA COMMERCIALS

1 Michael Jackson 2 Lionel Richie 3 Glenn Frey
4 Robert Palmer 5 Linda Ronstadt 6 Tina Turner
7 David Bowie 8 Gloria Estefan 9 MC Hammer
10 Ray Charles

THE 10 ★
FIRST ARTISTS TO FEATURE IN A COCA-COLA TELEVISION COMMERCIAL

	ACT/JINGLE	YEAR
1	McGuire Sisters, *Pause for a Coke*	1958
2 =	Brothers Four*, *Refreshing New Feeling*	1960
=	Anita Bryant, *Refreshing New Feeling*	1960
=	Connie Francis, *Refreshing New Feeling*	1960
5 =	Fortunes, *Things Go Better With Coke*	1963
=	Limeliters*, *Things Go Better With Coke*	1963
7	Ray Charles, *Things Go Better With Coke*	1969
8 =	Bobby Goldsboro, *It's the Real Thing*	1971
=	New Seekers*, *It's the Real Thing*	1971
10	Dottie West*, *It's the Real Thing (Country Sunshine)*	1972

* Artist(s) provided only the audio soundtrack for the commercial

ALL IN THE FAMILY
David Cassidy and real-life stepmother Shirley Jones starred in the popular TV series The Partridge Family, *screened from 1970 to 1974.*

TOP 10 ★
HIGHEST-RATED NETWORKED MUSIC TELEVISION SERIES IN THE US, 1950–99

	PROGRAMME	YEAR	PERCENT OF TV AUDIENCE*
1	*Stop the Music*	1951	34.0
2	*Your Hit Parade*	1958	33.6
3	*The Perry Como Show*	1956	32.6
4	*Name That Tune*	1958	26.7
5	*The Dean Martin Show*	1966	24.8
6	*The Sonny & Cher Hour*	1973	23.3
7	*The Partridge Family*	1972	22.6
8	*The Glen Campbell Goodtime Hour*	1968	22.5
9	*The Johnny Cash Show*	1969	21.8
10	*Cher*	1975	21.3

* Percentage of American households with TV sets watching the broadcast: the total number of households rose from 3.8 million in 1950 to 99.4 million in 1999.

© 2000, Nielsen Media Research

What was unique about *The Milky Way* cartoon?
see p.186 for the answer

A It was the first non-Disney animation to win an Oscar
B It was the first animated movie made in color
C It was the longest movie ever made

Top Videos

DVD SALES IN THE US, 1999

DVD/LABEL

1 **The Matrix**, Warner

2 **Blade**, New Line/Warner

3 **Lethal Weapon 4**, Warner

4 **Enemy of the State**, Touchstone/Buena Vista

5 **Armageddon**, Touchstone/Buena Vista

6 **Titanic**, Paramount

7 **Saving Private Ryan**, DreamWorks

8 **Rush Hour**, New Line/Warner

8 **The Mummy**, Universal

10 **The Mask of Zorro**, Columbia TriStar

Source: *VideoScan*

DVD was launched in the US in March 1997. In that year, total sales of DVD players was 315,136. This increased in 1998 to 1,089,261, and in 1999 to 4,019,389, as traditional videotape recordings, which had been the industry standard for almost 25 years, became progressively eclipsed by DVD. It is predicted that worldwide shipments of DVD discs will rise from 77 million units in 1999 to over 2 billion by 2005, by which time 144 million players will be instaled globally.

MOVIE SALES ON VIDEO IN THE US, 1999

MOVIE/LABEL

1 **Austin Powers: International Man of Mystery**, New Line/Warner

2 **Armageddon**, Touchstone/Buena Vista

3 **A Bug's Life**, Walt Disney/Buena Vista

4 **Blade**, New Line/Warner

5 **Mulan**, Walt Disney/Buena Vista

6 **The Wedding Singer**, New Line/Warner

7 **You've Got M@il**, Warner

8 **The Lion King II: Sinba's Pride**, Walt Disney/Buena Vista

9 **There's Something About Mary**, Fox

10 **Ever After: A Cinderella Story**, Fox

Source: *VideoScan*

VIDEO-RENTING COUNTRIES

COUNTRY	AVERAGE NO. OF RENTALS PER VHS HOUSEHOLD, 1998
1 South Korea	88.6
2 Taiwan	57.4
3 USA	39.1
4 South Africa	37.7
5 India	37.3
6 Philippines	33.9
7 Australia	31.2
8 Canada	29.3
9 Japan	22.0
10 Pakistan	18.8

This list is at odds with the list of European countries because here only those homes that have a VHS video player are included in the statistics.

Source: Screen Digest

COUNTRIES WITH THE MOST VCRs

COUNTRY	VIDEO HOUSEHOLDS
1 US	91,602,000
2 Japan	38,982,000
3 Germany	31,425,000
4 China	23,956,000
5 Brazil	21,330,000
6 UK	21,306,000
7 France	18,903,000
8 Russia	14,555,000
9 Italy	12,706,000
10 South Korea	11,616,000

Source: Screen Digest

The 1980s has rightly been described as the "video decade": according to estimates published by *Screen Digest*, the period from 1980 to 1990 saw an increase of more than 17 times in the number of video recorders in use in the world, from 7,687,000 to 210,159,000. Since 1992, more than one-third of all world homes with television have also had video.

BESTSELLING MUSIC VIDEOS OF 1999 IN THE US

VIDEO/ARTIST

1 **'N The Mix with 'N Sync**, 'N Sync

2 **Night Out With the Backstreet Boys**, Backstreet Boys

3 **All Access Video**, Backstreet Boys

4 **Homecoming - Live in Orlando**, Backstreet Boys

5 **Cunning Stunts**, Metallica

6 **Family Values Tour '98**, Various Artists

7 **Second Coming**, Kiss

8 **Kennedy Center Homecoming**, Bill & Gloria Gaither

8 **Live**, Shania Twain

10 **Live at Wembley**, Spice Girls

Source: *VideoScan*

BESTSELLING VIDEOS OF THE 1990s IN THE US*

YEAR	VIDEO/LABEL
1999	*Austin Powers: International Man of Mystery*, New Line/Warner
1998	*Titanic*, Paramount/20th Century Fox
1997	*Men in Black*, Columbia
1996	*Babe*, Universal
1995	*The Lion King*, Buena Vista
1994	*Aladdin*, Walt Disney
1993	*Beauty and the Beast*, Walt Disney
1992	*Fantasia*, Walt Disney
1991	*Pretty Woman*, Touchstone
1990	*Bambi*, Walt Disney

* By year

Background image: **VIDEOS TO RENT**

MARY, MARY
Blockbuster comedy There's Something About Mary, *starring Cameron Diaz in the title role, became the US's No. 2 video of 1999.*

TOP 10 ⭐
MOVIE RENTALS ON VIDEO, 1999

MOVIE/LABEL

1 *Enemy of the State*, Touchstone/Buena Vista

2 *There's Something About Mary*, Fox

3 *The Truman Show*, Paramount

4 *Elizabeth*, USA Home Entertainment

5 *Ronin*, MGM/Warner

6 *Armageddon*, Touchstone/Buena Vista

7 *Saving Private Ryan*, DreamWorks

8 *The Siege*, Fox

9 *Payback*, Paramount

10 *American History X*, New Line/Warner

Source: *VideoScan*

TOP 10 ⭐
BESTSELLING VIDEOS IN THE US*

	VIDEO/RELEASE	LABEL	SALES ($)
1	*Titanic*, Sep 9, 1998	Paramount	30,000,000
2	*The Lion King*, Mar 3, 1995	Buena Vista/ Disney	27,500,000
3	*Snow White*, Oct 28, 1994	Buena Vista/ Disney	27,000,000
4	*Aladdin*, Oct 1, 1993	Buena Vista/ Disney	25,000,000
5	*Independence Day*, Nov 19, 1996	Fox Video	21,955,000
6	*Jurassic Park*, Oct 4, 1994	MCA/Universal	21,500,000
7	*Toy Story*, Oct 29, 1996	Buena Vista/ Disney	21,000,000
8	*Beauty and the Beast*, Oct 30, 1992	Buena Vista/ Disney	20,000,000
9	*Pocahontas*, Feb 26, 1996	Buena Vista/ Disney	18,000,000
10	*Men in Black*, Nov 25, 1997	Columbia TriStar	18,000,000

* Since 1992

Source: Video Store *magazine*

TOP 10 ⭐
BESTSELLING CHILDREN'S VIDEOS OF 1999 IN THE US

VIDEO/LABEL

1 *The Lion King II – Simba's Pride*, Walt Disney/Buena Vista

2 *Mulan*, Walt Disney/Buena Vista

3 *The Lady and the Tramp*, Walt Disney/Buena Vista

4 *Mary-Kate & Ashley: Billboard Dad*, Dualstar/Warner

5 *Pokémon: I Choose You, Pikachu*, VIZ/Pioneer Entertainment

6 *The Rugrats Movie*, Nickelodeon/Paramount

7 *Teletubbies: Dance with the Teletubbies*, PBS/Warner

8 *101 Dalmatians*, Walt Disney/Buena Vista

9 *The Little Mermaid: The Special Edition*, Walt Disney/Buena Vista

10 *Teletubbies: Here Come the Teletubbies*, PBS/Warner

Source: *VideoScan*

TOP 10 ⭐
BESTSELLING SPORT VIDEOS OF 1999 IN THE US

VIDEO

1 WWF: *Austin 3:16 Uncensored*

2 WWF: *'Cause Stone Cold Said So*

3 WWF: *The Rock – Know Your Role*

4 WWF: *Hell Yeah – Stone Cold's Saga Continues*

5 WWF: *Best of Survivor Series – 1987-1997*

6 WWF: *Best of Raw Vol. 1*

7 WWF: *Best of Wrestlemania I–XIV*

8 WWF: *Sable Unleashed*

9 WWF: *Undertaker the Phenom*

10 WWF: *Wrestlemania 14*

All the bestselling sport videos were of wrestling matches. The highest placed non-wrestling video in 1999 was *Michael Jordan: His Airness* at No.12.

Source: *VideoScan*

Did You Know? A massive 60 million copies of the video of *Titanic* were shipped worldwide, making it the bestselling videocassette of all time.

195

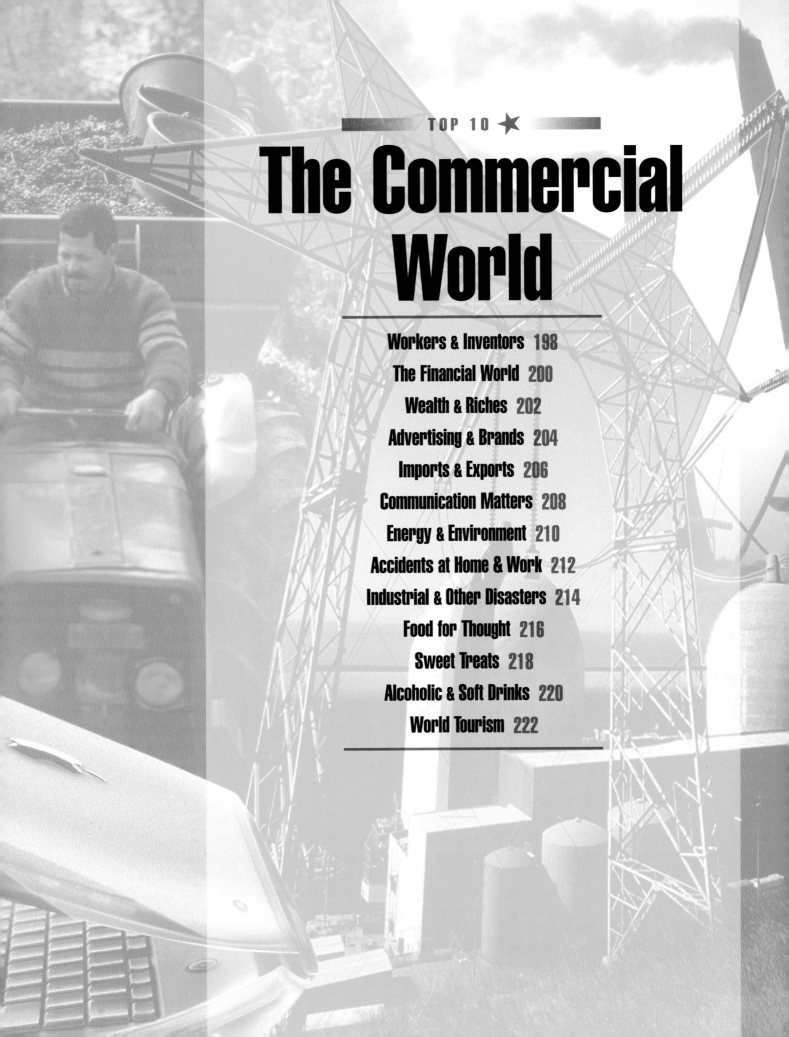

TOP 10 ★

The Commercial World

Workers & Inventors

COUNTRIES WITH THE MOST WORKERS

	COUNTRY	WORKERS*
1	China	736,000,000
2	India	423,000,000
3	US	136,000,000
4	Indonesia	94,000,000
5	Russia	78,000,000
6	Brazil	75,000,000
7	Japan	68,000,000
8	Bangladesh	63,000,000
9	Pakistan	48,000,000
10	Nigeria	47,000,000

* Based on people aged 15–64 who are currently
  employed; unpaid groups are not included.

Source: World Bank

COUNTRIES WITH THE HIGHEST PROPORTION OF FEMALE WORKERS*

	COUNTRY	LABOR FORCE PERCENTAGE
1	Latvia	50
2	=Belarus	49
	=Burundi	49
	=Estonia	49
	=Malawi	49
	=Moldova	49
	=Russia	49
	=Rwanda	49
	=Tanzania	49
	=Ukraine	49
	=Vietnam	49

* Based on people aged 15–64 who are currently
  employed; unpaid groups are not included

Source: World Bank

COUNTRIES WITH THE HIGHEST PROPORTION OF FARMERS

	COUNTRY	PERCENTAGE IN AGRICULTURE
1	Bhutan	93.9
2	Nepal	93.3
3	Burkina Faso	92.4
4	Rwanda	91.2
5	Burundi	90.7
6	=Niger	89.2
	=Mali	89.2
8	Ethiopia	85.3
9	Guinea Bissau	84.1
10	Uganda	83.1

Source: Food and Agriculture Organization of the
United Nations

EMPLOYERS IN THE US

	COMPANY	EMPLOYEES (1999)
1	Wal-Mart Stores	910,000
2	US Postal Services	859,484
3	General Motors	594,000
4	Ford Motor	345,175
5	United Parcel Service	333,000
6	Sears Roebuck	324,000
7	General Electric	293,000
8	IBM	291,067
9	McDonald's	284,000
10	K-mart	278,525

Source: Fortune 500/Universal Postal Union

HARD LABOR

India's huge work force relies on traditional manual
labor, but the country is increasingly becoming a
major center for computer technology.

TOP 10 ★
OCCUPATIONS IN THE US

JOB SECTOR*	EMPLOYEES#
1 Machine operators, assemblers, and inspectors	7,245,000
2 Sales workers (retail and personal services)	6,953,000
3 Food service	6,133,000
4 Construction trades	5,799,000
5 Handlers, equipment cleaners, helpers, and laborers	5,499,000
6 Teachers (except college and university)	4,924,000
7 Management-related	4,871,000
8 Sales supervisors and proprietors	4,866,000
9 Mechanics and repairers	4,759,000
10 Motor vehicle operators	4,149,000
US total (including occupations not in Top 10)	134,264,000

* Excluding general and miscellaneous group categories
\# As at August 1999
Source: US Bureau of Labor Statistics

THE 10 ★
FIRST PATENTS IN THE US

PATENTEE	PATENT	DATE
1 Samuel Hopkins	Making pot and pearl ash	July 31, 1790
2 Joseph S. Sampson	Candle making	Aug 6, 1790
3 Oliver Evans	Flour and meal making	Dec 18, 1790
4 =Francis Bailey	Punches for type	Jan 29, 1791
=Aaron Putnam	Improvement in distilling	Jan 29, 1791
6 John Stone	Driving piles	Mar 10, 1791
7 =Samuel Mullikin	Threshing machine	Mar 11, 1791
=Samuel Mullikin	Breaking hemp	Mar 11, 1791
=Samuel Mullikin	Polishing marble	Mar 11, 1791
=Samuel Mullikin	Raising nap on cloth	Mar 11, 1791

A patent is an exclusive license to manufacture and exploit a unique product or process for a fixed period. The world's first patent, by which the architect Filippo Brunelleschi was granted the exclusive license to make a barge crane to transport marble, was issued in Florence in 1421. Of the most prolific patentees in the US, Thomas Edison tops the bill with a massive 1,093 patents. Electricity, radio, and television feature prominently among the many patents credited to the most prolific patentees in the US, but their inventions also cover the Polaroid camera and the tape drive used in the Sony Walkman.

FACTORY-MADE

Despite the growth of the service sector, manufacturing remains a vital component of most developed economies, providing employment for countless workers.

THE 10 ★
FIRST WOMEN PATENTEES IN THE US

PATENTEE	PATENT	DATE
1 Mary Kies	Straw weaving with silk or thread	May 5, 1809
2 Mary Brush	Corset	July 21, 1815
3 Sophia Usher	Carbonated liquid	Sep 11, 1819
4 Julia Planton	Foot stove	Nov 4, 1822
5 Lucy Burnap	Weaving grass hats	Feb 16, 1823
6 Diana H. Tuttle	Accelerating spinning-wheel heads	May 17, 1824
7 Catharine Elliot	Manufacturing moccasins	Jan 26, 1825
8 Phoebe Collier	Sawing wheel-fellies (rims)	May 20, 1826
9 Elizabeth H. Buckley	Sheet-iron shovel	Feb 28, 1828
10 Henrietta Cooper	Whitening leghorn straw	Nov 12, 1828

THE 10 FIRST TRADEMARKS ISSUED IN THE US

(Issued to/product)

1 **Averill Chemical-Paint Company**, Liquid paint
2 **J.B. Baldy & Co.**, Mustard **3** **Ellis Branson**, Retail coal
4 **Tracy Coit**, Fish **5** **William Lanfair Ellis & Co.**, Oyster packing **6** **Evans, Clow, Dalzell & Co.**, Wrought-iron pipe **7** **W.E. Garrett & Sons**, Snuff
8 **William G. Hamilton**, Cartwheel **9** **John K. Hogg**, Soap
10 **Abraham P. Olzendam**, Woollen hose

All of these trademarks were registered on the same day, October 25, 1870, and are ranked only by the trademark numbers assigned to them.

Did You Know? Thomas Alva Edison (1847–1931) is the world's most prolific inventor, with 1,093 patents issued to him solely or jointly between June 1, 1869 and May 16, 1933.

The Financial World

CORPORATIONS IN THE US

CORPORATION	REVENUE* ($)
1 General Motors	176,558,000,000
2 Wal-Mart Stores	165,013,000,000
3 Ford Motor Company	162,558,000,000
4 Exxon Mobil	160,883,000,000
5 General Electric	111,630,000,000
6 IBM	87,548,000,000
7 Citigroup	82,005,000,000
8 AT&T	62,391,000,000
9 Philip Morris	61,751,000,000
10 Boeing	57,993,000,000

* In lastest year

Source: Forbes Global

Despite their involvement in new technologies, several of the corporations listed here have a history dating back to the late 19th century: AT&T – originally the American Telephone and Telegraph Company – dates from 1885, while General Electric was established in 1892, when the Edison General Electric Company and Thomson Houston Company were merged. Even portions of computer giant IBM have roots in the 1880s (although its name-change to International Business Machines dates from 1924). The Ford Motor Company was founded in 1903, General Motors in 1908, and Boeing in 1916.

TOP 10 ★

BANKS IN THE US

BANK	1998 REVENUE ($)
1 Bank of America	50,777,000,000
2 Chase Manhattan Corp.	32,379,000,000
3 Bank One Corp.	25,595,000,000
4 First Union Corp.	21,543,000,000
5 Wells Fargo	20,482,000,000
6 J. P. Morgan & Co.	18,425,000,000
7 Bankers Trust Corp.	12,048,000,000
8 Fleet Financial Group	10,002,000,000
9 National City Corp.	8,071,000,000
10 PNC Bank Corp.	7,936,000,000

Source: Fortune magazine

TOP 10 ★

SUPERMARKET GROUPS IN THE US

COMPANY	ANNUAL SALES ($)
1 Kroger Co.	45,400,000,000
2 Wal-Mart Supercenters	45,000,000,000
3 Albertson's	37,600,000,000
4 Safeway	28,400,000,000
5 Supervalu	20,800,000,000
6 Ahold USA	20,300,000,000
7 Fleming Cos.	14,700,000,000
8 Delhaize America	14,400,000,000
9 Winn-Dixie Stores	13,300,000,000
10 Publix Super Markets	12,900,000,000

Source: Supermarket News

TOP 10 ★

RICHEST COUNTRIES

COUNTRY	GDP PER CAPITA, 1998 ($)
1 Liechtenstein	50,000*
2 Luxembourg	43,570
3 Switzerland	40,080
4 Norway	34,330
5 Denmark	33,260
6 Japan	32,380
7 Singapore	30,060
8 US	29,340
9 Iceland	28,010
10 Austria	26,850
UK	21,400

* *World Bank estimate for the purpose of ranking*
Source: World Bank, World Development Indicators

GDP (Gross Domestic Product) is the total value of all the goods and services produced annually within a country (Gross National Product, or GNP, also includes income from overseas). Dividing GDP by the country's population produces GDP per capita, which is often used as a measure of how "rich" a country is.

EASTERN STAR

Despite recent economic setbacks, the wealth of cities such as Tokyo has helped Japan to maintain its prominent place among the world's richest countries.

TOP 10 ★

US COMPANIES MAKING THE GREATEST PROFIT PER SECOND

COMPANY	PROFIT PER SEC ($)
1 Ford Motor Company	699
2 General Electric	294
3 AT&T	202
4 Exxon Corporation	201
5 IBM	200
6 Intel Corporation	192
7 Citigroup	184
8 Philip Morris Companies, Inc.	170
9 Merck	166
10 BankAmerica Corporation	163

THE 10 ★
COUNTRIES MOST IN DEBT

	COUNTRY	TOTAL EXTERNAL DEBT ($)
1	Brazil	193,663,000,000
2	Mexico	149,690,000,000
3	China	146,697,000,000
4	South Korea	143,373,000,000
5	Indonesia	136,174,000,000
6	Russia	125,645,000,000
7	Argentina	123,221,000,000
8	India	94,404,000,000
9	Thailand	93,416,000,000
10	Turkey	91,205,000,000

Source: *World Bank*

The World Bank's annual debt calculations estimated the total indebtedness of low- and middle-income countries at $2.177 trillion in 1996.

THE 10 ★
POOREST COUNTRIES

	COUNTRY	GDP PER CAPITA, 1998 ($)
1	Ethiopia	100
2	Dem. Rep. of Congo	110
3 =	Sierra Leone	140
=	Burundi	140
5	Guinea-Bissau	160
6	Niger	190
7 =	Eritrea	200
=	Malawi	200
9 =	Mozambique	210
=	Nepal	210
=	Tanzania	210

Source: *World Bank*, Word Development Indicators

POVERTY-STRIKEN LAND

Factors including civil wars and severe droughts affecting their rural economies mean that several sub-Saharan African countries are among the world's poorest

TOP 10 ★
OLDEST ESTABLISHED COMPANIES IN THE US

	COMPANY/BUSINESS	FOUNDED
1	**J. E. Rhoads & Sons**, Conveyor belts	1702
2	**Covenant Life Assurance**, Insurance	1717
3	**Philadelphia Contributorship**, Insurance	1752
4	**Dexter Corporation**, Adhesives, etc.	1767
5 =	**D. Landreth Seed**, Seeds	1784
=	**Bank of New York**, Banking	1784
=	**Mutual Assurance**, Insurance	1784
=	**Bank of Boston**, Banking	1784
9 =	**Burns & Russell**, Building materials	1789
=	**George R. Ruhl & Sons**, Bakery supplies	1789

The Dexter Corporation of Windsor Locks, Connecticut, here in fourth place, is the oldest company listed on the US Stock Exchange. In addition to these businesses, there are a number of family farming concerns founded in the 17th century, among which the oldest is Tuttle Market Gardens of Dover Point, New Hampshire, which dates from 1640.

TOP 10 ★
INTERNATIONAL INDUSTRIAL COMPANIES

	COMPANY/ LOCATION/SECTOR	ANNUAL SALES ($)
1	**General Motors Corp.**, US, Transport	161,315,000,000
2	**DaimlerChrysler**, Germany, Transport	154,615,000,000
3	**Ford Motor Co.**, US, Transport	144,416,000,000
4	**Wal-Mart Stores, Inc.**, US, Retailing	139,208,000,000
5	**Mitsui and Co. Ltd.**, Japan, Trading	109,372,000,000
6	**Itochu Corp.**, Japan, Trading	108,749,100,000
7	**Mitsubishi Corp.**, Japan, Trading	107,184,000,000
8	**Exxon Corp.**, US, Oil, gas, fuel	100,697,000,000
9	**General Electric**, US, Electronics, electrical equipment	100,469,000,000
10	**Toyota Motor**, Japan, Transport	99,740,100,000

Source: Fortune Global 500

What was the fate of the *Cullinan* diamond?
see p.203 for the answer

A It became part of the British Crown Jewels
B It was stolen and never recovered
C It is owned by Elizabeth Taylor

Wealth & Riches

TAKING A BACK SEAT

Comedian Jerry Seinfeld formerly headed the richest entertainers' list with earnings of $225 million, but dropped out of the Top 10 with the end of his TV series.

TOP 10 ★
HIGHEST-EARNING ENTERTAINERS

ENTERTAINER	PROFESSION	1999 INCOME ($)
1 George Lucas	Film producer/director	400,000,000
2 Oprah Winfrey	TV host/producer	150,000,000
3 David Kelley	TV writer/producer (*Ally McBeal* etc.)	118,000,000
4 Tom Hanks	Film actor	71,000,000
5 =Backstreet Boys	Pop band	60,000,000
=Steven Spielberg	Film producer/director	60,000,000
7 Bruce Willis	Film actor	54,000,000
8 =David Copperfield	Illusionist	50,000,000
=Julia Roberts	Film actress	50,000,000
=The Rolling Stones	Rock band	50,000,000

Used by permission of Forbes magazine

TOP 10 ★
RICHEST RULERS

RULER/COUNTRY/ YEAR CAME TO POWER	ESTIMATED WEALTH ($)
1 Sultan Hassanal Bolkiah, Brunei, 1967	30,000,000,000
2 King Fahd bin Abdulaziz Al Saud, Saudi Arabia, 1982	28,000,000,000
3 Sheikh Zayed bin Sultan al-Nahyan, UAE (Abu Dhabi), 1966	20,000,000,000
4 Amir Jaber al-Ahmed al Jaber Al-Sabah, Kuwait, 1977	17,000,000,000
5 Sheikh Maktoum bin Rashid Al Maktoum, UAE (Dubai), 1990	12,000,000,000
6 President Saddam Hussein, Iraq, 1979	6,000,000,000
7 Queen Beatrix, Netherlands, 1980	5,200,000,000
8 Amir Hamad bin Khalifa Al Thani, Qatar, 1995	5,000,000,000
9 President Hafez Al-Assad, Syria, 1971	2,000,000,000
10 Queen Elizabeth II, UK, 1952	450,000,000

Based on data published in Forbes magazine

TOP 10 ★
RICHEST PEOPLE IN THE US

NAME/PROFESSION OR SOURCE	ASSETS ($)
1 William Henry Gates III, Computer software	58,400,000,000
2 Warren Edward Buffett, Textiles, etc.	29,400,000,000
3 Paul Gardner Allen, Computer software	21,000,000,000
4 Michael Dell, Computers	13,000,000,000
5 Steven Ballmer, Computer software	12,000,000,000
6 =Helen R. Walton, Retailing	11,000,000,000
=John T. Walton, Retailing	11,000,000,000
=Alice L. Walton, Retailing	11,000,000,000
=S. Robson Walton, Retailing	11,000,000,000
=Jim C. Walton, Retailing	11,000,000,000

Used by permission of Forbes magazine

TOP 10 ★
YOUNGEST BILLIONAIRES IN THE US

NAME/SOURCE OF WEALTH	ASSETS ($)	AGE
1 Daniel Morton Ziff, Ziff Brothers Investments	1,200,000,000	27
2 Jerry Yang, Yahoo!	3,700,000,000	30
3 =Pierre M. Omidyar, eBay	4,900,000,000	31
=Mark Cuban, Broadcast.com	1,200,000,000	31
5 =David Filo, Yahoo!	3,700,000,000	33
=Robert David Ziff, Ziff Brothers Investments	1,200,000,000	33
7 Michael Dell, Dell Computer Corp.	20,000,000,000	34
8 =Jeffrey P. Bezos, Amazon.com	7,800,000,000	35
=Dirk Edward Ziff, Ziff Brothers Investments	1,200,000,000	35
10 =Theodore W. Waitt, Gateway 2000 Computers	6,200,000,000	36
=William Wrigley Jr., Wrigley's Chewing Gum	2,700,000,000	36

Based on data published in Forbes magazine

Did You Know? The weight of diamonds is measured in carats (the word derives from the carob bean, which was once used as a measure). There are approximately 142 carats to the ounce.

MOST EXPENSIVE SINGLE DIAMONDS SOLD AT AUCTION

DIAMOND/SALE	PRICE ($)
1 *Star of the Season,* pear-shaped 100.10-carat "D" flawless diamond, Sotheby's, Geneva, May 17, 1995	16,548,750 (SF19,858,500)
2 *The Mouawad Splendor,* pear-shaped 11-sided 101.84-carat diamond, Sotheby's, Geneva, November 14, 1990	12,760,000 (SF15,950,000)
3 *Star of Happiness,* rectangular-cut 100.36-carat diamond, Sotheby's, Geneva, November 17, 1993	11,882,333 (SF17,823,500)
4 Fancy blue emerald-cut 20.17-carat diamond ring, Sotheby's, New York, October 18, 1994	9,902,500
5 *Eternal Light,* pear-shaped 85.91-carat pendant, Sotheby's, New York, April 19, 1988	9,130,000
6 Rectangular-cut fancy deep blue 13.49-carat diamond ring, Christie's, New York, April 13, 1995	7,482,500
7 Rectangular-cut 52.59-carat diamond ring, Christie's, New York, April 20, 1988	7,480,000
8 Fancy pink rectangular-cut 19.66-carat diamond, Christie's, Geneva, November 17, 1994	7,421,318 (SF9,573,500)
9 *The Jeddah Bride,* rectangular-cut 80.02-carat diamond, Sotheby's, New York, October 24, 1991	7,150,000
10 *The Agra Diamond,* fancy light pink cushion-shaped 32.24-carat diamond, Christie's, London, June 20, 1990	6,959,700 (£4,070,000)

COUNTRIES WITH THE MOST DOLLAR BILLIONAIRES*

COUNTRY	BILLIONAIRES
1 US	50
2 Germany	43
3 Japan	30
4 France	15
5 =China (Hong Kong)	13
=Switzerland	13
7 UK	12
8 Mexico	10
9 =Brazil	8
=Canada	8

* Individuals and families with a net worth of $1 billion or more

Based on data published in Forbes magazine

GOLD-PRODUCING COUNTRIES

COUNTRY	1998 PRODUCTION IN TONNES
1 South Africa	466.3
2 US	358.6
3 Australia	308.0
4 Canada	161.4
5 China	158.4
6 Indonesia	137.0
7 Russia	125.2
8 Peru	87.7
9 Uzbekistan	79.3
10 Ghana	72.1

As reported by Gold Fields Mineral Services Ltd., world-dominating gold producer South Africa saw its output fall yet again for the sixth consecutive year, although it has still held on to the top slot as the world's largest gold producer.

LARGEST ROUGH DIAMONDS

DIAMOND/DESCRIPTION	CARATS
1 *Cullinan*	3,106.00

Measuring roughly 4 x 2½ x 2 in (10 x 6.5 x 5 cm), and weighing 1 lb 6 oz (621 g), the Cullinan was unearthed in 1905, and bought by the Transvaal government for £150,000. It was presented to King Edward VII, who had it cut; the most important of the separate gems are among the British Crown Jewels.

2 *Excelsior*	995.20

Found at the Jagersfontein Mine on June 30, 1893, it was cut by the celebrated Amsterdam firm of Asscher in 1903, producing 21 superb stones.

3 *Star of Sierra Leone*	968.80

Found in Sierra Leone on St. Valentine's Day, 1972, the rough diamond weighed 8 oz (225 g) and measured 2½ x 1½ in (63.5 x 38.1 mm).

4 *Incomparable*	890.00

Discovered in 1980 at Mbuji-Mayi, Dem. Rep. of Congo (then Zaïre).

5 *Great Mogul*	787.50

When found in 1650 in the Gani Mine, India, it was presented to Shah Jehan, the builder of the Taj Mahal.

6 *Millennium Star*	777.00

Recently discovered near the village of Mbuji-Mayi in the Dem. Rep. of Congo, the polished stone cut from it is 203.04 carats and measures 2 x 1½ x ¾ in (50.06 x 36.56 x 18.5 mm).

7 *Woyie River*	770.00

Found in 1945 beside the Woyie River in Sierra Leone, it was cut into 30 stones. The largest of these, known as Victory and weighing 31.35 carats, was auctioned at Christie's, New York in 1984 for $880,000.

8 *Golden Jubilee*	755.50

Found in 1986 in the Premier Mine (the home of the Cullinan), the polished diamond cut from it is, at 545.67 carats, the largest in the world.

9 *Presidente Vargas*	726.60

Discovered in the Antonio River, Brazil, in 1938, it was named after the then President, Getulio Vargas.

10 *Jonker*	726.00

In 1934 Jacobus Jonker found this massive diamond. Acquired by Harry Winston, it was exhibited in the American Museum of Natural History.

WORTH ITS WEIGHT IN GOLD

International trade in gold is customarily carried out with either 32.15-troy ounce (1-kg) or 400-troy ounce (12.5-kg) gold bars.

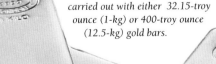

Advertising & Brands

TOP 10 ★ NETWORK TV ADVERTISERS IN THE US

	ADVERTISER	MEASURED NETWORK TV ADVERTISING ($)
1	General Motors Corp.	778,200,000
2	Proctor & Gamble Co.	670,400,000
3	Johnson & Johnson	420,500,000
4	Philip Morris Cos.	412,300,000
5	Ford Motor Co.	340,800,000
6	DaimlerChrysler	310,700,000
7	Unilever	294,000,000
8	Diageo	290,200,000
9	Walt Disney Co.	290,100,000
10	McDonald's Corp.	274,600,000

Source: Advertising Age

TOP 10 ★ CORPORATE ADVERTISERS IN THE US

	CORPORATION	TOTAL ADVERTISING EXPENDITURE ($)
1	General Motors Corp.	2,940,400,000
2	Proctor & Gamble Co.	2,650,300,000
3	Philip Morris Cos.	2,049,300,000
4	DaimlerChrysler	1,646,700,000
5	Sears, Roebuck & Co.	1,578,300,000
6	Ford Motor Co.	1,520,700,000
7	AT&T Corp.	1,428,000,000
8	Walt Disney Co.	1,358,700,000
9	PepsiCo	1,263,400,000
10	Diageo	1,205,700,000

Source: Advertising Age

TOP 10 ★ ADVERTISING CAMPAIGNS OF THE 20TH CENTURY*

	CAMPAIGN	COMPANY OR PRODUCT	FIRST YEAR
1	"Think small"	Volkswagen	1959
2	"The pause that refreshes"	Coca-Cola	1929
3	The Marlboro Man	Marlboro	1955
4	"Just do it"	Nike	1988
5	"You deserve a break today"	McDonald's	1971
6	"A diamond is forever"	DeBeers	1948
7	The Absolut bottle	Absolut vodka	1981
8	"Tastes great, less filling"	Miller Lite beer	1974
9	"Does she...or doesn't she?"	Clairol	1957
10	"We try harder"	Avis	1963

*Based on industry research
Source: Advertising Age

TOP 10 MOST VALUABLE FOOD AND DRINK BRANDS

(Brand name/industry/brand value in $)*

1 Coca-Cola, Beverages, 83,845,000,000 **2** McDonald's, Food, 26,231,000,000 **3** Nescafe, Switzerland, Beverages, 17,595,000,000 **4** Heinz, Food, 11,806,000,000 **5** Budweiser, Alcohol, 8,510,000,000 **6** Kelloggs, Food, 7,052,000,000 **7** Pepsi-Cola, Beverages, 5,932,000,000 **8** Wrigley's, Food, 4,404,000,000 **9** Burger King, Food, 2,806,000,000 **10** Moët & Chandon, France, Alcohol, 2,804,000,000

* US is country of origin unless otherwise stated
Source: Interbrand

BIG MAC

Global fast-food company McDonald's is ranked second only to Coca-Cola as one of the world's most valuable food and drink brands.

"SHOPPING MALL"

In 16th-century London, a croquet-like game called pall-mall (from the Italian *pallamaglio*, "ball to mallet") was played in long alleys in two parallel streets called Pall Mall and The Mall, where fashionable London society promenaded. By the 18th century, the game had fallen out of favor and Pall Mall had become renowned for its expensive shops. Later, "mall" became synonymous with any strolling and shopping area – especially the shopping malls of the United States.

WHY DO WE SAY?

Crowd cheers! Coke nears!
Game goes better refreshed.
Coca-Cola, never too sweet,
gives that special zing...refreshes best.

things go **better with Coke** Drink *Coca-Cola*

TOP 10 ★
COSMETIC AND TOILETRY BRANDS

	BRAND	MANUFACTURER	% OF WORLD MARKET BY VALUE
1	Nivea	Beiersdorf	2.20
2	Colgate	Colgate-Palmolive	2.01
3	Gillette	Gillette	1.87
4 =	Johnson's	Johnson & Johnson	1.25
=	Pantene Pro-V	Procter & Gamble	1.25
6	Clinique	Estée Lauder	0.86
7	Lux	Unilever	0.84
8	Oil of Olay	Procter & Gamble	0.82
9 =	Lancôme	L'Oréal	0.72
=	Revlon	Revlon	0.72

Source: *Euromonitor*

Many of the leading cosmetic brands are also among the oldest-established. Colgate was founded in the US in 1806 by William Colgate (1783–1857), who had emigrated from England. King Camp Gillette (1855–1932) made his first safety razors in 1895, while Johnson & Johnson's partnership dates back to 1885, Estée Lauder to 1946, Lux to 1900, and Revlon to 1932.

THE REAL THING

Bestselling, most advertised, and most valuable are only three of the many superlatives applied to Coca-Cola's world-beating status.

TOP 10 ★
MOST VALUABLE GLOBAL BRANDS

	BRAND NAME	INDUSTRY	BRAND VALUE ($)
1	Coca-Cola	Beverages	83,845,000,000
2	Microsoft	Software	56,654,000,000
3	IBM	Computers	43,781,000,000
4	General Electric	Diversified	33,502,000,000
5	Ford	Automobiles	33,197,000,000
6	Disney	Entertainment	32,275,000,000
7	Intel	Computers	30,021,000,000
8	McDonald's	Food	26,231,000,000
9	AT&T	Telecommunications	24,181,000,000
10	Marlboro	Tobacco	21,048,000,000

Source: *Interbrand*

Brand consultants Interbrand use a method of estimating value that takes account of the profitability of individual brands within a business (rather than the companies that own them), as well as such factors as their potential for growth.

TOP 10 ADVERTISERS BY BRAND IN THE US

(Brand/total advertising expenditure in $)

1 Chevrolet cars and trucks, 645,539,000 **2** MCI telephone services, 636,241,000 **3** Ford cars and trucks, 621,443,000 **4** Dodge cars and trucks, 602,754,000 **5** McDonald's restaurants, 571,748,000 **6** Sears stores, 571,364,000 **7** AT&T telephone services, 550,844,000 **8** Toyota cars and trucks, 500,020,000 **9** Buena Vista Pictures, 415,531,000 **10** Burger King, 407,492,000   Source: Advertising Age

TOP 10 ADVERTISERS BY CATEGORY IN THE US

(Category/total advertising expenditure in $)

1 Automotive, 14,073,500,000 **2** Retail, 11,572,500,000 **3** Movies and media, 4,121,900,000 **4** Financial, 3,849,500,000 **5** Medicines and proprietary remedies, 3,563,500,000 **6** Food and food products (not confections), 3,335,300,000 **7** Telecommunications, 3,220,500,000 **8** Restaurants and fast food, 3,163,500,000 **9** Travel, public transportation, hotels, and resorts, 2,997,100,000 **10** Local services and amusements, 2,741,700,000

Source: Advertising Age

Imports & Exports

GOODS EXPORTED FROM THE US

PRODUCT	TOTAL VALUE OF 1998 EXPORTS ($)
1 Electrical machinery	65,412,000,000
2 ADP equipment, office machinery	40,745,000,000
3 Airplanes	35,328,000,000
4 General industrial machinery	30,044,000,000
5 Power generating machinery	28,566,000,000
6 Specialized industrial machinery	27,317,000,000
7 Scientific instruments	24,143,000,000
8 Television, VCR, etc.	23,401,000,000
9 Chemicals - plastics	16,616,000,000
10 Airplane parts	15,046,000,000

Source: *US Census Bureau,* Statistical Abstract of the United States: 1999

EXPORT MARKETS FOR GOODS FROM THE US

COUNTRY	TOTAL VALUE OF 1998 EXPORTS ($)
1 Canada	156,307,600,000
2 Mexico	79,010,100,000
3 Japan	57,887,900,000
4 UK	39,070,200,000
5 Germany	26,641,900,000
6 Netherlands	19,003,800,000
7 Taiwan	18,157,100,000
8 France	17,728,000,000
9 South Korea	16,538,300,000
10 Singapore	15,673,500,000

Source: *US Census Bureau,* Statistical Abstract of the United States: 1999

In 1901, the US exported merchandise valued at $1,488,000,000, of which $106,000,000 went to Canada and £631,000,000 to the UK, its then leading trading partner. By 1946, the situation had reversed, Canada receiving $1,442,000,000-worth of goods compared with the UK's $855,000,000 out of a US total of $9,738,000,000. Canada has remained the USA's principal export market since that year.

GOODS IMPORTED TO THE US

PRODUCT	TOTAL VALUE OF 1998 IMPORTS ($)
1 Electrical machinery	79,366,000,000
2 ADP equipment, office machinery	76,846,000,000
3 Crude oil	54,226,000,000
4 Clothing	53,743,000,000
5 Television, VCR, etc.	36,771,000,000
6 General industrial machinery	28,802,000,000
7 Power-generating machinery	28,132,000,000
8 Specialized industrial machinery	21,182,000,000
9 Chemicals - organic	18,300,000,000
10 Toys, games, and sporting goods	17,374,000,000

Source: *US Census Bureau,* Statistical Abstract of the United States: 1999

EXPORT STATES IN THE US

STATE	TOTAL VALUE OF 1998 EXPORTS ($)
1 California	95,768,000,000
2 Texas	78,875,300,000
3 Washington	38,249,100,000
4 New York	37,383,500,000
5 Michigan	28,977,400,000
6 Illinois	28,914,200,000
7 Ohio	24,851,700,000
8 Florida	24,452,000,000
9 Louisiana	16,836,100,000
10 Pennsylvania	15,974,200,000

Source: *US Census Bureau,* Statistical Abstract of the United States: 1999

Total exports in 1998 were estimated to value $682,977,000,000, a 73 percent increase since 1990, with the Top 10 states responsible for 57 percent of the national total. Of the 50 states, 44 exported goods worth $1 billion or more. With 1998 exports of $276,400,000, Hawaii is bottom among exporting states.

COUNTRIES FOR DUTY-FREE SHOPPING

COUNTRY	ANNUAL SALES ($)
1 UK	2,480,000,000
2 US	1,775,000,000
3 Finland	1,046,000,000
4 Germany	885,000,000
5 France	724,000,000
6 South Korea	704,000,000
7 Denmark	652,000,000
8 Sweden	620,000,000
9 US Virgin Islands	601,000,000
10 Japan	491,000,000

Source: *Generation AB*

Duty-free sales began in 1951 with the opening of a small kiosk at Shannon Airport in Ireland, where transatlantic flights stopped for refueling on the final leg of their journey to New York. This has grown into a huge international business of which Europe takes almost half (49.8 percent) of global sales, Asia and Oceania 20.9 percent, the Americas 28.4 percent, and the whole of Africa just 1 percent.

DUTY-FREE FERRY OPERATORS

FERRY OPERATOR/LOCATION	ANNUAL SALES ($)
1 P & O Stena Line, UK	320,000,000
2 Eurotunnel, UK/France	280,000,000
3 Silja Ferries, Finland	260,000,000
4 Viking Line Ferries, Finland	210,000,000
5 Stena Line, Sweden	185,000,000
6 Scandlines, Denmark	*
7 Color Line, Norway	114,900,000
8 Seafrance, France	89,000,000
9 Hoverspeed, UK	75,000,000
10 Brittany Ferries, France	*

* Precise figure confidential

Source: *Generation AB*

UK and Scandinavian ferry services have long led this sector of the world markets.

CALL OF DUTY

Worldwide, duty-free sales have virtually doubled during the past decade and now exceed $20 billion. The top 10 countries account for almost half the total.

TOP 10 ★
DUTY-FREE AIRPORTS

	AIRPORT/LOCATION	ANNUAL SALES ($)
1	**London Heathrow**, UK	433,200,000
2	**Amsterdam Schiphol**, Netherlands	361,800,000
3	**Paris Charles De Gaulle**, France	320,700,000
4	**Frankfurt**, Germany	260,500,000
5	**Singapore Changi**, Singapore	250,000,000
6	**Honolulu**, Hawaii	242,500,000
7	**London Gatwick**, UK	208,300,000
8 =	**Copenhagen**, Denmark	200,000,000
=	**Tel Aviv Ben Gurion**, Israel	200,000,000
10	**São Paulo**, Brazil	*

* Precise figure confidential

Source: *Generation AB*

SCENT OF MONEY

Women's fragrances were once the foremost duty- and tax-free item, but since 1990 they have been overtaken by cigarettes.

TOP 10 DUTY-FREE SHOPS

(Shop/location)

1 **London Heathrow Airport**, UK
2 **Silja Ferries**, Finland **3** **P & O Stena Line**, UK **4** **Amsterdam Schiphol Airport**, Netherlands **5** **Viking Line Ferries**, Finland **6** **Paris Charles De Gaulle Airport**, France **7** **London Gatwick Airport**, UK **8** **Frankfurt Airport**, Germany **9** **Eurotunnel**, UK/France **10** **Stena Line**, Sweden

Source: *Generation AB*

In 1998, total global duty- and tax-free sales were worth $20.5 billion, down 2.2 percent on 1997 sales. Under recently introduced EC laws, duty-free sales in member countries have been axed since July 1999.

TOP 10 ★
DUTY-FREE PRODUCTS

	PRODUCT	SALES ($)
1	Cigarettes	2,477,000,000
2	Women's fragrances	2,157,000,000
3	Scotch whisky	1,423,000,000
4	Jewelry	1,331,000,000
5	Women's cosmetics	1,267,000,000
6	Confectionery	1,096,000,000
7	Men's fragrances and toiletries	995,000,000
8	Accessories	984,000,000
9	Leather goods (handbags, belts, etc)	890,000,000
10	Cognac	807,000,000

Source: *Generation AB*

Did You Know? Bestselling perfume Chanel No. 5 was invented in 1921 by Ernest Beaux. It was socalled because it was the fifth sample he submitted to Coco Chanel.

Communication Matters

	COUNTRY	MINUTES PER HEAD	TOTAL MINUTES OUTGOING CALLS PER ANNUM
1	US	90.3	24,593,000,000
2	UK	38.7	5,820,000,000
3	Canada	158.8	4,805,000,000
4	Germany	57.4	4,711,000,000
5	France	56.9	3,400,000,000
6	Italy	47.1	2,705,000,000
7	Switzerland	266.8	1,901,000,000
8	Japan	14.9	1,895,000,000
9	Netherlands	114.6	1,805,000,000
10	Spain	45.7	1,803,000,000

Source: *International Telecommunication Union*

TOP 10 ★
LETTER-SENDING COUNTRIES

	COUNTRY	AVERAGE NO. OF LETTER POST ITEMS SENT PER INHABITANT*
1	Vatican City	6,700.0
2	US	728.9
3	Norway	554.9
4	Sweden	502.8
5	France	435.9
6	Austria	371.6
7	Belgium	345.7
8	Luxembourg	339.7
9	Denmark	334.7
10	UK	324.9

* In 1998 or latest year for which data available

FIRST PAST THE POST

India's high population and tradition of bureaucracy combine to make it the world leader in number of post offices. The country's postal service employs some 600,000 people.

TOP 10 ★
COUNTRIES WITH THE MOST POST OFFICES

	COUNTRY	POST OFFICES*
1	India	153,021
2	China	112,204
3	Russia	43,900
4	US	38,159
5	Japan	24,678
6	Indonesia	20,139
7	UK	18,760
8	France	17,038
9	Turkey	16,984
10	Ukraine	15,227

* 1998 or latest year available
Source: *Universal Postal Union*

TOP 10 ★
COUNTRIES WITH THE HIGHEST RATIO OF CELLULAR MOBILE PHONE USERS

	COUNTRY	SUBSCRIBERS*	MOBILE PHONES PER 1,000 INHABITANTS*
1	Finland	2,966,000	577.0
2	Sweden	4,527,000	511.5
3	Norway	2,081,000	471.9
4	Italy	20,300,000	352.9
5	Denmark	1,854,000	351.1
6	Australia	6,000,000	323.8
7	Japan	39,786,000	315.7
8	Portugal	3,075,000	311.9
9	South Korea	13,988,000	304.2
10	Austria	2,270,000	281.3
	US	64,541,000	241.2

* Figures partly Siemens estimates
Source: *Siemens AG*

TOP 10 ★
COUNTRIES WITH THE MOST TELEPHONES

	COUNTRY	TELEPHONE LINES PER 100 INHABITANTS*
1	Luxembourg	71.00
2	Sweden	69.64
3	US	67.66
4	Switzerland	67.41
5	Norway	65.42
6	Denmark	65.38
7	Iceland	62.86
8	Canada	61.51
9	Netherlands	58.45
10	Hong Kong	58.36

* Figures partly Siemens estimates
Source: *Siemens AG*

The world average "teledensity" is 14.36 phone lines per 100 inhabitants. On a continental basis, Oceania (Australia, New Zealand, and their neighbors) has the highest ratio of telephone lines per 100 people – an average of 41.19 – followed by Europe with 36.74. The Americas as a whole have an average of 32.70, because even the high US figure fails to compensate for the much lower numbers in Central and South America.

Did You Know? In 1876 Elisha Gray attempted to patent the telephone, only to discover that Alexander Graham Bell had beaten him to it by a matter of hours. Undaunted, he invented the telautograph, a pen-driven precursor of the fax machine.

VATICAN POST

The list of the countries sending the most letters per person is headed by the Vatican City, with an average of over 27 per person daily, or almost 10,000 annually. The Vatican's population (which is variable, but seldom exceeds 750) is small, and this statistical anomaly results in part from the large numbers of official missives dispatched via the Holy See's post office and its 32 mailboxes, but mainly because Rome's inhabitants have discovered that mail posted there and bearing Vatican stamps is treated as priority and so is delivered more promptly.

SNAP SHOTS★

TOP 10 ★
ONLINE LANGUAGES

	LANGUAGE	NUMBER*
1	English	91,969,000
2	Japanese	9,000,000
3	French	7,100,000
4	German	6,900,000
5	Chinese (Mandarin)	5,600,000
6 =	Korean	3,300,000
=	Swedish	3,300,000
8	Italian	3,200,000
9	Finnish	1,430,000
10	Russian	1,300,000

* Of individuals accessing the Internet in this language
Source: NOP survey

TOP 10 ★
BUSIEST INTERNET SITES

	SITE	HITS*
1	Yahoo	32,263,000
2	AOL.com	30,545,000
3	msn.com	25,579,000
4	geocities.com	23,270,000
5	lycos.com	18,099,000
6	passport.com	17,793,000
7	microsoft.com	16,182,000
8	netscape.com	15,524,000
9	bluemountain.com	14,755,000
10	tripod.com	14,661,000

* Number of accesses during December 1999
Source: PC Data Online

One of the principal aims of the Internet is the dissemination of information, but information about its own users is rather patchy and erratic.

TOP 10 ★
COUNTRIES WITH THE MOST INTERNET USERS

	COUNTRY	PERCENTAGE OF POPULATION	INTERNET USERS*
1	US	41	110,825,000
2	Japan	14	18,156,000
3	UK	23	13,975,000
4	Canada	44	13,277,000
5	Germany	15	12,285,000
6	Australia	36	6,837,000
7	Brazil	4	6,790,000
8	China	0.5	6,308,000
9	France	10	5,696,000
10	South Korea	12	5,688,000
	World total	4.2	259,000,000

* Estimates for weekly usage as at end of 1999
Source: Computer Industry Almanac, Inc.

"CYBERSPACE"

The English word cybernetics – the communication and control of living things or machines – was coined in 1948 by American mathematician Norbert Wiener (1894–1964). He may have derived it from the French word cybernétique – the art of governing – created in 1834 by André Marie Ampère. From that, the term "cyberspace" was invented by American science-fiction writer William Gibson in his 1982 short story Burning Chrome, and developed in his 1984 novel Neuromancer. The term now refers to the ethereal electronic space that the Internet is thought to occupy.

WHY DO WE SAY?

LAPTOP OF LUXURY

Ever-increasing power, reducing costs, and the growth of the Internet have resulted in the global explosion of the computer industry.

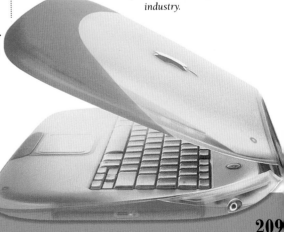

TOP 10 COUNTRIES WITH THE MOST COMPUTERS
(Country/computers)

1 US, 164,100,000   **2** Japan, 49,900,000   **3** Germany, 30,600,000
4 UK, 26,000,000   **5** France, 21,800,000   **6** Italy, 17,500,000   **7** Canada, 16,000,000
8 China, 15,900,000   **9** = Australia, 10,600,000;   = South Korea, 10,600,000

Source: Computer Industry Almanac, Inc.
Computer industry estimates put the number of computers in the world at 98 million in 1990, 222 million in 1995, and 579 million in 2000 – a sixfold increase over the decade.

Energy & Environment

POWER TO THE PEOPLE

In the 20th century, the creation of national grids for the transmission of electricity brought power to even the remotest communities.

TOP 10 ★
ELECTRICITY-CONSUMING COUNTRIES

	COUNTRY	CONSUMPTION KW/HR
1	US	3,278,500,000,000
2	China	955,980,000,000
3	Japan	904,600,000,000
4	Russia	712,400,000,000
5	Germany	477,270,000,000
6	Canada	475,120,000,000
7	India	397,280,000,000
8	France	375,550,000,000
9	Brazil	322,650,000,000
10	UK	309,590,000,000

Source: *Energy Information Administration*

TOP 10 ★
ITEMS OF DOMESTIC GARBAGE IN THE US

	ITEM	TONS PER ANNUM
1	Yard trimmings	29,750,000
2	Corrugated boxes	28,800,000
3	Food waste	14,000,000
4	Newspapers	13,100,000
5	Miscellaneous durables	12,000,000
6	Wood packaging	10,600,000
7	Furniture and furnishings	7,200,000
8	Other commercial printing	7,100,000
9	Office-type papers	6,800,000
10	Paper folding cartons	5,300,000

Source: *Environmental Protection Agency*

THE 10 ★
COUNTRIES EMITTING THE MOST SULFUR DIOXIDE

	COUNTRY	ANNUAL SO_2 EMISSIONS PER HEAD LB	OZ	KG
1	Czech Republic	329	6	149.4
2	Former Yugoslavia	304	11	138.2
3	Bulgaria	257	8	116.8
4	Canada	229	4	104.0
5	Hungary	179	7	81.4
6 =	Romania	174	10	79.2
=	US	174	10	79.2
8	Poland	156	12	71.1
9	Slovakia	154	5	70.0
10	Belarus	126	12	57.5

Source: *World Resources Institute*

Sulfur dioxide, the principal cause of acid rain, is produced by fuel combustion in factories and especially by power stations.

THE 10 ★
COUNTRIES EMITTING THE MOST CARBON DIOXIDE

	COUNTRY	ANNUAL CO_2 EMISSIONS PER HEAD (TONS)
1	Qatar	57.50
2	United Arab Emirates	39.89
3	Kuwait	27.81
4	Luxembourg	22.17
5	US	21.68
6	Singapore	21.43
7	Bahrain	20.42
8	Trinidad and Tobago	19.17
9	Australia	18.68
10	Brunei	18.60

Source: *Carbon Dioxide Information Analysis Center*

CO_2 emissions derive from three principal sources – fossil fuel burning, cement manufacturing, and gas flaring.

TOP 10 ★
COAL-CONSUMING COUNTRIES

	COUNTRY	1998 CONSUMPTION IN TONS OF OIL EQUIVALENT
1	China	678,170,800
2	US	588,137,400
3	India	169,267,200
4	Russia	113,285,600
5	Japan	97,416,800
6	South Africa	96,865,800
7	Germany	93,339,400
8	Poland	67,111,800
9	Australia	50,771,600
10	UK	44,851,400

Source: *BP Statistical Review of World Energy 1999*

POWER PLANT

Opened in 1985–86, Pacific Gas and Electric's Diablo Canyon Nuclear Power Station, California, is one of the US's 104 reactors.

TOP 10 COUNTRIES WITH THE MOST NUCLEAR REACTORS

(Country/reactors)

1 US, 104 **2** France, 58 **3** Japan, 53 **4** UK, 35 **5** Russia, 29 **6** Germany, 20 **7** Ukraine, 16 **8** South Korea, 15 **9** Canada, 14 **10** Sweden, 12

Source: *International Atomic Energy Agency*
There are some 434 nuclear power stations in operation in a total of 32 countries around the world, with a further 36 under construction. Lithuania has the greatest reliance on nuclear power, obtaining 77.2 percent of its electricity from nuclear sources.

TOP 10 ⭐
ENERGY-CONSUMING COUNTRIES

COUNTRY	OIL	GAS	1998 ENERGY CONSUMPTION* COAL	NUCLEAR	HEP#	TOTAL
1 US	939.6	607.4	588.1	201.6	29.4	2,365.8
2 China	209.7	19.1	678.1	4.2	18.8	930.0
3 Russia	134.7	361.7	113.2	29.6	14.9	654.3
4 Japan	281.0	68.8	97.4	92.5	10.4	550.1
5 Germany	150.5	78.9	93.3	45.9	1.9	370.6
6 India	94.8	23.0	169.2	3.0	7.9	298.2
7 France	104.1	37.1	16.6	110.2	6.2	274.5
8 UK	88.7	88.0	44.8	28.4	0.7	250.7
9 Canada	91.7	69.7	28.5	20.3	31.5	241.6
10 South Korea	102.8	15.5	39.7	25.4	0.5	184.1
World	3,734.0	2,222.0	2,445.7	690.5	249.0	9,342.0

* Millions of tons of oil equivalent   # Hydroelectric power
Source: BP Statistical Review of World Energy 1999

THE 10 MOST DEFORESTING COUNTRIES

(Country/average annual forest loss 1990–95 in sq miles/sq km)

1 Brazil, 9,862/25,544 **2** Indonesia, 4,186/10,844 **3** Dem. Rep. of Congo, 2,857/7,400 **4** Bolivia, 2,244/5,814 **5** Mexico, 1,961/5,080 **6** Venezuela, 1,943/5,034 **7** Malaysia, 1,545/ 4,002 **8** Myanmar, 1,495/3,874 **9** Sudan, 1,361/3,526 **10** Thailand, 1,271/3,294

Source: *Food and Agriculture Organization of the United Nations*

TOP 10 ⭐
NATURAL GAS-CONSUMING COUNTRIES

COUNTRY	1998 CONSUMPTION BILLION CU FT	BILLION CU M
1 US	24,005.4	612.4
2 Russia	14,297.9	364.7
3 UK	3,479.7	88.8
4 Germany	3,118.3	79.6
5 Canada	2,756.8	70.3
6 Japan	2,722.0	69.4
7 Ukraine	2,695.8	68.8
8 Italy	2,242.9	57.2
9 Iran	2,025.1	51.7
10 Saudi Arabia	1,803.0	46.0
World total	87,816.6	2,240.2

Source: BP Statistical Review of World Energy 1999

TOP 10 ⭐
OIL-CONSUMING COUNTRIES

COUNTRY	1998 CONSUMPTION TONS
1 US	939,611,000
2 Japan	281,010,000
3 China	209,710,600
4 Germany	150,533,200
5 Russia	134,774,600
6 Italy	104,359,400
7 France	104,168,500
8 South Korea	102,816,600
9 =Brazil	88,711,000
=Canada	91,712,300

Source: BP Statistical Review of World Energy 1999

In which year was Coca-Cola introduced?
see p.220 for the answer
A 1886
B 1902
C 1927

Accidents at Home & Work

MOST COMMON CAUSES OF INJURY AT WORK IN THE US

	CAUSE	DAYS LOST
1	Over-exertion	27,700,000
2	Contact with objects, equipment	27,000,000
3	Over-exertion in lifting	16,200,000
4	Struck by object	13,100,000
5	Fall to same level	10,800,000
6	Struck against object	7,000,000
7	Fall to lower level	5,400,000
8	Exposure to harmful substances	4,600,000
9	Caught in equipment or object	4,400,000
10	Repetitive motion	4,100,000

Source: *US Bureau of Labor Statistics*

The risk of sustaining an injury at work varies according to both type and size of establishment. Exposure to dangerous equipment and materials results in the highest incidence being encountered in manufacturing industries, with some three-fifths of the total, followed by agriculture, forestry, and fishing.

DANGER ON DECK

Exposure to extreme weather conditions and other hazards places fishing among the world's most dangerous industries.

THE 10 MOST DANGEROUS JOBS IN THE US
(Job sector/fatalities per year)

1 Agriculture, forestry, fishing, 831 **2** Special trade contractors, 679 **3** Trucking and warehousing, 562 **4** Heavy construction, other than building, 271 **5** Wholesale trade, 228 **6** General building contractors, 212 **7** Business services, 194 **8** Lumber and wood products, 170 **9** Public order and safety, 149 **10** Mining, 146

Source: *US Bureau of Labor Statistics*

MOST COMMON CAUSES OF ACCIDENTAL DEATH IN THE US

	CAUSE	DEATHS
1	Motor vehicle accidents (traffic)	42,522
2	Falls	14,986
3	Poisoning by drugs and medicines	8,431
4	Fires and flames	3,741
5	Drowning	3,488
6	Inhalation and ingestion of objects	3,206
7	Complications due to medical procedures	2,919
8	Motor vehicle accidents (nontraffic)	1,127
9	Air and space transport accidents	1,061
10	Firearms, unspecified	947

Source: *US National Center for Health Statistics*

TYPES OF WORKPLACE INJURIES OR ILLNESS CAUSING ABSENCE FROM WORK IN THE US

	INJURY OR ILLNESS	DAYS LOST
1	Sprains, strains	43,600,000
2	Bruises, contusions	9,000,000
3	Cuts, lacerations	7,300,000
4	Fractures	6,500,000
5	Multiple traumatic injuries	3,300,000
6 =	Heat burns	1,600,000
=	Carpel tunnel syndrome	1,600,000
8	Tendonitis	1,000,000
9	Chemical burns	700,000
10	Amputations	600,000

Source: *US Bureau of Labor Statistics*

The Department of Labor's Bureau of Statistics conducts an annual survey of workplace injuries. The one covering 1998 estimated that there were some 5.9 million injuries, a rate equivalent to 6.7 cases per 100 full-time workers. Of these, 2.8 million incidents resulted in one or more lost workdays for recuperation, restricted duties, or both.

THE 10 MOST ACCIDENT-PRONE COUNTRIES
(Country/accidental death rate per 100,000)*

1 South Korea, 120.2 **2** Moldova, 114.0 **3** Russia, 112.3 **4** South Africa, 99.4 **5** Lithuania, 95.0 **6** Estonia, 94.5 **7** Latvia, 94.1 **8** Ukraine, 89.0 **9** Belarus, 82.0 **10** Slovenia, 56.5 US, 35.5

* *Traffic accidents, accidental falls, and other accidents*
Source: *UN Demographic Yearbook*

DOMESTIC INFERNO
A combination of deliberate and accidental fires, many of which result from avoidable causes, contributes to losses of life and property.

THE 10 ★
ARTICLES MOST FREQUENTLY INVOLVED IN ACCIDENTS IN THE HOME

	ARTICLE	ACCIDENTS PER ANNUM*
1	Construction feature	775,000
2	Furniture	329,000
3	Person	230,000
4	Outdoor surface	194,000
5	Clothing/footwear	191,000
6	Building/raw materials	159,000
7	Furnishings	145,000
8	Cooking/kitchen equipment	134,000
9	Animal/insect	113,000
10	Food/drink	109,000
	Total	2,502,000

* National estimates based on actual Home Accident Surveillance System figures for sample population

THE 10 ★
MOST COMMON CAUSES OF DOMESTIC FIRES IN THE US*

	CAUSE	APPROX. NO. OF FIRES PER ANNUM
1	Cooking equipment	95,300
2	Heating equipment	65,900
3	Incendiary or suspicious causes	50,700
4	Other equipment	43,900
5	Electrical distribution system	39,200
6	Appliance, tool, or air conditioning	30,100
7	Smoking materials	22,000
8	Open flame, torch	20,500
9	Child playing	19,800
10	Exposure to other hostile fire	15,700

* Survey conducted by the NFIRS and NFPA covering the period 1993–97

Source: *National Fire Protection Association*

THE 10 ANIMALS MOST INVOLVED IN ACCIDENTS IN THE UK
(Animal/injuries caused per annum*)

❶ **Dog**, 66,528 ❷ **Cat**, 14,150 ❸ **Bee and wasp**, 14,035 ❹ **Other insect**, 9,658 ❺ **Horse, pony, donkey**, 3,302 ❻ **Rabbit, hamster, etc.**, 2,976 ❼ **Wild creature**, 960 ❽ **Wild bird**, 826 ❾ **Cow, bull, calf**, 730 ❿ **Chicken, swan, duck, etc.**, 653

* National estimates based on actual Home Accident Surveillance System figures for sample population

"HAZARD"

Before it came to mean a risk, hazard was a dice game, popular in Europe since the 14th century. It comes from the Arabic word *al* (the) and *zahr* (dice). The uncertainty of casting the dice led to adoption of *al-zahr* in Spanish as *azahr*, an unexpected accident. In French this became *hasard*, and in the English *hazard*. **WHY DO WE SAY?**

Did You Know? In the US, in a single year, a total of 162 people aged 65 and over were treated for skateboarding injuries.

213

Industrial & Other Disasters

WORST DISASTERS AT SPORTS VENUES IN THE 20TH CENTURY

LOCATION/DATE/TYPE	NO. KILLED
1 **Hong Kong Jockey Club**, Feb 26, 1918, Stand collapse and fire	604
2 **Lenin Stadium**, Moscow, Oct 20, 1982, Crush in soccer stadium	340
3 **Lima**, Peru, May 24, 1964, Riot in soccer stadium	320
4 **Sinceljo**, Colombia, Jan 20, 1980, Bullring stand collapse	222
5 **Hillsborough**, Sheffield, UK, Apr 15, 1989, Crush in soccer stadium	96
6 **Guatemala City**, Guatemala, Oct 16, 1996, Stampede in Mateo Flores National Stadium during World Cup soccer qualifying match, Guatemala v Costa Rica, with 127 injured	83
7 **Le Mans**, France, June 11, 1955, Racing car crash	82
8 **Katmandu**, Nepal, Mar 12, 1988, Stampede in soccer stadium	80
9 **Buenos Aires**, Argentina, May 23, 1968, Riot in soccer stadium	74
10 **Ibrox Park**, Glasgow, Scotland, Jan 2, 1971, Barrier collapse in soccer stadium	66

Before the Ibrox Park disaster, the worst accident at a British stadium was caused by the collapse of a stand at Burnden Park, Bolton, on March 9, 1946, in an FA Cup Tie against Stoke City, which left 33 dead and 400 injured. If stunt-flying is included as a "sport," the worst airshow disaster of all time occurred at the Ramstein Air Force base, Germany, on August 28, 1988, when three fighters in an Italian aerobatic team collided, one of them crashing into the crowd, leaving 70 dead and 150 injured. Such tragedies are not an exclusively modern phenomenon: during the reign of Roman Emperor Antoninus Pius (AD 138–161), a stand at the Circus Maximus collapsed during a gladiatorial spectacle and 1,162 spectators were killed.

WORST MINING DISASTERS

LOCATION/DATE	NO. KILLED
1 **Hinkeiko**, China, Apr 26, 1942	1,549
2 **Courrières**, France, Mar 10, 1906	1,060
3 **Omuta**, Japan, Nov 9, 1963	447
4 **Senghenydd**, UK, Oct 14, 1913	439
5 **Coalbrook**, South Africa, Jan 21, 1960	437
6 **Wankie**, Rhodesia, June 6, 1972	427
7 **Dhanbad**, India, May 28, 1965	375
8 **Chasnala**, India, Dec 27, 1975	372
9 **Monongah**, US, Dec 6, 1907	362
10 **Barnsley**, UK, Dec 12, 1866	361*

* Including 27 killed the following day while searching for survivors

A mine disaster at the Fushun mines, Manchuria, in February 1931 may have resulted in up to 3,000 deaths, but information was suppressed by the Chinese government. Soviet security was also responsible for obscuring details of an explosion at the East German Johanngeorgendstadt uranium mine on November 29, 1949, when as many as 3,700 may have died. Among the most tragic disasters of this century was a mine disaster at Aberfan, Wales, on October 20, 1966. Waste from the local mine had been building up for many years to become a heap some 800 ft (244 m) in height. Weakened by the presence of a spring, a huge volume of slurry suddenly flowed down and engulfed the local school, killing 116 children.

WORST FIRES AT THEATER AND ENTERTAINMENT VENUES*

LOCATION/DATE/TYPE	NO. KILLED
1 **Canton**, China, May 25, 1845, Theater	1,670
2 **Shanghai**, China, June 1871, Theater	900
3 **Vienna**, Austria, Dec 8, 1881, Ring Theater	640–850
4 **St. Petersburg**, Russia, Feb 14, 1836, Lehmann Circus	800
5 **Antoung**, China, Feb 13, 1937, Movie theater	658
6 **Chicago**, Illinois, Dec 30, 1903, Iroquois Theater	591
7 **Boston**, Mass., Nov 28, 1942, Cocoanut Grove Night Club	491
8 **Abadan**, Iran, Aug 20, 1978, Theater	422
9 **Niteroi**, Brazil, Dec 17, 1961, Circus	323
10 **Brooklyn Theater**, New York, Dec 5, 1876	295

* 19th and 20th centuries, excluding sports stadiums and race tracks

All the worst theater disasters have been caused by fire. The figure given for the first entry in this list is a conservative estimate, some sources putting the figure as high as 2,500, but, even in recent times, reports of disasters in China are often unreliable.

WORST FIRES OF THE 20TH CENTURY*

LOCATION/DATE/TYPE	NO. KILLED	LOCATION/DATE/TYPE	NO. KILLED
1 **Kwanto**, Japan, Sep 1, 1923, Following earthquake	60,000	**6** =**Lagunillas**, Venezuela, Nov 14, 1939, Oil refinery and city	over 500
2 **Chungking**, China, Sep 2, 1949, Docks	1,700	=**Mandi Dabwali**, India, Dec 23, 1995, School tent	over 500
3 **Hakodate**, Japan, Mar 22, 1934, City	1,500	**8** **Hoboken**, New Jersey, US, June 30, 1900, Docks	326
4 **San Francisco**, US, Apr 18, 1906, Following earthquake	600–700	**9** **Brussels**, Belgium, May 22, 1967, Department store	322
5 **Cloquet**, Minnesota, US, Oct 12, 1918, Forest	559	**10** **Columbus**, Ohio, US, Apr 21, 1930, State Penitentiary	320

* Excluding sports and entertainment venues, mining disasters, and the results of military action

Did You Know? One of the worst fires in history was that which engulfed the wooden London Bridge on July 11, 1212, with some 3,000 victims burned, crushed, or drowned in the ensuing panic.

THE 10 ★
WORST COMMERCIAL AND INDUSTRIAL DISASTERS*

	LOCATION/DATE	TYPE	NO. KILLED
1	**Bhopal**, India, Dec 3, 1984	Methyl isocyante gas escape at Union Carbide plant	up to 3,000
2	**Oppau**, Germany, Sep 21, 1921	Chemical plant explosion	561
3	**Mexico City**, Mexico Nov 20, 1984	Explosion at a PEMEX liquified petroleum gas plant	540
4	**Seoul**, Korea, June 29, 1995	Collapse of Sampoong department store	501
5	**Brussels**, Belgium May 22, 1967	Fire in l'Innovation department store	322
6	**Novosibirsk**, USSR Apr 1979#	Anthrax infection following accident at biological and chemical warfare plant	up to 300
7	**Guadalajara**, Mexico Apr 22, 1992	Explosions caused by gas leak into sewers	230
8	**São Paulo**, Brazil Feb 1, 1974	Fire in Joelma bank and office building	227
9	**Oakdale**, US, May 18, 1918	Chemical plant explosion	193
10	**Bangkok**, Thailand, May 10, 1993	Fire engulfed a four-story doll factory	187

* *Including industrial sites, factories, offices, and stores; excluding military, mining, marine, and other transport disasters* # *Precise date unknown*

THE 10 ★
WORST EXPLOSIONS*

	LOCATION/DATE	TYPE	NO. KILLED
1	**Rhodes**, Greece, 1856#	Lightning strike of gunpowder store	4,000
2	**Brescia**, Italy, 1769#	Arsenal	over 3,000
3	**Salang Tunnel**, Afghanistan, Nov 3, 1982	Gasoline tanker collision	over 2,000
4	**Lanchow**, China, Oct 26, 1935	Arsenal	2,000
5	**Halifax**, Nova Scotia, Dec 6, 1917	Ammunition ship *Mont Blanc*	1,963
6	**Memphis**, Tenn., Apr 27, 1865	*Sultana* boiler explosion	1,547
7	**Bombay**, India, Apr 14, 1944	Ammunition ship *Fort Stikine*	1,376
8	**Cali**, Colombia, Aug 7, 1956	Ammunition trucks	up to 1,200
9	**Chelyabinsk**, USSR, June 3, 1989	Liquid gas beside railroad	up to 800
10	**Texas City**, Texas, Apr 16, 1947	Ammonium nitrate on cargo ships	576

* *Excluding mining disasters, terrorist and military bombs, and natural explosions such as volcanoes* # *Precise date unknown*

TROUBLE IN STORE

Some 1,500 people were inside the Sampoong Department Store, Seoul, when it collapsed, leaving over a third of them dead and as many as 900 injured.

THE 10 FIRST HEINZ'S "57 VARIETIES"

(Product/year introduced)

1 Horseradish, 1869 **2** = Sour gherkins, 1870; = Sour mixed pickles, 1870; = Chow chow pickle, 1870; = Sour onions, 1870; = Prepared mustard, 1870; = Sauerkraut in crocks, 1870 **8** = Heinz and Noble catsup, 1873; = Vinegar, 1873 **10** Tomato ketchup, 1876

LABOR SAVER

When Heinz was restructured in 1876, its first product was tomato ketchup. Although a staple product in every American household, until then making it involved stirring a huge cauldron over an open fire for a day.

TOP 10

HOTTEST CHILES

EXAMPLES OF CHILES	SCOVILLE UNITS
1 Datil, Habanero, Scotch Bonnet	100,000–350,000
2 Chiltepin, Santaka, Thai	50,000–100,000
3 Aji, Cayenne, Piquin, Tabasco	30,000–50,000
4 de Arbol	15,000–30,000
5 Serrano, Yellow Wax	5,000–15,000
6 Chipotle, Jalapeno, Mirasol	2,500–5,000
7 Cascabel, Sandia, Rocotillo	1,500–2,500
8 Ancho, Espanola, Pasilla, Poblano	1,000–1,500
9 Anaheim, New Mexico	500–1,000
10 Cherry, Peperoncini	100–500

Hot peppers contain substances called capsaicinoids, which determine how "hot" they are. In 1912 pharmacist Wilbur Scoville pioneered a test, based on which chiles are ranked by Scoville Units. According to this scale, one part of capsaicin (the principal capsaicinoid) per million equals 15,000 Scoville Units.

TOP 10 ★

FOOD AND DRINK ITEMS CONSUMED IN THE US BY WEIGHT

PRODUCT	AVERAGE ANNUAL CONSUMPTION PER CAPITA		
	LB	OZ	KG
1 Dairy products	579	12	262.9
2 Vegetables for processing	230	6	104.5
3 Flour and cereal products	200	1	90.7
4 Fresh vegetables	185	9	84.1
5 Fruit for processing	161	8	73.2
6 Caloric sweeteners	154	1	69.8
7 Fresh fruit	133	3	60.4
8 Red meat	111	0	50.3
9 Fats and oils	65	9	29.7
10 Poultry	64	12	29.3

Source: *United States Department of Agriculture/Economic Research Service*

HEINZ
57
VARIETIES

HEINZ
ESTD 1869 ESTD
TOMATO
KETCH

★ TOP 10 ★
MEAT-EATING COUNTRIES

	COUNTRY	ANNUAL CONSUMPTION PER CAPITA		
		LB	OZ	KG
1	US	258	2	117.1
2	Cyprus	242	1	109.8
3	Bahamas	231	7	105.0
4	New Zealand	229	4	104.0
5	Australia	222	10	101.0
6	Austria	221	12	100.6
7	Spain	218	0	98.9
8	Denmark	214	4	97.2
9	Yugoslavia	208	8	94.6
10	Slovenia	206	2	93.5

Source: Meat and Livestock Commission

There is a huge range in levels of meat consumption around the world, from the No. 1 meat consumer, the US, at 258 lb (117.1 kg) per person per year, to India, where the figure may be just 7 lb (3.4 kg).

★ TOP 10 ★
BEEF-CONSUMING COUNTRIES

	COUNTRY	ANNUAL CONSUMPTION PER CAPITA		
		LB	OZ	KG
1	Uruguay	129	10	58.8
2	Argentina	111	5	50.5
3	US	95	7	43.3
4	Paraguay	87	11	39.8
5	Australia	82	10	37.5
6	New Zealand	80	14	36.7
7	Mongolia	78	14	35.8
8	Canada	71	10	32.5
9	Bahamas	70	12	32.1
10	French Polynesia	68	1	30.9

Source: Meat and Livestock Commission

★ TOP 10 ★
PORK-CONSUMING COUNTRIES

	COUNTRY	ANNUAL CONSUMPTION PER CAPITA		
		LB	OZ	KG
1	Austria	140	14	63.9
2	Yugoslavia	132	7	60.1
3	Denmark	126	8	57.4
4	Spain	123	4	56.2
5	Hungary	116	6	52.8
6	Cyprus	115	4	52.3
7	Germany	114	6	51.9
8	Slovakia	106	4	48.2
9	Netherlands	105	2	47.7
10	Czech Republic	98	5	44.6
	US	61	8	27.9

Source: Meat and Livestock Commission

★ TOP 10 ★
FISH-CONSUMING COUNTRIES

	COUNTRY	ANNUAL CONSUMPTION PER CAPITA *		
		LB	OZ	KG
1	Maldives	338	3	153.4
2	Iceland	211	0	95.7
3	Kiribati	173	4	78.6
4	Japan	167	12	76.1
5	Seychelles	133	6	60.5
6	Portugal	129	7	58.7
7	Norway	120	6	54.6
8	Malaysia	119	4	54.1
9	French Polynesia	114	3	51.8
10	South Korea	113	12	51.6
	US	50	15	23.1

* Combines sea and freshwater fish totals

Source: Food and Agriculture Organization of the UN

FISH DISH
The national popularity of sushi (raw fish and rice) and other recipes help to make Japan one of the world's leading fish consumers.

★ TOP 10 ★
POULTRY-CONSUMING COUNTRIES

	COUNTRY	ANNUAL CONSUMPTION PER CAPITA		
		LB	OZ	KG
1	Antigua & Barbuda	142	6	69.6
2	Saint Lucia	120	5	54.6
3	Bahamas	113	5	51.5
4	Brunei	111	8	50.6
5	St. Kitts & Nevis	110	14	50.3
6	US	99	13	45.3
7=	Israel	97	0	44.0
=	Saint Vincent	97	0	44.0
9	Barbados	95	3	43.2
10	Dominica	89	4	40.5

Source: Meat and Livestock Commission

Sweet Treats

A MARS A DAY ...

Mars's first product, the Milky Way bar, was renamed Mars bar when launched in the UK in 1932. The name did not appear in the US until 1940, when a new bar was introduced.

THE 10 ★
FIRST MARS PRODUCTS

	PRODUCT	YEAR INTRODUCED
1 =	Milky Way bar	1923
=	Snickers bar (non-chocolate)	1923
3	Snickers bar (chocolate)	1930
4	3 Musketeers bar	1932
5	Maltesers	1937
6	Kitekat (catfood; now Whiskas)	1939
7	Mars almond bar	1940
8	M&M's plain chocolate candies	1941
9	Uncle Ben's converted brand rice	1942
10 =	M&M's peanut chocolate candies	1954
=	Pal (dogfood)	1954

American candy manufacturer Franklin C. Mars set up his first business in Tacoma, Washington, in 1911, and formed the Mar-O-Bar company in Minneapolis in 1922, with the first of its products, the Milky Way bar. The founder's son, Forrest E. Mars, set up in the UK in 1932, merging the firm with its American counterpart in 1964. Strangely, outside the US the Milky Way bar is known as a Mars bar, while in the UK a Milky Way is a rather different product, introduced in 1935. In the UK, the Snickers bar began life as a Marathon, but was renamed to bring it in line with the US.

TOP 10 ★
SUGAR-CONSUMING COUNTRIES

	COUNTRY	ANNUAL CONSUMPTION PER CAPITA		
		LB	OZ	KG
1	Israel	220	14	100.2
2	Belize	156	1	70.8
3	Trinidad and Tobago	134	11	61.1
4	Cuba	129	7	58.7
5	Barbados	127	14	58.0
6	Brazil	124	9	56.5
7	Swaziland	119	8	54.2
8 =	Costa Rica	118	3	53.6
=	Malta	118	3	53.6
10	Iceland	117	8	53.3
	World average	44	8	20.2
	US	71	10	32.5

Source: *Food and Agriculture Organization of the United Nations*

TOP 10 ★
CHOCOLATE BRANDS IN THE US

	BRAND/MANUFACTURER	MARKET SHARE % (1998)
1	Snickers, Mars	10.6
2	Reese's Peanut Butter Cup, Hershey Chocolate	8.7
3	M&Ms, Mars	5.1
4	Kit Kat, Hershey Chocolate	4.5
5	Russell Stover, Russell Stover Candies	4.0
6	Milky Way, Mars	3.7
7 =	Twix, Mars	2.9
=	York, Hershey Chocolate	2.9
9	Hershey's Milk Chocolate, Hershey Chocolate	2.8
10 =	Three Musketeers, Mars	2.6
=	Hershey's Bar with Almonds, Hershey Chocolate	2.6

Source: *Euromonitor*

TOP 10 ★
CANDY MANUFACTURERS IN THE US*

	MANUFACTURER	MARKET SHARE %*
1	Hershey Chocolate	26.2
2	Mars	19.9
3	Nestlé	5.7
4	William Wrigley Jr. Co.	4.8
5	Warner-Lambert	3.8
6	RJR Nabisco	3.7
7	Russell Stover Candies	3.5
8	Favorite Brands	2.8
9	Brach & Brock Confections	1.9
10	Tootsie Roll Industries	1.6

* *Based on $ sales volume*

Source: *Euromonitor*

Background image: **CHOCOLATE SELECTION**

TOP 10 ★
CHOCOLATE-CONSUMING NATIONS

	COUNTRY	TOTAL COCOA CONSUMPTION TONS
1	US	721,000
2	Germany	318,700
3	UK	211,600
4	France	195,400
5	Japan	137,000
6	Brazil	132,700
7	Russia	131,500
8	Italy	100,500
9	Canada	86,000
10	Spain	76,800
	World	2,999,600

Europe has the highest intake of the continents, with a cocoa consumption of 1,490,000 tons; the Americas are next with 1,158,000; then Asia and Oceania with 326,000; and lastly Africa, where only 65,000 tons are consumed across the entire continent.

TOP 10 ★
ICE CREAM-CONSUMING COUNTRIES

	COUNTRY	PRODUCTION PER CAPITA PINTS	LITERS
1	New Zealand	55.98	26.48
2	US	46.59	22.04
3	Canada	39.70	18.78
4	Australia	37.83	17.90
5	Belgium	31.09	14.71
6	Sweden	29.66	14.03
7	Finland	29.42	13.92
8	Norway	28.20	13.34
9	Denmark	21.64	10.24
10	Israel	15.93	7.23

Source: *International Dairy Foods Association*

Global statistics for ice cream consumption are hard to come by, but this list presents recent and reliable estimates for per capita production of ice ceam and related products.

TOP 10 ★
SUGAR PRODUCERS, 1999

	COUNTRY	TONNES*
1	Brazil	20,995,000
2	India	16,826,000
3	China	8,958,000
4	US	7,556,000
5	Australia	5,778,000
6	Mexico	4,985,000
7	France	4,891,000
8	Thailand	4,314,000
9	Germany	4,054,000
10	Pakistan	3,817,000
	World	133,089,042

* *Raw centrifugal sugar*

Source: *Food and Agriculture Organization of the United Nations*

TOP 10 CONSUMERS OF KELLOGG'S CORNFLAKES*

1 Ireland 2 UK 3 Australia
4 Denmark 5 Sweden 6 Norway
7 Canada 8 US 9 Mexico
10 Venezuela

* Based on per capita consumption
In 1894, the brothers Will Keith Kellogg and Dr. John Harvey Kellogg discovered, by accident, that boiled and rolled wheat dough turned into flakes if left overnight; once baked, they became a tasty cereal. In 1898, they replaced wheat with corn, thereby creating the Cornflakes we know today. Will Keith Kellogg went into business manufacturing Cornflakes, with his distinctive signature on the packet. Today, Cornflakes remain Kellogg's bestselling product.

CEREAL SUCCESS
One of the world's most popular breakfast foods, Kellogg's Cornflakes have a history spanning more than a century.

Alcoholic & Soft Drinks

TOP 10 ★
SOFT DRINK BRANDS IN THE US

	BRAND	ANNUAL SALES (GALLONS)*
1	Coca-Cola Classic	3,122,100,000
2	Pepsi	2,199,200,000
3	Diet Coke	1,303,400,000
4	Mountain Dew	1,017,600,000
5	Sprite	992,800,000
6	Dr. Pepper	899,100,000
7	Diet Pepsi	759,600,000
8	7-Up	316,400,000
9	Caffeine-Free Diet Coke	272,800,000
10	Minute Maid Regular and Diet	189,400,000

* Wholesale sales

Source: *Beverage Marketing Corporation*

TOP 10 ★
SOFT DRINK-CONSUMING COUNTRIES*

	COUNTRY	ANNUAL CONSUMPTION PER CAPITA	
		PINTS	LITERS
1	US	447.6	212
2 =	Iceland	290.4	138
=	Mexico	290.4	138
4	Malta	267.6	127
5	Norway	254.4	121
6	Canada	246.0	117
7	Australia	242.4	115
8	Israel	232.8	110
9	Chile	223.2	106
10	Ireland	222.0	103

* Carbonated only

Source: *Zenith International*

As one might expect, affluent Western countries feature prominently in this list and, despite the spread of the so-called "Coca-Cola culture," former Eastern Bloc and Third World countries rank very low – some African nations recording extremely low consumption figures of less than 2 pints (1 liter) per annum.

THE 10 FIRST COCA-COLA PRODUCTS
(Product/date introduced)

1 **Coca-Cola**, May 1886 2 **Fanta**, June 1960 3 **Sprite**, Feb 1961 4 **TAB**, May 1963 5 **Fresca**, Feb 1966 6 **Mr. PiBB***, June 1972 7 **Hi-C Soft Drinks**, Aug 1977 8 **Mello Yello**, Mar 1979 9 **Ramblin' Root Beer**, June 1979 10 **Diet Coke**, July 1982

* Mr. PiBB without Sugar launched Sep 1974; changed name to Sugar-free Mr. PiBB, 1975

TOP 10 ★
ALCOHOL-CONSUMING COUNTRIES

	COUNTRY	ANNUAL CONSUMPTION PER CAPITA (100 PERCENT ALCOHOL)	
		PINTS	LITERS
1	Luxembourg	28.1	13.3
2	Portugal	23.6	11.2
3 =	France	22.8	10.8
=	Ireland	22.8	10.8
5	Germany	22.3	10.6
6	Czech Republic	21.5	10.2
7	Spain	21.2	10.1
8 =	Denmark	20.0	9.5
=	Romania	20.0	9.5
10	Hungary	19.8	9.4
	US	13.7	6.5

Source: *Productschap voor Gedistilleerde Dranken*

TOP 10 BRANDS OF IMPORTED BEER IN THE US
(Brand/country/1998 imports in gallons)

1 **Corona Extra**, Mexico, 53,800,000 2 **Heineken**, Germany, 42,300,000 3 **LaBatt's**, Canada, 12,300,000 4 **Becks**, Germany, 10,300,000 5 **Molson Ice**, Canada, 9,900,000 6 **Guinness/Stout**, Ireland, 8,400,000 7 **Tecate**, Mexico, 8,300,000 8 **= Molsen**, Canada, 8,200,000; **= Foster's**, Australia, 8,200,000 10 **Bass**, England, 6,300,000

Source: *Beverage Marketing Corporation*

GRAPE HARVEST
Although Italy's wine production has led the world, it has recently been overtaken by that of France, which produced almost 6 million tons in 1999.

TOP 10 ★
WINE-DRINKING COUNTRIES

	COUNTRY	ANNUAL CONSUMPTION PER CAPITA	
		PINTS	LITERS
1	Luxembourg	147.4	70.0
2	France	122.6	58.1
3	Portugal	112.3	53.2
4	Italy	109.8	52.0
5	Switzerland	91.2	43.2
6	Argentina	81.8	38.8
7	Greece	75.7	35.9
8	Spain	75.1	35.6
9	Austria	63.5	30.1
10	Denmark	61.2	29.0
	US	15.6	7.4

Source: *Productschap voor Gedistilleerde Dranken*

The US still does not make it into the Top 10 or even Top 30 wine-drinking countries in the world.

TOP 10 ★
BEER-DRINKING COUNTRIES

	COUNTRY	ANNUAL CONSUMPTION PER CAPITA	
		PINTS	LITERS
1	Czech Republic	341.6	161.8
2	Ireland	317.7	150.5
3	Germany	268.9	127.4
4	Luxembourg	234.1	110.9
5	Austria	229.3	108.6
6	Denmark	221.6	105.0
7	UK	209.9	99.4
8	Belgium	206.9	98.0
9	Australia	199.4	94.5
10	Slovak Republic	193.8	91.8
	US	173.0	82.0

Source: *Productschap voor Gedistilleerde Dranken*

Despite its position as the world's leading producer of beer, the US misses being placed in the Top 10 – it is ranked in 13th position.

HERE FOR THE BEER

During the 1990s, beer consumption in Ireland rose by 20 percent, elevating the country from eighth to second place among the world's beer consumers.

TOP 10 ★
CHAMPAGNE-IMPORTING COUNTRIES

	COUNTRY	BOTTLES IMPORTED (1999)
1	UK	32,261,232
2	US	23,700,839
3	Germany	17,496,865
4	Belgium	10,753,197
5	Italy	9,431,994
6	Switzerland	8,658,165
7	Japan	3,946,155
8	Canada	2,462,938
9	Spain	1,731,055
10	Australia	1,686,231

In 1998 France consumed 179,004,405 bottles of champagne and exported 113,453,686. In that year Canada increased its imports by a record 45 percent, entering the Top 10 for the first time.

TOP 10 ★
MILK-DRINKING COUNTRIES*

	COUNTRY	ANNUAL CONSUMPTION PER CAPITA	
		PINTS	LITERS
1	Iceland	314.8	149.1
2 =Finland		294.1	139.3
=Ireland		294.1	139.3
4	Norway	244.5	115.8
5	UK	241.7	114.4
6	Sweden	138.6	113.0
7	New Zealand	209.9	99.4
8	US	202.7	96.0
9	Spain	193.3	91.5
10	Switzerland	192.6	91.2

* Those reporting to the International Dairy Federation
Source: *National Dairy Council*

TOP 10 ★
COFFEE-DRINKING COUNTRIES

	COUNTRY	ANNUAL CONSUMPTION PER CAPITA			
		LB	OZ	KG	CUPS*
1	Finland	25	13	11.71	1,756
2	Denmark	21	14	9.57	1,435
3	Norway	20	15	9.52	1,428
4	Sweden	18	10	8.47	1,270
5	Austria	17	11	8.04	1,206
6	Netherlands	17	3	7.82	1,173
7	Germany	15	9	7.07	1,060
8	Switzerland	15	1	6.85	1,027
9	France	11	14	5.39	808
10	Italy	11	5	5.13	772

* Based on 150 cups per 2 lb 3 oz (1 kg)
Source: *International Coffee Organization*

Did You Know? Until the invention of pasteurization, milk-drinkers risked contracting the disease scrofula. It was known as "King's Evil," because it was believed the only cure was to be touched by a king.

World Tourism

TOP 10 ★

TOURIST DESTINATIONS

COUNTRY	TOTAL VISITORS, 1999
1 France	71,400,000
2 Spain	51,958,000
3 US	46,983,000
4 China	37,480,000*
5 Italy	35,839,000
6 UK	25,740,000
7 Mexico	20,216,000
8 Canada	19,556,000
9 Poland	17,940,000
10 Austria	17,630,000

* Includes 10,433,000 vistors to Hong Kong

Source: *World Tourism Organization*

TOP 10 ★

TOURIST EARNING COUNTRIES

COUNTRY	TOTAL RECEIPTS ($), 1999
1 US	73,000,000,000
2 Italy	31,000,000,000
3 Spain	25,179,000,000*
4 France	24,657,000,000*
5 UK	20,972,000,000
6 China	14,099,000,000
7 Austria	11,259,000,000
8 Canada	10,282,000,000
9 Germany	9,570,000,000#
10 Mexico	7,850,000,000

* Estimates based on first nine months

 # Estimates based on first seven months

Source: *World Tourism Organization*

TOP 10 MOST VISITED US STATES AND TERRITORIES

(State/overseas visitors)

1 Florida, 6,067,000   **2** California, 5,972,000
3 New York, 5,285,000   **4** Hawaii, 2,796,000   **5** Nevada, 1,920,000
6 Illinois, 1,256,000   **7** Massachusetts, 1,161,000   **8** Texas, 1,114,000
9 Guam, 1,043,000   **10** = Arizona, 853,000; = New Jersey, 1853,000

Source: *Tourism Industries/International Trade Administration, Department of Commerce*

"FERRIS WHEEL"

Pennsylvania bridge engineer George W. Ferris gave his name to the Ferris wheels that are popular attractions at many of the world's amusement parks. He invented the first one for the Chicago Columbian Exposition of 1893. It had a diameter of 250 ft (76 m), its 36 wooden cars carried up to 60 people, and its 45-ft (14-m) axle was the largest steel object ever forged. Modern versions, such as the BA London Eye, opened in 2000, have improved on Ferris's original.

WHY DO WE SAY?

TOP 10 ★

OLDEST ROLLERCOASTERS*

ROLLERCOASTER/LOCATION		YEAR FOUNDED
1	**Leap-the-Dips**, Lakemont Park, Altoona, PA	1902
2	**Scenic Railway**, Luna Park, Melbourne, Australia	1912
3	**Rutschbanen**, Tivoli, Copenhagen, Denmark	1914
4	**Jack Rabbit**, Clemington Amusement Park, Clemington, NJ	1919
5 =	**Jack Rabbit**, Sea Breeze Park, Rochester, NY	1920
=	**Scenic Railway**, Dreamland, Margate, UK	1920
7 =	**Jack Rabbit**, Kennywood, West Mifflin, PA	1921
=	**Roller Coaster**, Lagoon, Farmington, UT	1921
9 =	**Big Dipper**, Blackpool Pleasure Beach, Blackpool, UK	1923
=	**Thunderhawk**, Dorney Park, Aleentown, PA	1923
=	**Zippin Pippin**, Libertyland, Memphis, TN	1923

* In operation at same location since founded

Leap-the-Dips at Lakemont Park, Altoona, Pennslyvania, was out of operation from 1985 but was restored and reopened in 1999.

IT JUST KEEPS ROLLING ALONG

In operation since 1914, the Rutschbanen in Copenhagen's Tivoli Gardens is Europe's oldest working rollercoaster. The oldest American one predates this by twelve years.

TOP 10 ⭐
FASTEST ROLLERCOASTERS IN THE US

ROLLERCOASTER/ LOCATION/YEAR OPENED	SPEED MPH	KM/H
1 **Superman: The Escape**, Six Flags Magic Mountain, Valencia, CA, 1997	100	161
2 **Millennium Force**, Cedar Point, Sandusky, OH, 2000	92	148
3 **Goliath**, Six Flags Magic Mountain, Valencia, CA, 2000	85	137
4 =**Desperado**, Buffalo Bill's Resort and Casino, Primm, NV, 1994	80	129
=**Steel Phantom**, Kennywood Park, West Mifflin, PA, 1991	80	129
=**Superman: The Ride of Steel**, Six Flags, Darien Lake, NY, 1999	80	129
7 **Son of Beast**, Paramount's Kings Island, Cincinnati, OH, 2000	78	126
8 =**Mamba**, Worlds of Fun, Kansas City, MO, 1998	75	121
=**Steel Force**, Dorney Park, Allentown, PA, 1997	75	121
10 **Wild Thing**, Valleyfair!, Skakopee, MN, 1996	74	119

TOP 10 ⭐
OLDEST AMUSEMENT PARKS

PARK/LOCATION	YEAR FOUNDED
1 **Bakken**, Klampenborg, Denmark	1583
2 **The Prater**, Vienna, Austria	1766
3 **Blackgang Chine Cliff Top Theme Park**, Ventnor, Isle of Wight, UK	1842
4 **Tivoli**, Copenhagen, Denmark	1843
5 **Lake Compounce Amusement Park**, Bristol, CT	1846
6 **Hanayashiki**, Tokyo, Japan	1853
7 **Grand Pier**, Teignmouth, UK	1865
8 **Blackpool Central Pier**, Blackpool, UK	1868
9 **Cedar Point**, Sandusky, OH	1870
10 **Clacton Pier**, Clacton, UK	1871

TOP 10 US AMUSEMENT AND THEME PARKS, 1999

PARK/LOCATION	ESTIMATED ATTENDANCE
1 **The Magic Kingdom***, Lake Buena Vista, FL	15,200,000
2 **Disneyland**, Anaheim, CA	13,450,000
3 **Epcot***, Lake Buena Vista, FL	10,100,000
4 **Disney-MGM Studios***, Lake Buena Vista, FL	8,700,000
5 **Disney's Animal Kingdom***, Lake Buena Vista, FL	8,600,000
6 **Universal Studios Florida**, Orlando, FL	8,100,000
7 **Universal Studios Hollywood**, Universal City, CA	5,100,000
8 **Sea World of Florida**, Orlando, FL	4,700,000
9 **Busch Gardens**, Tampa Bay, FL	3,900,000
10 **Six Flags Great Adventure**, Jackson, NJ	3,800,000

* *Walt Disney World*

Source: Amusement Business

TOP 10 ⭐
COUNTRIES OF ORIGIN OF VISITORS TO THE US

COUNTRY	VISITORS TO THE US, 1998
1 **Canada**	13,421,832
2 **Mexico**	9,276,000
3 **Japan**	4,885,369
4 **UK**	3,974,976
5 **Germany**	1,901,938
6 **France**	1,013,222
7 **Brazil**	909,477
8 **Venezuela**	540,685
9 **Italy**	610,796
10 **South Korea**	364,061

Source: *Tourism Industries/International Trade Administration, Department of Commerce*

The number of inbound Canadian tourists in 1998 actually represented an 11.3 percent drop on the 15,127,000 of the previous year, while those from South Korea plummeted by 51.2 percent, from 746,550.

TOP 10 ⭐
ACTIVITIES BY US TOURISTS

ACTIVITY	% OF US RESIDENT TOURISTS PARTICIPATING, 1998
1 **Shopping**	33
2 **Outdoor**	17
3 **Historical/museums**	15
4 **Beaches**	11
5 **Cultural events/festivals**	10
6 **National/State Parks**	9
7 =**Theme/amusement parks**	8
=**Nightlife/dancing**	8
9 **Gambling**	7
10 **Sports events**	6

Source: Tourism Works for America Report

This survey is of persons taking trips of 50 miles or more from home. Of these, some 40 percent were of 2–3 nights' duration, and 24 percent 4–9 nights; 15 percent of people stayed away for one night, 8 percent for 10 nights or more, and 13 percent did not stay overnight. Golf, tennis, and skiing collectively accounted for just 4 percent of the activities in which US tourists participated.

Background image: **FRANCE**

Did You Know? The first roller coaster, invented by Lemarcus Adna Thompson in 1884, was installed at Coney Island, Brooklyn, New York.

Speed Records

FIRST AMERICAN HOLDERS OF THE LAND SPEED RECORD

	DRIVER*/CAR/LOCATION	DATE	MPH	KM/H
1	William Vanderbilt, *Mors*, Albis, France	Aug 5, 1902	76.08	121.72
2	Henry Ford, *Ford Arrow*, Lake St. Clair, Michigan	Jan 12, 1904	91.37	146.19
3	Fred Marriott, *Stanley Rocket*, Daytona Beach, Florida	Jan 23, 1906	121.57	195.65
4	Barney Oldfield, *Benz*, Daytona Beach, Florida	Mar 16, 1910	131.27	210.03
5	Bob Burman, *Benz*, Daytona Beach, Florida	Apr 23, 1911	141.37	226.19
6	Ralph de Palma, *Packard*, Daytona Beach, Florida	Feb 17, 1919	149.87	239.79
7	Tommy Milton, *Duesenberg*, Daytona Beach, Florida	Apr 27, 1920	156.03	249.64
8	Ray Keech, *White Triplex*, Daytona Beach, Florida	Apr 22, 1928	207.55	332.08
9	Craig Breedlove, *Spirit of America*, Bonneville Salt Flats, Utah	Aug 5, 1963	407.45	651.92
10	Tom Green, *Wingfoot Express*, Bonneville Salt Flats, Utah	Oct 2, 1964	413.20	661.12

* Excluding those who subsequently broke their own records

ICE RACER

In 1904 Henry Ford set the land speed record – although it was actually achieved on ice – on the frozen Lake St. Clair. A former employee of Thomas Edison, Ford (standing) had established the Ford Motor Company the previous year.

FASTEST PRODUCTION MOTORCYCLES

	MAKE/MODEL	MPH	KM/H
1	Suzuki GSX1300R Hayabusa	192	309
2 =	Honda CBR1100XX Blackbird	181	291
=	Honda RC45(m)	181	291
4 =	Harris Yamaha YZR500	180	289
=	Kawasaki ZZR1100 D7	180	289
6	Bimota YB10 Biposto	176	283
7	Suzuki GSX-R1100WP(d)	174	280
8	Suzuki GSX-R750-WV	173	279
9 =	Bimota Furano	173	278
=	Kawasaki ZZR1100 C1	173	278

Since Honda (1940s), Suzuki and Yamaha (1950s), and Kawasaki (1960s) were established as motorcycle manufacturers, their machines have dominated the world's superbike league.

LATEST HOLDERS OF THE MOTORCYCLE SPEED RECORD

	RIDER/MOTORCYCLE	YEAR	MPH	KM/H
1	Dave Campos, Twin 1,491cc Ruxton Harley-Davidson Easyrider	1990	322.15	518.45
2	Donald A. Vesco, Twin 1,016cc Kawasaki Lightning Bolt	1978	318.60	512.73
3	Donald A. Vesco, 1,496cc Yamaha Silver Bird	1975	302.93	487.50
4	Calvin Rayborn, 1,480cc Harley-Davidson	1970	264.96	426.40
5	Calvin Rayborn, 1,480cc Harley-Davidson	1970	254.99	410.37
6	Donald A. Vesco, 700cc Yamaha	1970	251.82	405.25
7	Robert Leppan, 1,298cc Triumph	1966	245.62	395.27
8	William A. Johnson, 667cc Triumph	1962	224.57	361.40
9	Wilhelm Herz, 499cc NSU	1956	210.08	338.08
10	Russell Wright, 998cc Vincent HRD	1955	184.95	297.64

All the records listed here were achieved at the Bonneville Salt Flats, Utah, with the exception of No. 10, which was attained at Christchurch, New Zealand. To break a Fédération Internationale Motorcycliste record, the motorcycle has to cover a measured distance, making two runs within one hour and taking the average of the two. American Motorcycling Association records require a turnaround within two hours. Although all those listed were specially adapted for their record attempts, the two most recent had two engines and were stretched to 21 ft (6.4 m) and 23 ft (7 m) respectively.

Did You Know? The last steam vehicle to hold the land speed record was the Stanley Rocket, in which Fred Marriott achieved 121.57 mph (195.65 km/h) in Daytona Beach, Florida, on Jan 23, 1906.

THE 10 ★
FIRST HOLDERS
OF THE LAND SPEED RECORD

DRIVER/CAR/LOCATION	DATE	MPH	KM/H
1 Gaston de Chasseloup-Laubat, *Jeantaud*, Achères, France	Dec 18, 1898	39.24	62.78
2 Camile Jenatzy, *Jenatzy*, Achères, France	Jan 17, 1899	41.42	66.27
3 Gaston de Chasseloup-Laubat, *Jeantaud*, Achères, France	Jan 17, 1899	43.69	69.90
4 Camile Jenatzy, *Jenatzy*, Achères, France	Jan 27, 1899	49.92	79.37
5 Gaston de Chasseloup-Laubat, *Jeantaud*, Achères, France	Mar 4, 1899	57.60	92.16
6 Camile Jenatzy, *Jenatzy*, Achères, France	Apr 29, 1899	65.79	105.26
7 Leon Serpollet, *Serpollet*, Nice, France	Apr 13, 1902	75.06	120.09
8 William Vanderbilt, *Mors*, Albis, France	Aug 5, 1902	76.08	121.72
9 Henri Fournier, *Mors*, Dourdan, France	Nov 5, 1902	76.60	122.56
10 M. Augières, *Mors*, Dourdan, France	Nov 17, 1902	77.13	123.40

The first official land speed records were all broken within three years, the first six of them by rival French racers Comte Gaston de Chasseloup-Laubat and Camile Jenatzy. Both the *Jeantaud* and the *Jenatzy* were electrically powered.

TOP 10 FASTEST PRODUCTION CARS
(Model/country of manufacture/top speed in mph#/km/h#)*

1 McLaren F1, UK, 240/386
2 Lister Storm, UK, 201/323 **3** Lamborghini Diablo GT, Italy, 200/341 **4** Ferrari 550 Maranello, Italy, 199/320
5 Renault Espace F1, France, 194/312 **6** = Ascari Ecosse, Italy, >190/305; = Pagani Zonda, Italy, >190/305 **8** = Callaway C12, US, 190/305; = Porsche 911 Turbo, Germany, 190/305
10 Aston Martin DB7 Vantage, UK, 185/297

* Fastest of each manufacturer
 # May vary according to specification modifications to meet national legal requirements
Source: Auto Express

THE 10 ★
LATEST HOLDERS
OF THE LAND SPEED RECORD

DRIVER/CAR	DATE	MPH	KM/H
1 Andy Green, *Thrust SSC**	Oct 15, 1997	763.04	1,227.99
2 Richard Noble, *Thrust 2**	Oct 4, 1983	633.47	1,013.47
3 Gary Gabelich, *The Blue Flame*	Oct 23, 1970	622.41	995.85
4 Craig Breedlove, *Spirit of America – Sonic 1*	Nov 15, 1965	600.60	960.96
5 Art Arfons, *Green Monster*	Nov 7, 1965	576.55	922.48
6 Craig Breedlove, *Spirit of America – Sonic 1*	Nov 2, 1965	555.48	888.76
7 Art Arfons, *Green Monster*	Oct 27, 1964	536.71	858.73
8 Craig Breedlove, *Spirit of America*	Oct 15, 1964	526.28	842.04
9 Craig Breedlove, *Spirit of America*	Oct 13, 1964	468.72	749.95
10 Art Arfons, *Green Monster*	Oct 5, 1964	434.02	694.43

* Location, Black Rock Desert, Nevada. All other speeds were achieved at Bonneville Salt Flats, Utah.

TOP 10 PRODUCTION CARS WITH
THE FASTEST 0–60MPH TIMES
(Model/country of manufacture/seconds taken#)*

1 Renault Espace F1, France, 2.8 **2** McLaren F1, UK, 3.2
3 Caterham Superlight R500, UK, 3.5 **4** Porsche 911 Turbo, Germany, 3.6 **5** Lamborghini Diablo GT, Italy, 3.8 **6** Westfield FW400, UK, 4.0 **7** = Ascari Ecosse, Italy, 4.1; = Marcos Mantis, UK, 4.1 **9** = AC Cobra Superblower, UK, 4.2; = Callaway C12, US, 4.2; = TVR Tuscan Speed Six, UK, 4.2

* Fastest of each manufacturer
 # May vary according to specification modifications to meet national legal requirements
Source: Auto Express

RED HOT

One of the fastest cars ever built (with a top speed of 199 mph/320 km/h), the Ferrari 550M (Maranello) has been acclaimed as the best-handling car in the world.

Cars & Road Transportation

FIRST COUNTRIES TO MAKE SEAT BELTS COMPULSORY

	COUNTRY	INTRODUCED
1	Czechoslovakia	Jan 1969
2	Ivory Coast	Jan 1970
3	Japan	Dec 1971
4	Australia	Jan 1972
5	=Brazil	June 1972
	=New Zealand	June 1972
7	Puerto Rico	Jan 1974
8	Spain	Oct 1974
9	Sweden	Jan 1975
10	=Netherlands	June 1975
	=Belgium	June 1975
	=Luxembourg	June 1975

Seat belts, long in use on airplanes, were not designed for use in private cars until the 1950s. Ford was the first manufacturer in Europe to use anchor points, and belts were first installed as standard equipment in Swedish Volvos from 1959.

LIGHT TRUCKS OF 1999 IN THE US

	TRUCK	SALES
1	Ford Pickup	869,004
2	Chevrolet Pickup	636,150
3	Dodge Ram Pickup	428,930
4	Ford Explorer	428,772
5	Ford Ranger	348,358
6	Jeep Grand Cherokee	300,031
7	Dodge Caravan	293,100
8	Chevrolet S-10	233,669
9	Ford Expedition	233,125
10	Chevrolet Blazer	232,140

Source: *Ward's AutoInfoBank*

The Ford F-series was launched on January 16, 1948. Since then, more than 26 million have been produced, over 8 million of which are still on the road. It has been America's bestselling truck every year since 1976 and bestselling vehicle (including cars) since 1981.

MOST COMMON TYPES OF PROPERTY LOST ON THE NEW YORK TRANSIT AUTHORITY, 1997–98

	TYPE
1	Backpacks
2	Radios/Walkmans
3	Eyeglasses
4	Wallets and purses
5	Cameras
6	Keys
7	Cellular phones
8	Watches
9	Inline skates
10	Jewelry

Source: *New York City Transit Authority*

Cellular phones are increasingly among the most mislaid items in New York and internationally.

MOTOR VEHICLE-OWNING COUNTRIES

	COUNTRY	CARS	COMMERCIAL VEHICLES	TOTAL
1	US	134,981,000	65,465,000	200,446,000
2	Japan	44,680,000	22,173,463	66,853,463
3	Germany	40,499,442	3,061,874	43,561,316
4	Italy	30,000,000	2,806,500	32,806,500
5	France	25,100,000	5,195,000	30,295,000
6	UK	24,306,781	3,635,176	27,941,957
7	Russia	13,638,600	9,856,000	23,494,600
8	Spain	14,212,259	3,071,621	17,283,880
9	Canada	13,182,996	3,484,616	16,667,612
10	Brazil	12,000,000	3,160,689	15,160,689
	World total	477,010,289	169,748,819	646,759,108

FRENCH JAM

France has one of the world's highest ratios of cars to people and can claim a record traffic jam of 190 miles (176 km), which occurred between Paris and Lyons.

COUNTRIES PRODUCING THE MOST MOTOR VEHICLES

	COUNTRY	CARS	COMMERCIAL VEHICLES	TOTAL
1	US	5,554,390	6,451,689	12,006,079
2	Japan	8,055,736	1,994,029	10,049,792
3	Germany	5,348,115	378,673	5,726,788
4	France	2,603,021	351,139	2,954,160
5	Spain	2,216,571	609,492	2,826,063
6	Canada	1,122,287	1,050,375	2,172,662
7	UK	1,748,277	232,793	1,981,070
8	South Korea	1,625,125	329,369	1,954,494
9	Italy	1,402,382	290,355	1,692,737
10	China	507,103	1,120,726	1,627,829

Source: *Ward's Motor Vehicle Facts and Figures*

A CAR IS BORN

Japan's car production, which places increasing reliance on advanced robotic technology, closely rivals that of world leader the US.

TOP 10 BESTSELLING CARS OF ALL TIME

	MANUFACTURER/MODEL	FIRST YEAR PRODUCED	ESTIMATED NO. MADE
1	Toyota Corolla	1966	23,000,000
2	Volkswagen Beetle	1937*	21,376,331
3	Lada Riva	1972	19,000,000
4	Volkswagen Golf	1974	18,453,646
5	Ford Model T	1908	16,536,075
6	Nissan Sunny/Pulsar	1966	13,571,100
7 =	Ford Escort/Orion	1967	12,000,000
=	Honda Civic	1972	12,000,000
9	Mazda 323	1977	9,500,000
10	Renault 4	1961	8,100,000

* Original model still produced in Mexico and Brazil

Estimates of manufacturers' output of their bestselling models vary from the vague to the unusually precise: 16,536,075 of the Model T Ford, with 15,007,033 produced in the US and the rest in Canada and the UK in 1908–27.

BESTSELLING CARS OF 1999 IN THE US

	MODEL	1999 SALES
1	Toyota Camry	448,162
2	Honda Accord	404,192
3	Ford Taurus	368,327
4	Honda Civic	318,308
5	Ford Escort	260,486
6	Toyota Corolla	249,128
7	Pontiac Grand Am	234,936
8	Chevrolet Malibu	218,540
9	Saturn S-series	207,977
10	Ford Mustang	166,915

Source: *Ward's AutoInfoBank*

THE CAR IN FRONT ...

The Toyota Motor Company was started in 1937, in Koromo, Japan, by Kiichiro Toyoda. Its Corolla model became the world's bestselling car.

COR 163

Road Accidents & Disasters

THE 10 ★
COUNTRIES WITH THE HIGHEST NUMBER OF ROAD DEATHS

	COUNTRY	TOTAL DEATHS*
1	US	41,967
2	Thailand	15,176
3	South Korea	13,343
4	Japan	11,254
5	Germany	8,549
6	France	8,444
7	Poland	7,310
8	Brazil	6,759
9	Turkey	6,735
10	Italy	6,724

In latest year for which figures are available

Based on the ratio of fatalities to distance traveled, road deaths in the US have declined markedly from 24.1 deaths per 100 million vehicle miles traveled in 1921, to under 1.6 today.

THE 10 SAFEST CAR COLORS
(Color/light reflection percentage)

❶ White, 84.0 ❷ Cream, 68.8 ❸ Ivory, 66.7 ❹ Light pink, 66.5 ❺ Yellow, 57.0 ❻ Pink, 51.6 ❼ = Buff, 51.5; = Light gray, 51.5 ❾ Light green, 45.2 ❿ Aluminum gray, 41.0

Source: *Mansell Color Company Inc., published by the National Safety Council*

DRIVEN TO DESTRUCTION

In an average year in the US, over 6 million motor vehicle accidents are reported, 4 million involving property and 3 million resulting in injuries.

THE 10 ★
COUNTRIES WITH THE MOST DEATHS BY MOTOR ACCIDENTS

	COUNTRY	DEATH RATE PER 100,000 POPULATION
1	South Africa	99.4
2	Latvia	35.3
3	South Korea	33.1
4	Estonia	26.7
5	Russia	23.6
6	Portugal	22.8
7	Lithuania	22.1
8	Greece	21.3
9	Venezuela	20.7
10=	El Salvador	20.3
=	Kuwait	20.3

Source: *United Nations*

THE 10 ★
STATES WITH THE MOST MOTOR VEHICLE FATALITIES

	STATE	TOTAL FATALITIES (1998)
1	Texas	3,577
2	California	3,494
3	Florida	2,824
4	North Carolina	1,596
5	Georgia	1,569
6	New York	1,498
7	Pennsylvania	1,481
8	Ohio	1,422
9	Illinois	1,393
10	Michigan	1,367

ACCIDENT BLACKSPOT

Black cars are reputed to be the least safe because they are less visible at night, but types of vehicle and age and experience of drivers are equally salient factors.

SEARCHING FOR SURVIVORS

The 1995 underground gas explosion at Taegu, South Korea, destroyed scores of vehicles, leaving 110 dead and 250 injured.

THE 10 ★
WORST MOTOR VEHICLE AND ROAD DISASTERS

LOCATION/DATE/INCIDENT	NO. KILLED

1 Afghanistan, Nov 3, 1982 — over 2,000
Following a collision with a Soviet army truck, a gasoline tanker exploded in the 1.7-mile (2.7-km) Salang Tunnel. Some authorities have put the death toll from the explosion, fire, and fumes as high as 3,000.

2 Colombia, Aug 7, 1956 — 1,200
Seven army ammunition trucks exploded at night in the center of Cali, destroying eight city blocks, including a barracks where 500 soldiers were sleeping.

3 Thailand, Feb 15, 1990 — over 150
A dynamite truck exploded.

4 Nepal, Nov 23, 1974 — 148
Hindu pilgrims were killed when a suspension bridge over the Mahahali River collapsed.

5 Egypt, Aug 9, 1973 — 127
A bus drove into an irrigation canal.

6 Togo, Dec 6, 1965 — over 125
Two trucks collided with dancers during a festival at Sotouboua.

7 Spain, July 11, 1978 — over 120
A liquid gas tanker exploded in a campsite at San Carlos de la Rapita.

8 South Korea, Apr 28, 1995 — 110
An undergound explosion destroyed vehicles and caused about 100 cars and buses to plunge into the pit it created.

9 =The Gambia, Nov 12, 1992 — c.100
After brake failure, a bus carrying passengers to a dock plunged into a river.

=Kenya, early Dec 1992 — c.100
A bus carrying 112 people skidded, hit a bridge, and plunged into a river.

The worst motor racing accident occurred on June 13, 1955, at Le Mans, France, when Pierre Levegh's Mercedes-Benz 300 SLR went out of control, hit a wall, and exploded in mid-air, showering wreckage into the crowd and killing 82. The worst accident involving a single car was on Dec 17, 1956: 12 people were killed when their car was hit by a train near Phoenix, Arizona.

THE 10 WORST YEARS FOR FATAL MOTOR VEHICLE ACCIDENTS IN THE US

(Year/fatalities*)

1 1972, 54,589 **2** 1973, 54,052 **3** 1969, 53,543 **4** 1968, 52,725 **5** 1970, 52,627
6 1971, 52,542 **7** 1979, 51,093 **8** 1980, 51,091 **9** 1966, 50,894 **10** 1967, 50,724

* Traffic fatalities occurring within 30 days of accident

THE 10 ★
MOST VULNERABLE AGES FOR ROAD FATALITIES IN THE US

	AGE GROUP	1998 DEATHS	POPULATION	DEATH RATE PER 100,000
1	16–20	5,727	19,420,000	29.48
2	21–24	3,769	13,892,000	27.13
3	74+	4,137	16,006,000	25.85
4	25–34	6,928	38,774,000	17.87
5	65–74	3,132	18,395,000	17.03
6	35–44	6,696	44,520,000	15.04
7	55–64	3,202	22,676,000	14.12
8	45–54	4,785	34,585,000	13.84
9	10–15	1,437	23,135,000	6.21
10	5–9	796	19,921,000	4.00

Source: *National Highway Traffic Safety Administration*

THE 10 ★
MOST COMMON COLLISIONS IN THE US

	OBJECT OR EVENT	COLLISIONS (1998)
1	Another vehicle, at an angle	2,266,000
2	Another vehicle, rear end	1,872,000
3	Parked motor vehicle	323,000
4	Another vehicle, sideswipe	291,000
5	Animal	260,000
6	Culvert/curb/ditch	193,000
7	Pole or post	173,000
8	Shrubbery/tree	130,000
9	Rollover	112,000
10	Guard rail	100,000

Following on from this Top 10, the next most common event is a head-on collision, with 87,000 cases. Relatively uncommon incidents in 1998 were crashes into bridges (16,000) and collisions with trains (2,000).

On what did Henry Ford set the land speed record in 1904?
see p.226 for the answer

A A beach
B A racetrack
C A frozen lake

Rail Transportation

Amtrak

TOP 10 ★
LONGEST RAIL NETWORKS

	LOCATION	TOTAL RAIL LENGTH	
		MILES	KM
1	US	149,129	240,000
2	Russia	93,205	150,000
3	Canada	42,112	67,773
4	China	40,327	64,900
5	India	39,093	62,915
6	Germany	28,769	46,300
7	Australia	23,962	38,563
8	Argentina	23,506	37,830
9	France	19,901	32,027
10	Mexico	19,292	31,048

RAILROAD

Although the US still has the longest rail network in the world, US rail mileage has declined considerably since its 1916 peak of 254,000 miles (408,773 km).

THE 10 ★
WORST RAIL DISASTERS IN THE US

LOCATION/DATE/INCIDENT	NO. KILLED

1 =Chatsworth, Illinois, Aug 10, 1887 — 101
A trestle bridge caught fire and collapsed as the Toledo, Peoria & Western train was passing over. In the crash, 81 people were killed immediately and a further 20 died later, while as many as 372 were injured.

=Nashville, Tennessee, July 9, 1918 — 101
On the Nashville, Chattanooga, and St. Louis Railway, a head-on collision resulted in a deathtoll that remains equal to the worst in US history, with an additional 171 people injured.

3 Brooklyn, New York, Nov 1, 1918 — 97
A subway train was derailed in the Malbone Street tunnel.

4 =Eden, Colorado, Aug 7, 1904 — 96
A bridge washed away during a flood smashed Steele's Hollow Bridge as the World's Fair Express was crossing.

=Wellington, Washington, Mar 1, 1910 — 96
On February 25, two electric trains were held up by a snowdrift that blocked Cascade Tunnel, forcing the passengers to camp in the cars. At dawn on March 1st, an avalanche swept them into a canyon.

6 =Bolivar, Texas, Sep 8, 1900 — 85
A train traveling from Beaumont encountered the hurricane that destroyed Galveston, killing 6,000. Attempts to load the train onto a ferry were abandoned, and it off set back to Beaumont, but was destroyed by the storm.

=Woodbridge, New Jersey, Feb 6, 1951 — 85
A Pennsylvania Railroad's Broker Special, traveling at excessive speed, passed over a temporary trestle, causing it to collapse. The rear cars of the train fell off the trestle, injuring a further 330.

8 =Ashtabula, Ohio, Dec 29, 1876 — 84
A bridge collapsed in a snow storm and the Lake Shore train fell into the Ashtabula River. The death toll may have been as high as 92.

9 =Frankford Junction, Pennsylvania, Sep 6, 1943 — 79
Pennsylvania's worst railroad accident occurred when a wheel locked and the train was derailed, with 100 injured.

=Richmond Hill, New York, Nov 22, 1950 — 79
A Long Island Railroad commuter train rammed into the rear of another, leaving 79 dead and 352 injured.

Did You Know? The world's first passenger rail fatality occurred on the Stockton and Darlington Railway on March 19, 1828, when a boiler explosion killed the driver, John Gillespie.

TOP 10 ★
FASTEST RAIL JOURNEYS*

JOURNEY/COUNTRY/TRAIN	DISTANCE		SPEED	
	MILES	KM	MPH	KM/H
1 **Hiroshima–Kokura**, Japan, Nozomi 500	119.3	192.0	162.7	261.8
2 **Massy–St. Pierre des Corps**, France, 7 TGV	128.5	206.9	157.4	253.3
3 **Brussels–Paris**, Belgium/France, Thalys 9342	194.7	313.4	140.7	226.5
4 **Madrid–Seville**, Spain, 5 AVE	292.4	470.5	129.9	209.1
5 **Karlsruhe–Mannheim**, Germany, 2 trains	44.1	71.0	120.4	193.8
6 **London–York**, UK, 1 IC225	188.5	303.4	112.0	180.2
7 **Skövde–Södertälje**, Sweden, 3 X2000	172.1	277.0	106.4	171.3
8 **Piacenza–Parma**, Italy, ES 9325	35.4	57.0	106.2	171.0
9 **North Philadelphia–Newark Penn**, US, 1 NE Direct	76.0	122.4	95.0	153.0
10 **Salo–Karjaa**, Finland, S220 132	33.0	53.1	94.3	151.7

* Fastest journey for each country; all those in the Top 10 have other similarly or equally fast services   Source: Railway Gazette International

THE 10 FIRST CITIES IN NORTH AMERICA TO HAVE SUBWAY SYSTEMS
(City/year opened)

1 **New York**, 1867　2 **Chicago**, 1892
3 **Boston**, 1901　4 **Philadelphia**, 1908　5 **Toronto**, 1954
6 **Cleveland**, 1955　7 **Montreal**, 1966　8 **San Francisco**, 1972
9 **Washington, D.C.**, 1976
10 **Atlanta**, 1979

TOP 10 ★
BUSIEST UNDERGROUND RAILROAD NETWORKS

CITY	YEAR OPENED	TRACK LENGTH MILES	KM	STATIONS	PASSENGERS PER ANNUM
1 **Moscow**	1935	153	243.6	150	3,183,900,000
2 **Tokyo**	1927	106	169.1	154	2,112,700,000
3 **Mexico City**	1969	112	177.7	154	1,422,600,000
4 **Seoul**	1974	84	133.0	112	1,354,000,000
5 **Paris**	1900	127	201.4	372	1,170,000,000
6 **New York**	1867	249	398.0	469	1,100,000,000
7 **Osaka**	1933	66	105.8	99	988,600,000
8 **St. Petersburg**	1955	58	91.7	50	850,000,000
9 **Hong Kong**	1979	27	43.2	38	804,000,000
10 **London**	1863	247	392.0	245	784,000,000

THE 10 ★
WORST RAIL DISASTERS

LOCATION/DATE/INCIDENT	NO. KILLED

1 **Bagmati River**, India, June 6, 1981 — *c.*800
The carriages of a train traveling from Samastipur to Banmukhi in Bihar plunged off a bridge over the Bagmati River, near Mansi, when the driver braked, apparently to avoid hitting a sacred cow. Although the official death toll was said to have been 268, many authorities have claimed that the train was so massively overcrowded that the actual figure was in excess of 800, making it probably the worst rail disaster of all time.

2 **Chelyabinsk**, Russia, June 3, 1989 — up to 800
Two passenger trains, laden with vacationers heading to and from Black Sea resorts, were destroyed when liquid gas from a nearby pipeline exploded.

3 **Guadalajara**, Mexico, Jan 18, 1915 — over 600
A train derailed on a steep incline, but political strife in the country meant that full details of the disaster were suppressed.

4 **Modane**, France, Dec 12, 1917 — 573
A troop-carrying train ran out of control and was derailed. It has been claimed that the train was overloaded and that as many as 1,000 may have died.

5 **Balvano**, Italy, Mar 2, 1944 — 521
A heavily laden train stalled in the Armi Tunnel, and many passengers were asphyxiated. Like the disaster at Torre (No. 6), wartime secrecy prevented full details from being published.

6 **Torre**, Spain, Jan 3, 1944 — over 500
A double collision and fire in a tunnel resulted in many deaths – some have put the total as high as 800.

7 **Awash**, Ethiopia, Jan 13, 1985 — 428
A derailment hurled a train laden with some 1,000 passengers into a ravine.

8 **Cireau**, Romania, Jan 7, 1917 — 374
An overcrowded passenger train crashed into a military train and was derailed.

9 **Quipungo**, Angola, May 31, 1993 — 355
A trail was derailed by UNITA guerrilla action.

10 **Sangi**, Pakistan, Jan 4, 1990 — 306
A train was diverted on to the wrong line, resulting in a fatal collision.

PARIS METRO
Now 100 years old, the Paris Metro – with its distinctive Art Deco entrances – is among the world's longest and most used underground railroad systems.

Water Transportation

TOP 10 ★
BUSIEST PORTS*
PORT/LOCATION

1	**Hong Kong**, China	
2	**Singapore**	
3	**Kaohsiung**, Taiwan	
4	**Rotterdam**, Netherlands	
5	**Pusan**, South Korea	
6	**New York/New Jersey**, USA	
7	**Long Beach**, USA	
8	**Hamburg**, Germany	
9	**Antwerp**, Belgium	
10	**Los Angeles**, USA	

* Handling the most TEUs (Twenty-ft Equivalent Units)

Source: *International Association of Ports & Harbors*

TOP 10 ★
LARGEST CRUISE SHIPS

SHIP/YEAR BUILT/ COUNTRY	PASSENGER CAPACITY	GROSS TONNAGE
1 =*Explorer of the Seas*, 2000, Finland	3,840	142,000
=*Voyager of the Seas*, 1999, Finland	3,840	142,000
3 *Grand Princess*, 1998, Italy	3,300	108,806
4 *Carnival Triumph*, 1999, Italy	3,473	101,672
5 *Carnival Destiny*, 1996, Italy	3,336	101,353
6 *Disney Magic*, 1998, Italy	2,500	83,338
7 *Disney Wonder*, 1999, Italy	6,000	83,308
8 *Rhapsody of the Seas*, 1997, France	2,416	78,491
9 *Vision of the Seas*, 1995, Italy	2,416	78,340
10 *Sun Princess*, 1995, Italy	2,272	77,441

Source: *Lloyd's Register of Shipping, MIPG/PPMS*

PORT OF CALL

Singapore's substantial and well-protected harbor has contributed to the city-state's status as the most important commercial center in Southeast Asia.

"WOMEN AND CHILDREN FIRST"

The movie *Titanic* brought home to many the significance of a ship built with insufficient lifeboats, requiring choices to be made as to who would have a seat to safety and who would have to take their chances in the sea. The first such incident involved the sinking of the *Birkenhead* off South Africa in 1852. The 20 women and children on board were placed in the only three lifeboats that were serviceable, while the British soldiers remained on deck, 445 of them drowning in the incident. This subsequently became a naval tradition known to all as the "Birkenhead Drill."

WHY DO WE SAY ?

FLOATING GIANT

One of the world's largest cruise ships, the 1997 French-built Rhapsody of the Seas is also one of the longest afloat, at 915 ft 2 in (278.94 m).

THE 10 ★
WORST PASSENGER FERRY DISASTERS OF THE 20TH CENTURY

	FERRY/LOCATION/DATE	NO. KILLED
1	**Dona Paz**, Philippines, Dec 20, 1987	up to 3,000
2	**Neptune**, Haiti, Feb 17, 1992	1,800
3	**Toya Maru**, Japan, Sep 26, 1954	1,172
4	**Don Juan**, Philippines, Apr 22, 1980	over 1,000
5	**Estonia**, Baltic Sea, Sep 28, 1994	909
6	**Samia**, Bangladesh, May 25, 1986	600
7	**MV Bukoba**, Lake Victoria, Tanzania, May 21, 1996	549
8	**Salem Express**, Egypt, Dec 14, 1991	480
9	**Tampomas II**, Indonesia, Jan 27, 1981	431
10	**Nam Yung Ho**, South Korea, Dec 15, 1970	323

The *Dona Paz* sank in the Tabias Strait, Philippines, after the ferry was struck by the oil tanker *MV Victor*. The loss of life may have been much higher than the official figure (up to 4,386 has been suggested by some authorities).

THE 10 ★
WORST OIL TANKER SPILLS

TANKER(S)/LOCATION/DATE	APPROX. SPILLAGE TONS
1 *Atlantic Empress* and *Aegean Captain*, Trinidad, July 19, 1979	331,000
2 *Castillio de Bellver*, Cape Town, South Africa, Aug 6, 1983	281,000
3 *Olympic Bravery*, Ushant, France, Jan 24, 1976	276,000
4 *Showa-Maru*, Malacca, Malaya, June 7, 1975	261,000
5 *Amoco Cadiz*, Finistère, France, Mar 16, 1978	246,000
6 *Odyssey*, Atlantic, off Canada, Nov 10, 1988	154,000
7 *Torrey Canyon*, Isles of Scilly, UK, Mar 18, 1967	132,000
8 *Sea Star*, Gulf of Oman, Dec 19, 1972	127,000
9 *Irenes Serenada*, Pilos, Greece, Feb 23, 1980	112,000
10 *Urquiola*, Corunna, Spain, May 12, 1976	111,000

THE 10 ★
WORST MARINE DISASTERS OF THE 20TH CENTURY

LOCATION/DATE/INCIDENT	APPROX. NO. KILLED
1 **Off Gdansk**, Poland, Jan 30, 1945	up to 7,800

The German liner Wilhelm Gustloff, *crowded with refugees, was torpedoed by a Soviet submarine, S-13. The precise death toll remains uncertain, but is in the range of 5,348 to 7,800.*

2 **Off Cape Rixhöft** (Rozeewie), Poland, Apr 16, 1945	6,800

The German ship Goya, *carrying evacuees from Gdansk, was torpedoed in the Baltic.*

3 **Off Yingkow**, China, Nov 1947	over 6,000

The boilers of an unidentified Chinese troop ship, carrying Nationalist soldiers from Manchuria, exploded, detonating ammunition.

4 **Lübeck**, Germany, May 3, 1945	5,000

The German ship Cap Arcona, *carrying concentration camp survivors, was bombed and sunk by British aircraft.*

5 **Off St. Nazaire**, France, June 17, 1940	3,050

The British troop ship Lancastria *sank.*

6 **Off Stolpmünde** (Ustka), Poland, Feb 9, 1945	3,000

German war-wounded and refugees were lost when the Steuben *was torpedoed by the same Russian submarine that had sunk the* Wilhelm Gustloff.

LOCATION/DATE/INCIDENT	APPROX. NO. KILLED
7 **Tabias Strait**, Philippines, Dec 20, 1987	up to 3,000

The ferry Dona Paz *was struck by oil tanker MV Victor.*

8 **Woosung**, China, Dec 3, 1948	over 2,750

The overloaded steamship Kiangya, *carrying refugees, struck a Japanese mine.*

9 **Lübeck**, Germany, May 3, 1945	2,750

The refugee ship Thielbeck *sank during the British bombardment of Lübeck harbor in the closing weeks of World War II.*

10 **South Atlantic**, Sep 12, 1942	2,279

The British passenger vessel Laconia, *carrying Italian prisoners-of-war, was sunk by German U-boat U-156.*

Other disasters occurring during wartime and resulting in losses of more than 1,000 include the explosion of *Mont Blanc*, a French ammunition ship, following its collision with the Belgian steamer *Imo* on December 6, 1917, with 1,635 lost; the sinking of the British cruiser *HMS Hood* by the German battleship *Bismarck* on May 24, 1941, with 1,418 killed; and the torpedoing by German submarine *U-20* of the *Lusitania*, a British passenger liner, on May 7, 1915, with the loss of 1,198 civilians.

ENVIRONMENTAL DISASTER
The 1979 collision of the Atlantic Empress and the Aegean Captain off Trinidad resulted in the worst oil spill of all time.

Air Records

FIRST TRANSATLANTIC FLIGHTS

AIRCRAFT/CREW/COUNTRY	CROSSING	DATE*
1 **US Navy/Curtiss flying boat** *NC-4*, Lt.-Cdr. Albert Cushing Read and crew of five, US	Trepassy Harbor, Newfoundland, to Lisbon, Portugal	May 16–27, 1919
2 **Twin Rolls-Royce-engined converted Vickers Vimy bomber**#, Capt. John Alcock and Lt. Arthur Whitten Brown, UK	St. John's, Newfoundland, to Galway, Ireland	June 14–15, 1919
3 **British** *R-34* **airship**+, Maj. George Herbert Scott and crew of 30, UK	East Fortune, Scotland, to Roosevelt Field, New York	July 2–6, 1919
4 **Fairey IIID seaplane** *Santa Cruz*, Adm. Gago Coutinho and Cdr. Sacadura Cabral, Portugal	Lisbon, Portugal, to Recife, Brazil	Mar 30–June 5, 1922
5 **Two Douglas seaplanes,** *Chicago* **and** *New Orleans*, Lt. Lowell H. Smith and Leslie P. Arnold/ Erik Nelson and John Harding, US	Orkneys, Scotland, to Labrador, Canada	Aug 2–31, 1924
6 *Los Angeles*, **a renamed German-built** *ZR 3* **airship**, Dr. Hugo Eckener, with 31 passengers and crew, Germany	Friedrichshafen, Germany, to Lakehurst, New Jersey	Oct 12–15, 1924
7 *Plus Ultra*, **a Dornier Wal twin-engined flying boat**, Capt. Julio Ruiz and crew, Spain	Huelva, Spain, to Recife, Brazil	Jan 22–Feb 10, 1926
8 *Santa Maria*, **a Savoia-Marchetti S.55 flying boat**, Francesco Marquis de Pinedo, Capt. Carlo del Prete, and Lt. Vitale Zacchetti, Italy	Cagliari, Sardinia, to Recife, Brazil	Feb 8–24, 1927
9 **Dornier Wal flying boat**, Sarmento de Beires and Jorge de Castilho, Portugal	Lisbon, Portugal, to Natal, Brazil	Mar 16–17, 1927
10 **Savoia-Marchetti flying boat**, João De Barros and crew, Brazil	Genoa, Italy, to Natal, Brazil	Apr 28–May 14, 1927

* *All dates refer to the actual Atlantic legs of the journeys; some started earlier and ended beyond their first transatlantic landfalls* # *First nonstop flight* + *First east–west flight*

FIRST PEOPLE TO FLY IN HEAVIER-THAN-AIR AIRCRAFT

PILOT/COUNTRY/AIRCRAFT	DATE
1 **Orville Wright**, US, *Wright Flyer I*	Dec 17, 1903
2 **Wilbur Wright**, US, *Wright Flyer I*	Dec 17, 1903
3 **Alberto Santos-Dumont**, Brazil, *No. 14-bis*	Oct 23, 1906
4 **Charles Voisin**, France, *Voisin-Delagrange I*	Mar 30, 1907
5 **Henri Farman**, UK, later France, *Voisin-Farman I-bis*	Oct 7, 1907
6 **Léon Delagrange**, France, *Voisin-Delagrange I*	Nov 5, 1907
7 **Robert Esnault-Pelterie**, France, *REP No. 1*	Nov 16, 1907
8 **Charles W. Furnas***, US, *Wright Flyer III*	May 14, 1908
9 **Louis Blériot**, France, *Blériot VIII*	June 29, 1908
10 **Glenn Hammond Curtiss**, US, *AEA June Bug*	July 4, 1908

* *As a passenger in a plane piloted by Wilbur Wright, Furnas was the first airplane passenger in the US.*

"MACH NUMBER"

A Mach number is a unit of speed, related to the speed of sound, that varies according to such factors as altitude and the moisture content of the air. In dry air at sea level, Mach 1 is 763.67 mph (1,229 km/h). The land speed record set in 1997 was undertaken early in the morning, when high humidity and a cool temperature lower the speed of sound. The word Mach derives from the name of Ernst Mach (1838–1916), an Austrian physicist and philosopher.

WHY DO WE SAY?

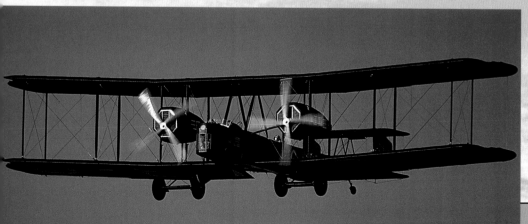

COAST TO COAST

A previous transatlantic crossing had been made as a series of "hops," but Alcock and Brown's Vickers Vimy flight of 1919 was the first nonstop crossing.

TOP 10 ★
FASTEST X-15 FLIGHTS

	PILOT/DATE	MACH*	SPEED MPH	KM/H
1	William J. Knight, Oct 3, 1967	6.70	4,520	7,274
2	William J. Knight, Nov 18, 1966	6.33	4,261	6,857
3	Joseph A. Walker, June 27, 1962	5.92	4,105	6,606
4	Robert M. White, Nov 9, 1961	6.04	4,094	6,589
5	Robert A. Rushworth, Dec 5, 1963	6.06	4,018	6,466
6	Neil A. Armstrong, June 26, 1962	5.74	3,989	6,420
7	John B. McKay, June 22, 1965	5.64	3,938	6,388
8	Robert A. Rushworth, July 18, 1963	5.63	3,925	6,317
9	Joseph A. Walker, June 25, 1963	5.51	3,911	6,294
10	William H. Dana, Oct 4, 1967	5.53	3,910	6,293

* Mach no. varies with altitude – the list is ranked on actual speed

FASTEST AIRCRAFT

The speeds attained by the rocket-powered X-15 and X-15A-2 aircraft remain the greatest by piloted vehicles in the Earth's atmosphere. They were air-launched by being released from B-52 bombers, and so do not qualify for the official air speed record, for which aircraft must take off and land under their own power. An X-15 also set an unofficial altitude record when, on August 22, 1963, Joseph A. Walker piloted one to 354,200 ft (107,960 m) – some 67 miles (108 km) high. The pioneering work of the pilots of the X-15s laid the foundations of US spaceflight.

SNAP SHOTS

U.S. AIR FORC

THE 10 ★
FIRST FLIGHTS OF MORE THAN ONE HOUR

	PILOT	DURATION	DATE		PILOT	DURATION	DATE
1	Orville Wright	1:2:15	Sep 9, 1908	7	Wilbur Wright*	1:4:26	Oct 6, 1908
2	Orville Wright	1:5:52	Sep 10, 1908	8	Wilbur Wright	1:9:45	Oct 10, 1908
3	Orville Wright	1:10:0	Sep 11, 1908	9	Wilbur Wright	1:54:53	Dec 18, 1908
4	Orville Wright	1:15:20	Sep 12, 1908	10	Wilbur Wright	2:20:23	Dec 31, 1908
5	Wilbur Wright	1:31:25	Sep 21, 1908				
6	Wilbur Wright	1:7:24	Sep 28, 1908				

* First ever flight of more than one hour with a passenger (M. A. Fordyce)

THE 10 ★
FIRST ROCKET AND JET AIRCRAFT

	AIRCRAFT/COUNTRY	FIRST FLIGHT
1	Heinkel He 176*, Germany	June 20, 1939
2	Heinkel He 178, Germany	Aug 27, 1939
3	DFS 194*, Germany	Aug 1940#
4	Caproni-Campini N-1, Italy	Aug 28, 1940
5	Heinkel He 280V-1, Germany	Apr 2, 1941
6	Gloster E.28/39, UK	May 15, 1941
7	Messerschmitt Me 163 Komet*, Germany	Aug 13, 1941
8	Messerschmitt Me 262V-3, Germany	July 18, 1942
9	Bell XP-59A Airacomet, US	Oct 1, 1942
10	Gloster Meteor F Mk 1, UK	Mar 5, 1943

* Rocket-powered   # Precise date unknown

TOP 10 ★
BIGGEST AIRSHIPS EVER BUILT

	AIRSHIP	COUNTRY	YEAR	VOLUME CU FT	CU M	LENGTH FT	M
1=	Hindenburg	Germany	1936	7,062,934	200,000	804	245
=	Graf Zeppelin II	Germany	1938	7,062,934	200,000	804	245
3=	Akron	US	1931	6,500,000	184,060	785	239
=	Macon	US	1933	6,500,000	184,060	785	239
5	R101	UK	1930	5,500,000	155,744	777	237
6	Graf Zeppelin	Germany	1928	3,708,040	105,000	776	237
7	L72	Germany	1920	2,419,055	68,500	743	226
8	R100	UK	1929	5,500,000	155,743	709	216
9	R38	UK*	1921	2,724,000	77,136	699	213
10=	L70	Germany	1918	2,418,700	62,200	694	212
=	L71	Germany	1918	2,418,700	62,200	694	212

* UK-built, but sold to US Navy

The giant airships in this list ultimately suffered unfortunate fates: the *Hindenburg*, *Akron*, *Macon*, *R101*, *L72*, and *R38* crashed, the *L70* was shot down, and the remainder were broken up for scrap.

Background image: HEINKEL HE 178

In whch incident did 36 people die in the US in 1937?
see p.238 for the answer

A *Hindenburg* explosion
B Airplane crash
C Baseball stand collapse

Air Transportation

THE 10 ★
WORST AIRSHIP DISASTERS

LOCATION/DATE/INCIDENT	NO. KILLED
1 Off the Atlantic coast, US, Apr 4, 1933	73
US Navy airship Akron crashed into the sea in a storm, leaving only three survivors in the world's worst airship tragedy.	
2 Over the Mediterranean, Dec 21, 1923	52
French airship Dixmude is assumed to have been struck by lightning and to have broken up and crashed into the sea. Wreckage, believed to be from the airship, was found off Sicily 10 years later.	
3 Near Beauvais, France, Oct 5, 1930	50
British airship R101 crashed into a hillside leaving 48 dead, with two dying later, and six survivors.	
4 Off the coast near Hull, UK, Aug 24, 1921	44
Airship R38, sold by the British government to the US and renamed USN ZR-2, broke in two on a training and test flight.	
5 Lakehurst, New Jersey, May 6, 1937	36
German Zeppelin Hindenburg caught fire when mooring.	
6 Hampton Roads, Virginia, Feb 21, 1922	34
Roma, an Italian airship bought by the US Army, crashed, killing all but 11 men on board.	
7 Berlin, Germany, Oct 17, 1913	28
German airship LZ18 crashed after engine failure during a test flight at Berlin-Johannisthal.	
8 Baltic Sea, Mar 30, 1917	23
German airship SL9 was struck by lightning on a flight from Seerappen to Seddin and crashed into the sea.	
9 Mouth of the Elbe River, Germany, Sep 3, 1915	19
German airship L10 was struck by lightning and plunged into the sea.	
10=Off Heligoland, Sep 9, 1913	14
German Navy airship L1 crashed into the sea, leaving six survivors.	
=Caldwell, Ohio, Sep 3, 1925	14
US dirigible Shenandoah, the first airship built in the US and the first to use safe helium instead of inflammable hydrogen, broke up in a storm, scattering sections over a large area of the Ohio countryside.	

THE 10 ★
WORST AIR DISASTERS CAUSED BY HIJACKINGS AND BOMBS

LOCATION/DATE/INCIDENT	NO. KILLED
1 Off the Irish coast, June 23, 1985	329
An Air India Boeing 747, on a flight from Vancouver to Delhi, exploded in midair, perhaps as a result of a terrorist bomb, resulting in the worst-ever air disaster over water.	
2 Lockerbie, Scotland, Dec 21, 1988	270
(See Worst Air Disasters, No. 10)	
3 Tenere Desert, Niger, Sep 19, 1989	170
A Union de Transports Ariens DC-10, flying out of Ndjamena, Chad, exploded over Niger. French investigators implicated Libyan and Syrian terrorists.	
4 Baiyun Airport, China, Oct 2, 1990	132
A Xiamen Airlines Boeing 737 was hijacked in flight and, during an enforced landing, crashed into a taxiing 757.	
5 Comoro Islands, Indian Ocean, Nov 23, 1996	127
An Ethiopian Airlines Boeing 767 was hijacked and ditched in the sea when it ran out of fuel.	
6 Andaman Sea, off Myanmar (Burma), Nov 29, 1987	115
A Korean Air Boeing 707 exploded in midair. Two North Korean terrorists were captured, one of whom committed suicide, while the other was sentenced to death but later pardoned.	
7 Near Abu Dhabi, United Arab Emirates, Sep 23, 1983	111
A Gulf Air Boeing 737 exploded as it prepared to land. Evidence indicated that the explosion had been caused by a bomb in the cargo hold.	
8 Near El Dorado Airport, Bogota, Colombia, Nov 27, 1989	110
An AVIANCA Boeing 727 exploded soon after takeoff in a drug cartel-related bombing.	
9 Near Johor Baharu, Malaysia, Dec 4, 1977	100
A Malaysian Airline System Boeing 737 plunged to earth and exploded. Investigators concluded that the pilots had been shot.	
10 Near Kefallinia, Greece, Sep 8, 1974	88
A Trans World Airlines Boeing 707 plunged into the Ionian Sea after an explosion resulted in loss of control.	

"BLACK BOX"
During World War II, the British Royal Air Force slang term for the radar apparatus that aided navigators and bomb-aimers was "black box," the mystery and secrecy surrounding this invention emphasized by its color. The name was later applied to the flight data recorder on a modern airliner, the device that records all the aircraft's principal actions. In fact, to make them easier to find after a crash, black boxes are now customarily painted a luminous orange.

WHY DO WE SAY?

FIERY FINALE
Astonishingly, 61 of the 97 people on board the Hindenburg survived its explosion, but the awesome and terrible images of the catastrophe ended the airship era.

Background image: **CHARLES DE GAULLE AIRPORT, PARIS, FRANCE**

TOP 10 ★
BUSIEST INTERNATIONAL AIRPORTS

	AIRPORT/LOCATION	PASSENGERS PER ANNUM
1	**London Heathrow**, London, UK	50,612,000
2	**Frankfurt**, Frankfurt, Germany	32,333,000
3	**Charles de Gaulle**, Paris, France	31,549,000
4	**Schiphol**, Amsterdam, Netherlands	30,832,000
5	**Hong Kong**, Hong Kong, China	28,316,000
6	**London Gatwick**, Gatwick, UK	24,835,000
7	**Singapore International**, Singapore	23,799,000
8	**New Tokyo International (Narita)**, Tokyo, Japan	22,941,000
9	**J. F. Kennedy International**, New York, US	17,378,000
10	**Zurich**, Zurich, Switzerland	16,747,000

Source: *International Civil Aviation Organization*

In addition to New York's JFK, only six airports in the US handle more than 5 million international passengers a year: notably Miami, Los Angeles, Chicago O'Hare, San Francisco, Honolulu, and New York Newark.

THE 10 ★
WORST AIR DISASTERS

LOCATION/DATE/INCIDENT	NO. KILLED

1 Tenerife, Canary Islands, Mar 27, 1977 — 583
Two Boeing 747s (Pan Am and KLM, carrying 364 passengers and 16 crew and 230 passengers and 11 crew, respectively) collided and caught fire on the runway of Los Rodeos airport after the pilots received incorrect control-tower instructions.

2 Mt. Ogura, Japan, Aug 12, 1985 — 520
A JAL Boeing 747 on an internal flight from Tokyo to Osaka crashed, killing all but four on board in the worst-ever disaster involving a single aircraft.

3 Charkhi Dadri, India, Nov 12, 1996 — 349
Soon after taking off from New Delhi's Indira Gandhi International Airport, a Saudi Airways Boeing 747 collided with a Kazakh Airlines Ilyushin IL76 cargo aircraft on its descent and exploded, killing all 312 on the Boeing and 37 on the Ilyushin in the world's worst midair crash.

4 Paris, France, Mar 3, 1974 — 346
A Turkish Airlines DC-10 crashed at Ermenonville, north of Paris, immediately after takeoff for London, with many English rugby supporters among the dead.

5 Off the Irish coast, June 23, 1985 — 329
An Air India Boeing 747 on a flight from Vancouver to Delhi exploded in midair, perhaps as a result of a terrorist bomb.

6 Riyadh, Saudi Arabia, Aug 19, 1980 — 301
A Saudia (Saudi Arabian) Airlines Lockheed Tristar caught fire during an emergency landing.

7 Kinshasa, Zaïre, Jan 8, 1996 — 298
A Zaïrean Antonov-32 cargo plane crashed shortly after takeoff, killing shoppers in a market.

8 Off the Iranian coast, July 3, 1988 — 290
An Iran Air A300 airbus was shot down in error by a missile fired by the USS Vincennes.

9 Chicago, US, May 25, 1979 — 273
An engine fell off an American Airlines DC-10 as it took off from Chicago O'Hare airport; the plane plunged out of control, killing all 271 on board and two on the ground, in the US's worst-ever air disaster.

10 Lockerbie, Scotland, Dec 21, 1988 — 270
Pan Am Flight 103 from London Heathrow to New York exploded in midair as a result of a terrorist bomb, killing 243 passengers, 16 crew, and 11 on the ground in the UK's worst-ever air disaster.

TOP 10 COUNTRIES WITH THE MOST AIRPORTS
(Country/airports)

1. **US**, 14,459
2. **Brazil**, 3,265
3. **Russia**, 2,517
4. **Mexico**, 1,805
5. **Argentina**, 1,374
6. **Canada**, 1,395
7. **Bolivia**, 1,130
8. **Colombia**, 1,120
9. **Paraguay**, 941
10. **South Africa**, 749

Source: *Central Intelligence Agency*
Airports, as defined by the CIA, range in size from those with paved runways over 10,000 ft (3,048 m) in length to those with only short landing strips. Among European countries those with the most airports are Germany (618), France (474), and the UK (387).

TOP 10 AIRLINE-USING COUNTRIES
(Country/passenger miles per annum*/passenger km per annum*)

1. **US**, 599.332 billion/964.533 billion
2. **UK**, 98.111 billion/157.895 billion
3. **Japan**, 93.856 billion/151.048 billion
4. **Germany**, 53.555 billion/86.189 billion
5. **France**, 52.614 billion/84.675 billion
6. **Australia**, 47.145 billion/75.873 billion
7. **China**, 45.337 billion/72.964 billion
8. **Netherlands**, 41.424 billion/66.666 billion
9. **Canada**, 38.439 billion/61.862 billion
10. **Rep. of Korea**, 36.892 billion/59.372 billion

* *Total distance traveled by scheduled aircraft of national airlines multiplied by number of passengers carried*
Source: *International Civil Aviation Organization*

Which country has the world's fastest scheduled rail service?
see p.232 for the answer

A France
B USA
C Japan

see p.232 for the answer

SYDNEY 2000

Indigenous Australian creatures welcome the world to the 27th Olympiad, held in Sydney from September 15 to October 1, 2000.

© SOCOG 1996

TOP 10 ★

LONGEST-STANDING CURRENT OLYMPIC TRACK AND FIELD RECORDS

	EVENT	WINNING DISTANCE, TIME, OR SCORE	COMPETITOR/ COUNTRY	DATE SET
1	Men's long jump	8.90 m	Bob Beamon, US	Oct 18, 1968
2	Women's shot put	22.41 m	Ilona Slupianek, East Germany	July 24, 1980
3	Women's 800 meters	1 min 53.43 sec	Nadezhda Olizarenko, USSR	July 27, 1980
4 =	Women's 4 x 100 meters	41.60 sec	East Germany	Aug 1, 1980
=	Men's 1500 meters	3 min 32.53 sec	Sebastian Coe, GB	Aug 1, 1980
6	Women's marathon	2 hr 24 min 52 sec	Joan Benoit, US	Aug 5, 1984
7	Decathlon	8,847 points	Daley Thompson, GB	Aug 9, 1984
8	Men's 5,000 meters	13 min 05.59 sec	Said Aouita, Morocco	Aug 11, 1984
9	Men's marathon	2 hr 9 min 21 sec	Carlos Lopes, Portugal	Aug 12, 1984
10 =	Men's shot put	22.47 m	Ulf Timmermann, East Germany	Sep 23, 1988
=	Men's 20-km walk	1 hr 19 min 57 sec	Jozef Pribilinec, Czechoslovakia	Sep 23, 1988

Bob Beamon's record-breaking jump in 1968 is regarded as one of the greatest achievements in athletics. He was aided by Mexico City's rarefied atmosphere, but to add a staggering 21¼ in (55.25 cm) to the old record, and win the competition by 28½ in (72.39 cm), was no mean feat. Beamon's jump of 29 ft 2½ in (8.90 m) was the first beyond both 28 and 29 ft (8.53 and 8.84 m). The next 28-ft (8.53-m) jump in the Olympics was not until 1980, 12 years after Beamon's leap.

THE 10 OLYMPIC DECATHLON EVENTS

1 100 meters **2** Long jump **3** Shot put **4** High jump **5** 400 meters
6 110 meter hurdles **7** Discus
8 Pole vault **9** Javelin **10** 1500 meters

TOP 10 ★

OLYMPIC SPORTS IN WHICH GREAT BRITAIN HAS WON THE MOST MEDALS

	SPORT	MEDALS GOLD	SILVER	BRONZE	TOTAL
1	Track and field	47	79	57	183
2	Swimming	18	23	30	71
3 =	Cycling	9	21	16	46
=	Tennis	16	14	16	46
5	Shooting	13	14	18	45
6	Boxing	12	10	21	43
7	Rowing	19	15	7	41
8	Yachting	14	12	9	35
9	Equestrian	5	7	9	21
10	Wrestling	3	4	10	17

TOP 10 ★

OLYMPIC SPORTS IN WHICH THE US HAS WON THE MOST MEDALS

	SPORT	MEDALS GOLD	SILVER	BRONZE	TOTAL
1	Track and field	299	216	177	692
2	Swimming	230	176	137	543
3	Diving	46	40	41	127
4	Wrestling	46	38	25	109
5	Boxing	47	21	34	102
6	Shooting	45	26	21	92
7	Gymnastics	26	23	28	77
8	Rowing	29	28	19	76
9	Yachting	16	19	16	51
10	Speed skating	22	16	10	48

Background image: **THE OLYMPIC STADIUM IN SYDNEY**

TOP 10 ⭐
COUNTRIES WITH THE MOST SUMMER OLYMPICS MEDALS, 1896–1996

	COUNTRY	GOLD	SILVER	BRONZE	TOTAL
1	US	833	634	548	2,015
2	Soviet Union*	485	395	354	1,234
3	Great Britain	177	233	225	635
4	France	176	181	205	562
5	Germany#	151	181	184	516
6	Sweden	134	152	173	459
7	Italy	166	136	142	444
8	Hungary	142	128	155	425
9	East Germany	153	130	127	410
10	Australia	87	85	122	294

* Includes Unified Team of 1992; does not include Russia since this date

Not including West/East Germany 1968–88

The medals table was led by the host nations at the first three Games: Greece in 1896, France in 1900, and the US in 1904. Germany led at the 1936 Games, after which the US and the Soviet Union vied for preeminence.

TOP 10 SUMMER OLYMPICS ATTENDED BY THE MOST COMPETITORS, 1896–1996

(City/year/competitors)

1. **Atlanta**, 1996, 10,310 2. **Barcelona**, 1992, 9,364 3. **Seoul**, 1988, 9,101
4. **Munich**, 1972, 7,156 5. **Los Angeles**, 1984, 7,058 6. **Montreal**, 1976, 6,085
7. **Mexico City**, 1968, 5,530 8. **Rome**, 1960, 5,346 9. **Moscow**, 1980, 5,326
10. **Tokyo**, 1964, 5,140

The first Games in 1896 were attended by just 311 competitors, all men, representing 13 countries. Women took part for the first time four years later at the Paris Games.

TOP 10 ⭐
MEDAL WINNERS IN A SUMMER OLYMPICS CAREER

	MEDALLIST	COUNTRY	SPORT	YEARS	GOLD	SILVER	BRONZE	TOTAL
1	Larissa Latynina	USSR	Gymnastics	1956–64	9	5	4	18
2	Nikolay Andrianov	USSR	Gymnastics	1972–80	7	5	3	15
3 =	Edoardo Mangiarotti	Italy	Fencing	1936–60	6	5	2	13
=	Takashi Ono	Japan	Gymnastics	1952–64	5	4	4	13
=	Boris Shakhlin	USSR	Gymnastics	1956–64	7	4	2	13
6 =	Sawao Kato	Japan	Gymnastics	1968–76	8	3	1	12
=	Paavo Nurmi	Finland	Athletics	1920–28	9	3	0	12
8 =	Viktor Chukarin	USSR	Gymnastics	1952–56	7	3	1	11
=	Vera Cáslavská	Czechoslovakia	Gymnastics	1964–68	7	4	0	11
=	Carl Osborn	US	Shooting	1912–24	5	4	2	11
=	Mark Spitz	US	Swimming	1968–72	9	1	1	11
=	Matt Biondi	US	Swimming	1984–92	8	2	1	11

"OLYMPICS"

What we call the Olympics is a modern revival of games that took place at Olympia in Greece from as early as 1370 BC, as part of a religious festival held every four years. Originally foot races were the only events, and the earliest record is that of Coroibis of Olis, winner of a 186-yd (170-m) race in 776 BC. New sports were progressively added, but the Games were banned in AD 393 by Emperor Theodosius I. The Olympics were reborn with the first modern games held in Athens in 1896. **WHY DO WE SAY?**

MEDAL WINNER
Russian gymnast Nikolay Andrianov's tally of 15 individual and team medals won in three Olympics makes him the most decorated male athlete of all time.

Did You Know? Several unusual Olympic events have been discontinued, including underwater swimming, long jump and high jump on horseback, club-swinging, and stone-throwing.

243

Sporting Heroes

MOST POINTS SCORED BY MICHAEL JORDAN IN A GAME

	TEAM	DATE	POINTS
1	Cleveland Cavaliers	Mar 28, 1990	69
2	Orlando Magic	Jan 16, 1993	64
3	Boston Celtics	Apr 20, 1986	63
4 =	Detroit Pistons	Mar 4, 1987	61
=	Atlanta Hawks	Apr 16, 1987	61
6	Detroit Pistons	Mar 3, 1988	59
7	New Jersey Nets	Feb 6, 1987	58
8	Washington Bullets	Dec 23, 1992	57
9 =	Philadelphia 76ers	Mar 24, 1987	56
=	Miami Heat	Apr 29, 1992	56

Source: *NBA*

SEASONS BY WAYNE GRETZKY

	SEASON	GOALS	ASSISTS	POINTS
1	1985–86	52	163	215
2	1981–82	92	120	212
3	1984–85	73	135	208
4	1983–84	87	118	205
5	1982–83	71	125	196
6	1986–87	62	121	183
7	1988–89	54	114	168
8	1980–81	55	109	164
9	1990–91	41	122	163
10	1987–88	40	109	149

Wayne Gretzky, who retired in 1999 after 20 seasons in the NHL, is considered to be the greatest ice-hockey player of all time. He gained more records than any player in history, including the most goals, assists, and points in a career.

ICE MAN

Wayne Gretzky (pictured here during his 1984–85 season with the Edmonton Oilers) holds more career records than any player in ice-hockey history.

THE 10 LATEST WINNERS OF THE *SPORTS ILLUSTRATED* "SPORTSMAN OF THE YEAR" AWARD

(Year/winner(s)/sport)

1 1999 United States Women's World Cup Squad, Soccer **2** 1998 Mark McGwire and Sammy Sosa, Baseball **3** 1997 Dean Smith, Basketball coach **4** 1996 Tiger Woods, Golf **5** 1995 Cal Ripken, Jr., Baseball **6** 1994 Johan Olav Koss and Bonnie Blair, Ice skating **7** 1993 Don Shula, Football coach **8** 1992 Arthur Ashe, Tennis **9** 1991 Michael Jordan, Basketball **10** 1990 Joe Montana, Football

THE 10 LATEST WINNERS OF THE BBC "SPORTS PERSONALITY OF THE YEAR" AWARD

(Year/winner/sport)

1 1999 Lennox Lewis, Boxing **2** 1998 Michael Owen, Soccer **3** 1997 Greg Rusedski, Tennis **4** 1996 Damon Hill, Motor racing **5** 1995 Jonathan Edwards, Track and Field **6** 1994 Damon Hill, Motor racing **7** 1993 Linford Christie, Track and Field **8** 1992 Nigel Mansell, Motor racing **9** 1991 Liz McColgan, Track and Field **10** 1990 Paul Gascoigne, Soccer

This annual award is based on a poll of BBC television viewers in the UK.

ON THE BALL

In many seasons during his exceptional career, Michael Jordan achieved an average of over 30 points per game, with those listed above standing out as his highest-scoring ones.

THE 10 ★
LATEST EVANDER HOLYFIELD WINS BY KNOCKOUT

	OPPONENT	ROUND	DATE
1	Michael Moorer	8	Nov 8, 1997
2	Mike Tyson	11*	Nov 9, 1996
3	Bobby Czyz	5	May 10, 1996
4	Riddick Bowe	8*	Nov 4, 1995
5	Bert Cooper	7	Nov 23, 1991
6	Buster Douglas	3	Oct 25, 1990
7	Seamus McDonagh	4*	June 1, 1990
8	Alex Stewart	8*	Nov 4, 1989
9	Adilson Rodrigues	2	July 15, 1989
10	Michael Dokes	10*	Mar 11, 1989

* Technical knockout

Born October 19, 1962, boxer Evander Holyfield won his first undisputed heavyweight title in 1990 when he defeated Buster Douglas. His 1993 defeat of Riddick Bowe (when Holyfield won on points) and his 1996 victory over Mike Tyson established him as the only fighter, apart from Muhammad Ali, to win the heavyweight title on three occasions.

TOP 10 ★
FASTEST 100-METER RUNS BY LINFORD CHRISTIE

	STADIUM/LOCATION	DATE	TIME SECS
1	Stuttgart, Germany	Aug 15, 1993	9.87
2	Victoria, Canada	Aug 23, 1994	9.91
3	Tokyo, Japan	Aug 25, 1991	9.92
4	Barcelona, Spain	Aug 1, 1992	9.96
5 =	Seoul, Korea	Sep 24, 1988	9.97
=	Stuttgart, Germany	Aug 15, 1993	9.97
=	Johannesburg, SA	Sep 23, 1995	9.97
8	Victoria, Canada	Aug 23, 1994	9.98
9	Tokyo, Japan	Aug 25, 1991	9.99
10 =	Barcelona, Spain	Aug 1, 1992	10.00
=	Stuttgart, Germany	Aug 14, 1993	10.00

Christie made his international debut for Great Britain in 1980, became the fastest runner outside the US in 1986, and won Olympic gold in 1992.

TOP 10 ★
LONGEST LONG JUMPS BY CARL LEWIS

	STADIUM/LOCATION	DATE	DISTANCE M
1	Tokyo, Japan	Aug 30, 1991	8.87
2 =	Indianapolis	June 19, 1983	8.79
=	New York*	Jan 27, 1984	8.79
4 =	Indianapolis	July 24, 1982	8.76
=	Indianapolis	July 18, 1988	8.76
6	Indianapolis	Aug 16, 1987	8.75
7	Seoul, Korea	Sep 26, 1988	8.72
8 =	Westwood	May 13, 1984	8.71
=	Los Angeles	June 19, 1984	8.71
10	Barcelona, Spain	Aug 5, 1992	8.68

* Indoor performance

All-round athlete Lewis won four gold medals at the 1984 Olympics, two in 1988, two in 1992, and his ninth in 1996.

THE 10 ★
LATEST WINNERS OF THE JESSE OWENS INTERNATIONAL TROPHY

YEAR	WINNER	SPORT
2000	Lance Armstrong	Track and field
1999	Marion Jones	Track and field
1998	Haile Gebrselassie	Track and field
1997	Michael Johnson	Track and field
1996	Michael Johnson	Track and field
1995	Johann Olav Koss	Speed skating
1994	Wang Junxia	Track and field
1993	Vitaly Scherbo	Gymnastics
1992	Mike Powell	Track and field
1991	Greg LeMond	Cycling

The Jesse Owens International Trophy, named in honor of American Olympic athlete Jesse (James Cleveland) Owens (1913–80), has been presented by the Amateur Athletic Association since 1981, when it was won by speed skater Eric Heiden. Michael Johnson is the only sportsperson to have won on two occasions, while Marion Jones, the 1999 winner, is only the fourth woman to receive the award.

POLES APART
Ukrainian pole-vaulter Sergei Bubka (b. 1963) has ruled his sport since winning the 1983 World Championship. He has set 35 world records, which is more than any other athlete in sports history.

TOP 10 ★
HIGHEST POLE VAULTS BY SERGEI BUBKA

	STADIUM/LOCATION	DATE	HEIGHT M
1	Donetsk, Ukraine*	Feb 21, 1993	6.15
2 =	Lievin, France*	Feb 13, 1993	6.14
=	Sestriere, Italy	July 31, 1994	6.14
4 =	Berlin, Germany*	Feb 21, 1992	6.13
=	Tokyo, Japan	Sep 19, 1992	6.13
6 =	Grenoble, France*	Mar 23, 1991	6.12
=	Padua, Italy	Aug 30, 1992	6.12
8 =	Donetsk, Ukraine*	Mar 19, 1991	6.11
=	Dijon, France	June 13, 1992	6.11
10 =	San Sebastian, Spain*	Mar 15, 1991	6.10
=	Malmo, Sweden	Aug 5, 1991	6.10

* Indoor performance

Did You Know? In little over a century, the world pole-vaulting record leaped from 3.62 m (achieved by Raymond Clapp of the US in 1898) to today's 6.14-m outdoor record.

Football Feats

LARGEST
NFL STADIUMS

STADIUM/HOME TEAM	CAPACITY
1 Pontiac Silverdome, Detroit Lions	80,311
2 FedExField, Washington Redskins	80,116
3 Giants Stadium, New York Giants*	79,469
4 Arrowhead Stadium, Kansas City Chiefs	79,409
5 Mile High Stadium, Denver Broncos	76,082
6 Ralph Wilson Stadium, Buffalo Bills	75,339
7 Pro Player Stadium, Miami Dolphins	74,916
8 Sun Devil Stadium, Arizona Cardinals	73,273
9 Alltel Stadium, Jacksonville Jaguars	73,000
10 Ericsson Stadium, Carolina Panthers	72,250

* Seating reduced to 77,803 for New York Jets games

Source: *National Football League*

The roof of the octagonal Pontiac Silverdome is the world's largest air-supported structure.

BIGGEST
WINNING MARGINS
IN THE SUPER BOWL

GAME*	YEAR	MARGIN
1 San Francisco 49ers v Denver Broncos	1990	45
2 Chicago Bears v New England Patriots	1986	36
3 Dallas Cowboys v Buffalo Bills	1993	35
4 Washington Redskins v Denver Broncos	1988	32
5 Los Angeles Raiders v Washington Redskins	1984	29
6 Green Bay Packers v Kansas City Chiefs	1967	25
7 San Francisco 49ers v San Diego Chargers	1995	23
8 San Francisco 49ers v Miami Dolphins	1985	22
9 Dallas Cowboys v Miami Dolphins	1972	21
10 =Green Bay Packers v Oakland Raiders	1968	19
=New York Giants v Denver Broncos	1987	19

* Winners first

MOST SUCCESSFUL
TEAMS*

TEAM	WINS	LOSSES	PTS
1 Dallas Cowboys	5	3	13
2 San Francisco 49ers	5	0	10
3 Pittsburgh Steelers	4	1	10
4 Washington Redskins	3	2	8
5 Denver Broncos	2	4	8
6 =Green Bay Packers	3	1	7
=Oakland/L.A. Raiders	3	1	7
8 Miami Dolphins	2	3	7
9 New York Giants	2	0	4
10 =Buffalo Bills	0	4	4
=Minnesota Vikings	0	4	4

* Based on two points for a Super Bowl win and one for a loss; wins take precedence over losses in determining ranking

Source: *National Football League*

MOST SUCCESSFUL
COACHES
IN AN NFL CAREER

COACH	GAMES WON
1 Don Shula	347
2 George Halas	324
3 Tom Landry	270
4 Curly Lambeau	229
5 Chuck Noll	209
6 Chuck Knox	193
7 Dan Reeves*	175
8 Paul Brown	170
9 Bud Grant	168
10 Marv Levy	154

* Still active

Source: *National Football League*

TOP COACH

Don Shula retired at the end of the 1995 season, having achieved an NFL record of coaching his team, the Miami Dolphins, to 347 wins.

Background image: **PONTIAC SILVERDOME**

PASSING GREAT
Jerry Rice, who joined the San Francisco 49ers in 1985, is one of the greatest-ever pass catchers and the player with the most career touchdowns.

TOP 10 — PLAYERS WITH THE MOST CAREER POINTS

	PLAYER	POINTS
1	George Blanda	2,002
2	Gary Anderson*	1,948
3	Morten Andersen*	1,840
4	Norm Johnson*	1,736
5	Nick Lowery	1,711
6	Jan Stenerud	1,699
7	Eddie Murray*	1,549
8	Pat Leahy	1,470
9	Jim Turner	1,439
10	Matt Bahr	1,422

* Still active 1999 season
Source: National Football League

TOP 10 — LONGEST CAREERS OF CURRENT NFL PLAYERS

	PLAYER	TEAM	YEARS
1	Wade Wilson	Oakland Raiders	19
2=	Morten Andersen	Atlanta Falcons	18
=	Gary Anderson	Minnesota Vikings	18
=	Norm Johnson	Philadelphia Eagles	18
5=	Darrell Green	Washington Redskins	17
=	Trey Junkin	Arizona Cardinals	17
=	Dan Marino	Miami Dolphins	17
=	Bruce Matthews	Tennessee Titans	17
=	Eddie Murray	Dallas Cowboys	17
=	Mike Horan	St. Louis Rams	17

Source: National Football League

TOP 10 — PLAYERS WITH THE MOST CAREER TOUCHDOWNS

	PLAYER	TOUCHDOWNS
1	Jerry Rice*	179
2	Emmitt Smith*	147
3	Marcus Allen	145
4	Jim Brown	126
5	Walter Payton	125
6	John Riggins	116
7	Lenny Moore	113
8	Don Hutson	105
9	Steve Largent	101
10	Franco Harris	100

* Still active
Source: National Football League

TOP 10 — PLAYERS WITH THE MOST PASSING YARDS IN AN NFL CAREER

	PLAYER	PASSING YARDS
1	Dan Marino*	61,243
2	John Elway	51,475
3	Warren Moon*	49,117
4	Fran Tarkenton	47,003
5	Dan Fouts	43,040
6	Joe Montana	40,551
7	Johnny Unitas	40,239
8	Dave Krieg	37,946
9	Boomer Esiason	37,920
10	Jim Kelly	35,467

* Still active 1999 season
Source: National Football League

TOP 10 — POINT SCORERS IN AN NFL SEASON

	PLAYER/TEAM/YEAR	GAMES WON
1	Paul Hornung, Green Bay Packers, 1960	176
2	Gary Anderson, Minnesota Vikings, 1998	164
3	Mark Moseley, Washington Redskins,1983	161
4	Gino Cappelletti, Boston Patriots, 1964	155*
5	Emmitt Smith, Dallas Cowboys, 1995	150
6	Chip Lohmiller, Washington Redskins, 1991	149
7	Gino Cappelletti, Boston Patriots, 1961	147
8	Paul Hornung, Green Bay Packers, 1961	146
9=	Jim Turner, New York Jets, 1968	145
=	John Kasay, Carolina Panthers, 1996	145
=	Mike Vanderjagt, Indianapolis Colts, 1999	145

* Including a two-point conversion
Source: National Football League

THE 10 LATEST ATTENDANCES OF NFL TEAMS*
(Year/attendance)

1 1999 16,206,640 2 1998 16,187,758 3 1997 15,769,193 4 1996 15,381,727
5 1995 15,834,468 6 1994 14,810,173 7 1993 14,781,450 8 1992 14,644,797
9 1991 14,654,706 10 1990 14,807,439

* Regular season only   Source: NFL

What sort of baskets were originally used in basketball?
see p.250 for the answer   A Fish   B Peach   C Bread

Athletic Achievements

TOP 10 ★
FASTEST WINNING TIMES
IN THE NEW YORK CITY MARATHON

MEN			
RUNNER/COUNTRY		YEAR	TIME*
1 **Juma Ikangaa**, Tanzania		1989	2.08.01
2 **John Kagwe**, Kenya		1997	2.08.12
3 **Alberto Salazar**, US		1981	2.08.13
4 **Steve Jones**, UK		1988	2.08.20
5 **John Kagwe**, Kenya		1998	2.08.45
6 **Rod Dixon**, New Zealand		1983	2.08.59
7 **Joseph Chebet**, Kenya		1999	2.09.14
8 **Salvador Garcia**, Mexico		1991	2.09.28
9 = **Alberto Salazar**, US		1982	2.09.29
= **Willie Mtolo**, South Africa		1992	2.09.29

WOMEN			
RUNNER/COUNTRY		YEAR	TIME*
1 **Lisa Ondieki**, Australia		1992	2.24.40
2 **Adriana Fernandez**, Mexico		1999	2.25.06
3 **Franca Fiacconi**, Italy		1998	2.25.17
4 **Allison Roe**, New Zealand		1981*	2.25.29
5 **Ingrid Kristiansen**, Norway		1989	2.25.30
6 **Grete Waitz**, Norway		1980	2.25.41
7 **Uta Pippig**, Germany		1993	2.26.24
8 **Grete Waitz**, Norway		1983	2.27.00
9 **Grete Waitz**, Norway		1982	2.27.14
10 **Liz McColgan**, Scotland		1991	2.27.23

* In 1981–83 the circuit was 170 yd (155 m) shorter.

TOP 10 LONGEST LONG JUMPS*

(Athlete/country/year/distance in meters)

1 **Mike Powell**, US, 1991, 8.95 **2** **Bob Beamon**, US, 1968, 8.90
3 **Carl Lewis**, US, 1991, 8.87 **4** **Robert Emmiyan**, USSR, 1987, 8.86
5 = **Larry Myricks**, US, 1988, 8.74; = **Eric Walder**, US, 1994, 8.74
7 **Ivan Pedroso**, Cuba, 1995, 8.71 **8** **Kareem Streete-Thompson**, US, 1994, 8.63
9 **James Beckford**, Jamaica, 1997, 8.62 **10** **Yago Lamela**#, Spain, 1999, 8.56

* Longest by each athlete only   # Indoor

JUMPING AHEAD

US athlete Mike Powell's long-jump record of 8.95 m, set in Tokyo on August 30, 1991, broke Bob Beamon's record, which had stood for 23 years.

TOP 10 ★
HIGHEST POLE VAULTS*

	ATHLETE/COUNTRY	YEAR	HEIGHT METERS
1	**Sergey Bubka**#, Ukraine	1993	6.15
2	**Maxin Tarasov**, Russia	1999	6.05
3	**Okkert Brits**, South Africa	1995	6.03
4 =	**Rodion Gataullin**#, USSR	1989	6.02
=	**Jeff Hartwig**, US	1999	6.02
6	**Igor Trandenkov**, Russia	1996	6.01
7 =	**Jeane Galfione**, France	1999	6.00
=	**Tim Lobinger**, Germany	1997	6.00
=	**Dmitri Markov**, Belarus	1998	6.00
10	**Lawrence Johnson**, US	1996	5.98

* Highest by each athlete only
 # Indoor

THE 10 ★
FIRST ATHLETES TO RUN A MILE
IN UNDER FOUR MINUTES

	ATHLETE/COUNTRY	LOCATION	MIN:SEC	DATE
1	**Roger Bannister**, UK	Oxford	3:59.4	May 6, 1954
2	**John Landy**, Australia	Turku, Finland	3:57.9	June 21, 1954
3	**Laszlo Tabori**, Hungary	London	3:59.0	May 28, 1955
4 =	**Chris Chataway**, UK	London	3:59.8	May 28, 1955
=	**Brian Hewson**, UK	London	3:59.8	May 28, 1955
6	**Jim Bailey**, Australia	Los Angeles	3:58.6	May 5, 1956
7	**Gunnar Nielsen**, Denmark	Compton, US	3:59.1	June 1, 1956
8	**Ron Delany**, Ireland	Compton, US	3:59.4	June 1, 1956
9	**Derek Ibbotson**, UK	London	3:59.4	Aug 6, 1956
10	**István Rózsavölgyi**, Hungary	Budapest	3:59.0	Aug 26, 1956

Within a little over two years of Roger Bannister's capturing the imagination of the world by shattering the four-minute-mile barrier, the number of athletes to do so had risen to 10.

TOP 10 ★
FASTEST WOMEN EVER*

ATHLETE/COUNTRY	YEAR	TIME
1 Florence Griffith-Joyner, US	1988	10.49
2 Marion Jones, US	1998	10.65
3 Christine Arron, France	1998	10.73
4 Merlene Ottey, Jamaica	1996	10.74
5 Evelyn Ashford, US	1984	10.76
6 Irina Privalova, Russia	1994	10.77
7 Dawn Sowell, US	1989	10.78
8 Inger Miller, US	1999	10.79
9 Marlies Göhr, East Germany	1983	10.81
10= Gail Devers, US	1992	10.82
= Gwen Torrence, US	1994	10.82

* Based on fastest time for the 100 meters

TOP 10 ★
FASTEST MEN EVER*

ATHLETE/COUNTRY	YEAR	TIME
1 Maurice Green, US	1999	9.79
2 = Donovan Bailey, Canada	1996	9.84
= Bruny Surin, Canada	1999	9.84
4 Leroy Burrell, US	1994	9.85
5 = Ato Boldon, Trinidad	1998	9.86
= Frank Fredericks, Namibia	1996	9.86
= Carl Lewis, US	1991	9.86
8 = Linford Christie, UK	1993	9.87
= Obadele Thompson, Barbados	1998	9.87
10 Dennis Mitchell, US	1991	9.91

* Based on fastest time for the 100 meters

TOP 10 HIGHEST HIGH JUMPS*
(Athlete/country/year/height in meters)

1 Javier Sotomayor, Cuba, 1993, 2.45 **2** = Patrik Sjöberg, Sweden, 1987, 2.42; = Carlo Thränhardt #, West Germany, 1988, 2.42 **4** Igor Paklin, USSR, 1985, 2.41 **5** = Rudolf Povarnitsyn, USSR, 1985, 2.40; = Sorin Matei, Romania, 1990, 2.40; = Charles Austin, US, 1991, 2.40; = Hollis Conway #, US, 1991, 2.40 **9** = Zhu Jianhua, China, 1984, 2.39; = Hollis Conway, US, 1989, 2.39; = Dietmar Mögenburg #, West Germany · 1985, 2.39; = Ralph Sonn #, Germany, 1991, 2.39

* Highest by each athlete only   # Indoor

TOP 10 ★
FASTEST TIMES IN THE BOSTON MARATHON

MEN

RUNNER/COUNTRY	YEAR	TIME
1 Cosmas Ndeti, Kenya	1994	2:07:15
2 Andres Espinosa, Mexico	1994	2:07:19
3 Moses Tanui, Kenya	1998	2:07:34
4 Joseph Chebet, Kenya	1998	2:07:37
5 Rob de Castella, Australia	1986	2:07:51
6 Gert Thys, South Africa	1998	2:07:52
7 Jackson Kipngok, Kenya	1994	2:08:08
8 Hwang Young-Cho, Korea	1994	2:08:09
9 Ibrahim Hussein, Kenya	1992	2:08:14
10 Gelindo Bordin, Italy	1990	2:08:19

WOMEN

RUNNER/COUNTRY	YEAR	TIME
1 Uta Pippig, Germany	1994	2:21:45
2 Joan Benoit, US	1983	2:22:43
3 Fatuma Roba, Ethiopia	1998	2:23:21
4 Fatuma Roba, Ethiopia	1999	2:23:25
5 Valentina Yegorova, Russia	1994	2:23:33
6 Olga Markova, CIS	1992	2:23:43
7 Wanda Panfil, Poland	1991	2:24:18
8 Rosa Mota, Portugal	1988	2:24:30
9 Ingrid Kristiansen, Norway	1989	2:24:33
10 Ingrid Kristiansen, Norway	1986	2:24:55

Source: *Boston Athletics Association*

FASTEST MAN ON EARTH
US sprinter Maurice Green broke the world 100-m record on June 16, 1999, trimming 5/100ths of a second off Donovan Bailey's record.

Did You Know? The marathon distance was established at the Olympics in London in 1908. It was to have been 26 miles, but 385 yards were added to ensure that the race started beneath the Royal Nursery at Windsor Castle.

Basketball Bests

BIGGEST ARENAS IN THE NBA

	ARENA/LOCATION	HOME TEAM	CAPACITY
1	The Alamodome, San Antonio, Texas	San Antonio Spurs	34,215
2	Charlotte Coliseum, Charlotte, North Carolina	Charlotte Hornets	23,799
3	The Palace of Auburn Hills, Auburn Hills, Michigan	Detroit Pistons	22,076
4	United Center, Chicago, Illinois	Chicago Bulls	21,711
5	MCI Center, Washington, DC	Washington Wizards	20,674
6	Gund Arena, Cleveland, Ohio	Cleveland Cavaliers	20,562
7	First Union Center, Philadelphia, Pennsylvania	Philadelphia 76ers	20,444
8	Continental Airlines Arena, East Rutherford, New Jersey	New Jersey Nets	20,049
9	The Rose Garden, Portland, Oregon	Portland Trailblazers	19,980
10	Delta Center, Salt Lake City, Utah	Utah Jazz	19,911

The smallest arena in the NBA is the 15,200 capacity Miami Arena, home of the Miami Heat. The largest ever NBA stadium was the Louisiana Superdome, used by The New Orleans Jazz (now the Utah Jazz) from 1975 to 1979, which was capable of holding crowds of 47,284.

Source: NBA

TOP 10 NCAA COACHES
(Coach/wins)

1 Dean Smith, 879   **2** Adolph Rupp, 876   **3** Jim Phelan*, 803   **4** Henry Iba, 767
5 Bob Knight*, 762   **6** Ed Diddle, 759   **7** Phog Allen, 746   **8** Norm Stewart, 731
9 Ray Meyer, 724   **10** Don Haskins, 719

* Still active 1999–2000 season   Source: NCAA

MOST SUCCESSFUL DIVISION 1 NCAA TEAMS

	COLLEGE	DIVISION 1 WINS
1	Kentucky	1,765
2	North Carolina	1,753
3	Kansas	1,708
4	Duke	1,606
5	St. John's	1,602
6	Temple	1,542
7	Syracuse	1,522
8	Pennsylvania	1,495
9	Oregon State	1,481
10	Indiana	1,472

Source: NCAA

POINT SCORERS IN AN NBA CAREER*

	PLAYER	TOTAL POINTS
1	Kareem Abdul-Jabbar	38,387
2	Wilt Chamberlain	31,419
3	Karl Malone #	31,041
4	Michael Jordan	29,277
5	Moses Malone	27,409
6	Elvin Hayes	27,313
7	Oscar Robertson	26,710
8	Dominique Wilkins	26,534
9	John Havlicek	26,395
10	Hakeem Olajuwon #	25,822

* Regular season games only
\# Still active at end of 1999–2000 season
Source: NBA

NBA COACHES

	COACH	GAMES WON*
1	Lenny Wilkens #	1,179
2	Pat Riley #	999
3	Bill Fitch	944
4	Red Auerbach	938
5	Dick Motta	935
6	Don Nelson #	926
7	Jack Ramsay	864
8	Cotton Fitzsimmons	832
9	Gene Shue	784
10	John MacLeod	707

* Regular season games only
\# Still active 1999–2000 season
Source: NBA

POINTS AVERAGES IN AN NBA SEASON

	PLAYER/TEAM	SEASON	AVERAGE
1	Wilt Chamberlain, Philadelphia 76ers	1961–62	50.4
2	Wilt Chamberlain, San Francisco Warriors	1962–63	44.8
3	Wilt Chamberlain, Philadelphia 76ers	1960–61	38.4
4	Elgin Baylor, Los Angeles Lakers	1961–62	38.3
5	Wilt Chamberlain, Philadelphia 76ers	1959–60	37.6
6	Michael Jordan, Chicago Bulls	1986–87	37.1
7	Wilt Chamberlain, San Francisco Warriors	1963–64	36.9
8	Rick Barry, San Francisco Warriors	1966–67	35.6
9	Michael Jordan, Chicago Bulls	1987–88	35.0
10=	Elgin Baylor, Los Angeles Lakers	1960–61	34.8
=	Kareem Abdul-Jabbar, Milwaukee Bucks	1971–72	34.8

Source: NBA

Did You Know? When basketball was invented in 1891, the peach baskets that were originally used had bases, and the balls had to be retrieved by ladder.

TOP 10 ATTENDANCES IN THE 1990s

(Years/total attendances for all games)

1 1997–8 20,373,079 **2** 1995–6 20,513,218
3 1996–7 20,304,629 **4** 1999–2000 20,058,536
5 1994–5 18,516,484 **6** 1993–4 17,984,014 **7** 1992–3
17,778,295 **8** 1989–90 17,368,659 **9** 1991–2 17,367,240
10 1990–1 16,876,125

Source: *NBA*

TOP 10 ★
POINTS SCORED IN THE WNBA

PLAYER/GAME	DATE	PTS
1 Cynthia Cooper, Houston v Sacramento	July 25, 1997	44
2 Cynthia Cooper, Houston v Charlotte	Aug 11, 1997	39
3 Jennifer Gillom, Phoenix v Cleveland	Aug 10, 1998	36
4 =Cynthia Cooper, Houston v Los Angeles	Aug 1, 1997	34
=Cynthia Cooper, Houston v Phoenix	Aug 7, 1997	34
=Ruthie Bolton-Holifield, Sacramento v Utah	Aug 8, 1997	34
=Ruthie Bolton-Holifield, Sacramento v Cleveland	Aug 12, 1997	34
=Cynthia Cooper, Houston v Sacramento	July 3, 1998	34
=Cynthia Cooper, Houston at Detroit	Aug 7, 1998	34
10 Linda Burgess, Sacramento v Utah	Aug 15, 1998	33

Source: *WNBA*

TOP 10 ★
FREE THROW PERCENTAGES

	PLAYER	ATTEMPTS	BASKETS	%
1	Mark Price	2,362	2,135	90.4
2	Rick Barry	4,243	3,818	90.0
3	Calvin Murphy	3,864	3,445	89.2
4	Scott Skiles	1,741	1,548	88.9
5	Larry Bird	4,471	3,960	88.6
6	Bill Sharman	3,559	3,143	88.3
7	Reggie Miller*	5,690	5,015	88.1
8	Ricky Pierce	3,871	3,389	87.5
9	Kiki Vandeweghe	3,997	3,484	87.2
10	Jeff Malone	3,383	2,947	87.1

* Still active at end of 1999–2000 season
Source: *NBA*

TOP 10 PLAYERS WITH THE MOST CAREER ASSISTS

(Player/assists)

1 John Stockton*, 13,790 **2** Magic Johnson,
10,141 **3** Oscar Robertson, 9,887 **4** Isiah
Thomas, 9,061 **5** Mark Jackson*, 8,574
6 Maurice Cheeks, 7,392 **7** Lenny
Wilkens, 7,211 **8** Bob
Cousy, 6,995 **9** Guy
Rodgers, 6,917
10 Nate Archibald, 6,476

* Still active at end of
1999–2000 season
Source: *NBA*

MAGIC TOUCH

*Magic (Earvin) Johnson
turned professional in
1979, becoming one of
the NBA's most
legendary players.*

TOP 10 ★
PLAYERS TO HAVE PLAYED MOST GAMES IN THE NBA AND ABA

	PLAYER	GAMES PLAYED*
1	Robert Parish	1,611
2	Kareem Abdul-Jabbar	1,560
3	Moses Malone	1,455
4	Buck Williams	1,348
5	Artis Gilmore	1,329
6	Elvin Hayes	1,303
7	Caldwell Jones	1,299
8	John Havlicek	1,270
9	John Stockton#	1,258
10	Paul Silas	1,254

* Regular season only
# Still active at end of 1999–2000 season
Source: *NBA*

Combat Sports

TOP 10 OLYMPIC JUDO COUNTRIES
(Country/medals)

1 Japan, 40 **2** Soviet Union*, 27 **3** France, 26 **4** South Korea, 25 **5** = Cuba, 15; = Great Britain, 15 **7** Netherlands, 10 **8** = Germany #, 9; = East Germany, 9 **10** = US, 8; = Poland, 8; = West Germany, 8; = Hungary, 8; = Brazil, 8

* Including United Team of 1992; excludes Russia since this date
 # Not including West Germany or East Germany 1968–88

FIGHTING FIT

Judo was first introduced as an Olympic sport for men at the 1964 Tokyo Games, and for women in 1992. Min Soo Kim, from South Korea, here wins bronze at the Olympic Games, Atlanta, 1996.

TOP 10 ★
OLYMPIC WRESTLING COUNTRIES/ GRECO-ROMAN

COUNTRY	GOLD	MEDALS SILVER	BRONZE	TOTAL
1 Soviet Union*	37	19	13	69
2 Finland	19	21	18	58
3 Sweden	19	16	19	54
4 Hungary	15	9	11	35
5 Bulgaria	8	14	7	29
6 Romania	6	8	13	27
7 Germany	4	13	8	25
8 Poland	5	8	6	19
9 Italy	5	4	9	18
10 Turkey	10	4	3	17
US	2	5	5	12

* Including United Team of 1992; excludes Russia since this date

TOP 10 ★
OLYMPIC WRESTLING COUNTRIES/FREESTYLE

COUNTRY	GOLD	MEDALS SILVER	BRONZE	TOTAL
1 US	44	33	22	99
2 Soviet Union*	31	17	15	63
3 Turkey	16	11	6	33
4 =Japan	16	9	7	32
=Bulgaria	7	16	9	32
6 Sweden	8	10	8	26
7 =Finland	8	7	10	25
=Iran	4	9	12	25
9 =Great Britain	3	4	10	17
=Hungary	4	7	6	17

* Including United Team of 1992; excludes Russia since this date

TOP 10 WRESTLING WEIGHT DIVISIONS
(Weight/limit lb/kg)

1 Heavyweight plus, over 220/over 100 **2** Heavyweight, 220/100 **3** Light-heavyweight, 198/90 **4** Middleweight, 181/82 **5** Welterweight, 163/74 **6** Lightweight, 150/68 **7** Featherweight, 137/62 **8** Bantamweight, 126/57 **9** Flyweight, 115/52 **10** Light-flyweight, 106/48

TOP 10 ★
HEAVIEST BOXING WEIGHT DIVISIONS

WEIGHT	LB	LIMIT KG
1 Heavyweight	over 190	over 86
2 Cruiserweight	190	86
3 Light-heavyweight	175	79
4 Super-middleweight	168	76
5 Middleweight	160	73
6 Junior-middleweight/ Super-welterweight	154	70
7 Welterweight	147	67
8 Junior-welterweight/ Super-lightweight	140	65
9 Lightweight	135	61
10 Junior-lightweight/ Super-featherweight	130	59

TOP 10 ★
BOXERS WITH THE MOST KNOCKOUTS IN A CAREER

BOXER*	CAREER	KOS
1 Archie Moore	1936–63	129
2 Young Stribling	1921–63	126
3 Billy Bird	1920–48	125
4 Sam Langford	1902–26	116
5 George Odwell	1930–45	114
6 Sugar Ray Robinson	1940–65	110
7 Sandy Saddler	1944–65	103
8 Henry Armstrong	1931–45	100
9 Jimmy Wilde	1911–23	99
10 Len Wickwar	1928–47	93

* All from the US except Jimmy Wilde, who was Welsh

TOP 10 ★
OLYMPIC FENCING COUNTRIES

COUNTRY	MEDALS GOLD	SILVER	BRONZE	TOTAL
1 France	38	34	32	104
2 Italy	37	36	24	97
3 Hungary	32	20	26	78
4 Soviet Union*	19	17	18	54
5 =Poland	4	7	9	19
=US	2	6	11	19
7 Germany	6	6	6	18
8 West Germany#	7	8	1	16
9 Belgium	5	3	5	13
10 Romania	2	3	6	11

* Including United Team of 1992; excludes Russia since this date

Not including West Germany or East Germany 1968–88

THE 10 LATEST WORLD HEAVYWEIGHT BOXING CHAMPIONS*
(Years/boxer)

1 1999–, Lennox Lewis **2** 1997–99, Evander Holyfield **3** 1996–97, Mike Tyson **4** 1995–96, Bruce Seldon **5** 1994–95, George Foreman **6** 1994, Michael Moorer **7** 1993–94, Evander Holyfield **8** 1992–93, Riddick Bowe **9** 1990–92, Evander Holyfield **10** 1990, James Douglas ** WBA only*

TOP 10 ★
FASTEST KNOCKOUTS IN WORLD TITLE FIGHTS

FIGHT (WINNERS FIRST)	WEIGHT	DATE	SEC*
1 Gerald McClellan v Jay Bell	Middleweight	Aug 7, 1993	20
2 James Warring v James Pritchard	Cruiserweight	Sep 6, 1991	24
3 Lloyd Honeyghan v Gene Hatcher	Welterweight	Aug 30, 1987	45
4 Mark Breland v Lee Seung-soon	Welterweight	Feb 4, 1989	54
5 Emile Pladner v Frankie Genaro	Flyweight	Mar 2, 1929	58
6 =Jackie Paterson v Peter Kane	Flyweight	June 19, 1943	61
=Bobby Czyz v David Sears	Light-heavyweight	Dec 26, 1986	61
8 Michael Dokes v Mike Weaver	Heavyweight	Dec 10, 1982	63
9 Tony Canzoneri v Al Singer	Lightweight	Nov 14, 1930	66
10 Marvin Hagler v Caveman Lee	Middleweight	Mar 7, 1982	67

* Duration of fight

WORLD CHAMPION
After a much-disputed previous contest, Lennox Lewis finally defeated Evander Holyfield in Las Vegas on December 12, 1999 to take the World Heavyweight title.

Baseball Teams

TOP 10 ★
AVERAGE ATTENDANCES IN 1999

	TEAM	ATTENDANCE
1	Colorado Rockies	42,976
2	Baltimore Orioles	42,901
3	Cleveland Indians	42,820
4	St. Louis Cardinals	40,960
5	New York Yankees	40,662
6	Atlanta Braves	40,554
7	Los Angeles Dodgers	38,247
8	Arizona Diamondbacks	37,234
9	Chicago Cubs	36,075
10	Seattle Mariners	35,999

Source: *Major League Baseball*

TOP 10 ★
BIGGEST SINGLE GAME WINS IN THE WORLD SERIES

	TEAMS (WINNERS FIRST)/GAME	DATE	SCORE
1	New York Yankees v New York Giants (Game 2)	Oct 2, 1936	18–4
2	New York Yankees v Pittsburgh Pirates (Game 2)	Oct 6, 1960	16–3
3 =	New York Yankees v New York Giants (Game 5)	Oct 9, 1951	13–1
=	New York Yankees v Pittsburgh Pirates (Game 6)	Oct 12, 1960	12–0
=	Detroit Tigers v St. Louis Cardinals (Game 6)	Oct 9, 1968	13–1
=	New York Yankees v Milwaukee Brewers (Game 6)	Oct 19, 1982	13–1
7 =	New York Yankees v Philadelphia Athletics (Game 6)	Oct 26, 1911	13–2
=	Atlanta Braves v New York Yankees (Game 1)	Oct 20, 1996	12–1
=	St. Louis Cardinals v Detroit Tigers (Game 7)	Oct 9, 1934	11–0
=	Chicago White Sox v Los Angeles Dodgers (Game 1)	Oct 1, 1959	11–0
=	Kansas City Royals v St. Louis Cardinals (Game 7)	Oct 27, 1985	11–0

Source: *Major League Baseball*

TOP 10 ★
TEAMS WITH THE MOST WORLD SERIES WINS

	TEAM*	WINS
1	New York Yankees	25
2 =	St. Louis Cardinals	9
=	Philadelphia/Kansas City/Oakland Athletics	9
4	Brooklyn/Los Angeles Dodgers	6
5 =	New York/San Francisco Giants	5
=	Boston Red Sox	5
=	Cincinnati Reds	5
=	Pittsburgh Pirates	5
9	Detroit Tigers	4
10 =	Boston/Milwaukee/Atlanta Braves	3
=	St. Louis/Baltimore Orioles	3
=	Washington Senators/Minnesota Twins	3

* *Teams separated by / indicate changes of franchise and are regarded as the same team for Major League record purposes*

Source: *Major League Baseball*

Major League Baseball started in the United States with the forming of the National League in 1876. The rival American League was started in 1901, and two years later Pittsburgh, champion of the National League, invited American League champion Boston to take part in a best-of-nine games series to establish the "real" champion. Boston won 5–3. The following year the National League champion, New York, refused to play Boston and there was no World Series, but it was resumed in 1905.

TOP 10 ★
BASEBALL TEAM PAYROLLS, 1999

	TEAM	AVERAGE SALARY ($)	TOTAL PAYROLL ($)
1	New York Yankees	3,217,914	91,990,955
2	Texas Rangers	2,813,666	80,801,598
3	Atlanta Braves	2,491,388	79,256,599
4	Los Angeles Dodgers	2,413,389	76,607,247
5	Baltimore Orioles	2,495,937	75,443,363
6	Cleveland Indians	2,166,075	73,531,692
7	Boston Red Sox	2,218,787	72,330,656
8	New York Mets	2,199,903	71,510,523
9	Arizona Diamondbacks	2,267,995	70,046,818
10	Houston Astros	1,722,192	56,389,000

Source: *Major League Baseball Commissioner's Office*

THE 10 LAST YEARS OF MAJOR LEAGUE PLAYERS' SALARIES
(Year/average salary in $)

1. 1999, 1,720,050
2. 1998, 1,441,406
3. 1997, 1,383,578
4. 1996, 1,176,967
5. 1995, 1,071,029
6. 1994, 1,188,679
7. 1993, 1,120,254
8. 1992, 1,084,408
9. 1991, 891,188
10. 1990, 578,930

Source: *Associated Press*

Did You Know? In 1869–70 the Cincinnati Red Stockings became the first baseball team to receive a regular salary. They received payments of $800, rising to $1,400 for the shortstop.

TOP 10 ★
OLDEST STADIUMS IN MAJOR LEAGUE BASEBALL

	STADIUM	HOME CLUB	FIRST GAME
1	Fenway Park	Boston Red Sox	Apr 20, 1912
2	Wrigley Field	Chicago Cubs	Apr 23, 1914
3	Yankee Stadium	New York Yankees	Apr 18, 1923
4	Dodger Stadium	Los Angeles Dodgers	Apr 10, 1962
5	Shea Stadium	New York Mets	Apr 17, 1964
6	Edison International Field of Anaheim*	Anaheim Angels	Apr 19, 1966
7	Busch Stadium	St. Louis Cardinals	May 12, 1966
8	Qualcomm Stadium#	San Diego Padres	Apr 5, 1968
9	Network Associates Coliseum+	Oakland Athletics	Apr 17, 1968
10	Cinergy Field	Cincinnati Reds	June 30, 1970

* Formerly known as Anaheim Stadium
# Formerly known as Jack Murphy Stadium
+ Formerly known as Oakland-Alameda County Coliseum

Source: Major League Baseball

TOP 10 ★
LAST WINNERS OF THE WORLD SERIES

YEAR*	WINNER/LEAGUE#	LOSER/LEAGUE#	SCORE
1999	New York, AL	Atlanta, NL	4–0
1998	New York, AL	San Diego, NL	4–0
1997	Florida, NL	Cleveland, AL	4–3
1996	New York, AL	Atlanta, NL	4–2
1995	Atlanta, NL	Cleveland, AL	4–2
1993	Toronto, AL	Philadelphia, NL	4–2
1992	Toronto, AL	Atlanta, NL	4–2
1991	Minnesota, AL	Atlanta, NL	4–2
1990	Cincinnati, NL	Oakland, AL	4–0
1989	Oakland, AL	San Francisco, NL	4–0

* The 1994 event was canceled due to a players' strike

# AL = American League
 NL = National League

TOP 10 ★
NEWEST MAJOR LEAGUE TEAMS

	TEAM	LEAGUE*	1ST SEASON
1 =	Arizona Diamondbacks	NL	1998
=	Tampa Bay Devil Rays	AL	1998
3 =	Colorado Rockies	NL	1993
=	Florida Marlins	NL	1993
5 =	Seattle Mariners	AL	1977
=	Toronto Blue Jays	AL	1977
7 =	Kansas City Royals	AL	1969
=	Montreal Expos	NL	1969
=	Seattle Pilots/ Milwaukee Brewers	AL	1969
10 =	Houston Astros	NL	1962
=	New York Mets	NL	1962

* AL = American League
 NL = National League

Source: Major League Baseball

TOP 10 ★
LARGEST MAJOR LEAGUE BALLPARKS*

	STADIUM	HOME TEAM	CAPACITY
1	Veterans Stadium	Philadelphia Phillies	62,411
2	Qualcomm Stadium	San Diego Padres	59,960
3	Yankee Stadium	New York Yankees	57,746
4	Dodger Stadium	Los Angeles Dodgers	56,000
5	Shea Stadium	New York Mets	55,775
6	Cinergy Field	Cincinnati Reds	52,953
7	SkyDome	Toronto Blue Jays	50,516
8	Coors Field	Colorado Rockies	50,249
9	Turner Field	Atlanta Braves	50,062
10	Busch Stadium	St. Louis Cardinals	49,738

* By capacity

Source: Major League Baseball

Stadium capacities vary constantly, some being adjusted according to the event: Veterans Stadium, for example, holds fewer for baseball games than for football games.

Baseball Stars

PLAYERS WITH THE MOST CAREER STRIKEOUTS

PLAYER	STRIKEOUTS
1 Nolan Ryan	5,714
2 Steve Carlton	4,136
3 Bert Blyleven	3,701
4 Tom Seaver	3,640
5 Don Sutton	3,574
6 Gaylord Perry	3,534
7 Walter Johnson	3,508
8 Phil Niekro	3,342
9 Roger Clemens*	3,316
10 Ferguson Jenkins	3,192

* Still active in 1999 season

Source: *Major League Baseball*

Nolan Ryan was known as the "Babe Ruth of strikeout pitchers," pitching faster (a record 101 mph) and longer (27 seasons – 1966 and 1968–93) than any previous player.

PLAYERS WITH THE HIGHEST CAREER BATTING AVERAGES

PLAYER	AT BAT	HITS	AVERAGE*
1 Ty Cobb	11,434	4,189	.366
2 Rogers Hornsby	8,173	2,930	.358
3 Joe Jackson	4,981	1,772	.356
4 Ed Delahanty	7,505	2,597	.346
5 Tris Speaker	10,195	3,514	.345
6 =Billy Hamilton	6,268	2,158	.344
=Ted Williams	7,706	2,654	.344
8 =Dan Brouthers	6,711	2,296	.342
=Harry Heilmann	7,787	2,660	.342
=Babe Ruth	8,399	2,873	.342

* Calculated by dividing the number of hits by the number of times a batter was at bat

Source: *Major League Baseball*

Second only to the legendary Ty Cobb, Rogers Hornsby stands as the best second-hitting baseman of all time, with an average of over .400 in a five-year period.

PLAYERS WITH THE MOST RUNS IN A CAREER*

PLAYER	RUNS
1 Ty Cobb	2,245
2 =Babe Ruth	2,174
=Hank Aaron	2,174
4 Pete Rose	2,165
5 Rickey Henderson#	2,103
6 Willie Mays	2,062
7 Stan Musial	1,949
8 Lou Gehrig	1,888
9 Tris Speaker	1,882
10 Mel Ott	1,859

* Regular season only, excluding World Series
# Still active in 1999 season

Source: *Major League Baseball*

Ty Cobb is also the only player ever to collect six hits in six at bats and hit three home runs in the same game, which he achieved on May 5, 1925, helping the Detroit Tigers to a 14–8 win over the St. Louis Browns.

PLAYERS WITH THE MOST CONSECUTIVE GAMES PLAYED

PLAYER	GAMES
1 Cal Ripken, Jr.	2,600
2 Lou Gehrig	2,130
3 Everett Scott	1,307
4 Steve Garvey	1,207
5 Billy Williams	1,117
6 Joe Sewell	1,103
7 Stan Musial	895
8 Eddie Yost	829
9 Gus Suhr	822
10 Nellie Fox	798

Source: *Major League Baseball*

Cal Ripken took himself out of the starting lineup on September 21, 1998, in a game between the Orioles and the Yankees, having played in every game since May 30, 1982.

PLAYERS WHO PLAYED THE MOST GAMES IN A CAREER

PLAYER	GAMES
1 Pete Rose	3,562
2 Carl Yastrzemski	3,308
3 Hank Aaron	3,298
4 Ty Cobb	3,034
5 =Stan Musial	3,026
=Eddie Murray	3,026
7 Willie Mays	2,992
8 Dave Winfield	2,973
9 Rusty Staub	2,951
10 Brooks Robinson	2,896

Source: *Major League Baseball*

Pete Rose is the only player to appear in over 500 games in five different positions: he was at first base in 939 games, second in 628, third in 634, left field in 671, and right field in 595.

PITCHERS WITH THE MOST CAREER WINS

PLAYER	WINS
1 Cy Young	509
2 Walter Johnson	417
3 =Grover Alexander	373
=Christy Mathewson	373
5 Warren Spahn	363
6 =Kid Nichols	361
=Pud Galvin	361
8 Tim Keefe	344
9 Steve Carlton	329
10 =Eddie Plank	326
=John Clarkson	326

Source: *Major League Baseball*

In the 1925 season, Walter Johnson became the only pitcher to win 20 games and achieve a batting average for the season of 0.433 in 97 at bats – the highest of any pitcher in baseball history.

Did You Know? The first Major League baseball player killed in a game was Raymond Chapman of the Cleveland Indians, struck by a pitch thrown by New York Yankees Carl Mays on August 16, 1920.

TOP 10 ⭐
HIGHEST PAID PLAYERS IN MAJOR LEAGUE BASEBALL, 1999

PLAYER	TEAM	EARNINGS ($)
1 Albert Belle	Baltimore Orioles	11,949,794
2 Pedro Martinez	Boston Red Sox	11,250,000
3 Kevin Brown	Los Angeles Dodgers	10,714,286
4 Greg Maddux	Atlanta Braves	10,600,000
5 Gary Sheffield	Los Angeles Dodgers	9,936,667
6 Bernie Williams	New York Yankees	9,857,143
7 Randy Johnson	Arizona Diamondbacks	9,650,000
8 David Cone	New York Yankees	9,500,000
9 Barry Bonds	San Francisco Giants	9,381,057
10 Mark McGwire	St. Louis Cardinals	9,308,667

The median salary for the 1999 season was $495,000, up from $427,500 in 1998.

Source: *Associated Press*

THE 10 ⭐
FIRST PITCHERS TO THROW PERFECT GAMES

PLAYER	MATCH	DATE
1 Lee Richmond	Worcester vs Cleveland	June 12, 1880
2 Monte Ward	Providence vs Buffalo	June 17, 1880
3 Cy Young	Boston vs Philadelphia	May 5, 1904
4 Addie Joss	Cleveland vs Chicago	Oct 2, 1908
5 Charlie Robertson	Chicago vs Detroit	Apr 30, 1922
6 Don Larsen*	New York vs Brooklyn	Oct 8, 1956
7 Jim Bunning	Philadelphia vs New York	June 21, 1964
8 Sandy Koufax	Los Angeles vs Chicago	Sept 9, 1965
9 Catfish Hunter	Oakland vs Minnesota	May 8, 1968
10 Len Barker	Cleveland vs Toronto	May 15, 1981

* *Larsen's perfect game was, uniquely, in the World Series*

Fourteen pitchers have thrown perfect games; that is, they have pitched in all nine innings, dismissing 27 opposing batters, and without conceding a run. The last player to pitch a perfect innings was Kenny Rogers, for Texas against California, on July 28, 1994.

Source: *Major League Baseball*

TOP 10 ⭐
PLAYERS MOST AT BAT IN A CAREER

PLAYER	AT BAT
1 Pete Rose	14,053
3 Hank Aaron	12.364
3 Carl Yastrzemski	11,988
4 Ty Cobb	11,434
5 Eddie Murray	11,336
6 Robin Yount	11,008
7 Dave Winfield	11,003
8 Stan Musial	10,906
9 Willie Mays	10,881
10 Paul Molitor	10,835

As well as his appearance in this roll of fame, Hank Aaron collected more bases than any other hitter in baseball history, overtaking Stan Musial's previous record of 6,134 in 1972, and going on to reach 6,856 in 1976.

TOP 10 ⭐
LOWEST EARNED RUN AVERAGES IN A CAREER

PLAYER	EARNED RUN AVERAGES
1 Ed Walsh	1.82
2 Addie Joss	1.89
3 Three Finger Brown	2.06
4 John Ward	2.10
5 Christy Mathewson	2.13
6 Rube Waddell	2.16
7 Walter Johnson	2.17
8 Orval Overall	2.23
9 Tommy Bond	2.25
10 Ed Reulbach	2.28

Source: *Major League Baseball*

Although Addie Joss died in 1911 at the age of 31, he had gained his place in this list and also the distinction of being the only pitcher to achieve two non-hitters against the same team, playing for the Cleveland Indians against the Chicago White Sox on October 2, 1908 and April 20, 1910.

THE 10 ⭐
FIRST PLAYERS TO HIT FOUR HOME RUNS IN ONE GAME

PLAYER	CLUB	DATE
1 Bobby Lowe	Boston	May 30, 1884
2 Ed Delahanty	Philadelphia	July 13, 1896
3 Lou Gehrig	New York	June 3, 1932
4 Chuck Klein	Philadelphia	July 10, 1936
5 Pat Seerey	Chicago	July 18, 1948
6 Gil Hodges	Brooklyn	Aug 31, 1950
7 Joe Adcock	Milwaukee	July 31, 1954
8 Rocky Colavito	Cleveland	June 10, 1959
9 Willie Mays	San Francisco	Apr 30, 1961
10 Mike Schmidt	Philadelphia	Apr 17, 1976

The only other players to score four homers in one game are Bob Horner, who did so for Atlanta on July 6, 1986, and Mark Whitten, for St. Louis on September 7, 1993.

Soccer Stars

TOP 10 ★
HIGHEST-SCORING WORLD CUP FINALS

	YEAR	GAMES	GOALS	AVERAGE PER GAME
1	1954	26	140	5.38
2	1938	18	84	4.66
3	1934	17	70	4.11
4	1950	22	88	4.00
5	1930	18	70	3.88
6	1958	35	126	3.60
7	1970	32	95	2.96
8	1982	52	146	2.81
9 =	1962	32	89	2.78
=	1966	32	89	2.78

The lowest-scoring World Cup was Italia '90, which produced just 115 goals from 52 matches at an average of 2.21 per game. The 1994 final between Brazil and Italy was the first World Cup final to fail to produce a goal, with Brazil wining 3–2 on penalties.

TOP 10 COUNTRIES WITH THE MOST PLAYERS SENT OFF IN THE FINAL STAGES OF THE WORLD CUP

(Country/dismissals)

1 = Brazil, 8; = Argentina, 8 **3** = Uruguay, 6; = Cameroon, 6 **5** = Germany/West Germany, 5; = Hungary, 5 **7** = Czechoslovakia, 4; = Holland, 4; = Italy, 4; = Mexico, 4

A total of 97 players have received their marching orders in the final stages of the World Cup since 1930. The South American nations account for 27 of them. Brazil, Czechoslovakia, Denmark, Hungary, and South Africa have each had three players sent off in a single game – Brazil twice (1938 and 1954).

TOP 10 ★
WORLD CUP ATTENDANCES

	MATCH (WINNERS FIRST)	VENUE	YEAR	ATTENDANCE
1	Brazil v Uruguay	Rio de Janeiro*	1950	199,854
2	Brazil v Spain	Rio de Janeiro	1950	152,772
3	Brazil v Yugoslavia	Rio de Janeiro	1950	142,409
4	Brazil v Sweden	Rio de Janeiro	1950	138,886
5	Mexico v Paraguay	Mexico City	1986	114,600
6	Argentina v West Germany	Mexico City*	1986	114,590
7 =	Mexico v Bulgaria	Mexico City	1986	114,580
=	Argentina v England	Mexico City	1986	114,580
9	Argentina v Belgium	Mexico City	1986	110,420
10	Mexico v Belgium	Mexico City	1986	110,000

*Final tie

The biggest crowd outside Mexico or Brazil was that of 98,270 at Wembley Stadium in 1966 for England's game against France. The attendance for the Brazil–Uruguay final in 1950 is the world's highest for a soccer match.

TOP 10 ★
COUNTRIES IN THE WORLD CUP*

	COUNTRY	WIN	R/U	3RD	4TH	TOTAL
1	Brazil	4	2	2	1	27
2	Germany/West Germany	3	3	2	1	26
3	Italy	3	2	1	1	21
4	Argentina	2	2	–	–	14
5	Uruguay	2	–	–	2	10
6	France	1	–	2	1	9
7	Sweden	–	1	2	1	8
8	Holland	–	2	–	1	7
9 =	Czechoslovakia	–	2	–	–	6
=	Hungary	–	2	–	–	6

* Based on 4 points for winning the tournament, 3 points for runner-up, 2 points for 3rd place, and 1 point for 4th; up to and including the 1998 World Cup

Did You Know? When Daniel Xuereb of France played in the 1986 finals, it meant that every letter of the alphabet had been used in players' last names in the World Cup.

TOP 10 ★
EUROPEAN CUP WINNERS

	COUNTRY	YEARS	WINS*		COUNTRY	YEARS	WINS*
1 =	England	1968–99	9	=	Scotland	1967	1
=	Italy	1961–96	9	=	Yugoslavia	1991	1
3	Spain	1956–98	8				
4	Holland	1970–95	6				
5	Germany	1974–97	5				
6	Portugal	1961–87	3				
7 =	France	1993	1				
=	Romania	1986	1				

* Of first and last win

The European Cup, now known as the European Champions' League Cup, has been competed for annually since 1956. It was won in that year, and the next four, by Real Madrid (who also won it in 1966 and 1998) – a total of seven times. Italy's AC Milan is their only close competitor, with five wins, while Ajax and Liverpool have each won the Cup on four occasions.

INTERNATIONAL STAR

Lothar Matthäus, Germany's World Cup-winning captain and European Footballer of the Year in 1990, has played for his country on 143 occasions. As a still-active player, he may yet improve on this figure.

TOP 10 ★
RICHEST SOCCER TEAMS

	CLUB/COUNTRY	INCOME (£)
1	Manchester United, England	87,939,000
2	Barcelona, Spain	58,862,000
3	Real Madrid, Spain	55,659,000
4	Juventus, Italy	53,223,000
5	Bayern Munich, Germany	51,619,000
6	AC Milan, Italy	47,480,000
7	Borussia Dortmund, Germany	42,199,000
8	Newcastle United, England	41,134,000
9	Liverpool, England	39,153,000
10	Inter Milan, Italy	39,071,000

A survey conducted by accountants Deloitte & Touche and football magazine *FourFourTwo* compared incomes of the world's top soccer teams during the 1997/8 season. It revealed the extent to which soccer has become a major business enterprise, with many teams generating considerably more revenue from commercial activities such as the sale of merchandise and income from TV rights than they receive from admissions to matches.

TOP 10 ★
EUROPEAN TEAMS WITH THE MOST DOMESTIC LEAGUE TITLES

	CLUB/COUNTRY	TITLES
1	Glasgow Rangers, Scotland	48
2	Linfield, Northern Ireland	42
3	Glasgow Celtic, Scotland	36
4	Rapid Vienna, Austria	*31
5	Benfica, Portugal	30
6 =	CSKA Sofia, Bulgaria	28
=	Olympiakos, Greece	28
8 =	Ajax, Holland	27
=	Real Madrid, Spain	27
10 =	Ferencvaros, Hungary	26
=	Jeunesse Esch, Luxembourg	26

* Rapid Vienna also won one German League title, in 1941

UNITED EFFORT

Manchester United confirmed their status as the world's richest team in 1999, and also captured the unique triple of League, Cup, and European Champions' League.

TOP 10 ★
MOST CAPPED INTERNATIONAL PLAYERS

	PLAYER/COUNTRY	YEARS	CAPS
1 =	Thomas Ravelli, Sweden	1981–97	143
=	Lothar Matthäus*, West Germany/Germany	1980–99	143
3	Majed Abdullah, Saudi Arabia	1978–94	140
4	Claudio Suarez*, Mexico	1982–99	131
5	Marcelo Balboa*, US	1988–98	127
6	Andoni Zubizarreta, Spain	1985–98	126
7	Peter Shilton, England	1970–90	125
8	Masami Ihara*, Japan	1988–99	123
9 =	Pat Jennings, Northern Ireland	1964–86	119
=	Gheorghe Hagi*, Romania	1983–99	119
=	Cobi Jones*, US	1982–99	119

* Still active in 1999

On Two Wheels

TOP 10 ★
FASTEST WORLD CHAMPIONSHIP RACES OF ALL TIME

	RIDER/COUNTRY	BIKE*	YEAR	AVERAGE SPEED MPH	KM/H
1	Barry Sheene, UK	Suzuki	1977	135.07	217.37
2	John Williams, UK	Suzuki	1976	133.49	214.83
3	Phil Read, UK	MV Agusta	1975	133.22	214.40
4	Wil Hartog, Holland	Suzuki	1978	132.90	213.88
5	Phil Read, UK	MV Agusta	1974	131.98	212.41
6	Giacomo Agostini, Italy	MV Agusta	1973	128.51	206.81
7	Walter Villa, Italy	Harley-Davidson	1977	127.03	204.43
8	Walter Villa, Italy	Harley-Davidson	1976	126.08	202.90
9	Giacomo Agostini, Italy	MV Agusta	1969	125.85	202.53
10	Kevin Schwartz, US	Suzuki	1991	125.34	201.72

* 500cc except for Nos. 7 and 8, which were 250cc

All races except for No. 10 were during the Belgian Grand Prix at the Spa-Francorchamps circuit. No. 10 was during the German Grand Prix at Hockenheim. The World Championships were first held in 1949, under the aegis of the Fédération Internationale Motorcycliste, when R. Leslie Graham (UK) won the 500cc class on an AJS.

TOP 10 ★
FASTEST WINNING SPEEDS OF THE DAYTONA 200

	RIDER/COUNTRY*	BIKE	YEAR	AVERAGE SPEED MPH	KM/H
1	Miguel Duhamel, Canada	Honda	1999	113.46	182.61
2	Kenny Roberts	Yamaha	1984	113.14	182.08
3	Kenny Roberts	Yamaha	1983	110.93	178.52
4	Graeme Crosby, New Zealand	Yamaha	1982	109.10	175.58
5	Steve Baker	Yamaha	1977	108.85	175.18
6	Johnny Cecotto, Venezuela	Yamaha	1976	108.77	175.05
7	Dale Singleton	Yamaha	1981	108.52	174.65
8	Kenny Roberts	Yamaha	1978	108.37	174.41
9	Kevin Schwartz	Suzuki	1988	107.80	173.49
10	Dale Singleton	Yamaha	1979	107.69	173.31

* From the US unless otherwise stated

The Daytona 200, which was first held in 1937, forms a round in the AMA (American Motorcyclist Association) Grand National Dirt Track series. It is raced over 57 laps of the 3.56-mile (5.73-km) Daytona International Speedway. The other non-US winners have been: Billy Matthews (Canada), Jaarno Saarinen (Finland), Giacomo Agostini (Italy), and Patrick Pons (France).

SUPERBIKE CHAMPION

British motorcycle legend Carl Fogarty (b. 1966) won his first Grand Prix in 1986. Up to the 2000 season, he had won a record 59 Superbike events.

TOP 10 ★
MOTORCYCLISTS WITH THE MOST WORLD TITLES

	RIDER/COUNTRY	YEARS	TITLES
1	Giacomo Agostini, Italy	1966–75	15
2	Angel Nieto, Spain	1969–84	13
3 =	Carlo Ubbiali, Italy	1951–60	9
=	Mike Hailwood, UK	1961–67	9
5 =	John Surtees, UK	1956–60	7
=	Phil Read, UK	1964–74	7
7 =	Geoff Duke, UK	1951–55	6
=	Jim Redman, Southern Rhodesia	1962–65	6
=	Klaus Enders, W. Germany	1967–74	6
10	Anton Mang, W. Germany	1980–87	5

THE 10 ★
LATEST WORLD CHAMPION SUPERBIKE RIDERS

YEAR	RIDER/COUNTRY	BIKE
1999	Carl Fogarty, UK	Ducati
1998	Carl Fogarty, UK	Ducati
1997	John Kocinski, US	Honda
1996	Troy Corser, Australia	Ducati
1995	Carl Fogarty, UK	Ducati
1994	Carl Fogarty, UK	Ducati
1993	Scott Russell, US	Kawasaki
1992	Doug Polen, US	Ducati
1991	Doug Polen, US	Ducati
1990	Raymond Roche, France	Ducati

TOP 10 — RIDERS WITH THE MOST GRAND PRIX RACE WINS

	RIDER/COUNTRY	YEARS	RACE WINS
1	Giacomo Agostini, Italy	1965–76	122
2	Angel Nieto, Spain	1969–85	90
3	Mike Hailwood, UK	1959–67	76
4	Rolf Biland, Switzerland	1975–90	56
5	Mick Doohan, Australia	1990–98	54
6	Phil Read, UK	1961–75	52
7	Jim Redman, Southern Rhodesia	1961–66	45
8	Anton Mang, West Germany	1976–88	42
9	Carlo Ubbiali, Italy	1950–60	39
10	John Surtees, UK	1955–60	38

TOP 10 — OLYMPIC CYCLING COUNTRIES

		MEDALS			
	COUNTRY	GOLD	SILVER	BRONZE	TOTAL
1	France	32	19	22	73
2	Italy	32	15	6	53
3	Great Britain	9	21	16	46
4	US	11	13	16	40
5	Netherlands	10	14	7	31
6	Germany*	8	9	9	26
7	Australia	6	11	8	25
8	Soviet Union#	11	4	9	24
9	Belgium	6	6	10	22
10	Denmark	6	6	10	21

* Not including West Germany or East Germany 1968–88
# Including United Team of 1992, exludes Russia since

TOP 10 500cc WORLD CHAMPIONSHIPS RIDERS, 1999

(Rider/country/points)

1 Alex Criville, Spain, 267 **2** Kenny Roberts, US, 220 **3** Tadayuki Okada, Japan, 211 **4** Max Biaggi, Italy, 194 **5** Sete Gibernau, Spain, 165 **6** Norick Abe, Japan, 136 **7** Carlos Checa, Spain, 125 **8** John Kocinski, US, 115 **9** Alex Barros, Brazil, 110 **10** Tetsuya Harada, Japan, 104

TOP 10 — TOUR DE FRANCE WINNERS

	RIDER/COUNTRY	WINS
1	Jacques Anquetil, France	5
=	Eddy Merckx, Belgium	5
=	Bernard Hinault, France	5
=	Miguel Indurain, Spain	5
5	Philippe Thys, Belgium	3
=	Louison Bobet, France	3
=	Greg LeMond, US	3
8	Lucien Petit-Breton, France	2
=	Firmin Lambot, Belgium	2
=	Ottavio Bottecchia, Italy	2
=	Nicholas Frantz, Luxembourg	2
=	André Leducq, France	2
=	Antonin Magne, France	2
=	Gino Bartali, Italy	2
=	Sylvere Maës, Belgium	2
=	Fausto Coppi, Italy	2
=	Bernard Thevenet, France	2
=	Laurent Fignon, France	2

TOUR DE FORCE

The 1999 Tour de France approaches the Eiffel Tower. The world's foremost cycle event, the Tour de France was first contested in 1903.

Auto Racing

DRIVERS WITH THE MOST WINSTON CUP WINS

DRIVER*/YEARS		WINS
1	Richard Petty, 1958–92	200
2	David Pearson, 1960–86	105
3 =Bobby Allison, 1975–88		84
=Darrell Waltrip#, 1975–92		84
5	Cale Yarborough, 1957–88	83
6	Dale Earnhardt#, 1979–99	74
7	Lee Petty, 1949–64	54
8 =Ned Jarrett, 1953–66		50
=Junior Johnson, 1953–66		50
10 =Rusty Wallace#, 1986–99		49
=Jeff Gordon#, 1994–99		49

* All from the US
# Still driving at the end of the 1999 season
Source: NASCAR

The Winston Cup is a season-long series of races organized by the National Association of Stock Car Auto Racing, Inc. (NASCAR). Races, which take place over enclosed circuits such as Daytona speedway, are among the most popular motor races in the US. The series started in 1949 (when it was won by Red Byron) as the Grand National series, but changed its name to the Winston Cup in 1970, when it was sponsored by the R. J. Reynolds tobacco company, manufacturers of Winston cigarettes.

TOP 10 MONTE CARLO RALLY-WINNING CARS*

(Car /wins)

❶ Lancia, 12 ❷ = Hotchkiss, 6;
= Renault, 6 ❹ Ford, 5 ❺ Porsche, 4
❻ = Mini-Cooper, 3; = Subaru, 3;
= Toyota, 3 ❾ = Citroën, 2;
= Delahaye, 2; = Fiat, 2; = Mitsubishi, 2;
= Opel, 2; = Saab, 2

* Up to and including 2000

The Monte Carlo Rally has been run since 1911 (with breaks in 1913–23, 1940–48, 1957, and 1974). The appearance of Hotchkiss in 2nd place is perhaps surprising, but it won the rally six times between 1932 and 1950.

NASCAR MONEYWINNERS OF ALL TIME*

DRIVER	TOTAL PRIZES ($)
1 Dale Earnhardt	36,526,665
2 Jeff Gordon	31,877,679
3 Mark Martin	22,269,442
4 Terry Labonte	21,258,305
5 Rusty Wallace	21,247,599
6 Dale Jarrett	21,113,115
7 Bill Elliott	21,107,134
8 Darrell Waltrip	18,170,338
9 Ricky Rudd	16,737,226
10 Geoffrey Bodine	14,013,963

* To January 1, 2000
Source: NASCAR

MONEYWINNERS AT THE INDIANAPOLIS 500, 1999

DRIVER*	TOTAL PRIZES ($)
1 Kenny Brack	1,465,190
2 Jeff Ward	583,150
3 Billy Boat	435,200
4 Arie Luyendyk	382,350
5 Buddy Lazier	285,100
6 John Hollansworth Jr.	265,400
7 Robbie Buhl	257,500
8 Robby Gordon	253,270
9 Raul Boesel	248,600
10 Robby McGehee	247,750
Total prize money for all drivers	9,047,150

* Chassis/engine for all drivers: Dallara/Oldsmobile Aurora
Source: Indianapolis Motor Speedway

Drivers are ranked here according to their winnings, which vary according to such designations as first using a brand of tire.

WINNERS OF THE INDIANAPOLIS 500 WITH THE HIGHEST STARTING POSITIONS*

DRIVER/YEAR	STARTING POSITON
1 =Ray Harroun, 1911	28
=Louis Meyer, 1936	28
3 Fred Frame, 1932	27
4 Johnny Rutherford, 1974	25
5 =Kelly Petillo, 1935	22
=George Souders, 1927	22
7 L. L. Corum and Joe Boyer, 1924	21
8 =Frank Lockart, 1926	20
=Tommy Milton, 1921	20
=Al Unser Jr., 1987	20

* Winners who have started from furthest back in the starting lineup

ALL-TIME CHAMPIONSHIP CAR VICTORY LEADERS WITH THE MOST RACE WINS

DRIVER/DATES		WINS
1	A. J. Foyt, Jr., 1960–81	67
2	Mario Andretti, 1965–93	52
3	Al Unser, 1965–87	39
4	Michael Andretti, 1986–97	38
5	Bobby Unser, 1966–81	35
6	Al Unser, Jr., 1984–95	31
7	Rick Mears, 1978–91	29
8	Johnny Rutherford, 1965–86	27
9	Rodger Ward, 1953–66	26
10	Gordon Johncock, 1965–83	25

Source: Championship Auto Racing Teams

Seventeen-year veteran Michael Andretti is the only leader on the list currently driving on the CART circuit. Colombian Juan Montoya seems likely to make the list in future.

TOP 10

FASTEST WINNING SPEEDS OF THE DAYTONA 500

	DRIVER*	CAR/YEAR	SPEED MPH	KM/H
1	Buddy Baker	Oldsmobile, 1980	177.602	285.823
2	Bill Elliott	Ford, 1987	176.263	283.668
3	Dale Earnhardt	Chevrolet, 1998	172.712	277.953
4	Bill Elliott	Ford, 1985	172.265	277.234
5	Dale Earnhardt	Chevrolet, 1998	172.071	276.921
6	Richard Petty	Buick, 1981	169.651	273.027
7	Derrike Cope	Chevrolet, 1990	165.761	266.766
8	Jeff Gordon	Chevrolet, 1999	161.551	259.991
9	A. J. Foyt	Mercury, 1972	161.550	259.990
10	Richard Petty	Plymouth, 1966	160.627	258.504#

* All winners from the US   # Race reduced to 495 miles (797 km)
Source: NASCAR

FASTEST WINNING TIMES OF THE INDIANAPOLIS 500

	DRIVER*	CAR/YEAR	SPEED MPH	KM/H
1	Arie Luyendyk, Holland	Lola-Chevrolet, 1990	185.984	299.307
2	Rick Mears	Chevrolet-Lumina, 1991	176.457	283.980
3	Bobby Rahal	March-Cosworth, 1986	170.722	274.750
4	Emerson Fittipaldi, Brazil	Penske-Chevrolet, 1989	167.581	269.695
5	Rick Mears	March-Cosworth, 1984	163.612	263.308
6	Mark Donohue	McLaren-Offenhauser, 1972	162.962	262.619
7	Al Unser	March-Cosworth, 1987	162.175	260.995
8	Tom Sneva	March-Cosworth, 1983	162.117	260.902
9	Gordon Johncock	Wildcat-Cosworth, 1982	162.029	260.760
10	Al Unser	Lola-Cosworth, 1978	161.363	259.689

* All US drivers unless otherwise stated
Source: Indianapolis Motor Speedway

TOP 10 CARS IN THE LE MANS 24-HOUR RACE

(Car/wins)

❶ Porsche, 15 ❷ Ferrari, 9 ❸ Jaguar, 7 ❹ Bentley, 5
❺ = Alfa Romeo, 4; = Ford, 4 ❼ Matra-Simca, 3 ❽ = Bugatti, 2;
= La Lorraine, 2; = Mercedes-Benz, 2; = Peugeot, 2

TOP 10

DRIVERS IN THE LE MANS 24-HOUR RACE

	DRIVER/COUNTRY	YEARS	WINS
1	Jacky Ickx, Belgium	1969–82	6
2	Derek Bell, UK	1975–87	5
3	=Olivier Gendebien, Belgium	1958–62	4
	=Henri Pescarolo, France	1972–84	4
5	=Woolf Barnato, UK	1928–30	3
	=Luigi Chinetti, Italy/US	1932–49	3
	=Phil Hill, US	1958–62	3
	=Klaus Ludwig, West Germany	1979–85	3
	=Al Holbert, US	1983–87	3
	=Yannick Dalmas, France	1992–95	3

The Le Mans 24-Hour Race is one of the most demanding in autosport. The first race, held on May 26–27, 1923, was won by André Lagache and René Leonard in a Chenard et Walcker.

TOP 10

FASTEST LE MANS 24-HOUR RACES

	DRIVERS/COUNTRY	CAR	YEAR	AVERAGE SPEED MPH	KM/H
1	Helmut Marko, Austria, Gijs van Lennep, Holland	Porsche	1971	138.133	222.304
2	Jan Lammers, Holland, Johnny Dumfries, Andy Wallace, UK	Jaguar	1988	137.737	221.665
3	Jochen Mass, Manuel Reuter, West Germany, Stanley Dickens, Sweden	Mercedes	1989	136.696	219.990
4	Dan Gurney, A. J. Foyt, US	Ford	1967	135.483	218.038
5	Geoff Brabham, Australia, Christophe Bouchot, Eric Hélary, France	Peugeot	1993	132.574	213.358
6	Klaus Ludwig, "John Winter" (Louis Krager), West Germany, Paulo Barilla, Italy	Porsche	1985	131.744	212.021
7	Chris Amon, Bruce McLaren, New Zealand,	Ford	1966	130.983	210.795
8	Vern Schuppan, Austria, Hurley Haywood, Al Holbert, US	Porsche	1983	130.693	210.330
9	Jean-Pierre Jassaud, Didier Pironi, France	Renault Alpine	1978	130.606	210.189
10	Jacky Ickx, Belgium Jackie Oliver, UK	Ford	1969	129.401	208.250

What type of sport did the highest-earning sportsman of 1999 make his fortune in?

see p278 for the answer

A Boxing
B Motor racing
C Basketball

Golfing Greats

TOP 10 PLAYERS TO WIN THE MOST MAJORS IN A CAREER

	PLAYER/COUNTRY*	BRITISH OPEN	US OPEN	MASTERS	PGA	TOTAL
1	Jack Nicklaus	3	4	6	5	18
2	Walter Hagen	4	2	0	5	11
3 =	Ben Hogan	1	4	2	2	9
=	Gary Player, South Africa	3	1	3	2	9
5	Tom Watson	5	1	2	0	8
6 =	Harry Vardon, England	6	1	0	0	7
=	Gene Sarazen	1	2	1	3	7
=	Bobby Jones	3	4	0	0	7
=	Sam Snead	1	0	3	3	7
=	Arnold Palmer	2	1	4	0	7

From the US unless otherwise stated

LOWEST FOUR-ROUND TOTALS IN THE BRITISH OPEN

	PLAYER/COUNTRY/VENUE	YEAR	TOTAL
1	Greg Norman, Australia, Sandwich	1993	267
2 =	Tom Watson, US, Turnberry	1977	268
=	Nick Price, Zimbabwe, Turnberry	1994	268
4 =	Jack Nicklaus, US, Turnberry	1977	269
=	Nick Faldo, England, Sandwich	1993	269
=	Jesper Parnevik, Sweden, Turnberry	1994	269
7 =	Nick Faldo, England, St. Andrews	1990	270
=	Bernhard Langer, Germany, Sandwich	1993	270
9 =	Tom Watson, US, Muirfield	1980	271
=	Fuzzy Zoeller, US, Turnberry	1994	271
=	Tom Lehman, US, Lytham	1996	271

LOWEST WINNING SCORES IN THE US MASTERS

	PLAYER/COUNTRY*	YEAR	SCORE
1	Tiger Woods	1997	270
2 =	Jack Nicklaus	1965	271
=	Raymond Floyd	1976	271
4 =	Ben Hogan	1953	274
=	Ben Crenshaw	1995	274
6 =	Severiano Ballesteros, Spain	1980	275
=	Fred Couples	1992	275
8 =	Arnold Palmer	1964	276
=	Jack Nicklaus	1975	276
=	Tom Watson	1977	276
=	Nick Faldo, England	1996	276

From the US unless otherwise stated

The US Masters is the only major played on the same course each year, in Augusta, Georgia. The course was built on the site of an old nursery, and the abundance of flowers, shrubs, and plants is a reminder of its former days, with each of the holes named after the plants growing adjacent to it.

WINNERS OF WOMEN'S MAJORS

	PLAYER*	TITLES
1	Patty Berg	16
2 =	Mickey Wright	13
=	Louise Suggs	13
4	Babe Zaharias	12
5	Betsy Rawls	8
6	JoAnne Carner	7
7 =	Kathy Whitworth	6
=	Pat Bradley	6
=	Julie Inkster	6
=	Glenna Collett Vare	6

All from the US

Women's majors once numbered six, but today consist of the US Open (first staged 1946), LPGA Championship (1955), Du Maurier Classic (1973; major status since 1979), and Dinah Shore Tournament (1972).

IRON LADY

US golfer Kathy Whitworth (b. 1939) scored a total of 88 tour wins, achieving victories in six majors, and was voted player of the year on seven occasions.

Did You Know? Mary, Queen of Scots (1542–87), is regarded as the first female golfer. In 1567, she was criticized for playing within two weeks of her husband Darnley's murder.

TOP 10 ★
LOWEST WINNING TOTALS IN THE US OPEN

PLAYER/COUNTRY*/VENUE	YEAR	SCORE
1 =Jack Nicklaus, Baltusrol	1980	272
=Lee Janzen, Baltusrol	1993	272
3 David Graham, Australia, Merion	1981	273
4 =Jack Nicklaus, Baltusrol	1967	275
=Lee Trevino, Oak Hill	1968	275
6 =Ben Hogan, Riviera	1948	276
=Fuzzy Zoeller, Winged Foot	1984	276
=Ernie Els, South Africa, Congressional	1997	276
9 =Jerry Pate, Atlanta	1976	277
=Scott Simpson, Olympic Club	1987	277

From the US unless otherwise stated

TOP 10 ★
PLAYERS WITH THE MOST CAREER WINS ON THE US TOUR

PLAYER*	TOUR WINS
1 Sam Snead	81
2 Jack Nicklaus	71
3 Ben Hogan	63
4 Arnold Palmer	60
5 Byron Nelson	52
6 Billy Casper	51
7 =Walter Hagen	40
=Cary Midlecoff	40
9 Gene Sarazen	38
10 Lloyd Mangrum	36

All from the US

For many years, Sam Snead's total of wins was held to be 84, but the PGA Tour amended his figure in 1990 after discrepancies had been found in their previous lists. They deducted 11 wins from his total, but added eight others that should have been included, giving a revised total of 81.

TOP 10 ★
MONEY-WINNING GOLFERS, 1999

PLAYER/COUNTRY*	WINNINGS ($)
1 Tiger Woods	6,981,836
2 David Duval	3,641,906
3 Davis Love III	2,475,328
4 Vijay Singh, Fiji	2,473,372
5 Colin Montgomerie, Scotland	2,281,884
6 Ernie Els, South Africa	2,151,574
7 Chris Perry	2,145,707
8 Hal Sutton	2,127,578
9 Payne Stewart	2,077,950
10 Justin Leonard	2,020,991

From the US unless otherwise stated

This list is based on winnings of the world's five top tours: US PGA Tour, European PGA Tour, PGA Tour of Japan, Australasian PGA Tour, and FNB Tour of South Africa.

TOP 10 ★
GOLFERS TO PLAY MOST STROKES AT ONE HOLE*

PLAYER/COUNTRY#/YEAR/EVENT	STROKES
1 Tommy Armour, 1927, Shawnee Open	23
2 Philippe Porquier, France, 1978, French Open	21
3 Ray Ainsley, 1938, US Open	19
4 =John Daly, 1998, Bay Hill Invitational	18
=Willie Chisolm, 1919, US Open	18
6 =Porky Oliver, 1953, Bing Crosby	16
=Ian Woosnam, Wales, 1986, French Open	16
8 Hermann Tissies, Germany, 1950, British Open	15
9 =Greg Norman, Australia, 1982, Martini International	14
=Orrin Vincent, 1992, Austrian Open	14

In a leading professional tournament
From the US unless otherwise stated

TOP 10 MONEY-WINNING GOLFERS OF ALL TIME

(Player/country/career winnings in $#)*

❶ **Greg Norman**, Australia, 12,507,322 ❷ **Davis Love III**, 12,487,463 ❸ **Payne Stewart**, 11,737,008 ❹ **Nick Price**, Zimbabwe, 11,386,236 ❺ **Tiger Woods**, 11,315,128 ❻ **Fred Couples**, 11,305,069 ❼ **Mark O'Meara**, 11,162,269 ❽ **Tom Kite**, 10,533,102 ❾ **Scott Hoch**, 10,308,995 ❿ **David Duval**, 10,047,947

From the US unless otherwise stated # *As at December 6, 1999*

DEATH OF A LEGEND

Payne Stewart (1957–99), one of the top professional golfers of the late 20th century, won 18 tournaments, including three major championships. In June 1999 he won his second US Open, by a single shot, with a 15-ft (4.57 m) putt. He was a leading money-winner and noted for his adherence to traditional golfing clothing of knickers and cap. On October 25, 1999, he was killed in a bizarre plane accident, when the Lear jet in which he was flying from Orlando, Florida, became depressurized and its pilots and passengers fell unconscious. The plane, shadowed by an F-16 fighter, flew on autopilot for some 1,400 miles (2,250 km) before crashing.

SNAP SHOTS

Background image: **THE CLUBHOUSE AT AUGUSTA, GEORGIA, US**

Horse Racing

MONEY-WINNING NORTH AMERICAN JOCKEYS IN A CAREER

JOCKEY	EARNINGS IN A CARER ($)
1 Chris McCarron	234,274,989
2 Pat Day	224,401,759
3 Laffit Pincay Jr.	207,472,414
4 Gary Stevens	187,176,371
5 Jerry Bailey	182,070,303
6 Eddie Delahoussaye	175,279,854
7 Angel Cordero Jr.	164,561,227
8 Jose Santos	134,527,287
9 Kent Desormeauc	128,148,779
10 Mike Smith	128,080,626

Source: *NTRA Communications*

MONEY-WINNING HORSES ALL TIME

HORSE/STARTS/WINS	WINNINGS ($)
1 Cigar, 33, 19	9,999,815
2 Skip Away, 38, 18	9,616,360
3 Silver Charm, 24, 12	6,944,369
4 Alysheba, 26, 11	6,679,242
5 John Henry, 83, 39	6,597,947
6 Singspiel, 20, 9	5,950,217
7 Best Pal, 47, 18	5,668,245
8 Taiki Blizzard, 22, 6	5,544,484
9 Sunday Silence, 14, 9	4,968,554
10 Easy Goer, 20, 14	4,873,770

Source: *National Thoroughbred Racing Association*

US JOCKEYS WITH THE MOST WINS IN A CAREER

JOCKEY	YEARS RIDING	WINS
1 Laffit Pincay Jr.	36	8,851
2 Willie Shoemaker	42	8,833
3 Pat Day	27	7,625
4 David Gall	42	7,396
5 Angel Cordero Jr.	35	7,057
6 Chris McCarron	26	6,853
7 Russell Baze	26	6,822
8 Jorge Velasquez	35	6,795
9 Sandy Hawley	31	6,449
10 Larry Snyder	37	6,388

Source: *NTRA Communications*

OLYMPIC EQUESTRIAN COUNTRIES

COUNTRY	GOLD	SILVER	BRONZE	TOTAL
1 West Germany/ Germany	31	17	20	68
2 Sweden	17	8	14	39
3 US	8	17	13	38
4 France	11	12	11	34
5 Italy	7	9	7	23
6 Great Britain	5	7	9	21
7 Switzerland	4	9	7	20
8 =Holland	6	7	2	15
=USSR	6	5	4	15
10 Belgium	4	2	5	11

TOP 10 MONEY-WINNING HORSES, 1999

(Horse/winnings in $)

1 Almutawakel, 3,290,000 **2** Cat Thief, 3,020,500 **3** Daylami, 2,190,000
4 Charismatic, 2,007,404 **5** Budroyale, 1,735,640 **6** Behrens, 1,735,000
7 Beautiful Pleasure, 1,716,404 **8** Silverbulletday, 1,707,640 **9** Menifee, 1,695,400
10 General Pleasure, 1,658,100

Source: *National Thoroughbred Racing Association*

JOCKEYS IN THE BREEDERS CUP

JOCKEY	YEARS	WINS
1 Pat Day	1984–99	11
2 =Mike Smith	1992–97	8
=Jerry Bailey	1991–99	8
4 =Eddie Delahoussaye	1984–93	7
=Laffit Pincay Jr.	1985–93	7
=Chris McCarron	1985–96	7
=Gary Stevens	1990–99	7
8 =Pat Valenzuela	1986–92	6
=Jose Santos	1986–97	6
10 Corey Nakatani	1996–99	5

Source: *The Breeders Cup*

Held at a different venue each year, the Breeders Cup is an end-of-season gathering with seven races run during the day, and with the season's best thoroughbreds competing in each category. Staged in October or November, there is $10 million prize money available, with $3 million going to the winner of the day's senior race, the Classic.

FASTEST WINNING TIMES OF THE KENTUCKY DERBY

HORSE	YEAR	TIME MINS	SECS
1 Secretariat	1973	1	59.2
2 Northern Dancer	1964	2	00.0
3 Spend A Buck	1985	2	00.2
4 Decidedly	1962	2	00.4
5 Proud Clarion	1967	2	00.6
6 Grindstone	1996	2	01.0
7 =Lucky Debonair	1965	2	01.2
=Affirmed	1978	2	01.2
=Thunder Gulch	1995	2	01.2
10 Whirlaway	1941	2	01.4

Source: *The Jockey Club*

The Kentucky Derby is held on the first Saturday in May at Churchill Downs, Louisville, Kentucky. The first leg of the Triple Crown, it was first raced in 1875 over a distance of 1 mile 4 furlongs, but after 1896 it was reduced to 1 mile 2 furlongs.

THE 10 LAST TRIPLE CROWN-WINNING HORSES*

(Horse/year)

1 **Affirmed**, 1978 2 **Seattle Slew**, 1977
3 **Secretariat**, 1973 4 **Citation**, 1948
5 **Assault**, 1946 6 **Count Fleet**, 1943
7 **Whirlaway**, 1941 8 **War
Admiral**, 1937 9 **Omaha**, 1935
10 **Gallant Fox**, 1930

* *Horses that have won the Kentucky Derby, the
Preakness Stakes, and the Belmont Stakes
in the same season*

TOP 10 ★
STEEPLECHASE TRAINERS IN NORTH AMERICA

	TRAINER	WINNINGS ($)	WINS
1	Jonathan Sheppard	866,389	26
2	Jack Fisher	509,695	19
3	Bruce Miller	539,946	14
4	Tom Voss	240,978	12
5	Sanna Neilson	306,220	11
6 =	Janet Elliot	382,720	10
=	Charlie Fenwick	225,453	10
8 =	Ricky Hendriks	117,990	9
=	Neil Morris	114,250	9
10	Toby Edwards	111,540	6

Source: Steeplechase Times/National Steeplechase
Association

TOP 10 JOCKEYS IN THE PRIX DE L'ARC DE TRIOMPHE

(Jockey/wins)

1 = **Jacko Doyasbère**, 4; = **Pat Eddery**, 4;
= **Freddy Head**, 4; = **Yves Saint-Martin**, 4
5 = **Enrico Camici**, 3; = **Charlie
Elliott**, 3; = **Olivier Peslier**, 3;
= **Lester Piggot**, 3; = **Roger
Poincelet**, 3; = **Charles Semblat**, 3

TOP 10 ★
JOCKEYS IN THE TRIPLE CROWN RACES

	JOCKEY	KENTUCKY	PREAKNESS	BELMONT	TOTAL
1	Eddie Arcaro	5	6	6	17
2	Bill Shoemaker	4	2	5	11
3 =	Bill Hartack	5	3	1	9
=	Earle Sande	3	1	5	9
5 =	Pat Day	1	5	2	8
=	Jimmy McLaughlin	1	1	6	8
7 =	Angel Cordero Jr.	3	2	1	6
=	Chas Kurtsinger	2	2	2	6
=	Ron Turcotte	2	2	2	6
=	Gary Stevens	3	1	2	6

The US Triple Crown consists of the Kentucky Derby, the Preakness Stakes, and the Belmont Stakes.
Since 1875, only 11 horses have won all three races in one season. The only jockey to complete the
Triple Crown twice is Eddie Arcaro, on Whirlaway in 1941 and Citation in 1948.

TOP 10 ★
MONEY-WINNING TROTTERS IN A HARNESS-RACING CAREER*

	HORSE	WINNINGS ($)
1	Moni Maker	4,175,503
2	Peace Corps	4,137,737
3	Ourasi	4,010,105
4	Mack Lobell	3,917,594
5	Reve d'Udon	3,611,351
6	Zoogin	3,428,311
7	Sea Cove	3,138,986
8	Ina Scot	2,897,044
9	Ideal du Gazeau	2,744,777
10	Vrai Lutin	2,612,429

* *A trotter is a horse whose diagonally opposite legs
move forward together.*

Harness racing is one of the oldest sports in the
US; its origins go back to the Colonial period,
when many races were held along the turnpikes
of New York and the New England colonies.
After growing in popularity in the nineteenth
century, the exotically titled governing body, the
National Association for the Promotion of the
Interests of the Trotting Turf (now the National
Trotting Association), was founded in 1870.

TOP 10 ★
MONEY-WINNING PACERS IN A HARNESS-RACING CAREER*

	HORSE	WINNINGS ($)
1	Nihilator	3,225,653
2	Artsplace	3,085,083
3	Presidential Ball	3,021,363
4	Matt's Scooter	2,944,591
5	On the Road Again	2,819,102
6	Riyadh	2,793,527
7	Beach Towel	2,570,357
8	Western Hanover	2,541,647
9	Cam's Card Shark	2,498,204
10	Pacific Rocket	2,333,401

* *A pacer's legs are extended laterally and with a
"swinging motion"; pacers usually travel faster
than trotters.*

Unlike thoroughbred racehorses, standardbred
harness-racing horses are trained to trot and
pace, but do not gallop. While widespread in the
United States, harness racing is also popular in
Australia and New Zealand, and, increasingly,
elsewhere in the globe.

Which sport was originally called "sphairistike"?

see p.271 for the answer

A Lawn tennis
B Polo
C Croquet

Hockey Headlines

GOAL SCORERS
IN AN NHL SEASON

PLAYER/TEAM		SEASON	GOALS
1	Wayne Gretzky, Edmonton Oilers	1981–82	92
2	Wayne Gretzky, Edmonton Oilers	1983–84	87
3	Brett Hull, St. Louis Blues	1990–91	86
4	Mario Lemieux, Pittsburgh Penguins	1988–89	85
5=	Phil Esposito, Boston Bruins	1970–71	76
=	Alexander Mogilny, Buffalo Sabres	1992–93	76
=	Teemu Selanne, Winnipeg Jets	1992–93	76
8	Wayne Gretzky, Edmonton Oilers	1984–85	73
9	Brett Hull, St. Louis Blues	1989–90	72
10=	Wayne Gretzky, Edmonton Oilers	1982–83	71
=	Jari Kurri, Edmonton Oilers	1984–85	71

BIGGEST NHL ARENAS

STADIUM/LOCATION	HOME TEAM	CAPACITY
1 Molson Center, Montreal	Montreal Canadiens	21,273
2= United Center, Chicago	Chicago Blackhawks	20,500
= Raleigh Entertainment & Sports Arena, Raleigh	Carolina Hurricanes	20,500
4= Canadian Airlines Saddledrome, Calgary	Calgary Flames	20,000
= Staples Center, Los Angeles	Los Angeles Kings	20,000
6 Joe Louis Arena, Detroit	Detroit Red Wings	19,983
7 MCI Center, Washington	Washington Capitals	19,740
8 First Union Center, Philadelphia	Philadelphia Flyers	19,511
9 Ice Palace, Tampa	Tampa Bay Lightning	19,500
10 Kiel Center, St. Louis	St. Louis Blues	19,260

TOP 10 TEAM SALARIES
IN THE NHL, 1999–2000

(Team/salary in $)

1 New York Rangers, 64,509,011 **2** Philadelphia Flyers, 52,233,976 **3** Detroit Red Wings, 48,545,849 **4** Dallas Stars, 43,659,500 **5** Colorado Avalanche, 41,130,000 **6** Florida Panthers, 41,032,423 **7** Chicago Blackhawks, 39,999,500 **8** St. Louis Blues, 39,032,072 **9** San Jose Sharks, 38,276,806 **10** Los Angeles Kings, 36,958,000

Source: *National Hockey League Players Association*

TOP 10 GOAL SCORERS
IN 1998–99

(Player/team/goals)

1 Teemu Selanne, Mighty Ducks of Anaheim, 47 **2** = Jaromir Jagr, Pittsburgh Penguins, 44; = Alexei Yashin, Ottawa Senators, 44; = Tony Amonte, Chicago Blackhawks, 44 **5** John LeClair, Philadelphia Flyers, 43 **6** Joe Sakic, Colorado Avalanche, 41 **7** = Eric Lindros, Philadelphia Flyers, 40; = Theoren Fleury, Colorado Avalanche, 40; = Miroslave Satan, Buffalo Sabres, 40 **10** = Paul Kariya, Mighty Ducks of Anaheim, 39; = Luc Robitaille, Los Angeles Kings, 39

Source: *National Hockey League*

GOAL TENDERS IN AN NHL CAREER*

PLAYER	SEASONS	GAMES WON
1 Terry Sawchuk	21	447
2 Jacques Plante	18	434
3 Tony Esposito	16	423
4 Patrick Roy#	14	412
5 Glenn Hall	18	407
6 Grant Fuhr#	18	398
7 Andy Moog	18	372
8 Rogie Vachon	16	355
9 Mike Vernon#	16	347
10 Tom Barrasso#	16	345

* Regular season only　　　*# Still active at start of 1999–2000 season*

BEST-PAID PLAYERS IN THE NHL,
1999–2000

PLAYER	TEAM	SALARY ($)
1 Jaromir Jagr	Pittsburgh Penguins	10,359,852
2 Paul Kariya	Anaheim Mighty Ducks	10,000,000
3 Peter Forsberg	Colorado Avalanche	9,000,000
4= Theoren Fleury	New York Rangers	8,500,000
= Eric Lindros	Philadelphia Flyers	8,500,000
6 Pavel Bure	Florida Panthers	8,000,000
7 Patrick Roy	Colorado Avalanche	7,500,000
8= Dominik Hasek	Buffalo Sabres	7,000,000
= Mats Sundin	Toronto Maple Leafs	7,000,000
10 Brian Leetch	New York Rangers	6,680,000

Source: *National Hockey League Players Association*

TOP 10 ★
WINNERS OF THE HART TROPHY

	PLAYER	YEARS	WINS
1	Wayne Gretzky	1980–89	9
2	Gordie Howe	1952–63	6
3	Eddie Shore	1933–38	4
4 =	Bobby Clarke	1973–76	3
=	Howie Morenz	1928–32	3
=	Bobby Orr	1970–72	3
=	Mario Lemieux	1988-96	3
8 =	Jean Beliveau	1956–64	2
=	Bill Cowley	1941–43	2
=	Phil Esposito	1969–74	2
=	Dominic Hasek	1997-98	2
=	Bobby Hull	1965–66	2
=	Guy Lafleur	1977–78	2
=	Mark Messier	1990–92	2
=	Stan Mikita	1967–68	2
=	Nels Stewart	1926–30	2

Source: *National Hockey League*

The Hart Trophy, named after Cecil Hart, former manager/coach of the Montreal Canadiens, has been awarded annually since 1924 to the player considered the most valuable to his team.

TOP 10 ★
TEAMS WITH THE MOST STANLEY CUP WINS

	TEAM	WINS
1	Montreal Canadiens	23
2	Toronto Maple Leafs	13
3	Detroit Red Wings	9
4 =	Boston Bruins	5
=	Edmonton Oilers	5
6 =	New York Islanders	4
=	New York Rangers	4
=	Ottawa Senators	4
9	Chicago Black Hawks	3
10 =	Philadelphia Flyers	2
=	Pittsburgh Penguins	2
=	Montreal Maroons	2

Source: *National Hockey League*

During his time as Governor General of Canada from 1888 to 1893, Sir Frederick Arthur Stanley (Lord Stanley of Preston and 16th Earl of Derby) became interested in ice hockey, and in 1893 presented a trophy to be contested by the best amateur teams in Canada. The first trophy went to the Montreal Amateur Athletic Association, who won it without a challenge from any other team.

TOP 10 ★
POINT SCORERS IN STANLEY CUP PLAY-OFF MATCHES

	PLAYER	TOTAL POINTS
1	Wayne Gretzky	382
2	Mark Messier*	295
3	Jari Kurri	233
4	Glenn Anderson	214
5	Paul Coffey*	196
6	Bryan Trottier	184
7	Jean Beliveau	176
8	Denis Savard	175
9	Doug Gilmour*	171
10	Denis Potvin	164

* Still active at start of 1999–2000 season

In his 20 playing seasons, Wayne Gretzky, who heads virtually every ice hockey league table, achieved some 61 NHL records, leading Edmonton to four Stanley Cups (1984–85 and 1987–88). In addition to scoring the most points, he leads for most goals and most assists in Stanley Cup matches. The Stanley Cup itself is a silver bowl. Each winning team has its club name and year engraved on a silver ring that is fitted to the Cup, and is obliged to return it in good condition.

TOP 10 ★
GOAL SCORERS IN AN NHL CAREER*

	PLAYER	SEASONS	GOALS
1	Wayne Gretzky	20	894
2	Gordie Howe	26	801
3	Marcel Dionne	18	731
4	Phil Esposito	18	717
5	Mike Gartner	19	708
6	Mario Lemieux	12	613
7 =	Bobby Hull	16	610
=	Mark Messier#	20	610
9	Dino Ciccarelli	19	608
10	Jari Kurri	17	601

* Regular season only

 # Still active at start of 1999–2000 season

TOP 10 ★
NHL GAMES TO PRODUCE THE MOST GOALS

	GAME	SCORE	DATE	TOTAL GOALS
1 =	Montreal Canadiens v Toronto St. Patricks	14—7	Jan 10, 1920	21
=	Edmonton Oilers v Chicago Black Hawks	12—9	Dec 11, 1985	21
3 =	Edmonton Oilers v Minnesota North Stars	12—8	Jan 4, 1984	20
=	Toronto Maple Leafs v Edmonton Oilers	11—9	Jan 8, 1986	20
5 =	Montreal Wanderers v Toronto Arenas	10—9	Dec 19, 1917	19
=	Montreal Canadiens v Quebec Bulldogs	16—3	Mar 3, 1920	19
=	Montreal Canadiens v Hamilton Tigers	13—3	Feb 26, 1921	19
=	Boston Bruins v New York Rangers	10—9	Mar 4, 1944	19
=	Boston Bruins v Detroit Red Wings	10—9	Mar 16, 1944	19
=	Vancouver Canucks v Minnesota North Stars	10—9	Oct 7, 1983	19

What were once used as targets in Olympic archery events?
see p.273 for the answer

A Rabbits
B Birds
C Goats

Tennis Triumphs

MEN WITH THE MOST WIMBLEDON TITLES

PLAYER/COUNTRY		YEARS	S	TITLES D	M	TOTAL
1	William Renshaw, UK	1880–89	7	7	0	14
2	Lawrence Doherty, UK	1897–1905	5	8	0	13
3	Reginald Doherty, UK	1897–1905	4	8	0	12
4	John Newcombe, Australia	1965–74	3	6	0	9
5 =	Ernest Renshaw, UK	1880–89	1	7	0	8
=	Tony Wilding, New Zealand	1907–14	4	4	0	8
7 =	Wilfred Baddeley, UK	1891–96	3	4	0	7
=	Bob Hewitt, Australia/S. Africa	1962–79	0	5	2	7
=	Rod Laver, Australia	1959–69	4	1	2	7
=	John McEnroe, US	1979–84	3	4	0	7

S – singles; D – doubles; M – mixed

TOP 10 TOURNAMENT WINNERS, MALE*

(Player/country/tournament wins)

1 Jimmy Connors, US, 109 **2** Ivan Lendl, Czechoslovakia, 94
3 John McEnroe, US, 77 **4** = Bjorn Borg, Sweden, 62;
= Guillermo Vilas, Argentina, 62 **6** Ilie Nastase, Romania, 57
7 Pete Sampras, US, 56 **8** Boris Becker, Germany, 49
9 Rod Laver, Australia, 47 **10** Thomas Muster, Austria, 44

* *Tournament leaders since Open Tennis introduced in 1968. Totals include ATP tour, Grand Prix, and WCT tournaments.*

WINNERS OF MEN'S GRAND SLAM SINGLES TITLES

PLAYER/COUNTRY		A	TITLES F	W	US	TOTAL
1	Roy Emerson, Australia	6	2	2	2	12
2 =	Björn Borg, Sweden	0	6	5	0	11
=	Rod Laver, Australia	3	2	4	2	11
=	Pete Sampras, US	2	0	5	4	11
5	Bill Tilden, US	0	0	3	7	10
6 =	Jimmy Connors, US	1	0	2	5	8
=	Ivan Lendl, Czechoslovakia	2	3	0	3	8
=	Fred Perry, UK	1	1	3	3	8
=	Ken Rosewall, Australia	4	2	0	2	8
10 =	Henri Cochet, France	0	4	2	1	7
=	René Lacoste, France	0	3	2	2	7
=	William Larned, US	0	0	0	7	7
=	John McEnroe, US	0	0	3	4	7
=	John Newcombe, Australia	2	0	3	2	7
=	William Renshaw, UK	0	0	7	0	7
=	Richard Sears, US	0	0	0	7	7
=	Mats Wilander, Sweden	3	3	0	1	7

A – Australian Open; F – French Open; W – Wimbledon; US – US Open

THE 10 LAST WINNERS OF THE US OPEN MEN'S CHAMPIONSHIP

(Year/winner/country)

1 1999, Andre Agassi, US **2** 1998, Patrick Rafter, Australia **3** 1997, Patrick Rafter, Australia **4** 1996, Pete Sampras, US
5 1995, Pete Sampras, US
6 1994, Andre Agassi, US
7 1993, Pete Sampras, US
8 1992, Stefan Edberg, Sweden
9 1991, Stefan Edberg, Sweden
10 1990, Pete Sampras, US

TOP 10 MALE PLAYERS*

(Player/country/weeks at No. 1)

1 Pete Sampras, US, 276 **2** Ivan Lendl, Czechoslovakia, 270 **3** Jimmy Connors, US, 268 **4** John McEnroe, US, 170 **5** Bjorn Borg, Sweden, 109 **6** Stefan Edberg, Sweden, 72 **7** Jim Courier, US, 58 **8** Andre Agassi, US, 47 **9** Ilie Nastase, Romania, 40 **10** Mats Wilander, Sweden, 20

* *Based on weeks at No. 1 in ATP rankings (1973 to 1999)*

TOP 10

WINNERS OF WOMEN'S GRAND SLAM SINGLES TITLES

	PLAYER/COUNTRY	A	F	W	US	TOTAL
1	**Margaret Court**, Australia	11	5	3	5	24
2	**Steffi Graf**, Germany	4	5	7	5	21
3	**Helen Wills-Moody**, US	0	4	8	7	19
4	=**Chris Evert-Lloyd**, US	2	7	3	6	18
	=**Martina Navratilova**, US	3	2	9	4	18
6	=**Billie Jean King**, US	1	1	6	4	12
	=**Suzanne Lenglen**, France	0	6	6	0	12
8	=**Maureen Connolly**, US	1	2	3	3	9
	=**Monica Seles**, US	4	3	0	2	9
10	**Molla Mallory**, US	0	0	0	8	8

TITLES: *A – Australian Open; F – French Open; W – Wimbledon; US – US Open*

TOP 10

TOURNAMENT WINNERS, FEMALE*

	PLAYER/COUNTRY	TOURNAMENT WINS
1	**Martina Navratilova**, US	167
2	**Chris Evert-Lloyd**, US	154
3	**Steffi Graf**, Germany	106
4	**Margaret Court**, Australia	92
5	**Billie Jean King**, US	67
6	**Evonne Goolagong Cawley**, Australia	65
7	**Virginia Wade**, UK	55
8	**Monica Seles**, US	43
9	**Conchita Martinez**, Spain	30
10	**Tracy Austin**, US	29

* *Tournament leaders since Open Tennis introduced in 1968*

TOP 10

DAVIS CUP WINNING TEAMS

	COUNTRY	WINS
1	**United States**	31
2	**Australia**	21
3	**France**	8
4	**Sweden**	7
5	**Australasia**	6
6	**British Isles**	5
7	**Great Britain**	4
8	**West Germany**	2
9	=**Germany**	1
	=**Czechoslovakia**	1
	=**Italy**	1
	=**South Africa**	1

South Africa's sole win was gained when, for political reasons, India refused to meet them in the 1974 final.

BRILLIANT CAREER

In 1995, Andre Agassi was the 12th player to be ranked world No. 1. In 1999, he became only the fifth male player to complete a Grand Slam.

TOP 10 CAREER MONEY-WINNING WOMEN*

(Player/country/winnings in $)

1 **Steffi Graf**, Germany, 20,646,410 2 **Martina Navratilova**, US, 20,344,061 3 **Arantxa Sanchez-Vicario**, Spain, 14,119,642 4 **Monica Seles**, US, 10,928,640 5 **Jana Novotna**, Czech Republic, 10,507,680 6 **Chris Evert-Lloyd**, US, 8,896,195 7 **Gabriela Sabatini**, Argentina, 8,785,850 8 **Martina Hingis**, Switzerland, 8,331,496 9 **Conchita Martinez**, Spain, 7,780,941 10 **Natasha Zvereva**, Belarus, 7,036,143

* *To end of 1999 season*

GOLDEN GIRL

German-born Steffi Graf was one of the youngest players ever ranked, aged just 13 in 1982. As her career progressed, she was first ranked No. 1 in 1987, and held the No. 1 ranking for a record 374 weeks. Aged just 19 in 1988, she became the youngest-ever winner of the Grand Slam, and also won Olympic gold at Seoul. She continued to win at least one Grand Slam title a year for the next 10 years, until knee injuries prevented her from competing. In 1999, after winning her sixth French Open championship, and her 22nd Grand Slam title, Steffi Graf announced her decision to retire. In 2000, her romantic involvement with Andre Agassi made press headlines.

SNAP SHOTS

Did You Know? Lawn tennis was patented in 1874 by Major Walter Clopton Wingfield, who originally called it "sphairistike" (from *sphaira*, Greek for ball).

Team Games

WINNERS OF THE TABLE TENNIS WORLD CHAMPIONSHIP

	COUNTRY	MEN'S	WOMEN'S	TOTAL
1	China	13	13	26
2	Japan	7	8	15
3	Hungary	12	–	12
4	Czechoslovakia	6	3	9
5	Romania	–	5	5
6	Sweden	4	–	4
7 =England		1	2	3
=US		1	2	3
9	Germany	–	2	2
10=Austria		1	–	1
=North Korea		–	1	1
=South Korea		–	1	1
=USSR		–	1	1

Originally a European event, it was later extended to a world championship.

TOP 10 POLO TEAMS WITH THE MOST BRITISH OPEN CHAMPIONSHIP WINS

(Team/wins)

1 = Stowell Park, 5; = Tramontana, 5
3 = Ellerston, 3; = Cowdray Park, 3;
= Pimms, 3; = Windsor Park, 3
7 = Casarejo, 2; = Jersey Lillies, 2;
= Woolmer's Park, 2; = Falcons, 2;
= Southfield, 2

TOP 10 COUNTIES WITH THE MOST WINS IN THE ALL-IRELAND HURLING CHAMPIONSHIPS

(County/wins)

1 Cork, 28 **2** Kilkenny, 25
3 Tipperary, 24 **4** Limerick, 7
5 = Dublin, 6; = Wexford, 6
7 = Galway, 4; = Offaly, 4 **9** Clare, 3
10 Waterford, 2

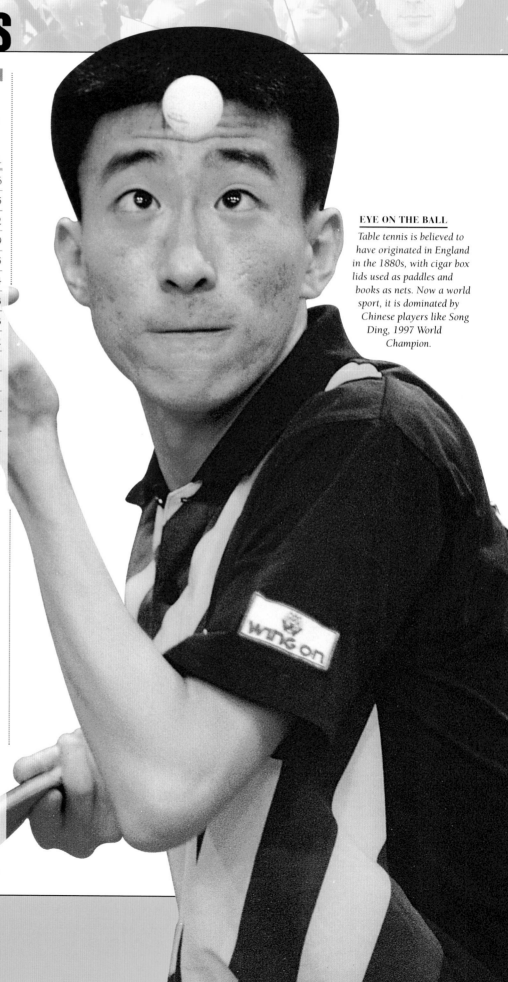

EYE ON THE BALL
Table tennis is believed to have originated in England in the 1880s, with cigar box lids used as paddles and books as nets. Now a world sport, it is dominated by Chinese players like Song Ding, 1997 World Champion.

LAST WINNERS OF THE ROLLER HOCKEY WORLD CHAMPIONSHIP

YEAR	WINNER
1999	Argentina
1997	Italy
1995	Argentina
1993	Portugal
1991	Portugal
1989	Spain
1988	Spain
1986	Spain
1984	Argentina
1982	Portugal

Roller hockey, a five-a-side game formerly called rink hockey, has been played for more than 100 years. The first international tournament was held in Paris in 1910, the first European Championships in Britain in 1926, and the men's World Championship biennially since 1936 (odd-numbered years since 1989). Portugal is the overall winner, with 14 titles to its credit.

OLYMPIC FIELD HOCKEY COUNTRIES

	COUNTRY	GOLD	SILVER	BRONZE	TOTAL
1	India	8	1	2	11
2	Great Britain*	3	2	5	10
3	Netherlands	2	2	5	9
4	Pakistan	3	3	2	8
5	Australia	2	3	2	7
6	Germany#	1	2	2	5
7 =	Spain	1	2	1	4
=	West Germany	1	3	–	4
9 =	South Korea	–	2	–	2
=	US	–	–	2	2
=	Soviet Union	–	–	2	2

* Including England, Ireland, Scotland, and Wales, which competed separately in the 1908 Olympics

\# Not including West Germany or East Germany 1968–88

OLYMPIC ARCHERY COUNTRIES

	COUNTRY	GOLD	SILVER	BRONZE	TOTAL
1	US	13	7	7	27
2	France	6	10	6	22
3	South Korea	10	6	3	19
4	Soviet Union	1	3	5	9
5	Great Britain	2	2	4	8
6	Finland	1	1	2	4
7 =	China	0	3	0	3
=	Italy	0	0	3	3
9 =	Sweden	0	2	0	2
=	Japan	0	1	1	2
=	Poland	0	1	1	2

Archery was introduced as an Olympic sport at the second modern Olympics, held in Paris in 1900. The format has changed considerably over succeeding Games, with events such as shooting live birds being discontinued in favor of target shooting. Individual and team events for men and women are now included in the program.

OLYMPIC VOLLEYBALL COUNTRIES

	COUNTRY	GOLD	SILVER	BRONZE	TOTAL
1	Soviet Union*	7	5	1	13
2	Japan	3	3	2	8
3	US	2	1	2	5
4 =	Cuba	2	–	1	3
=	Brazil	1	1	1	3
=	China	1	1	1	3
=	Poland	1	–	2	3
8 =	Netherlands	1	1	–	2
=	East Germany	–	2	–	2
=	Bulgaria	–	1	1	2
=	Czechoslovakia	–	1	1	2
=	Italy	–	1	1	2

* Includes United Team of 1992; excludes Russia since this date

UP AND OVER DOWN UNDER
Matther Allan (Carlton) and Steven King (Geelong) battle for possession in an Australian football match.

TOP 10 AUSTRALIAN FOOTBALL LEAGUE TEAMS

(Team/Grand Final wins)

❶ Carlton Blues, 16 ❷ Essendon Bombers, 15 ❸ Collingwood Magpies, 14 ❹ Melbourne Demons, 12 ❺ Richmond Tigers, 10 ❻ Hawthorn Hawks, 9 ❼ Fitzroy Lions, 8 ❽ Geelong Cats, 6 ❾ Kangaroos (North Melbourne), 4 ❿ South Melbourne, 3

OLYMPIC SHOOTING COUNTRIES

	COUNTRY	GOLD	SILVER	BRONZE	TOTAL
1	US	45	26	21	92
2	Soviet Union	22	17	81	57
3	Sweden	13	23	19	55
4	Great Britain	13	14	18	45
5	France	13	16	13	42
6	Norway	16	9	11	36
7	Switzerland	11	11	12	34
8	Italy	8	5	10	23
9	Greece	5	7	7	19
10 =	China	7	5	5	17
=	Finland	3	5	9	17

Did You Know? At the 1932 Los Angeles Olympics, India's field hockey team beat the US by a record 24–1 (with 12 of the goals scored by one player, Roop Singh), and Japan by 11–1.

Water Sports

WINNERS OF MEN'S WORLD WATER-SKIING TITLES

SKIER/COUNTRY	OVERALL	SLALOM	TRICKS	JUMP	TOTAL
1 Patrice Martin, France	6	0	4	0	10
2 Sammy Duvall, US	4	0	0	2	6
3 =Alfredo Mendoza, US	2	1	0	2	5
=Mike Suyderhoud, US	2	1	0	2	5
=Bob La Point, US	0	4	1	0	5
=Andy Mapple, UK	0	5	0	0	5
7 =George Athans, Canada	2	1	0	0	3
=Guy de Clercq, Belgium	1	0	0	2	3
=Wayne Grimditch, US	0	0	2	1	3
=Mike Hazelwood, UK	1	0	0	2	3
=Ricky McCormick, US	0	0	1	2	3
=Billy Spencer, US	1	1	1	0	3

TOP 10 ★

WINNERS OF WOMEN'S WORLD WATER-SKIING TITLES

SKIER/COUNTRY	OVERALL	SLALOM	TRICKS	JUMP	TOTAL
1 Liz Shetter, US	3	3	1	4	11
2 Willa McGuire, US	3	2	1	2	8
3 Cindy Todd, US	2	3	0	2	7
4 Deena Mapple, US	2	0	0	4	6
5 =Marina Doria, Switzerland	1	1	2	0	4
=Tawn Hahn, US	0	0	4	0	4
=Helena Kjellander, Sweden	0	4	0	0	4
=Natalya Ponomaryeva, USSR	1	0	3	0	4
9 =Maria Victoria Carrasco, Venezuela	0	0	3	0	3
=Yelena Milakova, Russia	2	0	0	1	3

TOP 10 POWERBOAT DRIVERS WITH MOST RACE WINS

(Owner/country/wins)

1 Bill Seebold, US, 912 **2 Jumbo McConnell**, US, 217 **3 Chip Hanuer**, US, 203 **4 Steve Curtis**, UK, 184 **5 Mikeal Frode**, Sweden, 152 **6 Neil Holmes**, UK, 147 **7 Peter Bloomfield**, UK, 126 **8 Renato Molinari**, Italy, 113 **9 Cees Van der Valden**, Netherlands, 98 **10 Bill Muney**, US, 96

Source: Raceboat International

TOP 10 COLLEGES IN THE INTERCOLLEGIATE ROWING ASSOCIATION REGATTA*

(College/first and last winning years/wins)

1 Cornell, 1896–1982, 24 **2 Navy**, 1921–84, 13 **3 = Washington**, 1923–97, 11; **= California**, 1928–99, 11 **5 Pennsylvania**, 1898–1989, 9 **6 = Wisconsin**, 1951–90, 7; **= Brown**, 1979–95, 7 **8 Syracuse**, 1904–78, 6 **9 Columbia**, 1895–1929, 4 **10 Princeton**, 1985–98, 3 ** Men's varsity eight-oared shells event*

TOP 10 ★

OLYMPIC YACHTING COUNTRIES

COUNTRY	MEDALS			
	GOLD	SILVER	BRONZE	TOTAL
1 US	16	19	16	51
2 Great Britain	14	12	9	35
3 Sweden	9	12	9	30
4 Norway	16	11	2	29
5 France	12	6	9	27
6 Denmark	10	8	4	22
7 Germany/West Germany	6	5	6	17
8 Netherlands	4	5	6	15
9 New Zealand	6	4	3	13
10 =Australia	3	2	7	12
=Soviet Union*	4	5	3	12
=Spain	9	2	1	12

* Includes United Team of 1992; excludes Russia since this date

TOP 10 ★

OLYMPIC ROWING COUNTRIES

COUNTRY	MEDALS			
	GOLD	SILVER	BRONZE	TOTAL
1 US	29	28	19	76
2 East Germany	33	7	8	48
3 Soviet Union*	12	20	11	43
4 Germany#	19	12	11	42
5 Great Britain	19	15	7	41
6 Italy	12	11	9	32
= Canada	8	12	12	32
8 France	4	14	12	30
9 Romania	12	10	7	29
10 Switzerland	6	7	9	22

* Includes United Team of 1992; excludes Russia since this date

 # Not including West Germany or East Germany 1968–88

Did You Know? John B. Kelly (1891–1960), father of actress Grace Kelly, later Princess Grace of Monaco, won three rowing gold medals at the 1920 and 1924 Olympics.

TOP 10 ★
OLYMPIC SWIMMING COUNTRIES

	COUNTRY	GOLD	MEDALS SILVER	BRONZE	TOTAL
1	US	230	176	137	543
2	Australia	41	37	47	125
3	East Germany	40	34	25	99
4	Soviet Union*	24	32	38	94
5	Germany#	19	33	34	86
6 =Great Britain		18	23	30	71
=Hungary		29	23	19	71
8	Sweden	13	21	21	55
9	Japan	15	18	19	52
10	Canada	11	17	20	48

* Includes United Team of 1992; excludes Russia since this date
 # Not including West Germany or East Germany 1968–88

The medal table includes medals for the synchronized swimming, diving, and water polo events that form part of the Olympic swimming program. Swimming has been part of the Olympics since the first modern games in 1896, at which only members of the Greek navy were eligible for one event – the 100-m (328-ft) swimming race for sailors. Events were held in the open water until 1908, when specially built pools were introduced.

TOP 10 ★
OLYMPIC CANOEING COUNTRIES

	COUNTRY	GOLD	MEDALS SILVER	BRONZE	TOTAL
1 =Hungary		10	23	20	53
=Soviet Union*		30	13	10	53
3	Germany#	18	15	12	45
4	Romania	9	10	12	31
5	East Germany	14	7	9	30
6	Sweden	14	10	4	28
7	France	2	6	14	22
8 =Bulgaria		4	3	8	15
=US		5	4	6	15
10	Canada	3	7	4	14

* Includes United Team of 1992; excludes Russia since this date
 # Not including West Germany or East Germany 1968–88

PADDLE POWER

Canoeing has been an Olympic sport since 1936. Six of Sweden's golds were won by one contestant, Gert Fredriksson, who also gained a silver and a bronze, in Games from 1948–60.

Winter Sports

SWISS ROLL
The bobsled event has been part of the Winter Olympics since 1924. Switzerland has won more medals than any other country.

MEN'S WORLD AND OLYMPIC FIGURE SKATING TITLES

	SKATER/COUNTRY	YEARS	TITLES
1	Ulrich Salchow, Sweden	1901–11	11
2	Karl Schäfer, Austria	1930–36	9
3	Richard Button, US	1948–52	7
4	Gillis Grafstrom, Sweden	1920–29	6
5 =	Hayes Jenkins, US	1953–56	5
=	Scott Hamilton, US	1981–84	5
7 =	Willy Bockl, Austria	1925–28	4
=	David Jenkins, US	1957–60	4
=	Ondrej Nepela, Czechoslovakia	1971–73	4
=	Kurt Browning, Canada	1989–93	4

TOP 10 OLYMPIC BOBSLEDDING COUNTRIES
(Country/medals)

① Switzerland, 26 **②** US, 14 **③** East Germany, 13
④ = Germany*, 11; = Italy, 11 **⑥** West Germany, 6 **⑦** UK, 4
⑧ = Austria, 3; = Soviet Union#, 3 **⑩** = Canada, 2; = Belgium, 2

* Not including West or East Germany 1968–88
# Includes United Team of 1992; excludes Russia since then

SKIERS WITH THE MOST ALPINE SKIING WORLD CUP TITLES (MALE)

	SKIER/COUNTRY	YEARS	TOTAL
1	Ingemar Stenmark, Sweden	1976–84	18
2	Pirmin Zurbriggen, Switzerland	1984–90	15
3	Marc Girardelli, Luxembourg	1984–94	11
4 =	Gustavo Thoeni, Italy	1971–74	9
=	Alberto Tomba, Italy	1988–95	9
6	Hermann Maier, Austria	1998–2000	8
7 =	Jean-Claude Killy, France	1967–68	6
=	Phil Mahre, US	1981–83	6
9 =	Luc Alphand, France	1997	5
=	Franz Klammer, Austria	1975–83	5

SKIERS WITH THE MOST ALPINE SKIING WORLD CUP TITLES (FEMALE)

	SKIER/COUNTRY	YEARS	TOTAL
1	Annemarie Moser-Pröll, Austria	1971–79	16
2	Vreni Schneider, Switzerland	1986–95	14
3	Katia Seizinger, Germany	1992–98	11
4	Erika Hess, Switzerland	1981–84	8
5	Michela Figini, Switzerland	1985–89	7
6	Lise-Marie Morerod, Switzerland	1975–78	6
7 =	Maria Walliser, Switzerland	1986–87	5
=	Hanni Wenzel, Liechtenstein	1974–80	5
9 =	Renate Goetschl, Germany	1997–2000	4
=	Nancy Greene, Canada	1967–68	4
=	Petra Kronberger, Austria	1990–92	4
=	Tamara McKinney, USA	1981–84	4
=	Carole Merle, France	1989–92	4

The Alpine Skiing World Cup was launched as an annual event in 1967, with the addition of the super-giant slalom in 1986. Points are awarded for performances over a series of selected races during the winter months at meetings worldwide. In addition to her 16 titles, Annemarie Moser-Pröll won a record 62 individual events in the period 1970–79, and went on to win gold for the Downhill event in the 1980 Olympic Games.

Did You Know? At the Third Winter Olympics, in Lake Placid, New York, in 1932, an early thaw meant that snow had to be taken to the venue from Canada by a fleet of trucks.

TOP 10 ★
WOMEN'S WORLD AND OLYMPIC FIGURE SKATING TITLES

SKATER/COUNTRY/YEARS	TITLES
1 Sonja Henie, Norway, 1927–36	13
2= Carol Heiss, US, 1956–60	6
=Herma Planck Szabo, Austria, 1922–26	6
=Katarina Witt, E. Germany, 1984–88	6
5=Lily Kronberger, Hungary, 1908–11	4
=Sjoukje Dijkstra, Holland, 1962–64	4
=Peggy Fleming, US, 1966–68	4
8=Meray Horvath, Hungary, 1912–14	3
=Tenley Albright, US, 1953–56	3
=Michelle Kwan, US, 1996–2000	3
=Annett Poetzsch, E. Gemany, 1978–80	3
=Beatrix Schuba, Austria, 1971–72	3
=Barbara Ann Scott, Canada, 1947–48	3
=Kristi Yamaguchi, US, 1991–92	3
=Madge Syers, GB, 1906–08	3

TOP 10 ★
OLYMPIC FIGURE SKATING COUNTRIES

COUNTRY	GOLD	SILVER	BRONZE	TOTAL
1 US	12	13	14	39
2 Soviet Union*	13	10	6	29
3 Austria	7	9	4	20
4 Canada	2	7	9	18
5 Great Britain	5	3	7	15
6 France	2	2	7	11
7=Sweden	5	3	2	10
=East Germany	3	3	4	10
9 Germany#	4	4	1	9
10=Norway	3	2	1	6
=Hungary	0	2	4	6

* *Includes United Team of 1992; excludes Russia since then*

\# *Not including West Germany or East Germany 1968–88*

Figure skating was part of the Summer Olympics in 1908 and 1920, becoming part of the Winter program in 1924.

TOP 10 ★
WINTER OLYMPIC MEDAL-WINNING COUNTRIES, 1908–98

COUNTRY	GOLD	SILVER	BRONZE	TOTAL
1 Norway	83	87	69	239
2 Soviet Union*	87	63	67	217
3 US	59	59	41	159
4 Austria	39	53	53	145
5 Finland	38	49	48	135
6 Germany#	66	38	32	116
7 East Germany	39	36	35	110
8 Sweden	39	28	35	102
9 Switzerland	29	31	32	92
10 Canada	25	25	28	79

* *Includes United Team of 1992; excludes Russia since then*

\# *Not including West or East Germany 1968–88*

Only skating and ice hockey were featured in the 1908 and 1920 Summer Olympics. The first Winter Olympics was held at Chamonix, France, in 1924.

TOP 10 ★
FASTEST WINNING TIMES OF THE IDITAROD DOG SLED RACE

WINNER	YEAR	DAY	HR	MIN	SEC
1 Doug Swingley	2000	9	0	58	6
2 Doug Swingley	1995	9	2	42	19
3 Jeff King	1996	9	5	43	19
4 Jeff King	1998	9	5	52	26
5 Martin Buser	1997	9	8	30	45
6 Doug Swingley	1999	9	14	31	7
7 Martin Buser	1994	10	13	2	39
8 Jeff King	1993	10	15	38	15
9 Martin Buser	1992	10	19	17	15
10 Susan Butcher	1990	11	1	53	28

Source: *Iditarod Trail Committee*

TOP DOUG

Doug Swingley from Simms, Montana, is one of the few non-Alaskans to win the grueling 1,158-mile (1,864-km) Anchorage-to-Nome Iditarod dog sled race.

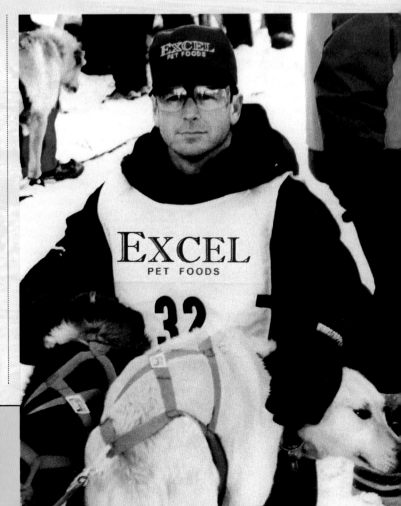

Background image: IDITAROD DOG SLED RACE, 1999

Sports Trivia

PARTICIPATION SPORTS, GAMES, AND PHYSICAL ACTIVITIES IN THE US

	ACTIVITY	NUMBER PARTICIPATING
1	Exercise walking	77,600,000
2	Swimming	58,200,000
3	Camping	46,500,000
4	Exercising with equipment	46,100,000
5	Fishing	43,600,000
6	Bicycle riding	43,500,000
7	Bowling	40,100,000
8	Billiards/pool	32,300,000
9	Basketball	29,400,000
10	Golf	27,500,000

* Participated more than once during the year

Source: *National Sporting Goods Association*

MOST COMMON SPORTS INJURIES

	COMMON NAME	MEDICAL TERM
1	Bruise	A soft tissue contusion
2	Sprained ankle	Sprain of the lateral ligament
3	Sprained knee	Sprain of the medial collateral ligament
4	Low back strain	Lumbar joint dysfunction
5	Hamstring tear	Muscle tear of the hamstrings
6	Jumper's knee	Patella tendinitis
7	Achilles tendinitis	Tendinitis of the Achilles tendon
8	Shin splints	Medial periostitis of the tibia
9	Tennis elbow	Lateral epicondylitis
10	Shoulder strain	Rotator cuff tendinitis

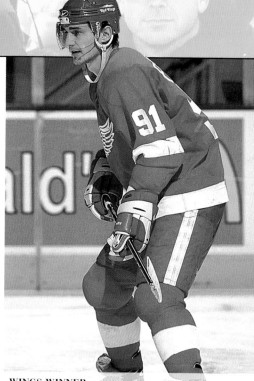

WINGS WINNER
Soviet-born Detroit Red Wings star Sergei Federov is one of the highest scoring and highest earning of all sports personalities.

SPORTING EVENTS WITH THE LARGEST TV AUDIENCES IN THE US

	EVENT	DATE	RATING
1	Super Bowl XVI	Jan 24, 1982	49.1
2	Super Bowl XVII	Jan 30, 1983	48.6
3	XVII Winter Olympics	Feb 23, 1994	48.5
4	Super Bowl XX	Jan 26, 1986	48.3
5	Super Bowl XII	Jan 15, 1978	47.2
6	Super Bowl XIII	Jan 21, 1979	47.1
7 =	Super Bowl XVIII	Jan 22, 1984	46.4
=	Super Bowl XIX	Jan 20, 1985	46.4
9	Super Bowl XIV	Jan 20, 1980	46.3
10	Super Bowl XXX	Jan 28, 1996	46.0

Source: *Nielsen Media Research*

Those listed here, along with ten further Super Bowls, back to VI in 1972, are among the Top 50 networked programs of all time in the US. In this extended list, the XVII Lillehammer, Norway, Winter Olympics makes two showings, on Feb 23 and Feb 25 1994 (the latter achieving a rating of 44.2). Despite the national enthusiasm (fueled by media interest in figure skater Nancy Kerrigan, who had been physically attacked before the Games), the US finished a disappointing 5th in the overall medals table.

HIGHEST-EARNING SPORTSMEN

	SPORTSMAN*	SPORT	1999 INCOME ($)
1	Michael Shumacher, Germany	Motor racing	49,000,000
2	Tiger Woods	Golf	47,000,000
3	Oscar De La Hoya	Boxing	43,500,000
4	Michael Jordan	Basketball	40,000,000
5	Evander Holyfield	Boxing	35,500,000
6	Mike Tyson	Boxing	33,000,000
7	Shaquille O'Neal	Basketball	31,000,000
8	Lennox Lewis, UK	Boxing	29,000,000
9	Dale Earnhardt	Stock car racing	26,500,000
10	Grant Hill	Basketball	23,000,000

* From the US unless otherwise stated   Source: *Forbes* magazine

TOP 10 COLLEGE SPORTS IN THE US

(Sport/participants in NCAA sports*)

1 Football, 54,793 **2** Outdoor track, 35,308
3 Soccer, 33,191 **4** Indoor track, 29,638 **5** Basketball, 28,829
6 Baseball, 24,806 **7** Cross-country, 21,000 **8** Swimming/diving, 16,737 **9** Tennis, 15,741 **10** Softball, 13,750

* In latest year for which figures available   Source: *NCAA*

Did You Know? The Tour de France bicycle race is believed to be watched by more spectators than any other sport, with some 10 million people lining the route during the three-week event.

THE 10 ★
LATEST TRIATHLON WORLD CHAMPIONS

MAN/COUNTRY	TIME	YEAR	TIME	WOMAN/COUNTRY
Dimitry Gaag, Kazahkstan	1:45:25	**1999**	1:55:28	**Loretta Harrop**, Australia
Simon Lessing, UK	1:55:31	**1998**	2:07:25	**Joanne King**, Australia
Chris McCormack, Australia	1:48:29	**1997**	1:59:22	**Emma Carney**, Australia
Simon Lessing, UK	1:39:50	**1996**	1:50:52	**Jackie Gallagher**, Australia
Simon Lessing, UK	1:48:29	**1995**	2:04:58	**Karen Smyers**, US
Spencer Smith, UK	1:51:04	**1994**	2:03:19	**Emma Carney**, Australia
Spencer Smith, UK	1:51:20	**1993**	2:07:41	**Michellie Jones**, Australia
Simon Lessing, UK	1:49:04	**1992**	2:02:08	**Michellie Jones**, Australia
Miles Stewart, Australia	1:48:20	**1991**	2:02:04	**Joanne Ritchie**, Canada
Greg Welch, Australia	1:51:37	**1990**	2:03:33	**Karen Smyers**, US

The Triathlon World Championship has been contested since 1989 and consists of a 1-mile (1.5-km) swim, a 25-mile (40-km) bike ride, and a 6¼-mile (10-km) run.

TOP 10 ★
ALL-AROUND CHAMPION COWBOYS

	COWBOY	YEARS	WINS
1	Ty Murray	1989–98	7
2=	Tom Ferguson	1974–79	6
=	Larry Mahan	1966–73	6
4	Jim Shoulders	1949–59	5
5=	Lewis Feild	1985–87	3
=	Dean Oliver	1963–65	3
7=	Joe Beaver	1995–96	2
=	Everett Bowman	1935–37	2
=	Louis Brooks	1943–44	2
=	Clay Carr	1930–33	2
=	Bill Linderman	1950–53	2
=	Phil Lyne	1971–72	2
=	Gerald Roberts	1942–48	2
=	Casey Tibbs	1951–55	2
=	Harry Tompkins	1952–60	2

The All-Around World Champion Cowboy title is presented by the Professional Rodeo Cowboys Association (PRCA) each year. The winner is the rodeo athlete who wins the most prize money in a single year in two or more events, with minimum earnings of $2,000 per event. During the 1990s, several winners earned more than $250,000 a year.

TOP 10 ★
FASTEST WINNING TIMES FOR THE HAWAII IRONMAN

	WINNER/COUNTRY*	YEAR	TIME HR:MIN:SEC
1	Luc Van Lierde, Belgium	1996	8:04:08
2	Mark Allen	1993	8:07:45
3	Mark Allen	1992	8:09:08
4	Mark Allen	1989	8:09:16
5	Luc Van Lierde	1999	8:17:17
6	Mark Allen	1991	8:18:32
7	Greg Welch, Australia	1994	8:20:27
8	Mark Allen	1995	8:20:34
9	Peter Reid, Canada	1998	8:24:20
10	Mark Allen	1990	8:28:17

From the US unless otherwise stated

In perhaps one of the most grueling sporting contests, competitors engage in a 2½-mile (3.86-km) swim, a 112-mile (180-km) cycle race, and a 26¼-mile (42.195-km) run.

DANGER BELOW

The risk of injury or becoming trapped underground has resulted in spelunking being ranked among the world's most hazardous sports.

TOP 10 ★
MOST DANGEROUS AMATEUR SPORTS

	SPORT	RISK FACTOR*
1	Powerboat racing	15
2	Ocean yacht racing	10
3	Cave diving	7
4	Spelunking	6
5=	Drag racing	5
=	Karting	5
7	Microlyte	4
8=	Hang gliding	3
=	Motor racing	3
=	Mountaineering	3

* Risk factor refers to the premium that insurance companies place on insuring someone for that activity – the higher the risk factor, the higher the premium

Source: *General Accident*

Index

Special US research:
Dafydd Rees

UK research assistants: Harriet Hart, Lucy Hemming

Thanks to the individuals, organizations, and publications listed below who kindly supplied information to enable me to prepare many of the lists.

Caroline Ash, Mark Atterton, John Bardsley, Richard Braddish, Lesley Coldham, Pete Compton, Stanley Coren, Luke Crampton, François Curiel, Sidney S. Culbert, Bonnie Fantasia, Christopher Forbes, Professor Ken Fox, Darryl Francis, Simon Gilbert, Russell E. Gough, Monica Grady, Stan Greenberg, Duncan Hislop, Andreas Hoerstemeier, Tony Hutson, Alan Jeffreys, Robert Lamb, Dr. Jaquie Lavin, Dr. Benjamin Lucas, John Malam, Ian Morrison, Vincent Nasso, Christiaan Rees, Linda Rees, Adrian Room, Bill Rudman, Joanne Schioppi, Robert Senior, Lisa E. Smith, Mitchell Symons, Tony Waltham, Professor Edward O. Wilson

Academy of Motion Picture Arts and Sciences, *Advertising Age,* American Athletic Association, American Film Institute, American Forestry Association, American Kennel Club, American Library Association, American Music Conference, American Pet Classics, American Theater Wing, *Amusement Business, Art Newspaper,* Art Institute of Chicago, Art Sales Index, Associated Press, Association of Tennis Professionals (ATP), Audit Bureau of Circulations, Beverage Marketing Corporation, *Billboard,* Boston Athletics Association, BPI, *BP Statistical Review of World Energy,* Breeders Cup, British Cave Research Association, British Columbia Vital Statistics Agency, British Library, Bureau of Federal Prisons, Bureau of Justice Statistics, Cannes Film Festival, Carbon Dioxide Information Analysis Center, Cat Fancier's Association, Center for Disease Control, Central Intelligence Agency, Central Statistics Office/An Príomh-Oifig Staidrimh, Ireland, Champagne Bureau, Championship Auto Racing Teams (CART), Channel Swimming Association, Christian Research, Christie's, *Classical Music,* Coca-Cola, Columbia University/ Pulitzer Prizes, Computer Industry Almanac, Inc., Country Music Association, *Crime in the United States, Criminal Statistics England & Wales,* Dateline International, Death Penalty Information Center, De Beers, Duncan's

American Radio, *Economist, Editor & Publisher Year Book,* Electoral Reform Society, Energy Information Administration, Environmental Protection Agency, Euromonitor, *FBI Uniform Crime Reports,* Feste Catalogue Index Database/ Alan Somerset, *Financial Times,* Fine Arts Museum, Boston, *Flight International,* Food and Agriculture Organization of the United Nations, Food Marketing Institute, *Forbes, Fortune,* Gemstone Publishing, Inc., General Accident, Generation AB, Gold Fields Mineral Services Ltd., H. J. Heinz, Hollywood Foreign Press Association (Golden Globe Awards), Home Office, UK, Indianapolis Motor Speedway, Iditarod Trail Committee, Interbrand, International Associatiion of Ports and Harbors, International Atomic Energy Agency, International Civil Aviation Organization, International Cocoa Organization, International Coffee Organization, International Commission on Large Dams, International Dairy Foods Association, International Game Fish Association, International Union for the Conservation of Nature, Inter-Parliamentary Union, Interpol, Jockey Club, Kellogg's, Korbel Champagne Cellars, League of American Theaters and Producers, Lloyds Register of Shipping/ MIPG/PPMS, Magazine Publishers of America, Major League Baseball, Mansell Color Company Inc., Mars, Inc., Meat and Livestock Commission, Metropolitan Opera House, New York, Modern Language Association of America, MRIB, M Street, MTV, NASA, National Academy of Recording Arts and Sciences (NARAS), National Academy of Television Arts and Sciences (Emmy Awards), National Ambulatory Medical Care Survey, National Association of Broadcasters, National Association of Stock Car Auto Racing, Inc (NASCAR), National Basketball Association (NBA), National Center for Health Statistics, National Climatic Data Center, National Collegiate Athletic Association (NCAA), National Dairy Council, National Fire Protection Association, National Football League (NFL), National Highway Traffic Safety Administration, National Hockey League (NHL), National Hockey League Players Association, National Hurricane Center, National Public Radio, National Safety Council, National Sporting Goods Association, National Steeplechase Association, National Thoroughbred Racing Association, National Trotting Association, New South Wales Registry of Births, Deaths and Marriages, New York City Transit Authority, New York Road Runners Club, Niagara Falls Museum,

ACNielsen MMS, Nielsen Media Research, Nobel Foundation, *NonProfit Times,* NOP, Northern Ireland Statistics and Research Agency, NPD TRSTS, Toy Tracking Service, Nua Ltd., Office for National Statistics, UK, Peabody Awards, PC Data Online, Pet Industry Joint Advisory Council, Phillips Group, Phobics Society, Popular Music Database, Produktschap voor Gedistilleerde Dranken, Professional Rodeo Cowboys Association (PRCA), Project Feeder Watch/Cornell Lab of Ornithology, Public Broadcasting System (PBS), *Publishers' Weekly, Raceboat International, Railway Gazette International,* Recording Industry Association of America (RIAA), Rock 'n' Roll Hall of Fame, Royal Aeronautical Society, *Screen Digest,* Shakespeare Birthplace Trust, Siemens AG, *Slimming World,* Songwriters Hall of Fame, Sotheby's, *Spaceflight, Sporting News, Sports Illustrated, Statistical Abstract of the United States,* Statistics Norway, STATS Inc., *Steeplechase Times,* Stockholm International Peace Research Institute, *Time,* Tourism Industries, International Trade Administration, Ty Inc., UNESCO, United Nations, Universal Postal Union, US Board on Geographic Names, US Bureau of Labor Statistics, US Bureau of Engraving and Printing, US Bureau of the Census, US Consumer Product Safety Commission, US Department of Agriculture/ Economic Research Service, US Department of Justice, US Department of the Interior, US Fish and Wildlife Service, US Geological Survey, US Mint, US Patent Office, US Social Security Administration, *Variety,* VideoScan, Inc., *Video Store,* Ward's Automotive, Whitbread Literary Awards, Women's National Basketball Association (WNBA), World Association of Newspapers, World Bank, World Health Organization, World Meteorological Organization, World Resources Institute, World Science Fiction Society, World Tourism Organization, Zenith International

Index
Patrica Coward

DK Picture Librarians
Denise O'Brien, Melanie Simmonds

Packager's acknowledgments:
Cooling Brown would like to thank the following: Pauline Clarke for design assistance; Peter Cooling for technical support; Carolyn MacKenzie for proof reading; Chris and Eleanor Bolus for the loan of the Beanie Babies.